Theory and Applications of Fuzzy Systems and Neural Networks

Theory and Applications of Fuzzy Systems and Neural Networks

Guest Editors

Alexander Gegov
Raheleh Jafari

MDPI

Basel • Beijing • Wuhan • Barcelona • Belgrade • Novi Sad • Cluj • Manchester

Guest Editors

Alexander Gegov
School of Computing
University of Portsmouth
Portsmouth
UK

Raheleh Jafari
School of Design
University of Leeds
Leeds
UK

Editorial Office
MDPI AG
Grosspeteranlage 5
4052 Basel, Switzerland

This is a reprint of the Special Issue, published open access by the journal *Electronics* (ISSN 2079-9292), freely accessible at: https://www.mdpi.com/journal/electronics/special_issues/FSNN.

For citation purposes, cite each article independently as indicated on the article page online and as indicated below:

Lastname, A.A.; Lastname, B.B. Article Title. *Journal Name* **Year**, *Volume Number*, Page Range.

ISBN 978-3-7258-4807-2 (Hbk)
ISBN 978-3-7258-4808-9 (PDF)
https://doi.org/10.3390/books978-3-7258-4808-9

Contents

About the Editors

Alexander Gegov

Dr Alexander Gegov is an Associate Professor of Computational Intelligence at the School of Computing, University of Portsmouth, UK. He holds a DSc in Artificial Intelligence, a PhD in Cybernetics, an MSc in Robotics and a BSc in Automatics. His research interests and expertise are in the development of artificial intelligence methods and their application for complex systems modelling.

Raheleh Jafari

Dr Raheleh Jafari is a Senior Research Fellow in Artificial Intelligence at the School of Design, University of Leeds, UK. She holds a PhD in Automatic Control, an MSc in Applied Mathematics and a BSc in Pure Mathematics. Her research interests and expertise are in the development of artificial intelligence methods and their application in robotics, automation and fashion technology.

electronics

MDPI

Review

Artificial Neural Networks and Deep Learning Techniques Applied to Radar Target Detection: A Review

Wen Jiang *, Yihui Ren, Ying Liu * and Jiaxu Leng

School of Computer Science and Technology, University of Chinese Academy of Sciences, Beijing 101400, China; renyihui18@mails.ucas.ac.cn (Y.R.); lengjx@cqupt.edu.cn (J.L.)
* Correspondence: jiangwen19@mails.ucas.ac.cn (W.J.); yingliu@ucas.ac.cn (Y.L.)

Abstract: Radar target detection (RTD) is a fundamental but important process of the radar system, which is designed to differentiate and measure targets from a complex background. Deep learning methods have gained great attention currently and have turned out to be feasible solutions in radar signal processing. Compared with the conventional RTD methods, deep learning-based methods can extract features automatically and yield more accurate results. Applying deep learning to RTD is considered as a novel concept. In this paper, we review the applications of deep learning in the field of RTD and summarize the possible limitations. This work is timely due to the increasing number of research works published in recent years. We hope that this survey will provide guidelines for future studies and applications of deep learning in RTD and related areas of radar signal processing.

Keywords: radar target detection; radar signal processing; deep learning models; artificial neural network; deep neural network

1. Introduction

Radar target detection (RTD) is widely used to determine whether there is a signal present in noise. Since radar signals reflected from targets are often immersed in complex backgrounds (e.g., noise, clutter, even jamming), traditional signal processing methods are often used to boost signal-to-noise ratio (SNR) [1], while constant false alarm rate (CFAR) is a useful method for detection in a noise environment based on hypothesis testing [2]. Traditional CFAR-based detection methods consider the models of target or environment as a stochastic process which is usually based on statistical theory [3]. However, due to the complex detection environment and diverse target types, finding targets in a complex scene is an extremely challenging task, and therefore a reliable and robust RTD method has been one of the key pursuits of research [4].

Deep learning is a rapidly developing technology which has dramatically brought a breakthrough in many fields such as image classification, natural language processing, speech recognition, etc. [5,6]. As a subset of machine learning, deep learning-based models attempt to extract features from large scale raw data automatically. The success of deep learning is mainly due to the availability of big data, the improvement of computational power, and the ability of data processing [7]. Various deep neural network (DNN) technologies have been successfully used, including deep neural networks (DNN), convolutional neural networks (CNN), recursive neural networks (RNN), deep belief networks (DBN), etc. [8].

Although deep learning technology has demonstrated an exciting trend over the past few years, its full potential for radar application has not yet been explored. In ref. [9], researchers grouped the radar application problems that can be solved by deep learning-based methods into three general categories: radar sensing, radar signal processing, and radar automatic target recognition (ATR), respectively, which are listed in Figure 1. Radar sensing and radar signal processing are the necessary prerequisites and procedures for radar ATR.

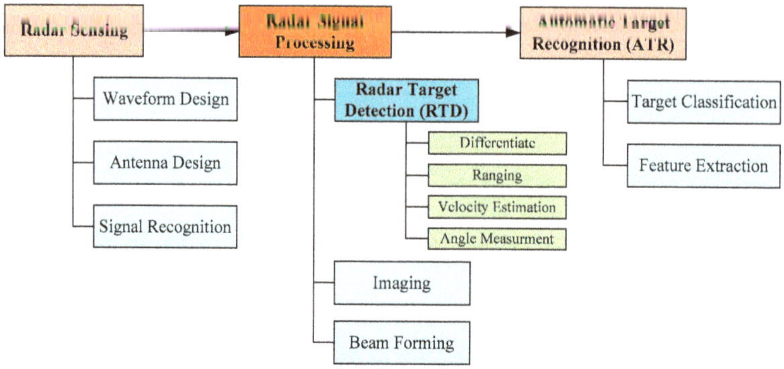

Figure 1. Radar tasks that can benefit from deep learning.

Deep learning methods have been fully applied in radar sensing. Wang et al. [10] applied CNNs to radar waveform recognition. According to [11,12], deep learning methods can solve the problem of high computational complexity of antenna parameter optimization. The design of array antennas has been addressed by artificial neural networks (ANN) [13]. Cognitive radar antenna selection has also been solved by deep learning methods [14,15]. Gao et al. [16] explored a feature extractor based on CNN and a stacked autoencoder (SAE) to recognize modulated signals of radar, including LFM, NLFM, BPSK, FRANK, COSTAS, P1, P2, P3 and P4, etc.

Automatic Target Recognition is the most straightforward and widely-used application of deep learning to radar, especially for synthetic aperture radar (SAR) [17–20]. Different "image-like" radar data have been well-studied for the purpose of feature extraction and classification of ATR. Deep learning models were built up on radar high-resolution range profiles (HRRP) for ATR [21–23]. ATR on radar Micro-Doppler signatures could also be considered in [24–28]. Deep learning can also be used for recognition of human activities using Micro-Doppler signatures, including hand gestures recognition [29–31], vital signs sensing [32–34], routine activities recognition [35–39], etc. Khalid et al. [40] investigated the use of radar Range-Doppler profiles for ATR with the Convolutional Long Short-Term Memory (CLSTM) model. A deep learning-based method on Range-Doppler radars is proposed to recognize human fall motions in [41].

Radar Signal Processing is an intermediate procedure between radar sensing and ATR. One of the most important purposes of radar signal processing is to detect targets. Machine learning-based classifiers algorithms, such as support vector machines (SVM) [42] and k-Nearest-Neighbour (kNN) [43], have been used for RTD [44,45]. As previously mentioned, RTD is a binary hypothesis testing which can be regarded as a binary classification problem, namely whether the target is present or absent. Based on this assumption, RTD can be regarded as an ATR application. As deep learning models have achieved good performance in ATR, it is feasible and reasonable to explore deep learning-based models in RTD. As one of the most reliable classifiers, ANN has been utilized to improve radar detection performance [46,47]. Many recent literatures utilize DNN to tackle RTD and also present performance improvements. Figure 2 illustrates the major developments and application of deep learning in RTD. Detailed descriptions of each algorithm will be presented later.

Applying deep learning technology to the field of RTD is a novel concept, yet by now, there is no paper which comprehensively summarizes and introduces the application and its development status. In this paper, we try to review the applications of ANN and deep learning methods in the classical radar system problem of target detection.

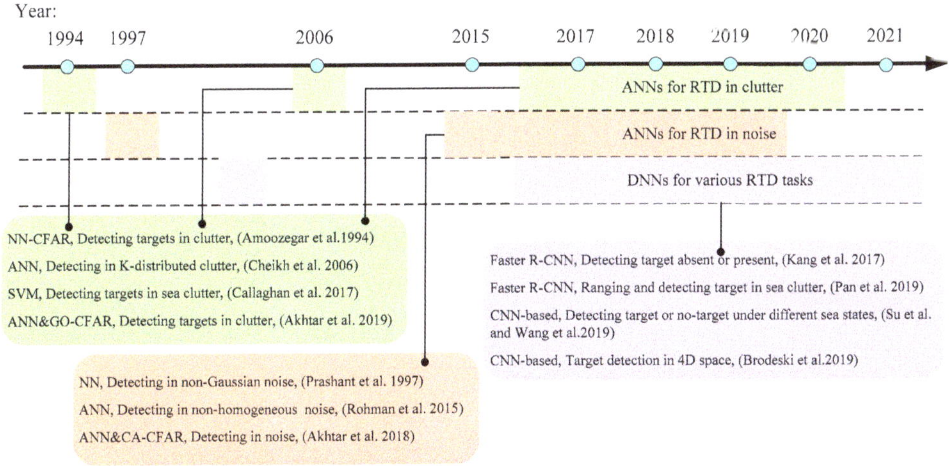

Figure 2. Major milestone of deep learning in RTD.

This review focuses on articles in online databases, e.g., IEEExplore, Open Science Elsevier, Scopus, Springer and Researchgate. Recent articles (available by July 2021) published in major journals of radar signal processing and major international conferences on artificial intelligence attract more attention; these include IEEE Signal Processing Magazine, IEEE Transactions on Antennas and Propagation, IEEE Transactions on Aerospace and Electronic Systems, IEEE Transactions on Geoscience and Remote Sensing, IEEE Geoscience and Remote Sensing Letters, IEEE Journal of Selected Topics in Signal Processing, IEEE Transactions on Signal Processing, ISPRS Journal of Photogrammetry and Remote Sensing, IEEE Radar Conference, International Conference on Radar, IEEE Conference on Computer Vision and Pattern Recognition, and IEEE International Conference on Computer Vision. In addition, a number of research papers from other sources are related to this topic and thus included in this review, and most of them were published between 2000 and 2020. These papers were selected by keywords in the titles and keywords of the studies, and they represent a wide range of: (a) methods from theoretical derivation to application research, (b) detection background from noise to clutter, (c) applications from maritime target detection to human motion detection, (d) data forms from radar received echoes to PPI images, and (e) comparative methods from neural networks to deep learning models. Lastly, only studies in the English language are included in the review.

The rest of this review is organized as follows: Section 2 introduces related work on RTD including traditional CFAR detectors, which are often used for performance comparisons. For completeness, in Section 3, we first recap on the basic methodology of ANN before applying it to practical applications, and we then recap the recent deep learning-based methods for. In Section 4, some open datasets are described as well as how to construct synthetic datasets, while Section 5 summarizes the research challenges and opportunities. Finally, conclusions are presented in Section 6.

2. Related Work on Radar Target Detection

2.1. Traditional Processing Methods for RTD

In a complex scenario of RTD, radar echo signals are often immersed in noise, jamming and clutter, etc., which is shown in Figure 3. During the typical pulse Doppler radar signal processing, the reflected radar signals are processed by a series of methods such as matched filtering, coherent accumulation, clutter suppression, CFAR detection, etc.

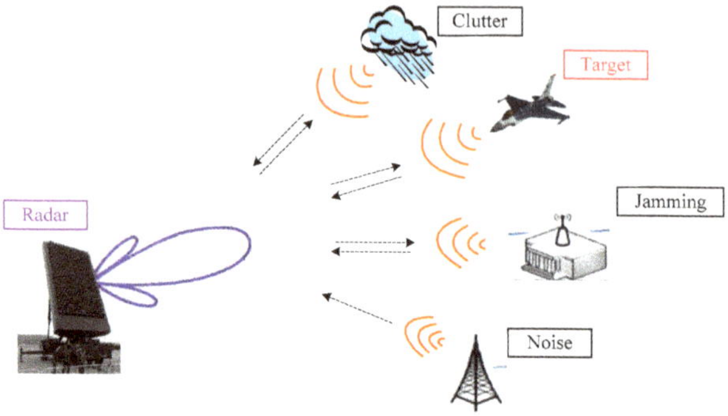

Figure 3. A schematic of RTD in a complex scene.

The received radar signals are sampled at a certain rate, and the pulses are compressed by the matched filter to obtain high range resolution and narrow pulse width. Moving target indication (MTI) is performed to suppress static clutter. Then, Doppler processing or coherent accumulation is applied over multiple pulses at each range unit to obtain the Range-Doppler spectrum. The reflected signal amplitude for each Range-Doppler is stored in separate cells, after which the CFAR detector is utilized to reveal one whose amplitude exceeds the threshold of detection. Thus, the corresponding information about velocity and position can be measured. The flowchart is presented in Figure 4.

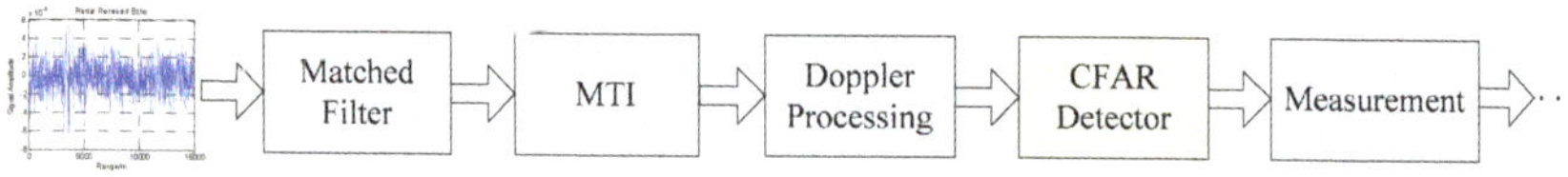

Figure 4. A signal processing diagram of the Pulse Doppler radar.

One of the most important purposes of designing a radar detector is to distinguish targets from noise, clutter and jamming signals. A decision must be made at the end of the detector as to whether the radar echo contains the target or not. The classical method is to establish an adaptive detection threshold based on statistical models, which varies according to noise and clutter energy. In order to minimize the false alarm rate (P_{fa}) and maximize the probability of detection (P_D), the Neyman-Pearson criterion is utilized for decision-making [2]. The typical performance requirement of a radar system will require $P_D \geq 0.8$ and $P_{fa} \leq 10e^{-4}$. This problem is commonly solved by applying a CFAR detector, which adaptively determines a local optimum threshold and maintains the P_{fa} to be constant as a predetermined value [48].

Figure 5 depicts a general CFAR detector, which is described as a shift register of length $2n + 1$. The input samples are sent into the detector cell by cell and the energy y in the cell under test (CUT) is estimated. The CFAR detector adjusts the statistic value z according to the variation of energy in $2n$ reference cells. The energy of the CUT is compared to the statistical result z of the CFAR processor scaled by a constant scale factor α. Thus, the detection threshold is represented as αz. Determining whether there is a target according to (1):

$$\begin{cases} y \leq \alpha z, & \textit{target absent} \\ y > \alpha z, & \textit{target present} \end{cases} \tag{1}$$

In order to find an adaptive detection threshold, many CFAR-based methods have been studied, which can adapt the threshold to the background changes, keeping a constant P_{fa}. The diagram of typical CFAR processors is also showed in Figure 5 [49].

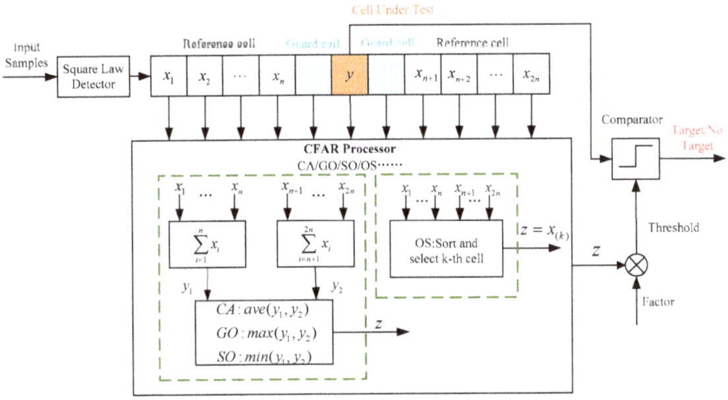

Figure 5. The diagram of typical CFAR detectors.

Compared with one-dimensional range detection, two-dimensional detection under phase-coherent accumulation includes range and Doppler detection, which is presented in Figure 6. x denotes the reference cells of range dimension, v denotes the reference cells of the Doppler dimension. The detection process of Doppler dimension is the same as that of range dimension.

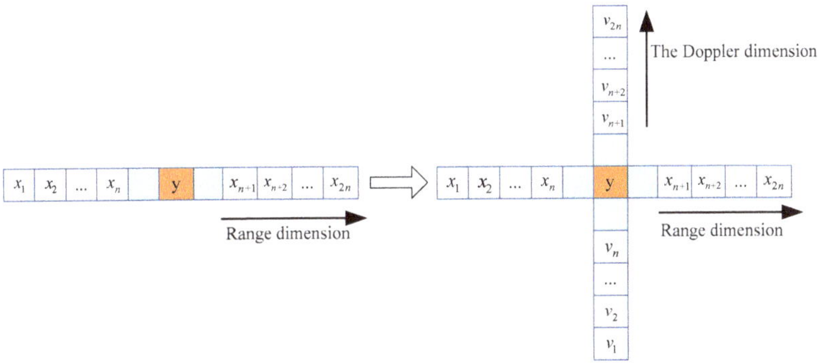

a) One dimensional detection area b) Two dimensional detection area

Figure 6. Schematic diagram of CFAR detection area, (**a**) One-dimensional detection area, (**b**) Two-dimensional detection area.

CFAR-based detectors have been well-studied over the past years, however, there still remains a trade-off between the various CFAR technologies. The cell averaging CFAR (CA-CFAR) is the most widely-used method which has the highest detectability in homogeneous background [50]. However, it also exhibits severe performance degradation in the presence of an interfering target or an abrupt change in clutter background [51]. The greatest CFAR (GO-CFAR) and the smallest CFAR (SO-CFAR) detectors were developed to improve the detection performance under various non-ideal conditions such as nonhomogeneous clutter background and multiple target environments [52]. Rohling et al. [53] developed an ordered statistics CFAR (OS-CFAR) to control the detecting threshold even though other interfering signals occurred in reference cell. As far as we know, CFAR methods are still under investigation, such as the censored mean level detector CFAR (CMLD-CFAR) and trimmed mean CFAR (TM-CFAR) detector [54], which were introduced to improve the anti-inference performance. However, each of those CFAR algorithms is only limited to some specific cases, lacking in generality.

2.2. Deficiencies and Challenges in Conventional Approaches

RTD is a rather complex problem in practical applications. Although conventional methods have been working well in some conditions, deficiencies and challenges still exist. Currently, the difficult problems of RTD still mainly lie in high-resolution processing of targets, clutter suppression, anti-jamming technology, and 'low-small-slow' target detection (low glancing angle, small size, slow or stationary), etc. [4].

Conventional CFAR-based methods in radar systems mainly depend on statistical hypothesis. (1) In the actual RTD, only the specific type of target under the specific background has good detection performance, because the predefined parameters of the detector, such as margin, threshold, sizes of the guard and reference windows, will determine the detection accuracy. However, radar always works in a diverse scene. (2) Furthermore, traditional methods are computationally expensive and not flexible because they process inputs cell-by-cell and need to manually change the window size to adaptive targets of different resolutions. (3) Most importantly, in most cases, neither the target nor the environment (noise, clutter, interference) have known statistical models. It is difficult to find suitable parameters to design the radar detector, not to mention predict its performance accurately.

In brief, traditional statistical methods are no longer applicable to complex scenes and the selection of the optimal parameter set is extremely challenging. It seems reasonable and inevitable to develop a data-driven deep learning approach for RTD.

3. Deep Learning Methods for Radar Target Detection

3.1. Artificial Neural Networks and Deep Learning-Based Models for RTD

ANN is motivated by the biological structure of the human brain. Generally, a neural network consists of neuron, weight vector, bias, activation function, etc. Multi-Layer Perceptron (MLP) is a type of neural network which consists of several hidden layers with neurons in layers being interconnected to each other [55]. Neural networks can be utilized in RTD due to their learning ability. In fact, the problem of RTD can be considered as a problem of pattern recognition, which fits well to the possibilities that an ANN provides [56]. Several approaches have suggested that considering ANNs as non-linear detectors could improve the detection performance. A typical ANN detector is shown in Figure 7. The output of each neuron can be given as (2):

$$X^{k+1} = f(W^k \cdot X^k + b^k) \tag{2}$$

where X^k is the input vector of the kth layer, W^k is the weight vector of the kth layer, b^k is an element of bias vector of the kth layer, $f(\cdot)$ is the activation function. ANN detector produces y_1 if the CUT contains a value larger than the sum of all the reference cells scaled by weights, otherwise, it would output y_2. Usually, a more complex ANN detector with multiple hidden layers would give better performance.

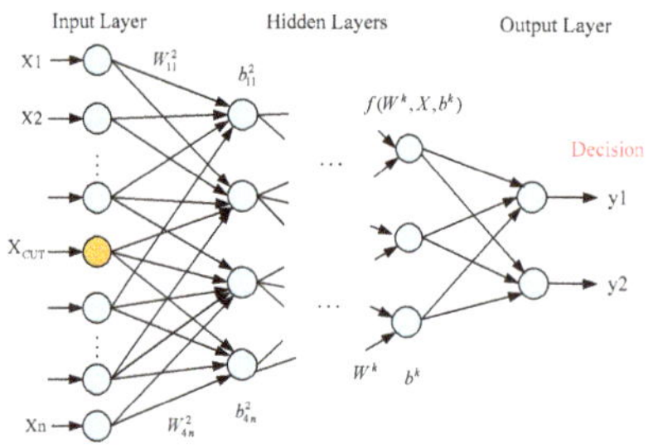

Figure 7. A typical architecture of a multi-layer ANN detector.

Using multiple layers to achieve more powerful generalization and abstractions, DNN outperforms all the machine learning methods. The traditional shallow neural network requires an empirical feature extraction process to decrease the networks' computational load. If the features have to be extracted automatically by the network, a deep network with powerful training capability is necessary. Currently, development in computer power and memory have made it possible to train very large-scaled networks. Various sizes of layers are used to provide different degrees of abstraction and generalization [57].

The increased popularity of deep learning has brought an increase in research publications related to RTD with deep learning models over the past few years. Specially designed network frameworks for RTD in noise environments and clutter backgrounds will be included in this work; in addition, several different DNNs will be reviewed in this paper, and each of them perform well for RTD. The increase in the number of related publications confirms the valid and increasing motivation of the research community on RTD tasks.

Next, we will review the recent articles using deep learning that address RTD in online databases. Table 1 summarizes the related works on RTD where we present the type of tasks and main contributions of each study. A more detailed description of the detection methods is provided in Table 2, where we summarize all the related papers, particularly highlighting the architecture of networks and the type of input and dataset. Unfortunately, a direct comparison for all methods is not possible because they were evaluated on different datasets.

Table 1. Summary of RTD tasks and methods in recent literature.

Task	Signal Processing Method	Detection Method	Main Contributions	Ref.	Year
Detecting signal in non-Gaussian noise	—	NN	NN is employed to detect signals in non-Gaussian noise.	[58]	1997
Detecting targets in non-homogeneous noise	CA-CFAR and OS-CFAR	ANN	ANN is employed to improve target detection performance by switching CA/OS CFAR.	[59]	2015
Detecting targets in noisy background	Pulse compression and CA-CFAR	ANN	ANN detector combined with CA-CFAR detector to offer a lower false alarm rate than CFAR.	[60]	2018
Detecting targets in clutter environment	Statistical parameters of target and clutter fluctuations	NN	A NN-CFAR detection scheme is presented to offer a robust performance in the face of loss of reference cells.	[61]	1994
Detecting signal in K-distributed clutter	CFAR	ANN	ANN-CFAR detector with MLP and RBF architecture is employed to detect signals in K-distributed clutter.	[62]	2006
Detecting targets in sea clutter	Pulse compression and Doppler processing	SVM&KNN	SVM and KNN are used for suppression of sea clutter.	[63]	2017
Detecting targets in sea clutter	—	SVM	SVM-based detector can flexibly control the false alarm rate.	[64]	2019
Detecting targets embedded in clutter	Doppler processing and GO-CFAR	ANN	ANN detector combined with GO-CFAR detector to offer a higher detection performance than CFAR.	[65]	2019
Detecting target absent or present	Pulse compression and Doppler processing	CNN	The classical CFAR detector is replaced by a CNN detector.	[66]	2019
Target detection in 4D space	Doppler processing	CNN	CNN is used to detect and localize in the 4D space of range, Doppler, azimuth and elevation.	[67]	2019

Table 1. Cont.

Task	Signal Processing Method	Detection Method	Main Contributions	Ref.	Year
Predicting targets' location and power distributions	—	Autoencoder	Construct input information and employ DNNs as radar models to learn conditional probability end-to-end from data.	[68]	2017
Ranging and detecting target from sea clutter	Pulse compression	Faster R-CNN	Faster R-CNN is applied to achieve the target detection and localization with low SCR.	[69]	2019
Detecting target absent or present	RDA and CFAR	Faster R-CNN	Faster R-CNN combined with CFAR to detect small-sized targets.	[70]	2017
Detecting targets in sea clutter	—	Faster R-CNN	Improved Faster R-CNN are used for target detection in navigation radar PPI images.	[71]	2019
Detecting targets in clutter	WVD	CNN	WVD-CNN detector is used for clutter analysis.	[72]	2002
Detecting target or no-target under different sea states	Pulse compression and STFT	CNN	CNNs are used for the detection of target micro-Doppler.	[73]	2019

RDA: Range Doppler Algorithm; WVD: Wigner-Ville Distribution; STFT: Short Time Fourier Transform; detection in 4D space: 4 dimension information of range, velocity, azimuth and elevation.

Table 2. Summary of RTD models in the literature.

Arch.	Name	Author	Model	Input	Activation Function	Pooling	Regularization	Optimization	Other Resources	Ref.
ANN	NN	Gandhi et al.	1 hidden layer	Radar received signals	Sigmoid	None	—	—	Simulated data	[58]
	ANN	Rohman et al.	2 hidden layers	CA, OS and CUT data	Log-sigmoid	None	—	—	Simulated data	[59]
	ANN	Akhtar et al.	2 hidden layers, 32 nodes NN	Pulse-Range maps	Hyperbolic tangent	None	—	SCG	Simulated data	[60]
	NN-CFAR	Amoozegar et al.	2 hidden layers	9 statistical parameters	Sigmoid	None	—	—	Simulated data	[61]
	ANN	Cheikh et al.	1 hidden layer	Range-Doppler maps	Sigmoid	None	—	—	Simulated data	[62]
	ANN	Akhtar et al.	4 hidden layers, 19 nodes in each layer	Range-Doppler maps	Hyperbolic tangent	None	—	SCG	Simulated data	[65]
DNN	CNN	Wang et al.	8 layers CNN	Range-Doppler maps	ReLU	Max	—	SGD	Simulated data	[66]
	RD-Net + Ang-Net	Brodeski et al.	CNN-based	Range-Doppler maps	ReLU	Max	Dropout	Adam	Collected data + Augmented data	[67]
	Faster R-CNN	Pan et al.	RPN + CNN + RoI	Pulse-Range images	ReLU	Max	Smooth L1 Dropout	GD	CSIR dataset	[69]
	CNN	Wang et al.	5 layers CNN	SAR images	Sigmoid	Average	—	—	MSTAR dataset	[74]
	GoogLeNet	Yang et al.	36 layers CNN	SAR images	ReLU	Max	Dropout	—	MSTAR dataset	[75]
	ANN + CNN	Zheng et al.	CNN-based	SAR images	ReLU	—	—	SGD	Sentinel-1 dataset [1]	[76]
	Faster R-CNN	Kang et al.	RPN + CNN + RoI	SAR images	ReLU	Max	—	—	Sentinel-1 dataset [1]	[70]

Table 2. Cont.

Arch. Name	Author	Model	Input	Activation Function	Pooling	Regularization	Optimization	Other Resources	Ref.
Faster R-CNN	Zhang et al.	RPN + CNN + RoI	Echo data and SAR images	ReLU	Max	——	——	Simulated data + MSTAR dataset	[77]
SSD	Zhao et al.	VGG16-based	SAR images	——	——	——	——	Gaofen-3 dataset	[78]
Faster R-CNN	Mou et al.	RPN + CNN + RoI	PPI images	ELUs	Max	——	Adam	Collected data	[71]
LeNet& GoogLeNet	Su et al.	7 layers & 22 layers CNN	Time-Frequency images	Sigmoid& ReLU	Max & Average	Dropout	SGD	IPIX measured data	[73]
DNN	Wheeler et al.	Autoencoder	Spatial raster and object list	ReLU	——	——	Ada	Collected and generated data	[68]
RD-Net + Ang-Net	Jiang et al.	CNN-based	Echo data	Soft-max	Max	Smooth L1	Adam	Simulated data	[49]

ReLU: Rectified Linear Units, ELUs: Exponential Linear Units, SCG: Scale conjugate gradient [79], GD: gradient descent, SGD: stochastic gradient descent [80], Adam: Adaptive Moment Estimation [81], Ada: Adadelta [82], CA: CA-CFAR, OS: OS-CFAR, CUT: Cell under test, RBF: Radial Basis Function. [1] https://scihub.copernicus.eu/ (accessed on 30 December 2021).

3.2. RTD in Noise Background

In the past decades, many approaches have been proposed to address the issue of RTD in diverse types of noise or clutter scenarios. Those approaches include complete descriptions of environmental statistics as well as statistical computing power. Recently, deep learning-based schemes were proposed to cope with the problem of RTD within noise backgrounds.

In practical application, the likelihood ratio can be obtained by sufficient statistics, which mainly depends on the probability density function of the noise, for example, Gaussian white noise. However, in a modern radar system, noise is usually non-Gaussian distribution, thus the likelihood ratio has a complex non-linear relation which makes it difficult to implement sufficient statistics [83,84]. Early in 1988, Gandhi and Kassam [85] analyzed the theoretical principle of CFAR processors in non-homogeneous backgrounds. This kind of processing can also be handled by ANN due to its ability to realize complicated nonlinear mappings on the data directly. In 1997, Gandhi and Ramaurti [58] were likely the first to employ neural networks to detect signals in non-Gaussian noise at some specified P_{fa}. With a detailed theoretical derivation, it was noted that the ANN detector's performance did not rely on the SNR, but actual relied on signal strength and noise common variations during training. By setting several non-Gaussian noise environments, the performance of the ANN detector has been shown to outperform the matched filter as well as the locally optimum detectors under some certain non-Gaussian noise environments. However, the computational power and the storage requirements are generally higher in the ANN detector.

In order to improve the detection performance of radar a in non-homogeneous environment, in 2015, Rohman et al. [59] presented a novel adaptive switch between the CA-CFAR and OS-CFAR detector by using the ANN structure with MLP which consisted of 2 hidden layers. The proposed architecture is illustrated in Figure 8. The inputs of ANN were calculated thresholds and the CUT value and the output was a preliminary threshold. Then, the nearest value between raw threshold and CA or OS-CFAR would be selected and utilized as the final threshold. The experiment's results showed that the combined approach is capable of switching between CA-CFAR and OS-CFAR properly in homogenous and non-homogeneous environments based on the best detection performance.

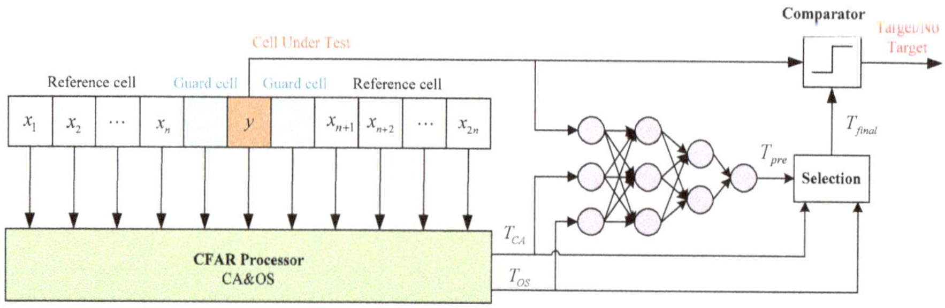

Figure 8. Design of ANN in switching CA/OS CFAR.

Additionally, a competent radar system must provide a high P_D with a low P_{fa}, which is the major principle of employing standard CFAR detectors. Akhtar and Olsen [60] presented an ANN, which is trained under a CA-CFAR detector for a fluctuating target detection procedure with a noise background. The ANN detector would output positive outcomes conditionally if a real target exists at a CUT and CA-CFAR returns a positive detection or the network would not return positive results. A prominent benefit of the ANN detector is that the outcome may be regarded as a measure of P_D, and not necessarily be either 0 or 1. It was also shown that such a scheme can obtain a slightly lower, or comparable target detection performance, but with a noticeably lower P_{fa} than that of the traditional CA-CFAR detector.

Taking into consideration that ANNs are confirmed to be able to approximate the CFAR detector, Amores et al. [86] further argued that the ANN can improve the robustness of a radar detector. Results show that although the detection performance of the trained network tends to increase as the number of hidden neurons increases, MLPs with one hidden layer with 23 units can implement very robust detectors for SNR lower than 10 dB. For more than 23 hidden neurons, the performance improvement is trivial, while the associated computational cost continues growing.

3.3. RTD in Clutter Background

Compared with a noise background, target detection in clutter background is a more common but challenging problem, because the signal returned from the targets are severely immersed by the backscatter from the clutter. According to theoretical analysis, the detection performance of CFAR detection increases as the number of reference cells increases; as the number approaches infinity, the CFAR detector approaches the optimal detector [87]. However, the serious degradation in P_D of the traditional CFAR detectors is due to a reduction in the number of available reference units. This decrease may be caused by high-resolution, the presence of interference signals, or clutter patches.

In the CFAR scheme, the need for a larger reference window, or more reference cells, results from the statistical requirements for the parameters which are used for representing the clutter background and the target fluctuation. The information loss caused by the window size reduction can be compensated for by introducing some extra parameters. Early in 1994, Amoozegar et al. [61] presented a NN-based CFAR detection method that provides a robust performance to compensate the loss of reference cells. The input layer contains nine specific statistical parameters which represent the features of target and clutter. A multi-layer feedforward neural network with sigmoid activation function was proposed to extract the features of target and clutter fluctuations. The results of experiments under diverse scenarios indicated that the NN-CFAR scheme consistently provides a superior robustness in responding to new environments and outperforms CA-CFAR detectors with small-sized reference windows.

To distinguish target from clutter, another meaningful method is to look for certain intrinsic features from the returned echoes to describe the difference between the targets and the clutter. Callaghan et al. [63] selected the magnitude of each Range-Doppler pixel as the feature from Range-Doppler maps and processed them by SVM and KNN algorithms to discriminate small maritime targets from sea clutter. Similarly, Li et al. [64] explored and extracted three practically discriminative features, namely the frequency peak to average ratio, the temporal Hurst exponent, and the temporal information entropy, from radar echo in time and frequency domains to construct feature space. An SVM-based detector which can flexibly control the P_{fa} was designed for target detection within sea clutter. Experimental results showed that the detection probability of the proposed detector is obviously higher than that of the classical detectors under the condition of low signal-to-clutter ratio (SCR) and low P_{fa} cases. All these statistical parameters which can depict the target and clutter characteristics may be embedded as the input of the NN-based detector in the literature [61].

However, because the characteristics of clutter highly rely on the actual environment and the parameters of radar, the above extracted parameters or features often become ineffective when the detection environment changes. Compared with machine learning methods which need to empirically select features, ANN is more suitable for extracting high-dimensional features, and has been adopted as a method of radar signal detection [88]. Following on from this work, Cheikh and Soltani [62] used different ANN architectures to assess the problem of RTD in a K-distributed clutter with thermal noise. They considered the MLP architecture with the genetic algorithm and back-propagation as the training methods, and the radial basis function (RBF) which has been largely used in signal processing was also adopted in the neuronal detector. A training set was used which can describe the clutter distribution well, and the architecture of the ANN-CFAR detector is depicted in Figure 9. The results show that the ANN-CFAR detector with MLP structure has better performance compared to the classical OS-CFAR and CA-CFAR detectors.

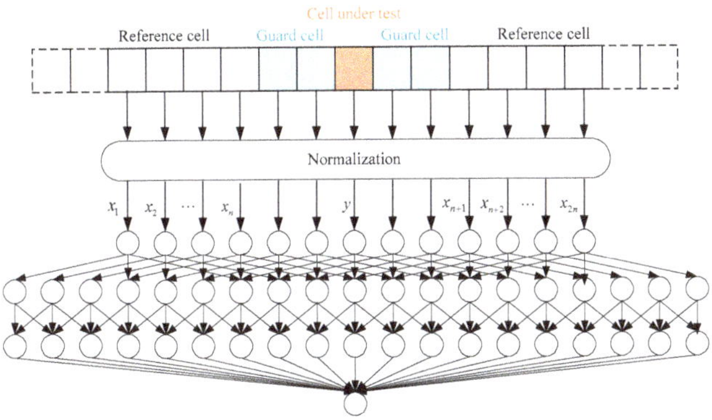

Figure 9. Artificial neural network detector structure.

Previous work, such as [58,61,62], attempted to improve the target detection performance on the basis of traditional CFAR methods. One objective in [59,60,69] is to replace the CFAR-based detector completely with neural networks to optimize the process of detection. In 2019, Akhtar and Olsen [65] continued to propose a more general training strategy where the conventional GO-CFAR detectors mutually work to detect targets in K-distributed clutter. This process would also be transferred into an ANN with four hidden layers and 19 nodes in each layer, with tanh as the activity function. The training strategy is related to [60] and the ANN structure is similar to that of [62], which is shown in Figure 9. The complete training data includes 2000 independent range-doppler maps with the average SNR over all CPIs ranging from −40 dB to 75 dB, while the average SCR varied from −60 dB to 60 dB. The experimental results show that, at least for specifically trained scenes, the overall detection performance of the ANN can significantly outperform a GO-CFAR detector, namely augment on P_D with reduction in P_{fa}.

From the above work, these ANN-based methods distinguish targets from a noise or clutter background and deliver better and more robust results than conventional statistical approaches. In addition, the multilayer architecture shows better performance, particularly in a mixed clutter environment. However, classical ANNs also have a major limitation; that is, due to the small number of neurons and layers, satisfactory performance may not be achieved when dealing with classification and regression problems.

3.4. Deep Learning for RTD with Different Data Forms

DNNs, such as CNN, RNN, etc., operate in a similar way to ANNs, but with more hidden layers and neurons. DNNs are capable of learning complex relationships from different types of data, which are more suitable to deal with large datasets and complex training algorithms. A basic CNN architecture consists of an input layer, a convolution layer, a pooling layer, a fully connected layer, and an output layer. The convolutional operation could generate local feature maps, and the pooling operation plays a role in obtaining the translation invariant [9]. The connections between these layers are more sparse than classical ANN structures.

CNNs are favored for computer vision tasks due to the grid structure of the input data, and the sparseness and locality of interactions between layers [89]. Typical optical image target detection algorithms based on CNNs are grouped into two categories: regional proposal-based and regression-based. The former contains R-CNN [90], SPP-Net [91], Fast RCNN [92] and Faster R-CNN [93], the latter contains YOLO [94], SSD [95], etc. Recently, these CNN-based methods have been widely used in RTD, which present faster speed, higher detection and position accuracy compared with CFAR.

Radar echo is a one-dimensional discrete time sequence, but a radar input data usually includes data of multiple range cells for a certain time, which determines that there are diverse forms of data for the detection network. The accuracy of deep learning also scales with the data. To accomplish this goal, the received radar signals are reshaped as various images to fit the CNN input format. Therefore, in addition to the original radar received signals, most researchers tried to detect and measure targets hidden in the noise background and clutter for multi-dimensional information with multiple CNN models based on range-Doppler spectrums, pulse-range maps, time-frequency images, synthetic aperture radar (SAR) images and plane position indicator (PPI) images as the inputs respectively, listed in Figure 10.

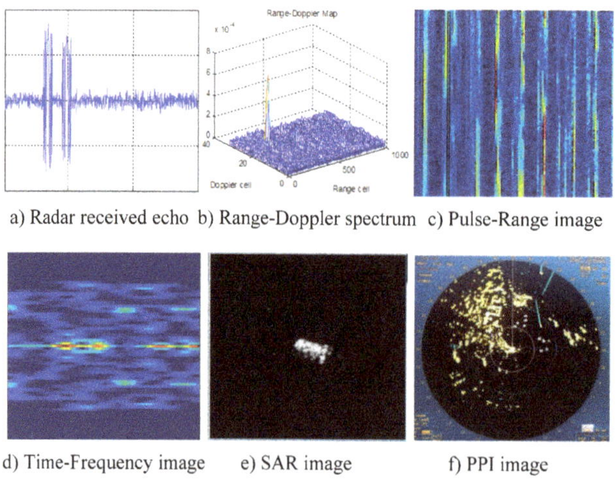

Figure 10. Input type of multiple CNN-based detectors, (**a**) Radar received echo; (**b**) Range-Doppler spectrum; (**c**) Pulse-Range image; (**d**) Time-Frequency image; (**e**) SAR image; (**f**) PPI image.

3.4.1. Radar Received Echo

Many studies have concluded that traditional signal processing methods of radar, serving as preprocessing methods of training data, is beneficial to extract features and improve the performance of detection. But actually, as the conventional processing methods, matched filtering and coherent accumulation are essentially convolution computations, and DNN models can extract features from inputs automatically, so it is feasible to detect targets from original radar echoes with DNNs. Jiang et al. [49] proposed a model for RTD based on CNN, which works with radar echo signal directly and therefore avoids the process of conventional signal processing. The proposed model explores the time and frequency domain of radar echo, which is presented in Figure 11. The echo signal is a one-dimensional discrete complex sequence, so the input data should be constructed as a radar echo cube to fit the network. The main goal of RTD is not only to distinguish the target from noise, but also to predict position and velocity. The RD-Detection Net is used to measure range and velocity, while azimuth and elevation are predicted by the Angle-Detection Net. The CNN-based model presented better accuracy and performance of detection than traditional approaches.

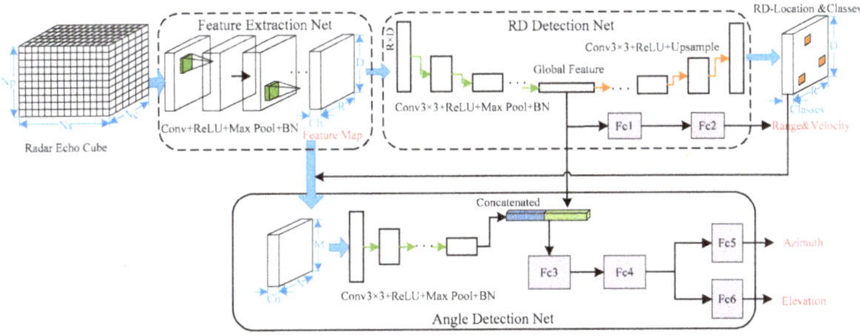

Figure 11. Structure of a CNN detector for RTD with radar echo data.

As in previous analyses, it is feasible and reasonable to implement a complete "end-to-end" multi-task RTD learning scheme, and a DNN-based learning scheme can also be utilized for more complex RTD tasks. For specific or more complex tasks, the received radar signals are transformed from the raw echo data to diverse data forms using different transform methods.

3.4.2. Range-Doppler Spectrum

Following the idea of image processing with CNN, a range-Doppler spectrum can be considered as an "image", then, the detector classifies the "image" as target absent or present, thus, the detection task could be treated as a classification task. Based on this idea, Wang et al. [66] designed a CNN target detector based on the range-Doppler spectrum and compared the proposed method with traditional CFAR detectors. The proposed network architecture presented in Figure 12 is an 8-layer CNN, including 2 convolutional layers, 2 ReLU layers, 2 max-pooling layers, and 2 fully connected layers. Different range-Doppler spectrum with multiple SNR values are constructed as the input of the CNN detector. The detector is actually a sliding window detector that slides over the Range-Doppler spectrum with a fixed window, and further decides whether the spectrum contains targets or just noise.

A deep learning method for automotive radar detection with non-image-like Range-Doppler data is proposed in [67], Brodeski et al. described a CNN model to detect and localize targets in the Range-Doppler-Azimuth-Elevation space. The training data was collected during the calibration process and augmented with raw radar data. Radar signals are transformed to the Range-Doppler domain by Doppler processing as the input to the network. When comparing with the conventional CA-CFAR method, the proposed approach outperformed the classical detection method while keeping the real-time abilities.

Their method for data construction was inspired by a simulation-based method for synthetic automotive scenes generation in [68].

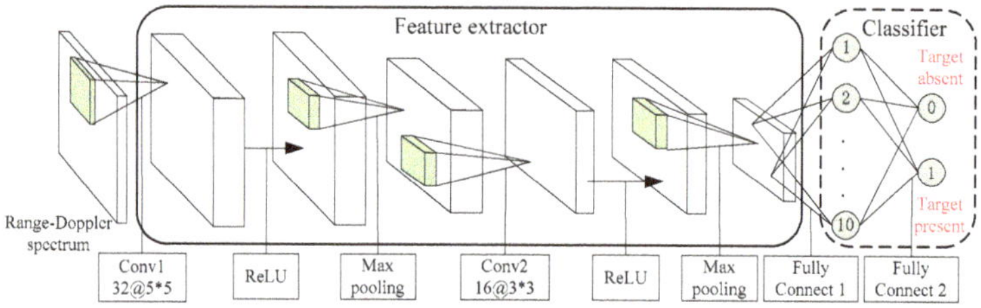

Figure 12. Structure of a CNN detector for RTD with Range-Doppler spectrum.

3.4.3. Pulse-Range Maps

Radar echoes also can be processed as pulse-range two-dimensional images for training and testing. Therefore, the problem of RTD can also be transformed into the target detection and location problem in Pulse-Range images. Pan et al. [69] introduced a CNN model for small marine target detection in strong sea clutter. A modified Faster R-CNN is utilized to extract the features of small targets and sea clutter, then the extracted features are utilized to detect and position the target in the pulse-range image. Figure 13 presents the DNN architecture for RTD based on Faster R-CNN with pulse-range images. This method proved to be easier to use in locating small targets from sea clutter and is able to obtain high P_D obviously, which overcomes the weakness of the traditional CFAR detection methods.

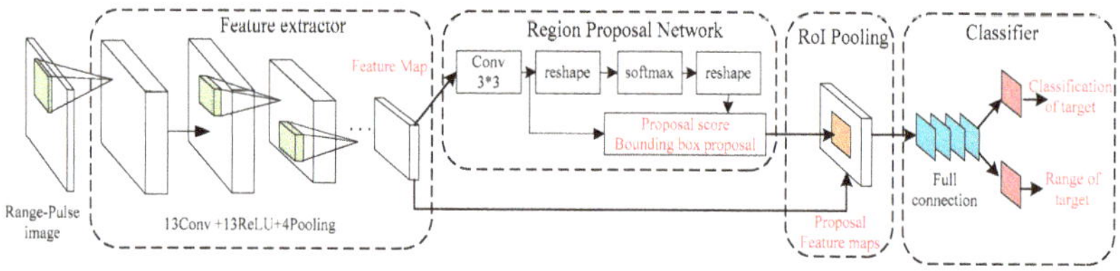

Figure 13. Faster R-CNN-based model for RTD with Pulse-Range images.

We can find that classic object detection methods based on CNNs, especially Faster R-CNN and SSD, which have been widely employed to RTD. Girshick et al. [92] transformed the detection task into a classification task and proposed Fast R-CNN structure. Ren et al. [93] depicted a new region proposal network (RPN) to implement the end-to-end target detection based on Faster R-CNN and RPN with shared convolutional features [96]. The target detection process of Fast R-CNN is performed in two steps; RPN proposes regions where are easy to find the target. Each region uses anchors to provide its possible course position, and then classifies the proposed target and fine-tunes its position by regression. The structure of Faster R-CNN is presented in Figure 14, and this architecture has been widely used as the basic framework for RTD, not only in Pulse-Range images, but also in SAR images and PPI images.

3.4.4. SAR Images

Some radar image signals, such as SAR data, can be inputted as images. Target detection based on SAR images is a key step in ATR, because SAR can provide high-resolution radar images of a wide range of scenarios including all-weather and all-day. However, as mentioned earlier, SAR imaging technology is another application branch of radar signal processing, and SAR images are widely-used in ATR. RTD tasks utilizing SAR images, as the input in this review will mainly focus on target feature extraction, target detection and location.

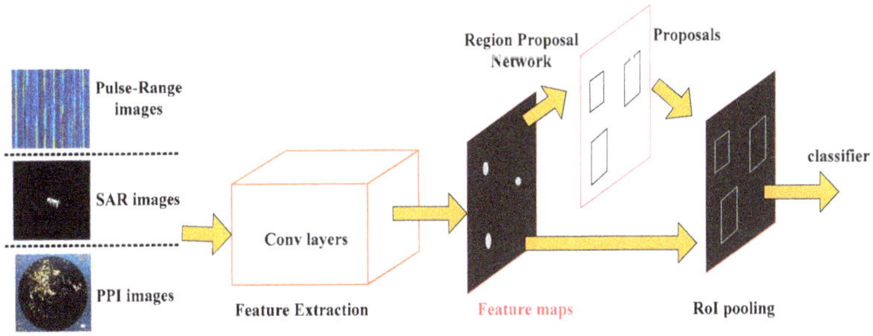

Figure 14. Basic structure of the Faster R-CNN.

CNN is a common deep learning architecture for target detection of SAR images. Wang et al. [74] presented a method and ideas of CNN in the research of target detection in SAR images, laying a foundation for future research. Yang et al. [75] adopted a DNN regression method for SAR images target detection based on the improved structure of YOLO [94]. This network is effective for extracting features with low resolution and complex composition. Zheng et al. [76] proposed a multi-feature target detection method in SAR imagers aiming at obtaining the target's actual position, which is presented in Figure 15. The CNN model was applied to capture deep features while the ANN was adopted to analyze hand-crafted features. Then, two sub-channel features are concatenated together in the main channel and the experimental results showed that the multi-features-based method outperformed other methods.

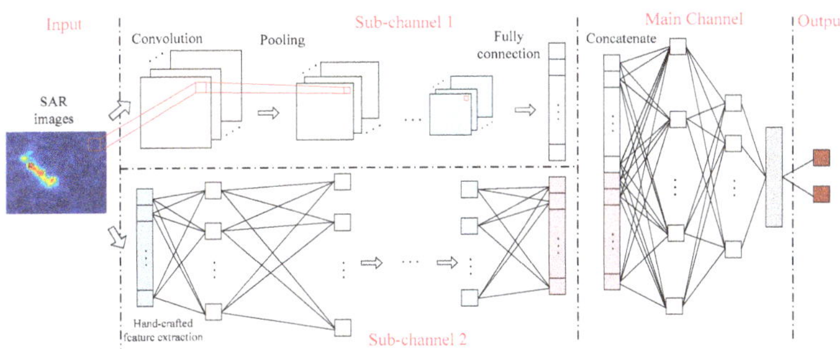

Figure 15. Structure of target detection model with multi-features in SAR images.

In addition, Faster R-CNN [93] was modified to improve detection performance in SAR images. Kang et al. [70] introduced a CNN-based detection method combining features and pixels in which the Faster R-CNN framework was modified by the traditional CFAR detection algorithm for small-sized targets detection, which is presented in Figure 16. For targets with clearer shape and structure, Faster R-CNN gave higher classification scores, while for those small-sized targets with smaller bounding boxes, the classification score was relatively low. CFAR was employed because this detector relies on the amplitude of the pixel rather than the shape or structure of the target. The combination of detectors based on deep features and pixels can improve the multi-scale target's detection performance. An SAR image is different from an optical image in that it reflects the electromagnetic characteristics of the target. Making full use of electromagnetic characteristics in feature extraction for RTD would help improve detection performance. Zhang et al. [77] fused electromagnetic and geometrical characteristics and involved the fused features in Faster R-CNN, and the architecture is presented in Figure 17. in their work, convolutional layers were utilized to extract geometric features of SAR images, just like the process of optical images. Meanwhile, SVM was applied to extract electromagnetic characteristics from the complex data.

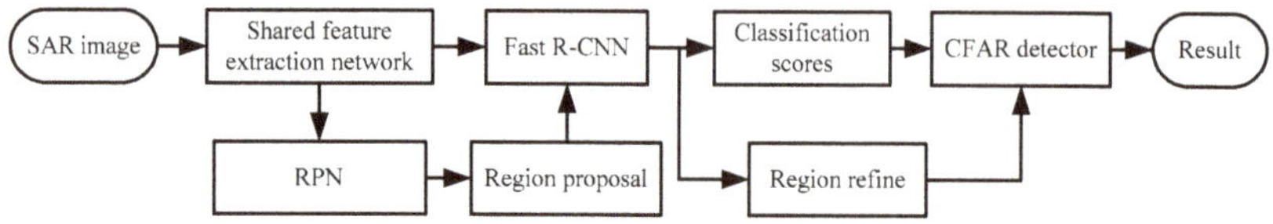

Figure 16. The flowchart of Faster R-CNN-based detector in SAR images.

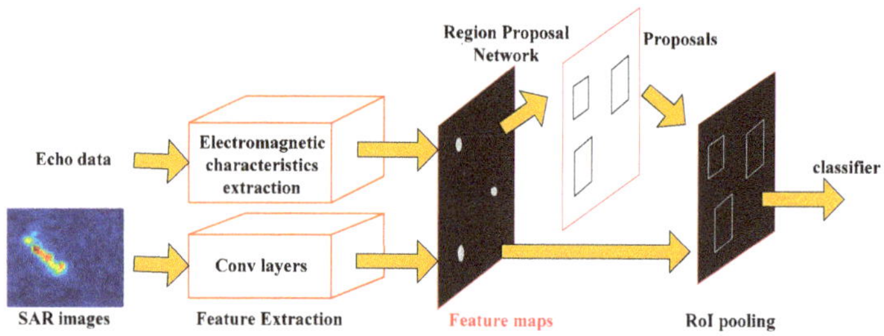

Figure 17. The structure of fused features of echo data and SAR images.

SSD is a single DNN designed to detect targets in images, which consists of the basic network and the auxiliary structure [95]. Zhao et al. [78] presented a SSD-based approach to deploy a maritime target detection network model of SAR on an embedded device. As shown in Figure 18, a truncated VGG-16 [97] is adopted as the backbone. The auxiliary structure generates the following key features for detection: convolution predictors, multi-scale feature maps, aspect ratios, and default boxes. Experiments based on the Gaofen-3 spaceborne SAR dataset showed that this approach has practicability and expansibility. Ma et al. [98] proposed a modified SSD model and designed a complete workflow for different targets detection in large-scale GF-3 SAR images.

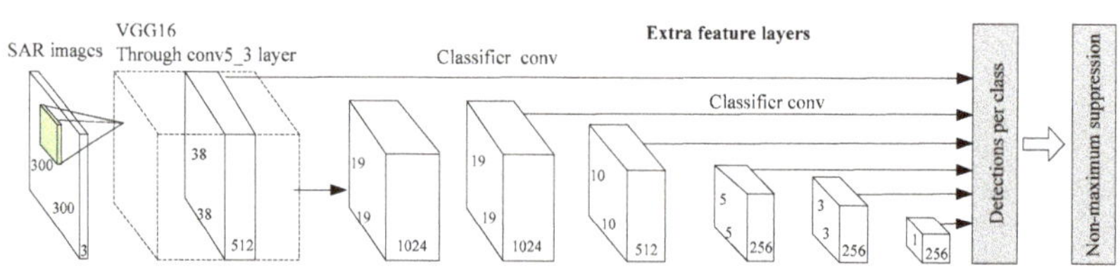

Figure 18. The structure of fused features in Faster R-CNN.

3.4.5. PPI Images

Although there are different visualizations of radar displays, such as P-display and A-display, they are all processed through radar signal processing and have a the similar process. Radar PPI images indicate all or part of the data of range, azimuth elevation or height. Mou et al. [71] proposed an improved Faster R-CNN method for marine target detection using radar PPI images. VGG16 and ResNet101 were used as backbone network models to extract target features. They modified Faster R-CNN in 4 aspects: (1) using the focal loss [99] instead of classification loss to overcome the deficiency of sample imbalance. (2) ROI Pooling is replaced by precise ROI Pooling [100] to reduce the precision loss in the process of scale unification and enhance the accuracy of pooling. (3) NMS is replaced by soft-NMS [101] to boost missing detection. (4) ReLU is replaced by ELUs [102] to speed up convergence and avoid gradient disappearance. Experimental results proved that compared with the traditional Faster R-CNN, the modified approach based on Faster R-CNN has better detection performance in stability and accuracy.

3.4.6. Time-Frequency Images

The development of micro-Doppler technology also provides a valid method for target detection [103,104]. Targets have the characteristics of micro-motion; due to the micro-motion of the targets, the amplitude and the phase of electromagnetic wave scattered by the moving parts change periodically or irregularly. This is, other words, the micro-motion signature induced by the high-speed moving parts of the targets, known as micro-Doppler.

The extraction of target micro-motion features is always one of the challenges in RTD. A common method for signal time-frequency analysis is Wigner-Ville distribution (WVD). Risueno et al. [72] introduced a WVD-CNN detector for RTD using less free weights than the conventional MLP scheme. Su et al. [73] investigated CNN-based methods (LeNet [105] and GoogLeNet [106] models) for maritime targets detection under different polarization and sea states. In this work, short-time Fourier transform (STFT) is adopted to convert the radar signal (IPIX measured data) to two-dimensional time-frequency images of the target and the clutter. According to the experiment results, LeNet is more efficient in echo signal preprocessing, while GoogLeNet has better detection performance under different polarization and sea states modes in P_D and P_{fa}.

3.5. *Summarization of Different Structures for RTD*

ANN-based models could be used as a kind of detectors to differentiate targets from noise or clutter with high detection performance, especially in a time-varying and non-homogeneous environment, the parameters of the background will change. The robustness of the detector is improved by training the network for different scenarios corresponding to different noise and clutter distribution parameters. Therefore, ANN-based detector is more robust and could provide a higher detection performance than the classical CFAR detector.

DNN-based models could be designed for different RTD tasks with different input forms. The purpose of RTD is to identify whether the radar echo undertested contains a signal from the target or only contains the noise, but more importantly, to obtain multi-dimensional information of position and motion. DNNs turned out to be qualified and excellent in RTD, and more complex architecture with different training ways for more complicated RTD scenes. In addition, various preprocessing methods of radar signal processing could extract features effectively, which could help to improve detection performance. A fusion of the traditional detection methods and the new concepts of deep learning methods has become a promising trend and solution in RTD application.

4. Summary of Datasets and Performance Evaluation

The effectiveness of deep learning-based methods depends largely on the available quantity of training data. The availability of a labelled dataset is regarded as a prerequisite for applying deep learning methods to a certain application. Although several publicly datasets are available for image processing, speech recognition, nature language processing, etc., there are very few ones for radar (except SAR images), not to mention the sampled radar data for RTD based on deep learning. In this review, we summarize IPIX and CSIR experimental datasets which have been used for RTD by some researchers. Although these two measured datasets have been used for RTD, they are not generally public because they are domain-specific. Therefore, we collect and summarize the related radar experimental parameters of these two datasets, which could help you to to understand the existing datasets or construct simulation datasets.

4.1. *Dataset Descriptions*

4.1.1. IPIX Database

The IPIX database is a widely-used database for sea-surface small target detection, sea clutter characteristic analysis and modeling. It was collected and maintained by Prof.

Haykin's research group at McMaster University. The IPIX database contains two data sets, one was collected by the popular intelligent pixel (IPIX) processing radar under the staring mode in the city of Dartmouth, Canada in 1993 [64,107], and the other came from IPIX radar in the Grimsby area of Canada in 1998 [108]. The Dartmouth database in 1993 contains 339 data sets which cover a wide range of wave and wind conditions. About 14 data files are particularly useful to test algorithms aiming at detecting small objects in sea clutter. All these target data files have a weak target in one of their range bins and are more than 2 min long, which (a subset) is available in [109]. The Grimsby experiment upgraded the quantization bits and measured sea clutter data from different range resolutions; in this way, weak clutter signals and strong targets can be observed simultaneously without large quantization errors or clipping. About 222 datasets in the Grimsby database focus specifically on the floating targets of various sizes, and the actual Grimsby data files are available in [110]. However, the related target information and auxiliary sea state information have yet to be released [111]. The parameters of IPIX radar, experimental parameters and sea state information are summarized in Table 3.

Table 3. IPIX radar and experimental parameters.

		IPIX Parameter		
Radar parameters	TX frequency (GHz)	9.39	Width of beam (°)	0.9 pencil beam
	Peak power (kW)	8	Antenna gain(dB)	45.7
	Pulse width(us)	0.2	Sampled range resolution (m)	15
	PRF (kHz)	0.8/1	Polarization mode	HH;HV;VH;VV
Experiment Summary	Year	1993 [1]		1998 [2]
	Longitude	63°25.41′ W		79°35′54.6″ W
	Latitude	44°36.72′ N		43°12′41.0″ N
	Height (m)	30		20
	Duration (s)	131		——
	Distance resolution (m)	30		3~60
	Target Type	Spherical buoyant apparatus		Floating boat
	Target range (m)	2660/5525/2655		——
	Target Azimuth (°)	128/130/170		——
	Quantization bits	8		10
Environmental parameters	SCR (dB)	0~6		——
	Observation direction	Upwind		——
	Significant wave height (m)	1.0/1.5/2.1		——
	Douglas sea state	2/3/4		——

[1] http://soma.ece.mcmaster.ca/ipix/dartmouth/datasets.html (accessed on 30 December 2021). [2] http://soma.mcmaster.ca/ipix.php (accessed on 30 December 2021).

There are limitations to using the IPIX database. These two datasets only cover restricted environmental conditions and limited relative positions, and related important auxiliary information was not recorded detailed, especially the measured data from 1998 [111]. The other limitation is that the radar echoes are only reflected from motionless floating objects, not mobile ships, so it is inevitable for researchers to add extra simulated target echo data. Li et al. [64] adopted the IPIX database to extract features for surface small target detection. Chen et al. [112] validated the proposed micromotion target detection method with a simulated IPIX dataset. Su et al. [72] used IPIX measured target signal and sea clutter data to conduct CNN training and testing schemes for maritime target detection. What is worth mentioning is that the results obtained in [72] are significantly worse than the simulated data. Besides the diversity of the measurements themselves, the low speed and acceleration of the targets in IPIX radar can also lead to degradation.

4.1.2. CSIR Database

The CSIR dataset was collected from two kinds of sea clutter and ship target echo measurement trials which were conducted by the Defense, Peace, Safety, and Security Unit of Council for Scientific and Industrial Research (CSIR) in the southwest coastline of South Africa. The first trial was conducted at the Overberg Test Range (OTR) near Arniston in July 2006 with the Fynment radar [113,114]. The second measurement trial was conducted on 4 November 2007 with an experimental monopulse radar deployed on top of Signal Hill in Cape Town [115,116]. Radar parameters and experimental parameters are demonstrated in Table 4.

Table 4. CSIR trial radar and experimental parameters.

	Items	Fynment Radar	Monopulse Radar
Radar parameters	TX frequency (GHz)	6.5~17.5	8.8
	Peak power (kW)	2	——
	PRF (kHz)	0~30	Adjustable
	Width of beam (°)	≤2	——
	Antenna gain(dB)	≥30	——
	Sampled range resolution (m)	15/45	15
	Gates	1~96	——
Experiment summary	Year	2006	2007
	Setup site	Overberg Test Range	Signal Hill
	Longitude	20°17′17.46″ E	18°23′53.76″ E
	Latitude	34°36′56.52″ S	33°55′15.62″ S
	Height (m)	67	294
	Grazing angle (°)	0.3~3	0.3~10
	Duration (s)	169.1	49.17
	Maximum target range (km)	15	60
	Target azimuth (°)	90° N~225° N	240°N~20° N
Environmental parameters	Mean wind speed (m/s)	0~10.3	0~20.58
	Wind direction	180° N~270° N	130° N~140° N,320° N~330° N
	Significant wave height (m)	1~3.8	1~6
	Swell direction	135° N~180° N	230° N~270° N

The CSIR dataset contains a large amount of sea clutter and target echo data, covering multiple parameter combination (various transmitted waveforms, azimuths and distances) under different environment conditions. The radar operating parameters, marine environment parameters, GPS auxiliary data and the types of cooperative target (inflatable boat, motor yacht and fishing boat) could make up the limitations of the IPIX database. A detailed trial designing scheme and trial data records are also maintained, which could provide reference and guidance for similar trials [108]. Currently, many research institutes are using the CSIR dataset in related research. In Pan's experiment [69], the dataset TFC15_008, collected from the Fynment radar was used to demonstrate that the DNN approach can easily detect small targets from sea clutter with low SCR and accurately locate the position of the targets compared with the traditional CFAR detection methods. Chen et al. [112] employed the CSIR database to validate the detection performance of marine maneuvering targets with translational motion.

In fact, from Table 2 in Section 2, we can conclude that most research teams construct and label radar datasets by simulation methods for deep RTD, besides SAR images, as the actual radar data was hard to obtain. The simulation parameters of radar waveform can also be referred from Tables 3 and 4.

4.2. Data Preprocessing and Construction

To boost target detection performance, appropriate preprocessing is necessary. According to the summarization of all related papers, radar received echoes, Pulse-Range maps, Range-Doppler spectrum and Time-Frequency images are widely-used in RTD.

All of them are transformed from raw radar echo by a train of signal processing methods or mathematical operations. In the signal processing process of a pulsed coherent radar, the received signals are processed by pulse compression, coherent accumulation, and clutter suppression. Therefore, to make a better comparison, we will discuss these inputs that are related to deep learning regarding RTD from the literature. Figure 19 shows the flow of the preprocessing of datasets for RTD.

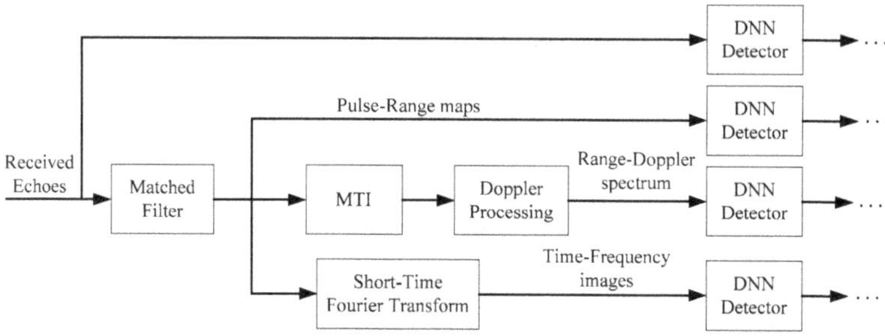

Figure 19. Preprocessing diagram of the dataset for the radar detection system.

4.2.1. Radar Received Echoes and Radar Cube

A typical pulsed radar system is considered in which a transmitted waveform $S(t)$ is emitted at a certain interval. The received echoes $S_r(t,k)$, which includes signals of a target and noise, are modulated by amplitudes, time delays, doppler frequency and then sampled at a given rate as (3):

$$S_r(t,k) = \sum_n \sigma_n S(t-\tau_n) e^{j\varphi_{n,k}} + W(t) \tag{3}$$

where $t = 1,2,\ldots,R$ (fast time). In the incoming radar echoes, σ_n denotes the reflectivity amplitude which can be calculated from the radar function, and τ_n is the time delay of target n, $W(t)$ is white Gaussian noise, an independent complex Gaussian random variable with mean zero. $e^{j\varphi_{n,k}}$ denotes the doppler shift for each target, for a target with a constant velocity, it can be defined as (4):

$$\varphi_{n,k} = \varphi_{n,k-1} + 2\pi f_c \frac{2v_n}{c} T_r \tag{4}$$

where $k = 1,\ldots,M$ (slow time), M is the total number of pulses in a coherent processing interval (CPI), assuming $\varphi_{n,0} = 0$ and v_n is the radial velocity of target n, f_c is the radar carrier frequency, T_r is the pulse repetition interval and c is the propagation velocity.

Simulations in a setting with fluctuating targets model and noise background are carried out to construct the radar received echoes for RTD. An example of how different targets stand out in different SNR is presented in Figure 20. The emitted pulse is assumed to be a unit vector which does not incorporate any beneficial compression gains or additional antenna gains. The targets are assumed to fluctuate slowly and follow the standard Swerling distribution, where the value of σ_n varies randomly. It is assumed to consider the impact of path propagation and other environmental effects indirectly. By time and frequency domain analysis of radar received echoes, targets or environment characteristics can be obtained.

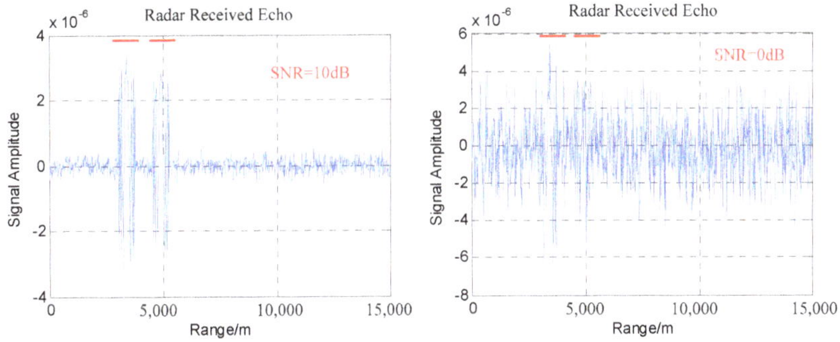

Figure 20. Example of simulated radar received echoes with different SNR, **left**: SNR = 10 dB, **right**: SNR = 0 dB.

Using raw data as the input to perform RTD training without any preprocessing method is a complete "end-to-end" task, and the radar echo cube enables the network to exploit the temporal and spatial correlation simultaneously [49], which is presented in Figure 21. Prashant et al. [58] used radar received echoes to detect signals in a non-Gaussian noise environment. However, for raw data, it may require a deeper network to extract target features; in other words, the increasing complex detection environment makes the "end-to-end" tasks more challenging.

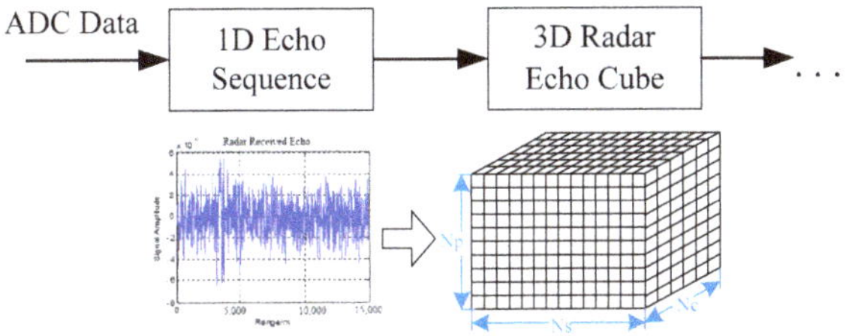

Figure 21. Data preprocessing for a radar echo cube.

4.2.2. Pulse-Range Maps

Radar emits multiple pulses in the CPI, and the reflected signals are integrated in a coherent or incoherent way. The axes of the original echo data can be labelled as 'fast' and 'slow' time, where fast time is utilized to calculate distance and slow time is used to calculate doppler velocity (see in Figure 22). Pulse compression is applied to the echo signal via a standard matched filtering operation, using the reference signal over the fast time, which is calculated as (5):

$$\hat{S}_r(t,k) = S^*(-t) * S_r(t,k) \quad (5)$$

The operation of pulse compression through matched filter can obtain a narrow pulse width and a high resolution of range profile, but has no impact on the radar detection range. Therefore, the problem of RTD can be converted into target detection and location in Pulse-Range maps. The upper part of Figure 22 shows an example of the Pulse-Range map. Akhtar et al. [60] used Pulse-Range maps to detect targets in a noisy background, and in [69], the Pulse-Range maps were applied to ranging and detecting targets from sea clutter.

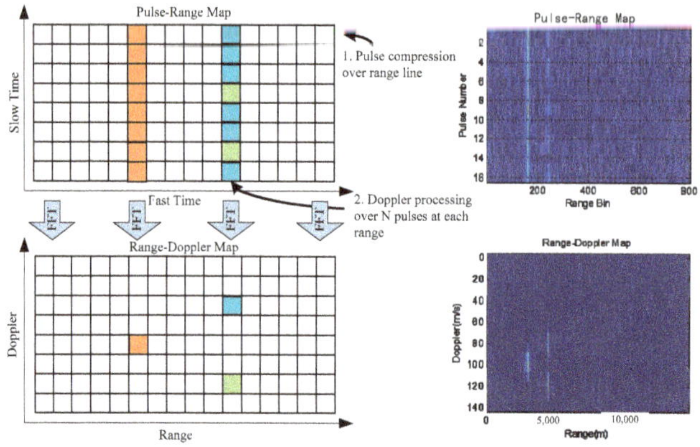

Figure 22. Schematic diagram of a pulse compression and Doppler processing.

4.2.3. Range-Doppler Maps

Subsequent to gathering all pulses, doppler processing is applied over multiple pulses by applying fast Fourier transform (FFT) over a slow time at each range. The slow time domain of $\hat{S}_r(t,k)$ is multiplied by a window function firstly and then FFT is used to yield a range-Doppler spectrum as (6):

$$\hat{S}_r(t,\omega) = F(win \times \hat{S}_r(t,k)) \tag{6}$$

where win is a windowing function, F denotes the discrete Fourier transform (DFT). Following DFT, targets with a steady pace will appear concentrated in doppler. An example of doppler processing after matched filtering is shown in Figure 22. The Range-Doppler map in Figure 22 shows three targets at different doppler bins, a close target at range 180 samples having a positive velocity, which indicates that the target is moving towards the radar (shown as orange grid in Figure 22), and 2 moving targets at the same range 250 samples but different doppler bins (shown as blue and green grids respectively). Multiple frames are extracted from the raw data, producing a sequence of Range-Doppler frames.

Range-Doppler maps with targets absent and present is presented in Figure 23. The target echo occupies multiple cells, forming a mountain-like shape in the spectrum. If the SNR is low, the two targets at the range of 250 samples are not obvious in the spectrum. Researchers often consider the Range-Doppler map as an image, and use a classifier to classify the image as target absent or present. Target present examples with different SNR can be generated By setting a different noise power. In Refs. [62,65–67], range-Doppler maps were utilized in various RTD tasks.

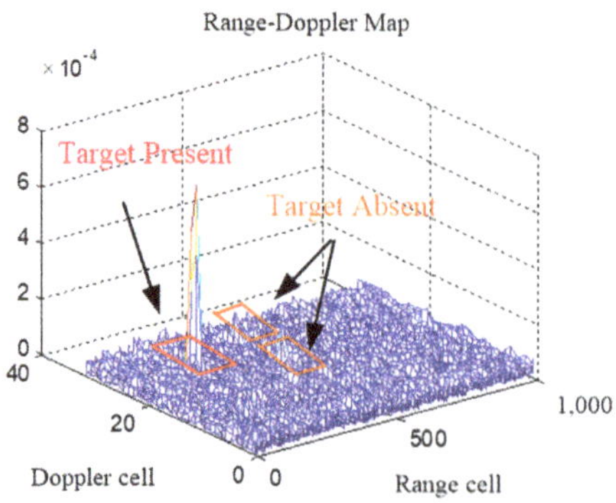

Figure 23. Target present and Target absent in Range-Doppler Map.

4.2.4. Time-Frequency Images

The time-frequency analysis method is an effective and powerful tool in analyzing time-varying non-stationary signals because of the time-varying characteristics of target micro-motion. After demodulation and pulse compression are applied on the radar echo, STFT is often adopted to convert the radar echo to two-dimensional time-frequency images, as shown in (7):

$$STFT(t,f) = \int_{-\infty}^{+\infty} \hat{S}_r(\delta,k)g^*(\delta - t)e^{-j2\pi f\delta}d\delta \quad (7)$$

where $g(t)$ is a narrow windowing function such as a Hamming window function. Since the micro-motion characteristics of targets differ from background noise or clutter, time-frequency images are utilized to build training and testing datasets. Su et al. [72] adopted a time-frequency analysis method to analyze micro-motion characteristics, thereby differentiating targets from clutter.

4.3. Performance Evaluation

RTD is a fundamental process for separating targets of interest from background noise. A primary goal of RTD is to satisfy two very contradictory requirements: acquire a high P_D with a low P_{fa}. Comparing the P_D under the same P_{fa} with the DNN-based detector and CFAR detector respectively is the common metric of detection performance [59,70]. P_D and P_{fa} are defined as (8) and (9):

$$P_D = \frac{N_{td}}{N_{total\_targets}} \quad (8)$$

$$P_{fa} = \frac{N_{fd}}{N_{de\_targets}} \quad (9)$$

where N_{td} is the total number of truly detected targets, $N_{total\_targets}$ denotes the total number of targets in the sample, N_{fd} is the total number of falsely detected targets (mistaken for targets), $N_{de\_targets}$ is the total number of non-targets in the sample.

4.4. Summarization of Dataset and Preprocessing

The actual radar data is not widely accessible at present because of the particularity of RTD tasks. Although a few of the existing datasets, such as, IPIX and CSIR, whose data have been used for sea surface targets detection and sea clutter characteristic analysis, most recent research on RTD still relies on synthetic or simulation data. In this section, we describe how to construct radar received echoes and preprocess three types of data which are widely used in RTD. Three types of data processed in radar signal processing are applied in different target detection tasks with respective characteristics. Since pulse compression could obtain a high resolution of the range profile, pulse-range maps are mainly used in radar ranging tasks. Range-Doppler maps are more commonly used in position and velocity measurement in complex scenarios with background noise or clutter because doppler processing could improve SNR effectively. The time-frequency analysis method is efficient and especially suitable for targets with distinct micro-motion characteristics. An example would be maritime target detection and recognition, which can make full use of the micro-motion information of the target and clutter.

5. Discussion

Although deep learning-based approaches have had some successful applications in the field of RTD, the following challenges remain:

5.1. Dataset Deficiency

One of the difficulties in applying deep learning-based methods to RTD is the lack of publicly available labelled data. The difference with other applications is the high cost of radar data collection. Currently, radar system simulation modeling is a method to solve the problem, but it is computationally demanding and extremely challenging to generate alternative data because multiple factors need to be considered, e.g., multiple attenuation, discrete cells and multipath reflections. In other words, even if all the above issues are avoided, relying on mathematical models for simulation is inevitable, which may introduce the problem of model fidelity. Similar inaccuracies have emerged in [72].

We still hope to get enough data for training from real-world radar systems, which will certainly make the detection model more reliable. In order to further advance the research of RTD in the absence of realistic radar data, the following approaches can be considered: (1) Data augmentation, which has been used in [67,68]; (2) Developing more robust deep learning-based algorithms with insufficient training data, such as generative adversarial networks (GAN) [117]; (3) Establishing more advanced RTD frameworks seems to be a new trend; (4) Developing learning-based methods, such as meta learning [118,119] and transfer learning [120,121], which can overcome the limitation of insufficient data and insensitivity to the changes of the radar detection environment.

5.2. Varied Models in Complex Tasks

Although the application of deep learning technology in RTD has made remarkable progress, the existing literatures on ANNs and DNNs of RTD are still relatively sparse and not mature enough. For instance, a common aspect found in many of the papers cited above is the moderate size of ANN, where the networks proposed in [58,61] contain only one hidden layer. In addition, although many other architectures have been proposed in DNN, only CNN is widely used in RTD. Therefore, there is plenty of room to explore various DNN in RTD. Signal processing system that can efficiently suppress target RCS fluctuations, noise, clutter, and jamming is always considered as one of the key directions of radar research and development. How to effectively distinguish targets from strong active jammed signals is still under investigation. How to verify other deep learning architectures can perform better in RTD also needs to be considered. These also imply that newer, more diverse but practical powerful learning schemes for more complex tasks are required urgently.

The advance in computing power allows the training of large-scaled deep learning models on massive data. Remarkable progress in deep learning algorithms and great advances in radar system would benefit each other. It is worth exploring replacing the entire radar signal processing by deep learning methods.

5.3. Integrated Training Methods

Much of the existing research shows that the deep fusion of traditional signal processing methods and deep learning-based schemes in RTD application is an evident trend [122]. For one thing, as a kind of data preprocessing method, traditional radar signal processing methods, such as pulse compression, coherent accumulation, STFT, etc., are beneficial to enhance features, thus improving the detection performance. For another, according to the previous review, neural networks combined with typical radar signal processing approaches (e.g., CFAR) as a learning strategy can help improve detection performance. In addition, we believe that models based on deep learning can provide an "end-to-end" framework for integrating perception, processing and decision making. Besides, studies of simulation process optimization, performance judgment criteria and other basic problems, such as model interpretability and generalization ability, are still under investigation.

6. Conclusions

Research efforts in artificial neural network and deep learning models in RTD has been discussed in this review. Various architectures of networks for various application schemes have been investigated. The results obtained have shown that deep learning-based detectors perform better than the traditional processing methods to some certain degree in some specific cases. Although the study of deep learning in the field of RTD is at the initial stage and still faces some challenges, there is no doubt that the research and usage of deep learning-based methods in RTD will contribute great improvement in the future. We wish to take a step towards making deep learning more applicable to the related fields of radar signal processing.

Author Contributions: Conceptualization, W.J. and Y.L.; methodology, W.J. and Y.R.; investigation, W.J. and Y.R.; resources, Y.L. and J.L.; writing—original draft preparation, W.J.; writing—review and editing, Y.L.; supervision, Y.L. All authors have read and agreed to the published version of the manuscript.

Funding: This research received no external funding.

Acknowledgments: This work was supported in part by the National Natural Science Foundation of China under Grant 71671178, 62176247, 62036007, 62050175, and 62102057. It was also supported by the Fundamental Research Funds for the Central Universities and the Science and Technology Research Program of Chongqing Municipal Education Commission (KJQN-202100627).

Conflicts of Interest: The authors declare no conflict of interest.

References

1. Richards, M.A. *Fundamentals of Radar Signal Processing*, 1st ed.; McGraw-Hill: New York, NY, USA, 2005.
2. Kay, S.M. *Fundamentals of Statistical Signal Processing: Detection Theory*; Prentice Hall PTR: Hoboken, NJ, USA, 1998; Volume 2.
3. Melvin, W.L.; Scheer, J.A. (Eds.) *Principles of Modern Radar*; SciTech Publishing: Raleigh, NC, USA, 2013.
4. Long, T.; Liang, Z.; Liu, Q. Advanced technology of high-resolution radar: Target detection, tracking, imaging, and recognition. *Sci. China Inf. Sci.* **2019**, *62*, 1–26. [CrossRef]
5. LeCun, Y.; Bengio, Y.; Hinton, G. Deep Learning. *Nature* **2015**, *521*, 436–444. [CrossRef]
6. Bengio, Y.; Courville, A.; Vincent, P. Representation Learning: A Review and New Perspectives. *IEEE Trans. Pattern Anal. Mach. Intell.* **2013**, *35*, 1798–1828. [CrossRef] [PubMed]
7. Xisto, L.T.; Sergio, L.A.; Nathan, I. Artificial Neural Networks and Machine Learning techniques applied to Ground Penetrating Radar: A review. *Appl. Comput. Inf.* **2018**, *17*, 296–308. [CrossRef]
8. Goodfellow, I.; Bengio, Y.; Courville, A. *Deep Learning*; The MIT Press: Cambridge, MA, USA, 2016.
9. Mason, E.; Yonel, B.; Yazici, B. Deep Learning for Radar. In Proceedings of the 2017 IEEE Radar Conference, Seattle, WA, USA, 8–12 May 2017. [CrossRef]
10. Wang, C.; Wang, J.; Zhang, X. Automatic Radar Waveform Recognition based on Time-frequency Analysis and Convolutional Neural Network. In Proceedings of the 2017 IEEE International Conference on Acoustics, Speech and Signal Processing (ICASSP), New Orleans, LA, USA, 5–9 March 2017; pp. 2437–2441.
11. Singhal, M.; Saini, G. Optimization of Antenna Parameters Using Artificial Neural Network: A Review. *Int. J. Comput. Trends Technol.* **2017**, *44*, 64–73. [CrossRef]
12. Kim, Y.; Keely, S.; Ghosh, J.; Ling, H. Application of Artificial Neural Networks to Broadband Antenna Design Based on a Parametric Frequency Model. *IEEE Trans. Antennas Propag.* **2007**, *55*, 669–674. [CrossRef]
13. Rawat, A.; Yadav, R.; Shrivastava, S. Neural network applications in smart antenna arrays: A review. *Int. J. Electron. Commun.* **2012**, *66*, 903–912. [CrossRef]
14. Elbir, A.M.; Mishra, K.V.; Eldar, Y.C. Cognitive radar antenna selection via deep learning. *IET Radar Sonar Navig.* **2019**, *13*, 871–880. [CrossRef]
15. Haykin, S. Cognitive radar: A way of the future. *IEEE Signal Process. Mag.* **2006**, *23*, 30–40. [CrossRef]
16. Gao, J.; Lu, Y.; Qi, J.; Shen, L. A Radar Signal Recognition System Based on Non-Negative Matrix Factorization Network and Improved Artificial Bee Colony Algorithm. *IEEE Access* **2019**, *7*, 117612–117626. [CrossRef]
17. Chen, S.; Wang, H. SAR Target Recognition based on Deep Learning. In Proceedings of the International Conference on Data Science and Advanced Analytics (DSAA), Shanghai, China, 30 October–1 November 2014.
18. Ding, J.; Chen, B.; Liu, H.; Huang, M. Convolutional Neural Network with Data Augmentation for SAR Target Recognition. *IEEE Geosci. Remote Sens. Lett.* **2016**, *13*, 364–368. [CrossRef]
19. Geng, J.; Fan, J.; Wang, H.; Ma, X.; Li, B.; Chen, F. High-resolution SAR Image Classification via Deep Convolutional Autoencoders. *IEEE Geosci. Remote Sens. Lett.* **2015**, *12*, 2351–2355. [CrossRef]
20. Liu, H.; Feng, B.; Chen, B.; Du, L. Radar high-resolution range profiles target recognition based on stable dictionary learning. *IET Radar Sonar Navig.* **2016**, *10*, 228–237. [CrossRef]
21. Liao, K.; Si, J.; Zhu, F.; He, X. Radar HRRP Target Recognition Based on Concatenated Deep Neural Networks. *IEEE Access* **2018**, *6*, 29211–29218. [CrossRef]
22. Feng, B.; Chen, B.; Liu, H. Radar HRRP target recognition with deep networks. *Pattern Recognit.* **2017**, *61*, 379–393. [CrossRef]
23. Yu, S.; Xie, Y. Application of a Convolutional Autoencoder to Half Space Radar HRRP Recognition. In Proceedings of the 2018 International Conference on Wavelet Analysis and Pattern Recognition, Chengdu, China, 15–18 July 2018.

24. Seyfioglu, M.S.; Gurbuz, S.Z. Deep Neural Network Initialization Methods for Micro-Doppler Classification with Low Training Sample Support. *IEEE Geosci. Remote Sens. Lett.* **2017**, *14*, 2462–2466. [CrossRef]
25. Kouemou, G. Radar Target Classification Technologies. In *Radar Technology*; InTech: Rijeka, Croatia, 2010.
26. Lombacher, J.; Hahn, M.; Dickmann, J.; Wöhler, C. Potential of Radar for Static Object Classification using Deep Learning Methods. In Proceedings of the 2016 IEEE MTT-S International Conference on Microwaves for Intty (ICMIM), San Diego, CA, USA, 19–20 May 2016.
27. Ningyuan, S.; Xiaolong, C.; Jian, G.; Xiaoqian, M.; Ningbo, L. Detection and Classification of Marine Target with Micro-motion Based on CNNs. *J. Radar* **2018**, *7*, 565–574. [CrossRef]
28. Mendis, G.J.; Wei, J.; Madanayake, A. Deep Learning Cognitive Radar for Micro UAS Detection and Classification. In Proceedings of the 2017 Cognitive Communications for Aerospace Applications Workshop (CCAA), Cleveland, OH, USA, 27–28 June 2017; pp. 1–5.
29. Kim, Y.; Moon, T. Human Detection and Activity Classification Based on Micro-Doppler Signatures Using Deep Convolutional Neural Networks. *IEEE Geosci. Remote Sens. Lett.* **2016**, *13*, 8–12. [CrossRef]
30. Jiang, W.; Ren, Y.; Liu, Y.; Wang, Z.; Wang, X. Recognition of Dynamic Hand Gesture Based on Mm-wave FMCW Radar Micro-Doppler Signatures. In Proceedings of the IEEE International Conference on Acoustics, Speech and Signal Processing, Toronto, ON, Canada, 6–11 June 2021.
31. Dong, X.; Zhao, Z.; Wang, Y.; Zeng, T.; Wang, J.; Sui, Y. FMCW Radar-Based Hand Gesture Recognition using Spatiotemporal Deformable and Context-Aware Convolutional 5D Feature Representation. *IEEE Trans. Geosci. Remote Sens.* **2021**. [CrossRef]
32. Lohman, B.; Boric-Lubecke, O.; Lubecke, V.M.; Ong, P.W.; Sondhi, M.M. A Digital Signal Processor for Doppler Radar Sensing of Vital Signs. *IEEE Eng. Med. Biol. Mag.* **2001**, *4*, 3359–3362. [CrossRef]
33. Wang, K.; Zeng, Z.; Sun, J. Through-Wall Detection of the Moving Paths and Vital Signs of Human Beings. *IEEE Geosci. Remote Sens. Lett.* **2018**, *16*, 717–721. [CrossRef]
34. Qiu, L.; Jin, T.; Lu, B.; Zhou, Z. An Isophase-Based Life Signal Extraction in Through-the-Wall Radar. *IEEE Geosci. Remote Sens. Lett.* **2016**, *14*, 193–197. [CrossRef]
35. Cardillo, E.; Li, C.; Caddemi, A. Millimeter-Wave Radar Cane: A Blind People Aid with Moving Human Recognition Capabilities. *IEEE J. Electromagn. RF Microw. Med. Biol.* **2021**. [CrossRef]
36. Chen, H.; Ye, W. Classification of Human Activity Based on Radar Signal Using 1-D Convolutional Neural Network. *IEEE Geosci. Remote Sens. Lett.* **2019**, *17*, 1178–1182. [CrossRef]
37. Barkat, M. On Adaptive Cell-averaging CFAR Radar Signal Detection. Ph.D. Thesis, Department of Electrical and Computer Engineering, Syracuse University, New York, NY, USA, 1987.
38. Seyfioğlu, M.; Özbayoğlu, A.; Gürbüz, S. Deep Convolutional Autoencoder for Radar-based Classification of Similar Aided and Unaided Human Activities. *IEEE Trans. Aerosp. Electron. Syst.* **2018**, *54*, 1709–1723. [CrossRef]
39. Park, J.; Rios, J.; Moon, T.; Kim, Y. Micro-Doppler based Classification of Human Activities on Water via Transfer Learning of Convolutional Neural Networks. *Sensors* **2016**, *16*, 19–90. [CrossRef] [PubMed]
40. Khalid, H.; Pollin, S.; Rykunov, M.; Bourdoux, A.; Sahli, H. Convolutional Long Short-Term Memory Networks for Doppler-Radar based Target Classification. In Proceedings of the 2019 IEEE Radar Conference, Boston, MA, USA, 22–26 April 2019. [CrossRef]
41. Jokanovic, B.; Amin, M. Fall Detection Using Deep Learning in Range-Doppler Radars. *IEEE Trans. Aerosp. Electron. Syst.* **2017**, *54*, 180–189. [CrossRef]
42. Cortes, C.; Vapnik, V.N. Support Vector Networks. *Mach. Learn.* **1995**, *20*, 273–297. [CrossRef]
43. Short, R.; Fukunaga, K. The optimal distance measure for nearest neighbor classification. *IEEE Trans. Inf. Theory* **1981**, *27*, 622–627. [CrossRef]
44. Mountrakis, G.; Im, J.; Ogole, C. Support vector machines in remote sensing: A review. *ISPRS J. Photogramm. Remote Sens.* **2011**, *66*, 247–259. [CrossRef]
45. Youngwook, K. Application of Machine Learning to Antenna Design and Radar Signal Processing: A Review. In Proceedings of the 2018 International Symposium on Antennas and Propagation (ISAP), Busan, Korea, 23–26 October 2018.
46. del Rey-Maestre, N.; Jarabo-Amores, M.P.; Mata-Moya, D.; Humanes, J.; Hoyo, P. Machine Learning Techniques for Coherent CFAR Detection Based on Statistical Modeling of UHF Passive Ground Clutter. *IEEE J. Sel. Top. Signal Proc.* **2018**, *12*, 104–118. [CrossRef]
47. Mata-Moya, D.; Del-Rey-Maestre, N.; Peláez-Sánchez, V.M.; Jarabo-Amores, M.-P.; Martín-De-Nicolás, J. MLP-CFAR for improving coherent radar detectors robustness in variable scenarios. *Expert Syst. Appl.* **2015**, *42*, 4878–4891. [CrossRef]
48. Cao, T.; Palmer, J.; Berry, P. False Alarm Control of CFAR Algorithms with Experimental Bistatic Radar Data. In Proceedings of the IEEE Radar Conference, Arlington, VA, USA, 10–14 May 2010; pp. 156–161.
49. Jiang, W.; Ren, Y.; Liu, Y.; Leng, J. A Method of Radar Target Detection Based on Convolutional Neural Network. *Neural Comput. Appl.* **2021**. [CrossRef]
50. Sciotti, M.; Lombardo, P. Performance Evaluation of Radar Detection Schemes based on CA-CFAR Against K-distributed Clutter. In Proceedings of the 2001 CIE International Conference on Radar, Beijing, China, 15–18 October 2001; pp. 345–349.
51. Gandhi, P.; Kassam, S. Optimality of the cell averaging CFAR detector. *IEEE Trans. Inf. Theory* **1994**, *40*, 1226–1228. [CrossRef]
52. Rohling, H. Radar CFAR Thresholding in Clutter and Multiple Target Situations. *IEEE Trans. Aerosp. Electron. Syst.* **1983**, *19*, 608–621. [CrossRef]

53. Rohling, H. New CFAR-Processor Based on An Ordered Statistic. In Proceedings of the IEEE 1985 International Radar Conference, Arlington, VA, USA, 6–9 May 1985.
54. Ritcey, J.A. Censored Mean-level Detector Analysis. *IEEE Trans. Aerosp. Electron. Syst.* **1986**, *AES-22*, 443–454. [CrossRef]
55. Reed, R.; Marks, R.J. *Neural Smithing: Supervised Learning in Feedforward Artificial Neural Networks*; MIT Press: Cambridge, MA, USA, 1999.
56. Bishop, C.M. *Pattern Recognition and Machine Learning*; Springer: Berlin/Heidelberg, Germany, 2006.
57. Google's AI Brain. Available online: http://research.google.com/teams/brain/ (accessed on 30 January 2017).
58. Gandhi, P.P.; Ramamurti, V. Neural networks for signal detection in non-Gaussian noise. *IEEE Trans. Signal Process.* **1997**, *45*, 2846–2851. [CrossRef]
59. Rohman, B.P.A.; Kurniawan, D.; Miftahushudur, M.T. Switching CA/OS CFAR using Neural Network for Radar Target Detection in Non-Homogeneous Environment. In Proceedings of the 2015 International Electronics Symposium (IES), Surabaya, Indonesia, 29–30 September 2015.
60. Akhtar, J.; Olsen, K.E. A Neural Network Target Detector with Partial CA-CFAR Supervised Training. In Proceedings of the 2018 International Conference on Radar (RADAR), Brisbane, QLD, Australia, 27–31 August 2018.
61. Amoozegar, F.; Sundareshan, M.K. A Robust Neural Network Scheme for CFAR Processing for Target Detection in Clutter Environment. In Proceedings of the American Control Conference, Baltimore, MD, USA, 29 June 1994.
62. Cheikh, K.; Soltani, F. Application of Neural Networks to Radar Signal Detection in K-distributed Clutter. *IEE Proc. Radar Sonar Navig.* **2006**, *153*, 460–466. [CrossRef]
63. Callaghan, D.; Burger, J.; Mishra, A.K. A Machine Learning Approach to Radar Sea Clutter Suppression. In Proceedings of the IEEE Radar Conference, Seattle, WA, USA, 8–12 May 2017. [CrossRef]
64. Li, Y.; Xie, P.; Tang, Z.; Jiang, T.; Qi, P. SVM-Based Sea-Surface Small Target Detection: A False-Alarm-Rate-Controllable Approach. *IEEE Geosci. Remote Sens. Lett.* **2019**, *16*, 1225–1229. [CrossRef]
65. Akhtar, J.; Olsen, K.E. GO-CFAR Trained Neural Network Target Detectors. In Proceedings of the 2019 IEEE Radar Conference, Boston, MA, USA, 22–26 April 2019. [CrossRef]
66. Wang, L.; Tang, J.; Liao, Q. A Study on Radar Target Detection Based on Deep Neural Networks. *IEEE Sens. Lett.* **2019**, *3*, 1–4. [CrossRef]
67. Brodeski, D.; Bilik, I.; Giryes, R. Deep Radar Detector. In Proceedings of the 2019 IEEE Radar Conference, Boston, MA, USA, 22–26 April 2019. [CrossRef]
68. Wheeler, T.A.; Holder, M.; Winner, H.; Kochenderfer, M.J. Deep Stochastic Radar Models. In Proceedings of the 28th IEEE Intelligent Vehicles Symposium, Los Angeles, CA, USA, 11–14 June 2017; Available online: Github.com/tawheeler/2017_iv_deep_radar (accessed on 20 December 2021).
69. Pan, M.; Chen, J.; Wang, S.; Dong, Z. A Novel Approach for Marine Small Target Detection Based on Deep Learning. In Proceedings of the IEEE 4th International Conference on Signal and Image Processing, Wuxi, China, 19–21 July 2019; pp. 395–399. [CrossRef]
70. Kang, M.; Leng, X.; Lin, Z.; Ji, K. A Modified Faster R-CNN based on CFAR Algorithm for SAR Ship Detection. In Proceedings of the 2017 International Workshop on Remote Sensing with Intelligent Processing (RSIP), Shanghai, China, 18–21 May 2017. [CrossRef]
71. Mou, X.; Chen, X.; Guan, J. Marine Target Detection Based on Improved Faster R-CNN for Navigation Radar PPI Images. In Proceedings of the 2019 International Conference on Control, Automation and Information Sciences, Chengdu, China, 23–26 October 2019.
72. Risueno, G.; Haykin, S.; Oliver, R. *Convolutional Neural Networks for Radar Detection*; Springer: Berlin/Heidelberg, Germany, 2002; pp. 1150–1155.
73. Su, N.; Chen, X.; Guan, J.; Li, Y. Deep CNN-Based Radar Detection for Real Maritime Target Under Different Sea States and Polarizations. In *Cognitive Systems and Signal Processing*; Springer: Singapore, 2019; Volume 1006. [CrossRef]
74. Wang, Y.; Zhang, Y.; Qu, H.; Tian, Q. Target Detection and Recognition Based on Convolutional Neural Network for SAR Image. In Proceedings of the 2018 11th International Congress on Image and Signal Processing, Biomedical Engineering and Informatics, Beijing, China, 13–15 October 2018.
75. Yang, T.; Zhu, J.; Liu, J. SAR Image Target Detection and Recognition based on Deep Network. In Proceedings of the 2019 SAR in Big Data Era, Beijing, China, 5–6 August 2019. [CrossRef]
76. Zheng, T.; Wang, J.; Lei, P. Deep Learning based Target Detection Method with Multi-features in SAR Imagery. In Proceedings of the 2019 6th Asia-Pacific Conference on Synthetic Aperture Radar (APSAR), Xiamen, China, 26–29 November 2019.
77. Zhang, J.; Xing, M.; Sun, G. A Fast Target Detection Method for SAR Image Based on Electromagnetic Characteristics. In Proceedings of the 2018 China International SAR Symposium (CISS), Shanghai, China, 10–12 October 2018.
78. Zhao, C.; Wang, P.; Wang, J.; Men, Z. A Marine Target Detector based on CNN and Embedded Device for GF-3 Images. In Proceedings of the 2019 6th Asia-Pacific Conference on Synthetic Aperture Radar (APSAR), Xiamen, China, 26–29 November 2019.
79. Moller, M.F. A Scaled Conjugate Gradient Algorithm for Fast Supervised Learning. *Neural Netw.* **1993**, *6*, 525–533. [CrossRef]
80. Robbins, H.; Monro, S. A Stochastic Approximation Method. *Ann. Math. Stat.* **1951**, *22*, 400–407. [CrossRef]
81. Kingma, D.; Ba, J. Adam: A Method for Stochastic Optimization. In Proceedings of the International Conference on Learning Representations, San Diego, CA, USA, 7–9 May 2015.

82. Zeiler, M.D. Adadelta: An Adaptive Learning Rate Method. *Comput. Sci.* **2012**. Available online: https://arxiv.org/abs/1212.5701v1 (accessed on 20 December 2021).
83. Kassam, S.A. *Signal Detection in Non-Gaussian Noise*; Springer: New York, NY, USA, 1988.
84. Garth, L.M.; Poor, H.V. Detection of Non-Gaussian Signals: A Paradigm for Modern Statistical Signal Processing. *Proc. IEEE* **1994**, *7*, 1061–1095. [CrossRef]
85. Gandhi, P.P.; Kassam, S.A. Analysis of CFAR processors in nonhomogeneous background. *IEEE Trans. Aerosp. Electron. Syst.* **1988**, *24*, 427–445. [CrossRef]
86. Jarabo-Amores, P.; Mata-Moya, D.; Zurera, M.R.; Nieto-Borge, J.C.; L'opez-Ferreras, F. A Neural Network Approach to Improve Radar Detector Robustness. In Proceedings of the 14th European Signal Processing Conference, Florence, Italy, 4–8 September 2006.
87. Galvez, N.; Pasciaroni, J.; Agamennoni, O.; Cousseau, J. Radar Signal Detector Implemented with Artificial Neural Networks. In Proceedings of the XIX Congreso Argentino de Control Automatico; 2004. Available online: https://www.researchgate.net/publication/236222896_RADAR_SIGNAL_DETECTOR_IMPLEMENTED_WITH_ARTIFICIAL_NEURAL_NETWORKS (accessed on 20 December 2021).
88. Wang, J.; Zheng, T.; Lei, P.; Wei, S. Study on Deep Learning in Radar. *Radars* **2018**, *7*, 395–411.
89. Huang, G.; Liu, Z.; Weinberger, K.Q. Densely Connected Convolutional Networks. In Proceedings of the 2017 IEEE Conference on Computer Vision and Pattern Recognition (CVPR), Honolulu, HI, USA, 21–26 July 2017; Volume 1, pp. 2261–2269.
90. Girshick, R.; Donahue, J.; Darrell, T.; Malik, J. Rich Feature Hierarchies for Accurate Object Detection and Semantic Segmentation. In Proceedings of the IEEE Conference on Computer Vision and Pattern Recognition, Columbus, OH, USA, 23–28 June 2014. [CrossRef]
91. He, K.; Zhang, X.; Ren, S.; Sun, J. Spatial Pyramid Pooling in Deep Convolutional Networks for Visual Recognition. *IEEE Trans. Pattern Anal. Mach. Intell.* **2015**, *37*, 1904–1916. [CrossRef]
92. Girshick, R. Fast R-CNN. In Proceedings of the 2015 IEEE International Conference on Computer Vision, Santiago, Chile, 7–13 December 2015. [CrossRef]
93. Ren, S.; He, K.; Girshick, R.; Sun, J. Faster R-CNN: Towards Real-Time Object Detection with Region Proposal Network. *IEEE Trans. Pattern Anal. Mach. Intell.* **2017**, *39*, 1137–1149. [CrossRef]
94. Redmon, J.; Divvala, S.; Girshick, R.; Farhadi, A. You Only Look Once: Unified, Real-Time Object Detection. In Proceedings of the IEEE Conference on Computer Vision and Pattern Recognition, Las Vegas, NV, USA, 27–30 June 2016; pp. 779–788.
95. Liu, W.; Anguelov, D.; Erhan, D. SSD: Single Shot Multi-box Detector. In *European Conference on Computer Vision*; Springer: Cham, Switzerland, 2016; pp. 21–37.
96. He, K.; Gkioxari, G.; Dollár, P.; Girshick, R. Mask R-CNN. In Proceedings of the IEEE International Conference on Computer Vision (ICCV), Venice, Italy, 22–29 October 2017; pp. 386–397.
97. Simonyan, K.; Zisserman, A. Very Deep Convolutional Networks for Large-scale Image Recognition. In Proceedings of the 3rd International Conference on Learning Representations, ICLR 2015, San Diego, CA, USA, 7–9 May 2015; pp. 1–14.
98. Ma, M.; Chen, J.; Liu, W.; Yang, W. Ship Classification and Detection Based on CNN Using GF-3 SAR Images. *Remote Sens.* **2018**, *10*, 2043. [CrossRef]
99. Lin, T.; Goyal, P.; Girshick, R.; He, K.; Dollár, P. Focal Loss for Dense Object Detection. In Proceedings of the 2017 IEEE International Conference on Computer Vision (ICCV), Venice, Italy, 22–29 October 2017; pp. 2999–3007.
100. Borui, J.; Ruixuan, L.; Jiayuan, M.; Tete, X.; Yuning, J. Acquisition of Localization Confidence for Accurate Object Detection. In Proceedings of the 15th European Conference on Computer Vision (ECCV), Munich, Germany, 8–14 September 2018.
101. Bodla, N.; Singh, B.; Chellappa, R.; Davis, L.S. Soft-NMS Improving Object Detection with One Line of Code. In Proceedings of the 2017 IEEE International Conference on Computer Vision (ICCV), Venice, Italy, 22–29 October 2017; pp. 5562–5570.
102. Djork-Arné, C.; Unterthiner, T.; Hochreiter, S. Fast and Accurate Deep Network Learning by Exponential Linear Units (ELUs). *Comput. Sci.* **2015**. Available online: https://arxiv.org/abs/1511.07289v1 (accessed on 20 December 2021).
103. Chen, X.; Guan, J.; He, Y. Applications and Prospect of Micro-motion Theory in the Detection of Sea Surface Target. *J. Radars* **2013**, *2*, 123–134. [CrossRef]
104. Chen, X.; Guan, J.; Bao, Z.; He, Y. Detection and Extraction of Target with Micro-Motion in Spiky Sea Clutter via Short-time Fractional Fourier Transform. *IEEE Trans. Geosci. Remote Sens.* **2014**, *52*, 1002–1018. [CrossRef]
105. LeCun, Y.; Bottou, L. Gradient-based Learning Applied to Document Recognition. *Proc. IEEE* **1998**, *86*, 2278–2324. [CrossRef]
106. Szegedy, C. Going Deeper with Convolutions. In Proceedings of the IEEE Conference on Computer Vision and Pattern Recognition, Boston, MA, USA, 7–12 June 2015; pp. 1–9.
107. Drosopoulos, A. *Description of the OHGR Database*; Defense Research Establishment: Ottawa, ON, Canada, 1994; Available online: https://www.researchgate.net/publication/235127506_Description_of_the_OHGR_database (accessed on 20 December 2021).
108. Ding, H.; Liu, N.; Dong, Y. Overview and Prospects of Radar Sea Clutter Measurement Experiments. *J. Radars* **2019**, *8*, 281–302.
109. IPIX Database in 1993: A Subset of the Dartmouth Database. Available online: http://soma.ece.mcmaster.ca/ipix/dartmouth/datasets.html (accessed on 20 August 2021).
110. The Grimsby Database. Available online: http://soma.mcmaster.ca/ipix.php (accessed on 20 August 2021).
111. Yan, L.; Sun, P.; Yi, L.; Han, N.; Tang, J. Modeling of Compound-gaussian Sea Clutter based on an Inverse Gaussian Distribution. *J. Radars* **2013**, *2*, 461–465. [CrossRef]

112. Chen, X.; Guan, J.; Huang, Y. Radon-linear Canonical Ambiguity Function-based Detection and Estimation Method for Marine Target with Micromotion. *IEEE Trans. Geosci. Remote Sens.* **2015**, *53*, 2225–2240. [CrossRef]
113. Inggs, M.; Griffiths, H.; Fioranelli, F.; Ritchie, M.; Woodbridge, K. Multistatic Radar: System Requirements and Experimental Validation. In Proceedings of the 2014 IEEE International Radar Conference, Lille, France, 13–17 October 2014; pp. 1–6.
114. Herselman, P.; Baker, C. Analysis of Calibrated Sea Clutter and Boat Reflectivity Data at C- and X-band in South African Coastal Waters. In Proceedings of the IET International Conference on Radar Systems, Edinburgh, UK, 15–18 October 2007. [CrossRef]
115. De Wind, H.J.; Cilliers, J.C.; Herselman, P.L. DataWare: Sea Clutter and Small Boat Radar Reflectivity Database. *IEEE Signal Process.* **2010**, *27*, 145–148. [CrossRef]
116. Herselman, P.; Barker, C.; de Wind, H.J. Analysis of X-band Calibrated Sea Clutter and Small Boat Reflectivity at Medium-to-low Grazing Angles. *Int. J. Navig. Obs.* **2008**, *2008*, 347518. [CrossRef]
117. Goodfellow, I.; Pouget-Abadie, J.; Mirza, M.; Xu, B. Generative Adversarial Networks. *Adv. Neural Inf. Processing Syst.* **2014**, 2672–2680. [CrossRef]
118. Hospedales, T.; Antoniou, A.; Micaelli, P.; Storkey, A. Meta-Learning in Neural Networks: A Survey. *arXiv* **2020**, arXiv:2004.05439. [CrossRef]
119. Ma, L.; Liu, Y.; Zhang, X.; Ye, Y.; Yin, G.; Johnson, B.A. Deep Learning in Remote Sensing Applications: A Meta-analysis and Review. *ISPRS J. Photogramm. Remote Sens.* **2019**, *152*, 166–177. [CrossRef]
120. Yosinski, J.; Clune, J.; Bengio, Y.; Lipson, H. How Transferable are Features in Deep Neural Networks. *Adv. Neural Inf. Proc. Syst.* **2014**, *2*, 3320–3328.
121. Oquab, M.; Bottou, L.; Laptev, I. Learning and Transferring Mid-Level Image Representations using Convolutional Neural Networks. In Proceedings of the IEEE Conference on Computer Vision and Pattern Recognition, Columbus, OH, USA, 23–28 June 2014. [CrossRef]
122. Evans, M.C.; Ruf, C.S. Toward the Detection and Imaging of Ocean Microplastics with a Spaceborne Radar. *IEEE Trans. Geosci. Remote Sens.* **2021**, 1–9. [CrossRef]

electronics

MDPI

Article

Grey Wolf Optimizer in Design Process of the Recurrent Wavelet Neural Controller Applied for Two-Mass System

Mateusz Zychlewicz, Radoslaw Stanislawski and Marcin Kaminski *

Department of Electrical Machines, Drives and Measurements, Faculty of Electrical Engineering, Wroclaw University of Science and Technology, 19 Smoluchowskiego St., 50-372 Wroclaw, Poland; mateusz.zychlewicz@pwr.edu.pl (M.Z.); radoslaw.stanislawski@pwr.edu.pl (R.S.)
* Correspondence: marcin.kaminski@pwr.edu.pl

Abstract: In this paper, an adaptive speed controller of the electrical drive is presented. The main part of the control structure is based on the Recurrent Wavelet Neural Network (RWNN). The mechanical part of the plant is considered as an elastic connection of two DC machines. Oscillation damping and robustness against parameter changes are achieved using network parameters updates (online). Moreover, the various combinations of the feedbacks from the state variables are considered. The initial weights of the neural network and the additional gains are tuned using a modified version of the Grey Wolf Optimizer. Convergence of the calculation is forced using a new definition. For theoretical analysis, numerical tests are presented. Then, the RWNN is implemented in a dSPACE card. Finally, the simulation results are verified experimentally.

Keywords: wavelet neural network; grey wolf optimizer; adaptive speed control; design process optimization; two-mass drive

1. Introduction

The reliability of the applied control methods is one of the main points of scientific work observed in research centers around the world. The advance of these algorithms is possible due to the fact that the computational power of the available programmable devices is now much higher and the tools are cheaper. Adaptive control theory is one of the many fields explored by scientists. Among the techniques applied in this field, neural networks (NNs) are the fastest-growing group—they find use in robotics [1], optimization of complex control schemes, e.g., predictive control [2], or combinations with other intelligent structures such as fuzzy systems [3]. They ensure a model-free design process and recalculation of internal coefficients under changes of the operating point. Due to these advantageous features, NNs are used in almost any engineering field. The real-life implementations also include electrical drives. In the literature, they are applied to control the speed of Permanent Magnet Synchronous Motors (PMSMs) [4], Induction Motors (IMs) [5], and systems with a complex mechanical part [6].

Neural networks theory proposes adaptation methods that can create models for engineering implementations. A significant division concerns the way the weights are recalculated. To implement offline learning, it is necessary to acquire patterns of data that represent the states of the controlled plant [7]. Then, after several pre-processing methods, the collected data are used for training. Through updating the weights online, adaptive structures for control solutions can be created [8]. Another point considered during the application of a neural network is its topology. The most basic arrangement is called Adaline [9]—a neuron with a linear activation function, which has inputs and weights connected to it. As shown in [10,11], when many linear neurons are connected in layers, a multi-layer perceptron is created, which is one of the most often used neural structures in control theory. A more advanced approach is related to recurrent connections in various parts of the network. Elman [12] and Jordan [13] networks are examples of the most common solutions in this group; for instance, the applicability of recurrent neural structures to electrical drives is presented in [14]. However, the significant point of the topology determination for a given issue is the activation function. The classical approach involves a sigmoidal transfer function [15]. Radial basis function can also be incorporated as the activation function [16], some modifications (recurrent feedbacks in the structure) are also included in the analyzed solutions [17]. The last group consists of wavelet functions [18]. Wavelet is a function whose value decays over a finite time. Every input neuron utilizes a wavelet that is translated and dilated from the mother wavelet function. The greatest advantage of wavelets is the function estimation. Given that, the neural network can approximate any function.

Wavelet neural networks are a combination of wavelets and neural networks. Neural networks have great learning (adaptation) capabilities, while wavelets are used in wavelet transform [19] (similar to Fourier). The wavelet transform changes the time-value system to a time-frequency system [20]. This ability can be used in neural networks to approximate complicated continuous functions. All wavelet functions use translation (μ) and dilatation (σ) coefficients, which facilitate searching the space for an appropriate value. In wavelet neural networks, translation and dilatation can be treated similarly to weights in classical networks, so they can change their value in time to better adapt to the current conditions. In control theory, this concept can be used to synthesize estimators [21], predictors [22], or controllers [23]. Adaptation algorithms can be used to update only the weights between layers [24] or weights as well as dilatation and translation parameters [25,26], which improves the efficiency of the learning algorithm. Recurrent wavelet networks adopt recursive connections in only one layer [27,28] or every layer [29,30].

Authors in [20] replace radial functions with wavelet functions. It has been shown that wavelet networks are better at approximating the desired functions, this comes with less computation power required. It is easier to determine parameters of such a network, e.g., the number of hidden layers or weights. Neural networks that use the wavelet function are also more accurate and faster converging than the well-known multi-layer perceptron (MLP). The authors also show the disadvantages of wavelet neural networks—a large number of input nodes is associated with a greater number of hidden layers, which can increase the complexity of computing. Paper [21] compares different neural networks used as battery state of charge estimators. Decomposing the signal helps to forecast the battery level more accurately. The output signal of classical neural networks is stable most of the time. However, fluctuations in the output values might be observed. Nevertheless, recurrent wavelet neural networks are accurate most of the time, there are no fluctuations in the estimated values. Recurrent wavelet neural networks are also more robust against external disturbances. A wavelet neural network, as well as wavelet decomposition, are applied in [25] to control a permanent magnet motor. Wavelet transform is used to decompose error signal into different frequency components. Meanwhile, a neural network is employed to calculate the gains of the speed controller. The results of this work are then compared to PI and PID controllers. Authors show that the applied algorithm performs much better in many different states of the drive and for different reference speeds.

The optimal selection of the control structure parameters, according to the reduction in the cost function values, can be achieved using methods based on observations of the populations in nature. Simple elementary data processing (without derivatives of the objective function), easy application to various problems, and multiple criteria analysis are the most often listed advantages of the mentioned techniques, which include the Cuckoo Search algorithm [31], Artificial Bee Colony algorithm [32], Particle Swarm Optimization [33] and Flower Pollination algorithm [34]. A general review of nature-inspired algorithms used for electric drive optimization has been provided by Hannan et al. in [35]. Recently, the Grey Wolf Optimizer (GWO) has been successfully used for optimization [36]. Formulas describe the behavior of wolves that try to find, surround, and get closer to the target [37,38]. The following modifications of the basic version of the GWO are analyzed in the literature (e.g., binary and multi-objective) [39,40]. Reduction in the area of searching in the application of the algorithm in the design process of the electrical machine (PM motor) can lead to faster results. For this purpose, new definitions of variable elements used in calculations are analyzed [41]. This was an inspiration for the new version of the modified Grey Wolf Optimizer (mGWO) described in this paper.

The implementation of the control algorithms based on artificial intelligence deals with the problems of mathematical terms and coefficient definitions in several design stages. The first concern is the proper determination of the gains used in the control structure. Their values can affect the precision of control and dynamics of the entire system. Classical methods of the control structure synthesis mostly require parameters and equations of the object to be known. Then, after some recalculations, the formulas are achieved. However, the application of the controllers based on neural networks or fuzzy models can be more complicated. A clear mathematical description of the topology of those controllers might be problematic (the transfer function of the closed control loop). Moreover, for controllers that contain reconfigurable parameters, advanced methods of analysis are used. Another issue refers to the nonlinearities of the plant. It needs to be considered during the design process, even though this is an additional design enhancement. In this paper, different combinations of the additional feedbacks (for better damping of the state variables oscillations observed in the two-mass system) used in the control structure are considered. The feedback loops presented in the literature include using the physically unobtainable signals calculated with state observers [42,43] or variations of the Kalman filter [44,45]. Internal recurrent connections in neural controllers are also tested [46]. Thus, multiple recalculations would be required. For the briefly mentioned above problems, the meta-heuristic algorithm can be a useful and efficient solution.

A separate issue of the neural controller applications is focused on the selection of the initial conditions. The systems often start with the random values of weights. After some time of operation, the adaptive law recalculates those coefficients. However, during the initial phase, high oscillations of the state variables can be observed. Assuming the application of the adaptive neural controller, it can be significant for the mechanical part. Unstable work (even over a short period) may lead to ruptures of the couplings and shafts connecting several parts of the system. This issue was also considered in this work, the GWO algorithm was used for the optimization of the starting point of the adaptive neural speed controller.

This paper contains seven essential sections. It starts with a short presentation of the problems and proposed tools used for solving the issue. Then, a description of the plant is shown. The next part of the manuscript is related to the mathematical details of the adaptive neural controller. The background of the GWO calculations and applied modification is presented in the following section. After the theoretical part, the tests (simulations and laboratory experiments) of the RWNN controller applied for an electrical drive with an elastic connection between the motor and the load machine are analyzed. The final element of the article stands concluding remarks.

2. Mathematical Model of the Controller and the Plant

Control structure described in this paper consists of the Recurrent Wavelet Neural Network applied to a two-mass drive as depicted in Figure 1. Mathematical model of mechanical part used in drive with elastic shaft can be characterized using following equations [6,14]:

$$\begin{cases} \frac{d\omega_1(t)}{dt} & = & \frac{m_e(t)-m_s(t)-m_{f1}(t)}{T_1} \\ \frac{d\omega_2(t)}{dt} & = & \frac{m_s(t)-m_L(t)-m_{f2}(t)}{T_2} \\ \frac{dm_s(t)}{dt} & = & \frac{\omega_1(t)-\omega_2(t)}{T_c} \end{cases} \tag{1}$$

where ω_1 and ω_2 are rotor speeds of motor and load, respectively, T_1, T_2, and T_c are mechanical time constants of the motor, the load, and the shaft, respectively, m_e and m_s are electromagnetic torque and shaft torque, respectively, m_L is load torque, and m_{f1} and m_{f2} are nonlinear functions that describe friction occurring in real electrical drives;

$$m_{fi} = (c \cdot \text{abs}(\omega_i) + d)\text{sgn}(\omega_i) \tag{2}$$

where c and d represent the viscous and the Coulomb friction coefficients, respectively.

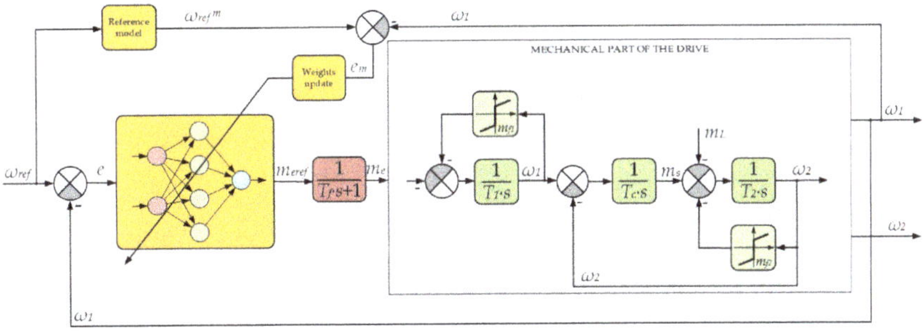

Figure 1. Schematic diagram of the adaptive control with the RWNN model.

Inner current loop is assumed to be simplified. It is represented using a first order inertial element with a current time constant T_f:

$$G_f(s) = \frac{1}{T_f s + 1} \tag{3}$$

A schematic diagram of the control structure is presented in Figure 1. The speed controller is based on a recurrent wavelet neural network. It is composed of four layers. The first layer ($L1$) is linear, it has two inputs—the error signal and its derivative. There is also an additional recurrent connection from the neuron output (z_i^1) to its input (h_i^1). It can be characterized by the following equation:

$$(L1)\begin{cases} h_i^1(k) = x_i(k) + w_i^{in}(k) z_i^1(k-1) \\ z_i^1(k) = h_i^1(k) \end{cases} \tag{4}$$

where x is the input signal; h^1 and z^1 are the neuron input and output, respectively; w^{in} is the connection weight; i is the index; and k is the sample number.

The second layer is the wavelet function layer ($L2$), in this part of the neural network the output of the input layer is processed according to the mother wavelet equation [47]:

$$(L2)\begin{cases} h_{ij}^2(k) = \frac{z_i^1(k) + \mu_{ij}(k)}{\sigma_{ij}(k)} \\ z_{ij}^2(k) = \lambda\left(h_{ij}^2(k)\right) \end{cases} \tag{5}$$

where h^2 and z^2 are the second layer's inputs and outputs, respectively, μ is the translation, σ is the dilatation coefficient, and i and j are indexes.

The mother wavelet used in this paper is the Mexican Hat Wavelet, it can be described using the undermentioned expression [48]:

$$\lambda(x) = (1 - 0.5x^2)\exp(-x^2) \tag{6}$$

where x is the input of the function and exp(.) represents the exponential function.

Then, the achieved values (from the second layer) are multiplied in the third layer ($L3$). Nodes in the mentioned layer have four inputs—two of them correspond to outputs from the second layer, the additional two signals are the recurrent connections from the third and the fourth layers:

$$(L3)\begin{cases} h_j^3(k) = \left(\prod_{j=1}^{n} z_j^{3r}(k) z_{1j}^2(k) z_{2j}^2(k)\right) z^{4r}(k) \\ z_j^3(k) = h_j^3(k) \end{cases} \tag{7}$$

where h^3 and z^3 are the third layer's inputs and outputs, respectively, and z^{3r} and z^{4r} are the outputs of the recurrent nodes:

$$(L3r)\begin{cases} h_i^{3r}(k) = w_j^{3r}(k) z_j^3(k-1) \\ z_j^3(k) = \theta\left(h_j^{3r}(k)\right) \end{cases} \tag{8}$$

$$(L4r)\begin{cases} h^{4r}(k) = w^{4r}(k) y_{nn}(k) \\ z^{4r}(k) = \vartheta\left(h^{4r}(k)\right) \end{cases} \tag{9}$$

where h^{3r}, z^{3r}, h^{4r}, and z^{4r} are the inputs and the outputs of the recurrent nodes in $L3$ and $L4$, respectively, w^{3r} and w^{4r} are the connection weights, and y_{nn} is the output of the controller.

In the above equations, θ and ϑ are nonlinear functions that help to propagate the signals back. These functions are defined as follows:

$$\theta(x) = \frac{1}{1 + \exp(-x)} \tag{10}$$

$$\vartheta(x) = \exp(-x^2) \tag{11}$$

The last neuron ($L4$) combines (sums) the output signals from the previous layer:

$$(L4)\begin{cases} h^4(k) = \sum_{j=1}^{n} w_j^{out}(k) z_j^3(k) \\ z^4(k) = h^4(k) = y_{nn}(k) \end{cases} \tag{12}$$

where h^4 and z^4 are the inputs and the outputs of the last layer, respectively, and w^{out} is the weight connection between neurons.

To achieve a proper operation of the controller, it is necessary to provide a learning process to update the weights of the neural network. This process consists of three parts—the forward pass, the backward pass, and the weights update. The forward pass of signals was explained at the beginning of this section. Details of the following stages are described below.

Adaptation is performed to reduce the cost function values—E. In this paper, for the RWNN, following formula was assumed [14]:

$$E(k) = 0.5 e_m^2(k) \tag{13}$$

$$e_m(k) = \omega_{ref}^m(k) - \omega_1(k) \tag{14}$$

where e_m is the difference between the reference model speed $\omega_{ref}{}^m$ and the actual motor speed ω_1.

To calculate new values of the parameters (weights), the gradient values with respect to all the layers need to be obtained. For the last layer, the gradient is calculated according to the following expression:

$$\delta^4(k) = \frac{\partial E(k)}{\partial y_{nn}(k)} \to e_m(k) \tag{15}$$

Then, the calculations use the chain rule applied for partial derivatives [27,30]. Values for the third layer are determined as:

$$\delta_j^3(k) = \frac{\partial E(k)}{\partial z_j^3(k)} = \frac{\partial E(k)}{\partial y_{nn}} \frac{\partial y_{nn}(k)}{\partial h^4(k)} \frac{\partial h^4(k)}{\partial z_j^3(k)} \rightarrow \delta^4 w_j^{out}(k) \tag{16}$$

Similarly, data processing is realized for the second layer:

$$\delta_{1j}^2(k) = \frac{\partial E(k)}{\partial z_{1j}^2(k)} = \frac{\partial E(k)}{\partial z_j^3(k)} \frac{\partial z_j^3(k)}{\partial h_j^3(k)} \frac{\partial h_j^3(k)}{\partial z_{1j}^2(k)} \rightarrow \delta_j^3 z^{4r}(k) z_j^{3r}(k) z_{2j}^2(k) \tag{17}$$

$$\delta_{2j}^2(k) = \frac{\partial E(k)}{\partial z_{1j}^2(k)} = \frac{\partial E(k)}{\partial z_j^3(k)} \frac{\partial z_j^3(k)}{\partial h_j^3(k)} \frac{\partial h_j^3(k)}{\partial z_{2j}^2(k)} \rightarrow \delta_j^3 z^{4r}(k) z_j^{3r}(k) z_{1j}^2(k) \tag{18}$$

Finally, for the input layer, gradient values are achieved using the formula:

$$\delta_{ij}^1(k) = \frac{\partial E(k)}{\partial z_i^1(k)} = \frac{\partial E(k)}{\partial z_{ij}^2(k)} \frac{\partial z_{ij}^2(k)}{\partial h_{ij}^2(k)} \frac{\partial h_{ij}^2(k)}{\partial z_i^1(k)} \rightarrow \delta_{ij}^2 \frac{\phi\vartheta(\phi)(1 - 0.5\phi^2) - \phi\vartheta(\phi)}{\sigma_{ij}(k)} \tag{19}$$

where:

$$\phi(k) = \frac{z_i^1(k) - \mu_{ij}(k)}{\sigma_{ij}(k)} \tag{20}$$

After the calculation of all the gradients, all variable parameters are updated in each iteration. In this work, all the weights, as well as the parameters of the wavelet function—translation (μ) and dilatation (σ)—are updated. Weights in the last recurrent layer are adjusted using the following expression:

$$\Delta w^{4r}(k) = \frac{\partial E(k)}{\partial w^{4r}(k)} = \frac{\partial E(k)}{\partial y_{nn}(k)} \frac{\partial y_{nn}(k)}{\partial h^{4r}(k)} \frac{\partial h^{4r}(k)}{\partial w^{4r}(k)} \rightarrow \delta^4 y_{nn}(k) \tag{21}$$

They are then updated according to the delta rule with the learning factor η:

$$w^{4r}(k+1) = w^{4r}(k) - \eta^{4r} \Delta w^{4r}(k) \tag{22}$$

Weights between the third and the last layer are recalculated using the following expression:

$$\Delta w_j^{out}(k) = \frac{\partial E(k)}{\partial w_j^{out}(k)} = \frac{\partial E(k)}{\partial y_{nn}(k)} \frac{\partial y_{nn}(k)}{\partial h^4(k)} \frac{\partial h^4(k)}{\partial w_j^{out}(k)} \rightarrow \delta^4 z_j^3(k) \tag{23}$$

Output weights are updated according to the adaptation law described using the expression presented:

$$w^{out}(k+1) = w^{out}(k) - \eta^{out} \Delta w_j^{out}(k) \tag{24}$$

Parameters in the recurrent nodes of the third layer are changed similarly to the previous ones:

$$\Delta w_j^{3r}(k) = \frac{\partial E(k)}{\partial w_j^{3r}(k)} = \frac{\partial E(k)}{\partial z_j^{3r}(k)} \frac{\partial z_j^{3r}(k)}{\partial h_j^{3r}(k)} \frac{\partial h_j^{3r}(k)}{\partial w_j^{3r}(k)} \rightarrow \delta_j^3 z^3(k-1) \tag{25}$$

The new values are obtained by the following expression:

$$w^{3r}(k+1) = w^{3r}(k) - \eta^{3r} \Delta w^{3r}(k) \tag{26}$$

Weights of the second and the third layer are fixed as once, thus there is no need to update those values. The parameters of the wavelet function are determined according to equations:

$$\Delta\mu_{ij}(k) = \frac{\partial E(k)}{\partial \mu_{ij}(k)} = \frac{\partial E(k)}{\partial z_{ij}^2(k)}\frac{\partial z_{ij}^2(k)}{\partial h_{ij}^2(k)}\frac{\partial h_{ij}^2(k)}{\partial \mu_{ij}(k)} \to \delta_{ij}^2\frac{\phi\vartheta(\phi)(1-0.5\phi^2)-\phi\vartheta(\phi)}{\sigma_{ij}(k)} \quad (27)$$

$$\Delta\sigma_{ij}(k) = \frac{\partial E(k)}{\partial \sigma_{ij}(k)} = \frac{\partial E(k)}{\partial z_{ij}^2(k)}\frac{\partial z_{ij}^2(k)}{\partial h_{ij}^2(k)}\frac{\partial h_{ij}^2(k)}{\partial \sigma_{ij}(k)} \to \delta_{ij}^2\frac{\phi\vartheta(\phi)(1-0.5\phi^2)-\phi\vartheta(\phi)}{\sigma_{ij}^2(k)} \quad (28)$$

Abovementioned values are applied in expressions:

$$\mu_{ij}(k+1) = \mu_{ij}(k) - \eta^{\mu}\Delta\mu_{ij}(k) \quad (29)$$

$$\sigma_{ij}(k+1) = \sigma_{ij}(k) - \eta^{\sigma}\Delta\sigma_{ij}(k) \quad (30)$$

The last parameters that need to be updated are recurrent weights that are present in the input neurons:

$$\Delta w_i^{in}(k) = \frac{\partial E(k)}{\partial w_i^{in}(k)} = \frac{\partial E(k)}{\partial z_i^1(k)}\frac{\partial z_i^1(k)}{\partial h_i^1(k)}\frac{\partial h_i^1(k)}{\partial w_i^{in}(k)} \to \delta^1 z_i^1(k-1) \quad (31)$$

$$w_i^{in}(k+1) = w_i^{in}(k) - \eta^{3r}\Delta w_i^{in}(k) \quad (32)$$

Constants η^{out}, η^{4r}, η^{3r}, η^{μ}, and η^{σ} correspond to learning rates used in Equations (24), (26), (29), (30) and (32), respectively. Based on the above mathematical description, the adaptive neural controller was designed. The details of the topology are presented in Figure 2.

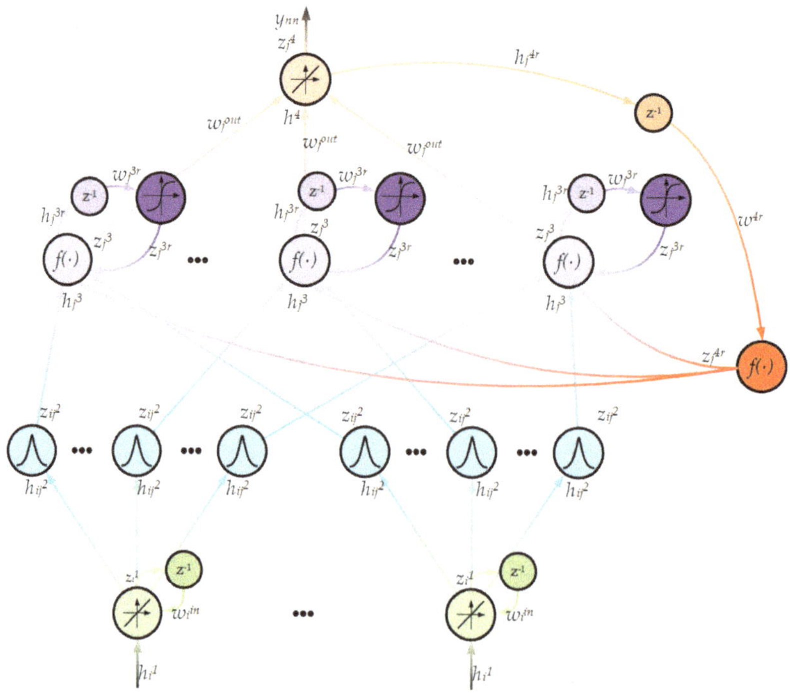

Figure 2. The recurrent wavelet neural network.

3. The Design Process of the Adaptive Neural Controller Using Grey Wolf Optimizer

The most basic process of establishing the initial values of weights and learning rates is to assign all the values using a pseudo-random number generator. Though it is easy, it comes with some disadvantages. The first few seconds of the operation of the system heavily depend on the initial values of these parameters. If they are too large, oscillations and overshoot may occur. On the other hand, when smaller values are applied, the network needs more time to adapt to the current state of the drive. To cope with this phenomenon, the initial values of the weights, the learning rates, and the gains in the control structure (an in-depth analysis of this topic is presented in Section 5) are chosen using a modified Grey Wolf Optimizer [36]. It should be noted that the optimization process is an offline operation performed before the start of the system, while backpropagation is constantly updating the weights of the controller during the system's operation.

Grey Wolf Optimizer is a nature-inspired metaheuristic algorithm. The most basic concept of the algorithm comes from observations of packs of wolves. When a pack tries to attack prey, they form a few smaller groups of wolves. All of them are led by an alpha wolf. Finally, the wolves approach their prey until they reach it.

In the algorithm, wolves are the points on the optimization plane, the prey is the investigated minimum of the function and the distance between the wolves and the prey is the value of the fitness function. In addition, some additional parameters are required to be established.

The current solution and the next point can be written as equations:

$$D = \left| C \cdot X_p(k_{iter}) - X(k_{iter}) \right| \tag{33}$$

$$X(k_{iter} + 1) = X_p(k_{iter}) - A \cdot D \tag{34}$$

where X_p are the optimal values from the previous iteration, X is the current iteration solution, and k_{iter} is the number of the current iteration.

Parameters A and C are adjusted in every iteration of the algorithm, according to the equations below:

$$C = 2 \cdot r_1 \tag{35}$$

$$A = 2 \cdot a \cdot r_2 \tag{36}$$

Values of r_1 and r_2 are random in the range of [0, 1]. The value of the parameter a is changed from 2 to 0, descending over the course of iterations [49].

$$a = 2\left(1 - \frac{k_{iter}}{k_{max}}\right) \tag{37}$$

When a is in the range of [1, 2], the algorithm is in the exploration state. The exploitation state lasts when a is in the range of [0, 1). In the exploration state, the algorithm seeks possible solutions in the search space while the exploitation results in narrowing the search plane. The modified formula for a allows for a longer exploration time so the final solution can be found more easily than in the classical GWO.

$$a = 2\left(1 - \frac{k_{iter}^2}{k_{max}^2}\right) \tag{38}$$

Figure 3 shows how different formulae for a influence the GWO algorithm. The horizontal axis shows the iteration count (T is the maximum value set), whilst the vertical axis shows the change of a over the course of iterations. The area covered in blue marks the exploitation phase and the red area denotes the exploration state. In the basic version of the GWO, the time for both stages is equal, while the modified version emphasizes searching for the new values for the algorithm. If a better solution is needed, the exploration stage must be extended by altering Equation (35).

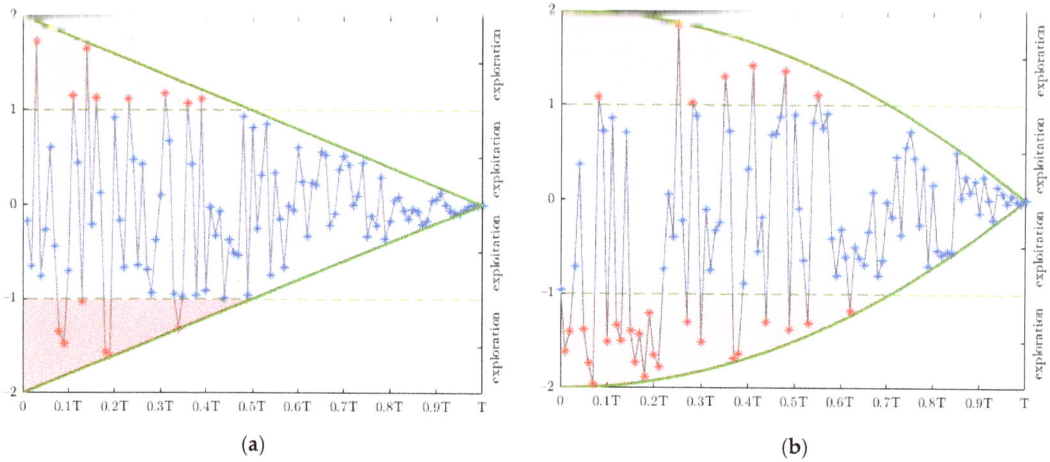

Figure 3. Changes of the *a* parameter in (**a**) the classical GWO, (**b**) the modified GWO.

The distance between the three best points (X_α, X_β, and X_δ) and the solution candidate can be calculated using Equations (39)–(41).

$$D_\alpha = |C_1 \cdot X_\alpha - X| \tag{39}$$

$$D_\beta = |C_2 \cdot X_\beta - X| \tag{40}$$

$$D_\delta = |C_3 \cdot X_\delta - X| \tag{41}$$

Later, the whole population is updated:

$$X_1 = X_1 - A_1 \cdot D_\alpha \tag{42}$$

$$X_2 = X_2 - A_2 \cdot D_\beta \tag{43}$$

$$X_3 = X_3 - A_3 \cdot D_\delta \tag{44}$$

$$X(k+1) = \frac{1}{3}\sum\nolimits_{i=1}^{3} X_i \tag{45}$$

The algorithm uses a fitness function that can be written as follows:

$$J_{GWO}(k_{iter}) = \frac{1}{t_{prob}}\sum\nolimits_{k=1}^{t_{prob}} \left|\omega_{ref}^{m}(k) - \omega_1(k)\right| \tag{46}$$

where ${\omega_{ref}}^{m}$ output of reference model.

All the steps of the GWO algorithm are pictured below in a block diagram in Figure 4.

Figure 5 shows examples of different transients of motor speed gathered during the optimization process. The transient from the third iteration has the greatest amplitude of oscillations and the settling time is the slowest amongst all the transients shown. With each consecutive iteration, the achieved results are improving—after 20 iterations, the speed transient oscillations are almost fully dampened and the overshoot issue is solved. The fitness function values for each of the presented transients are attached in Table 1.

Changes in the fitness function for both versions of the algorithm are depicted below in Figure 6. The crucial parameters of both algorithms are presented in Table 2. The only change that influences the results is the additional multiplications in the rate of change of a. After the first few iterations, the fitness function was lowering much faster for the modified version compared to the classical. Additionally, it can be seen that when the value of *a* is lower than 1, the convergence is faster. A value higher than 1 causes the algorithm to find a better value. After a few optimization runs, it was noticed that the modified Grey Wolf Optimizer can achieve similar values of the fitness function in less than half of the iterations required by the classic Grey Wolf Optimizer.

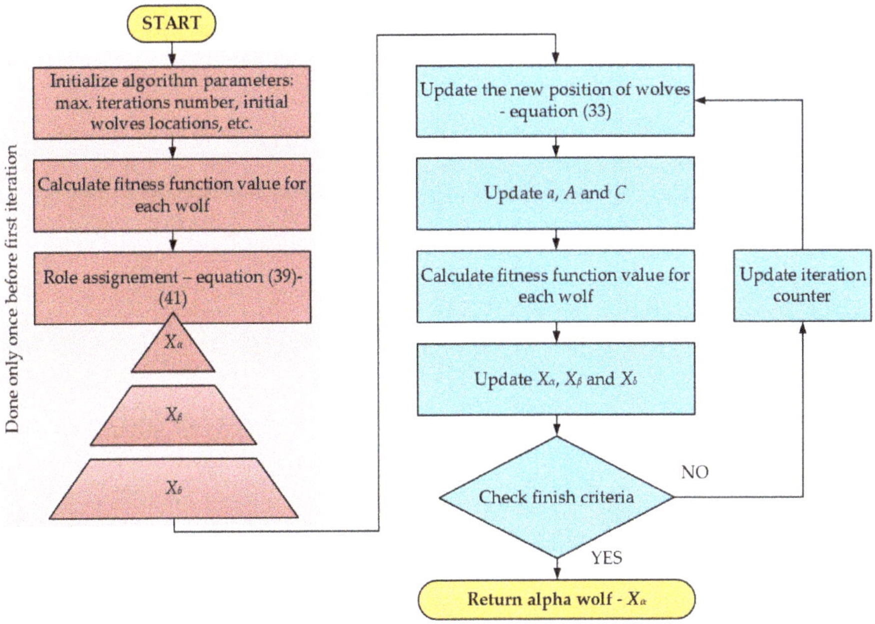

Figure 4. The Grey Wolf Optimizer.

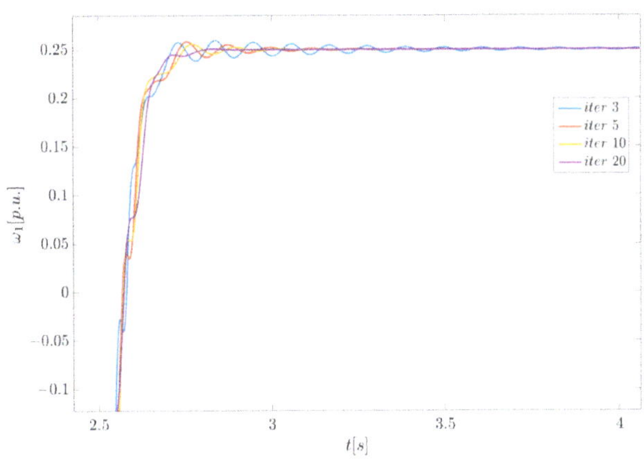

Figure 5. Speed transients' changes during optimization.

Table 1. The values of the fitness function.

Iteration	Fitness Function Value (*10^{-4})
3	0.1661
5	0.1052
10	0.0683
20	0.0164

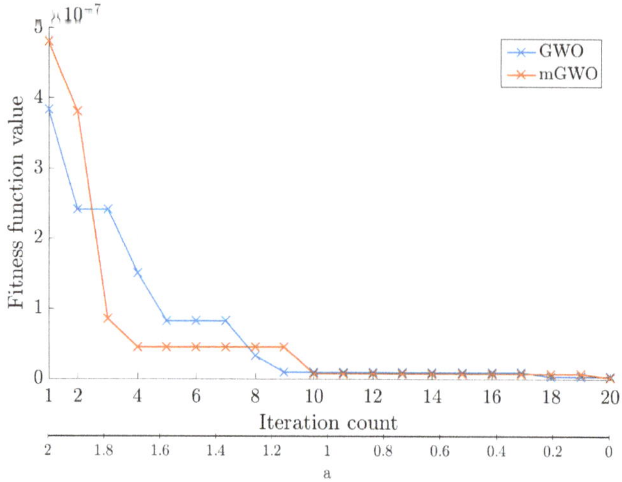

Figure 6. Comparison of fitness function for the GWO and the mGWO.

Table 2. Parameters of GWO and mGWO.

	GWO		mGWO
Number of iterations		20	
Population		40	
Rate of change of a parameter	$2\left(1-\frac{k_{iter}}{k_{max}}\right)$		$2\left(1-\frac{k_{iter}^2}{k_{max}^2}\right)$
Fitness function		$\frac{1}{t_{prob}}\sum_{k=1}^{t_{prob}}\left\vert\omega_{ref}^{m}(k)-\omega_1(k)\right\vert$	

The modified version of the algorithm can spend more time in the exploration state (red section of Figure 4) which means it is looking for the global extremum (minimum) longer. If one is found, in the exploitation phase the algorithm seeks the minimum value close to the extremum found. The longer the exploration phase lasts, the more accurate value should have been found, so the exploitation time (blue part of Figure 4) can be shortened.

The Grey Wolf Optimizer was implemented in Matlab software. For calculations, the machine with Intel Core 7-7700 CPU (3.60 GHz) with 16 GB of RAM and 64 bit Windows 10 was used. It took 12pprox.. 25.78 min to complete the optimization process for the modified version of the algorithm. The standard version is processed in about 17.52 min. During calculations an identical number of search agents and iterations were assumed—the exact parameters are presented in Table 2. An extended time needed for the optimization process is observed due to additional tasks (additional multiplications in the equation used for the value of a) in the code. However, these calculations are performed offline, therefore they do not affect the work of the whole system.

4. Simulation Tests

This section of the manuscript presents the numerical tests of the adaptive speed control structure based on the RWNN model. For all simulations, the sampling time equal to 100 µs is assumed, calculations take 20 s. Parameters of the two-mass system obtained through the identification of the real drive used in the experiment are as follows: $T_1 = T_2 = 0.203$ s and $T_c = 0.0012$ s.

Results acquired for the nominal parameters of the drive are presented in Figure 7. The observation of the operation of the control structure with the recurrent wavelet neural network controller makes it possible to state that the drive is working properly. There is no apparent overshoot or oscillations. Electromagnetic torque is produced rapidly.

Such a result can be achieved through the continuous adaptation of parameters of the neural controller.

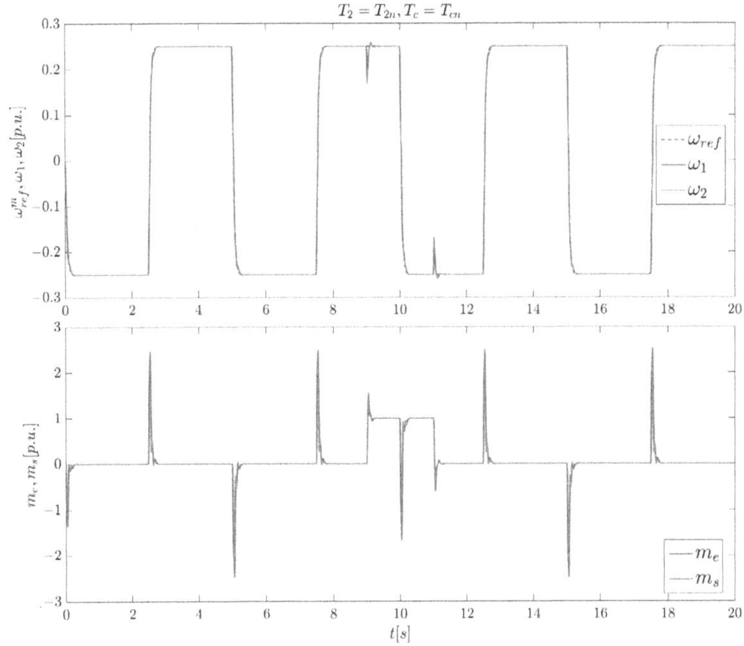

Figure 7. Speeds (ω_{ref}, ω_1, and ω_2) and torques (m_e and m_s)—transients for nominal parameters of drive.

Next, a set of simulations is carried out to verify how the changes in the drive's mechanical properties (time constants) affect the drive's performance. Figure 8 shows gathered results for an increased value of the mechanical time constant of the load machine (T_2 = 2 T_{2n}). In this case, there is a slight overshoot at the first phase, but it decays as simulation time passes. Slight oscillations can also be observed in electromagnetic and shaft torques, this is the effect of an increased time constant in a drive with elastic joints.

In Figure 9 the transients of the rotational speeds and torques of the drive with an increased value of the time constant of the shaft are presented. The increased time constant T_c introduces negligible oscillations in torques and speeds of the motor and the load. It is apparent that before and after switching the load torque the drive achieves the reference speed with high dynamics.

Figures 10 and 11 show the results achieved for decreased time constants of the load motor and the shaft, respectively. Transients of both speeds for the reduced time constants are similar to the results obtained for the nominal parameters of the drive, except the speed drop occurring directly after the change of the load (t_{L1} = 9 s, t_{L2} = 11 s) is smaller for the reduced value of the shaft stiffness time constant T_c. The difference can also be noticed in torques transients. The torque changes are as dynamic as with the nominal values, but oscillations can be seen in both instances, especially when the load torque is switched.

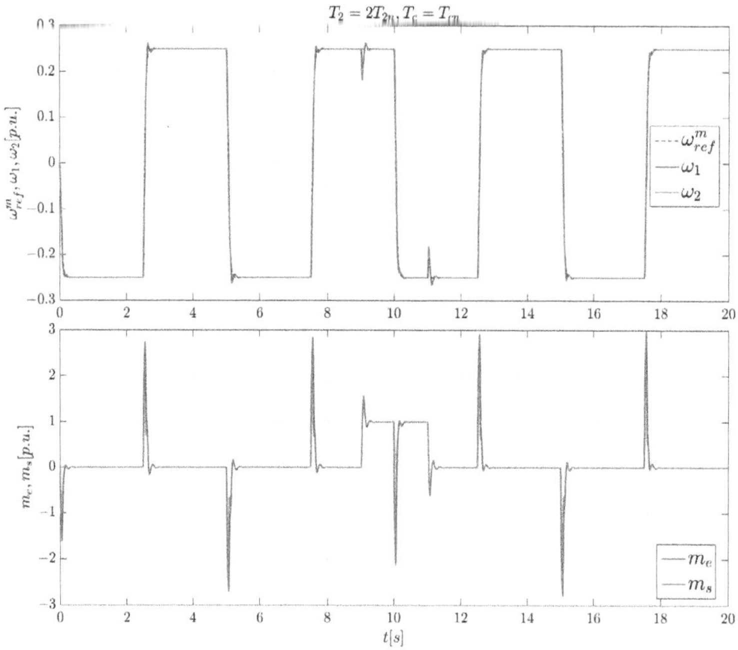

Figure 8. Speeds (ω_{ref}, ω_1, and ω_2) and torques (m_e and m_s)—transients for increased load time constant (T_2 = 2 T_{2n}).

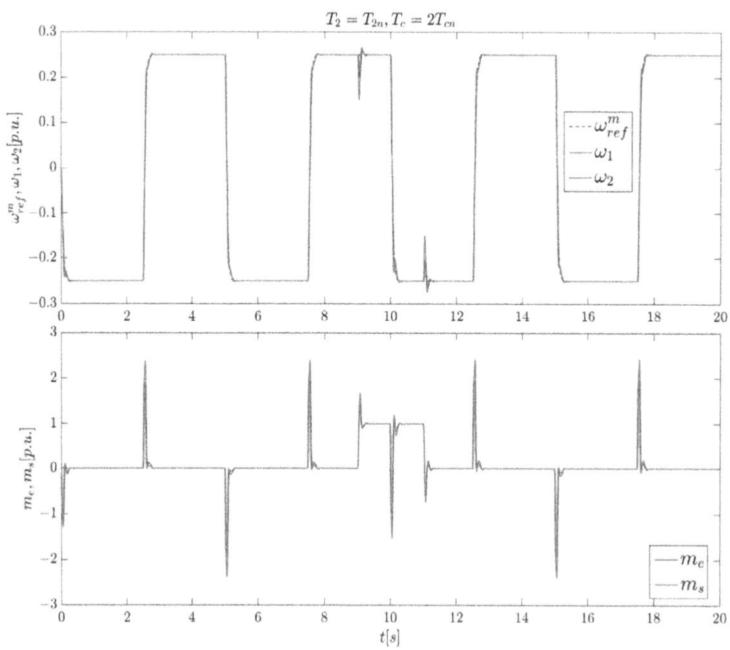

Figure 9. Speeds (ω_{ref}, ω_1, and ω_2) and torques (m_e and m_s)—transients for the increased stiffness time constant (T_c = 2 T_{cn}).

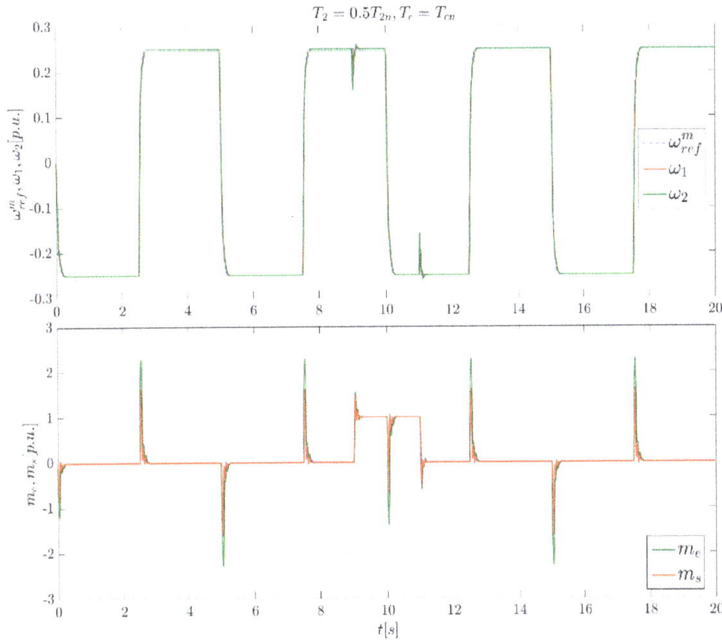

Figure 10. Speeds (ω_{ref}, ω_1, and ω_2) and torques (m_e and m_s)—transients for the decreased load time constant (T_2 = 0.5 T_{2n}).

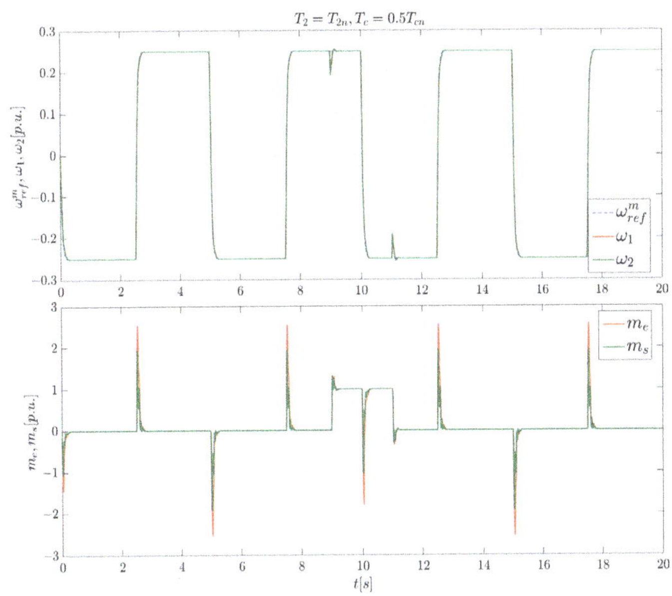

Figure 11. Speeds (ω_{ref}, ω_1, and ω_2) and torques (m_e and m_s)—transients for the decreased shaft time constant (T_c = 0.5 T_{cn}).

To verify the performance of the proposed control structure, RWNN was compared to the classical PI controller. Both systems were tested after changing the mechanical time constant of the load drive—T_{2n} = 2 T_{2n}. Comparison is depicted in Figure 12. The

PI controller was tuned according to the pole placement method—parameters were set according to the predefined design parameters—the damping coefficient and the reference resonant frequency. It should be added that both gains of the controller are depended on the proper identification of the plant. In comparison to the PI controller, structure with the RWNN ensures adaptive properties. As a result, rapid response to the parametric changes of the drive can be observed. It is due to the weights being constantly updated. Moreover, high overshoot can be noticed in the drive with the classical solution, which is not present in the adaptive structure.

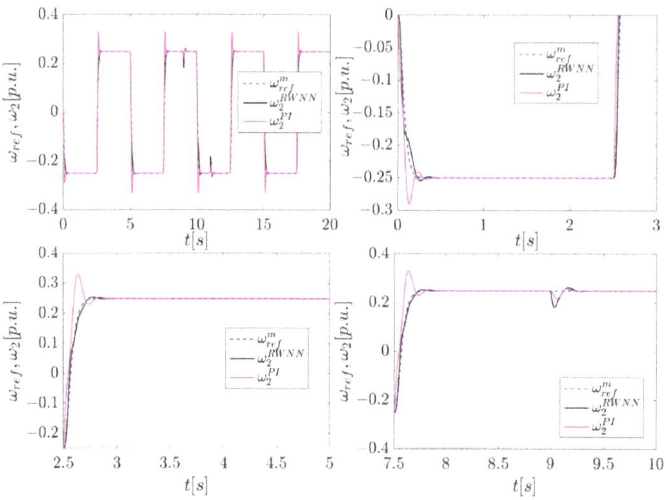

Figure 12. Results for RWNN controller and PI controller with increased load time constant—T_{2n} = 2 T_{2n}.

The impact of the learning rate value was also analyzed and shown in Figure 12. The results were gathered for the nominal parameters of the drive, but the outcome is similar when the parameters of the drive are changed.

Figure 13 shows how the drive behaves when different learning rates are applied to the controller where η_{mGWO} is the learning rate obtained from the mGWO optimization process (η_{mGWO} = 0.0982) and η_1 and η_2 are values 5 times lower and higher than the optimized value. Tests were performed for reduced and increased values of the learning rate. The speed of the drive is shaped in a similar way for the optimized and the greater learning rates, but oscillations are greater for the higher value. On the other hand, for the decreased value, it takes more time to reach the reference speed value. It was also observed that the bigger the value of the learning coefficient, the higher the maximum value of the overshoot, therefore results for any higher values are not shown in order not to blur the image.

Similar tests were carried out for the changes in the initial values of the weights of the controller. Figure 14 shows the changes in the speed of the motor speed when different initial values of weights were applied (red line indicates the load speed transient with the initial values optimized by the mGWO algorithm, the green line shows the situation, where the values of the weights were halved, and the yellow line shows the situation of a two-times increase in weights' value compared to the nominal ones).

As can be seen in Figure 14b, higher initial values cause greater overshoot in the starting process, and it takes more time to adapt the controller to the reference speed. On the other hand, when small values are applied the opposite is happening—there is an undershoot that needs to be corrected during the operation of the drive. The advantage of using the metaheuristic algorithm is the compromise between the two values with a long rise time and an overshoot that can be neglected as it is present only over a short period during the initial phase of the drive's operation.

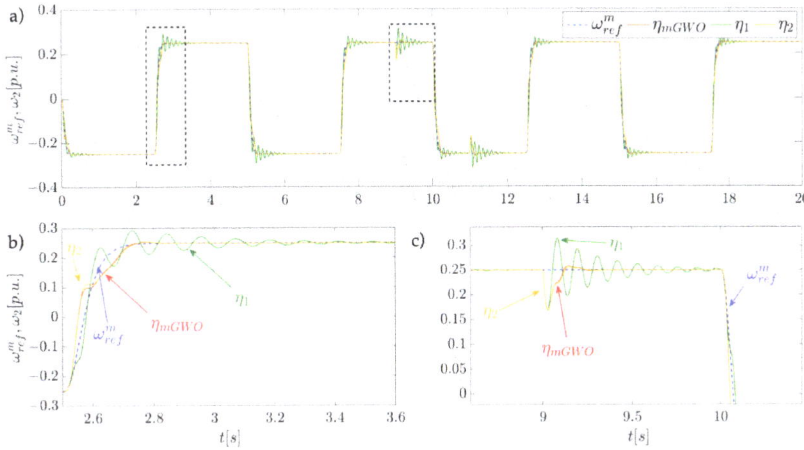

Figure 13. Influence of the learning rate parameter on the adaptation process (**a**), the initial part of the simulation (**b**), applying load torque (**c**).

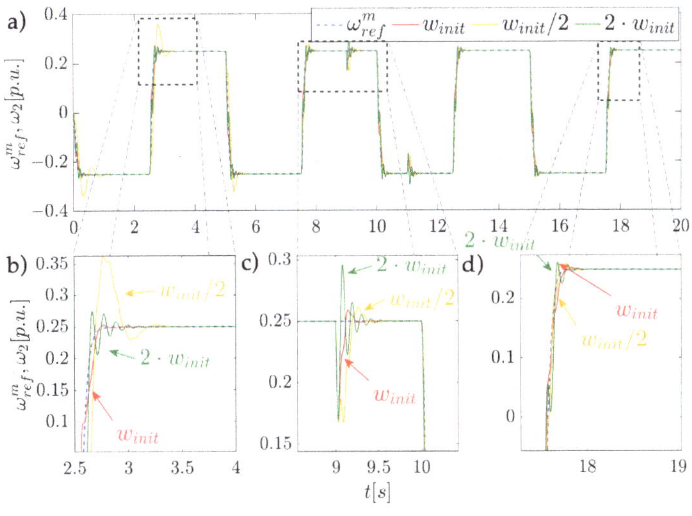

Figure 14. The impact of different initial values of weights in the adaptive speed controller based on the RWNN (**a**), the initial part of the simulation (**b**), applying load torque (**c**), the final part of the simulation (**d**).

In addition to transients, parameters of the step response were calculated for data presented in Figures 13 and 14 and presented in Table 3. The rise time of the signal can be calculated as the time it takes for the response to rise from 10% to 90% of the reference value. Settling time can be defined as the time it takes for the error to stay below 2%. Of the difference between reference speed and speed of the drive. All parameters were calculated for the first reversion from $\omega_{init} = -0.25$ p.u. to $\omega_{final} = 0.25$ p.u.

Table 3. Settling and rise times for different states of the drive.

Case	t_{rise} (s)	$t_{settling}$ (s)
η_{mGWO}, $w_{initGWO}$ (nominal)	0.186	0.25
$\eta_1 = 2\ \eta_{mGWO}$	0.189	0.69
$\eta_2 = 0.5\ \eta_{mGWO}$	0.191	0.27
$w_{init1} = 2\ w_{initGWO}$	0.190	0.34
$w_{init2} = 0.5\ w_{initGWO}$	0.263	0.40

The rise time for the nominal parameters, as well as for different learning rates applied, is almost equal. Lower initial values of the weights affect the time needed for adaptation, which results in lower rise time and higher overshoot in the first reversion of the drive. Even minimal changes of the analyzed parameters can influence the quality of the response (the settling time). The fastest response of the system can be observed for the neural network with parameters optimized with mGWO.

Initial weights of the controller also have an influence on the parameters of the step response. Rise time for increased initial values stays the same, but lowering them increases the value. Lower values of initial weights introduce overshoot which increases the rise time and settling time of the speed of the drive. Higher initial values of weights cause oscillations which increase the settling time.

5. The Influence of Additional Feedbacks in the Speed Loop

All previous tests were conducted for a structure with a classical negative speed feedback loop, where the speed of the motor was subtracted from the reference speed. In addition to the motor speed feedback, auxiliary feedbacks were applied with no additional gains present in these feedback loops. Additional loops can improve the characteristics of the drive in dynamical states, e.g., reversions. Supplementary feedback in the torque control loop provides better damping of torsional vibrations [50]. A signal from the difference in speeds inserted in a speed loop ensures good dynamical characteristics [51]. There are many possible feedback loop modifications, but for this study, the simplest were selected. The derivatives of the state variables could also be used, but they cause damping of high-frequency vibrations and a decline in the system's dynamical properties.

Results achieved for different feedbacks depicted in Figure 15 are presented in this section. By taking a look at Figure 16, only a small difference can be observed. Close-ups of different parts of the simulation are given in Figure 16b,c. First reversion shows that there are slight oscillations when additional feedback from the speed difference is applied (yellow graph). Green and red transients, indicating additional shaft torque and speed difference feedbacks and shaft torque feedback, respectively, are the closest to reference speed. The structure with no additional feedbacks has the highest error between the reference speed and the load speed. On the contrary, after switching the load at t_{L1} = 9 s, the red and green transients are the most distant from the set speed transient.

Oscillations are damped the most when the additional shaft torque feedback is applied (red and green transients in Figure 16b). During the simulations, all parameters of the recurrent wavelet neural network controller are updated, so the difference in speed transients is less visible at the end of the test. After applying the load, the structure with no additional feedbacks and with the feedback loop from the difference between the speeds perform the best. Near the end of the simulation tests in Figure 16c, it can be seen that all structures perform similarly. Drive with both loops (shaft torque and difference between speeds) achieves the best results overall.

To achieve the best results of the drive, it is suggested to implement the structure incorporating both the shaft torque feedback loop as well as the speed difference feedback loop. It is assumed that in the simulations all the state variables are accessible, and therefore they do not need to be estimated.

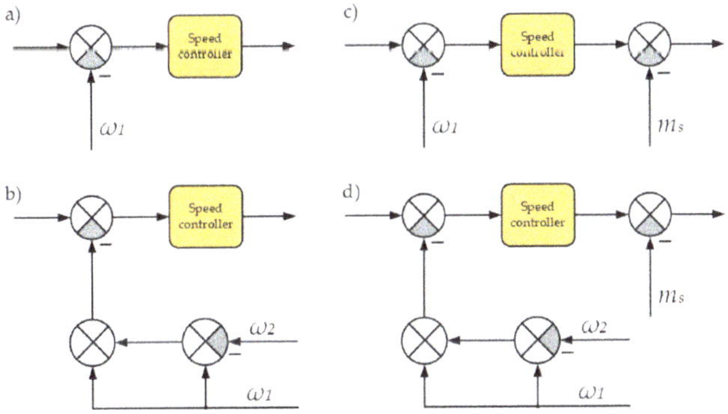

Figure 15. Combinations of feedbacks applied in the control structure, a classical feedback loop (**a**), an additional speed difference feedback (**b**), an additional shaft torque feedback (**c**) and a combination of speed and torque feedbacks (**d**).

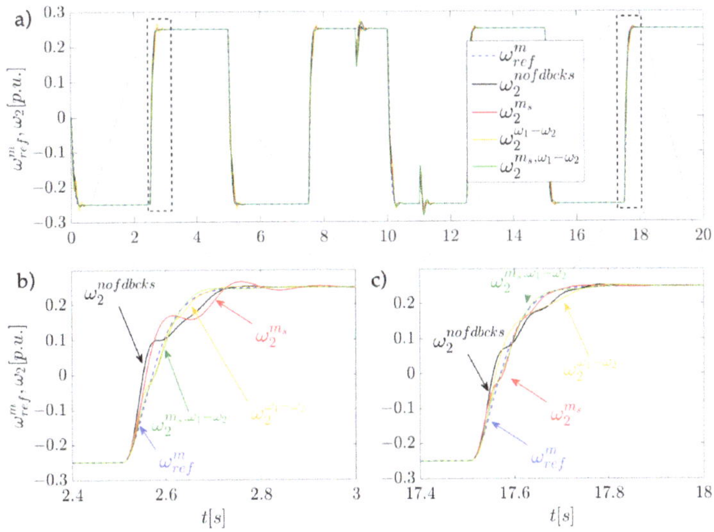

Figure 16. Comparison of speeds (ω_{ref} and ω_1) transients obtained for different connections of feedbacks (**a**), the initial part of the simulation (**b**), the final of the simulation (**c**).

6. Experimental Results

To confirm the theoretical tests, experimental studies on the laboratory stand were carried out. The laboratory system presented in Figure 17 consists of two DC motors coupled by a long steel shaft. To change the time constant of the load, motor flywheels can be added. Drive is powered through an H-bridge. Current measurements are conducted by LEM sensors and incremental encoders are mounted on both machines to measure the speed of the drive. The control algorithm is compiled on a PC and uploaded to a DSpace 1103 card with a digital signal processor. Everything is connected through a control panel. To simplify the process of compiling and uploading the algorithm to the processor, the controller was implemented as a Matlab Embedded Function.

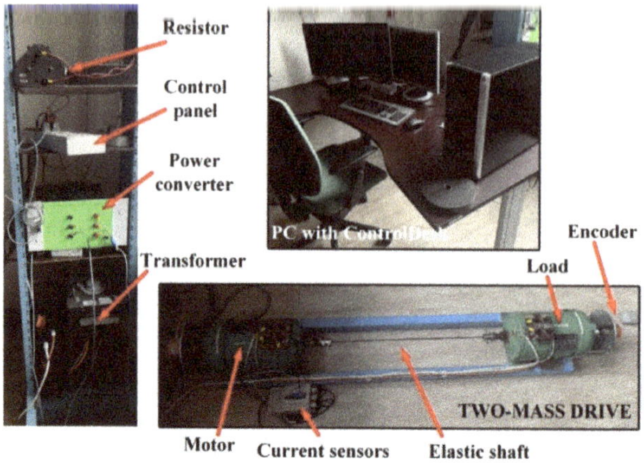

Figure 17. The laboratory setup.

The code is built using Matlab's built-in compiler. These data are then loaded to a ControlDesk virtual panel (which is a part of the dSPACE software). ControlDesk is used to capture signals from the dSPACE card, display the results and then save them in a *.mat file which can be read by Matlab. The nominal parameters of the experimental setup are presented in Table 4.

Table 4. Parameters of the experimental setup.

Motor Nominal Power	500 W
Load nominal power	500 W
Shaft length	600 mm
Shaft diameter	5 mm
Encoder impulse	36,000 pulses/rev

The experimental verification of the simulation tests can be found in Figure 18, presented transients match the results obtained in Section 4. The upper part of the graph shows the speeds of the motor and the load for nominal time constants of the drive. Reference speed of 25% of the nominal speed value was used with cyclic reversions occurring every 5 s.

The lower part of the graph shows the influence of an increased load time constant on the control structure. A small overshoot is observed, but it is gradually reduced with the adaptation process. The same can be noticed for the oscillations of speeds close to the setpoint, the frequency of oscillations decreases over the time of the experiment. The reaction to the load torque is comparable to the results achieved with the nominal parameters.

Settling time and rise time for nominal parameters in the experimental bench were also calculated. The calculated value of the rise time was equal to t_{rise} = 0.25 s, while the settling time was $t_{settling}$ = 0.38 s which is comparable to simulation results.

Another test was also carried out to see how an increased learning rate impacts the dynamics of the drive. As presented in Figure 19, when the higher value of learning rate is applied, the overshoot on the first reversion is substantially higher. After the controller updates all parameters, the overshoot is reduced to zero. The test proves the control structure's adaptive qualities. Other than that, the performance of the drive is exactly the same as in previous tests.

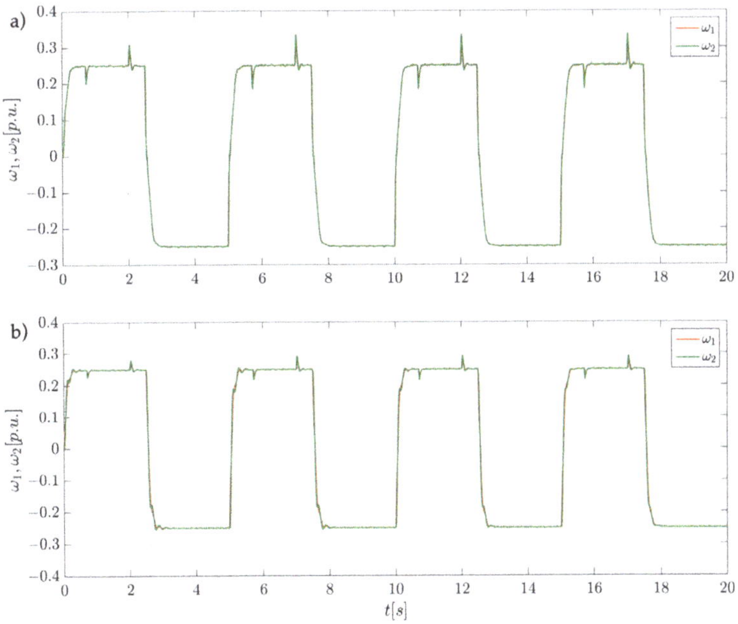

Figure 18. Transients of experimental results for nominal parameters of the drive (**a**) and increased load time constant (**b**).

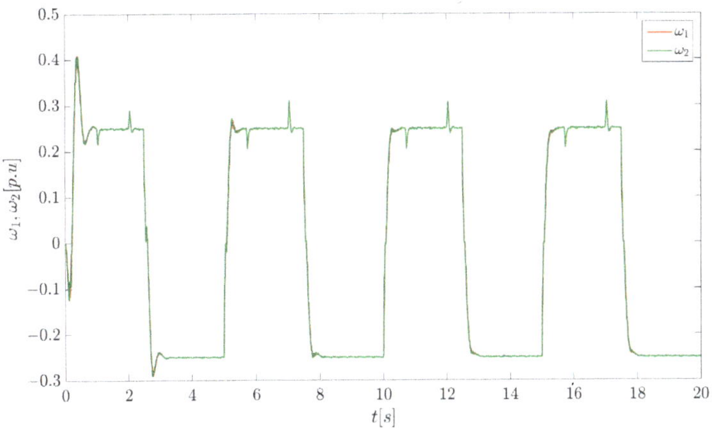

Figure 19. Results from the experimental setup obtained after increasing the value of the learning rate.

7. Concluding Remarks

In this paper, a recurrent wavelet neural network designed to control the electrical drive with an elastic shaft is investigated. Various combinations of state feedback signals from the plant are considered. It starts with only a basic connection from the motor speed, then additional solutions are analyzed. It can be important not only in theoretical assumptions, but also in real applications (economic aspects and reliability). One of the main points of the study is the application of the modified Grey Wolf Optimizer in the design process of the control structure. The efficiency of the proposed solutions was tested in simulations and experiments. Based on the obtained results, the main remarks presented below can be formulated.

- Recurrent wavelet neural network can form the basis of an adaptive speed controller designed for an electrical drive with a compound mechanical part.
- Presented results show that the adaptation is performed properly. As a result, overshoots are reduced, and oscillations are damped.
- Correct work of the control system is observed even when the parameters are changed.
- The Grey Wolf Optimizer can be used as a universal tool for solving issues observed in the design process of adaptive neural speed controllers for the drive.
- Proposed improvements (achieved through processing the data using the mGWO) expedite the process of the neural controller optimization.
- To effectively damp the oscillations of the state variables, implementation of an additional feedback loop is necessary.

Author Contributions: Conceptualization, M.K., R.S. and M.Z.; methodology, M.Z.; software, M.Z.; data curation, M.Z.; data, M.Z.; writing—original draft preparation, M.K., R.S. and M.Z.; writing—review and editing, M.K., R.S. and M.Z.; visualization, M.Z.; supervision, M.K.; funding acquisition, M.K. All authors have read and agreed to the published version of the manuscript.

Funding: This research received no external funding.

Institutional Review Board Statement: Not applicable.

Informed Consent Statement: Not applicable.

Data Availability Statement: The data presented in this study are available on request from the corresponding author.

Conflicts of Interest: The authors declare no conflict of interest.

References

1. Pedraza, L.F.; Hernández, H.A.; Hernández, C.A. Artificial Neural Network Controller for a Modular Robot Using a Software Defined Radio Communication System. *Electronics* **2020**, *9*, 1626. [CrossRef]
2. Yan, J.; Jin, L.; Yuan, Z.; Liu, Z. RNN for Receding Horizon Control of Redundant Robot Manipulators. *IEEE Trans. Ind. Electron.* **2022**, *69*, 1608–1619. [CrossRef]
3. Muthusamy, P.K.; Garratt, M.; Pota, H.; Muthusamy, R. Real-Time Adaptive Intelligent Control System for Quadcopter Unmanned Aerial Vehicles with Payload Uncertainties. *IEEE Trans. Ind. Electron.* **2022**, *69*, 1641–1653. [CrossRef]
4. Pajchrowski, T.; Zawirski, K. Application of artificial neural network to robust speed control of servodrive. *IEEE Trans. Ind. Electron.* **2007**, *54*, 200–207. [CrossRef]
5. Kaminski, M. Nature-Inspired Algorithm Implemented for Stable Radial Basis Function Neural Controller of Electric Drive with Induction Motor. *Energies* **2020**, *13*, 6541. [CrossRef]
6. Brock, S.; Łuczak, D.; Nowopolski, K.; Pajchrowski, T.; Zawirski, K. Two approaches to speed control for multi-mass system with variable mechanical parameters. *IEEE Trans. Ind. Electron.* **2017**, *64*, 3338–3347. [CrossRef]
7. Liu, G.; Xu, X.; Yu, X.; Wang, F. Graphite Classification Based on Improved Convolution Neural Network. *Processes* **2021**, *9*, 1995. [CrossRef]
8. Ruan, W.; Dong, Q.; Zhang, X.; Li, Z. Friction Compensation Control of Electromechanical Actuator Based on Neural Network Adaptive Sliding Mode. *Sensors* **2021**, *21*, 1508. [CrossRef]
9. Mohamed, Y.A.I.M. A Novel Direct Instantaneous Torque and Flux Control With an ADALINE-Based Motor Model for a High Performance DD-PMSM. *IEEE Trans. Power Electron.* **2007**, *22*, 2042–2049. [CrossRef]
10. Soufleri, E.; Roy, K. Network Compression via Mixed Precision Quantization Using a Multi-Layer Perceptron for the Bit-Width Allocation. *IEEE Access* **2021**, *9*, 135059–135068. [CrossRef]
11. Ke, K.-C.; Huang, M.-S. Quality Prediction for Injection Molding by Using a Multilayer Perceptron Neural Network. *Polymers* **2020**, *12*, 1812. [CrossRef]
12. Elman, J.L. Finding structure in time. *Cogn. Sci.* **1990**, *14*, 179–211. [CrossRef]
13. Jordan, M.I. Generic constraints on underspecified target trajectories. In Proceedings of the International Joint Conference on Neural Networks, Washington, DC, USA, 18–22 June 1989; Volume 1, pp. 217–225. [CrossRef]
14. Kamiński, M. Recurrent neural controller applied for two-mass system. In Proceedings of the International Conference on Methods and Models in Automation and Robotics (MMAR), Międzyzdroje, Poland, 29 August–1 September 2016; pp. 128–133. [CrossRef]
15. Chien, T.; Chen, C.; Huang, Y.; Lin, W. Stability and Almost Disturbance Decoupling Analysis of Nonlinear System Subject to Feedback Linearization and Feedforward Neural Network Controller. *IEEE Neural Netw.* **2008**, *19*, 1220–1230. [CrossRef]

16. Yipeng, L.; Wenkang, Y.; Ming, Z. Design of Adaptive Neural Network Backstepping Controller for Linear Motor Magnetic Levitation System. In Proceedings of the IEEE Industry Applications Society Annual Meeting, Baltimore, MD, USA, 29 September–3 October 2019; pp. 1–6. [CrossRef]
17. Han, H.; Zhang, L.; Hou, Y.; Qiao, J. Nonlinear Model Predictive Control Based on a Self-Organizing Recurrent Neural Network. *IEEE Trans. Neural Netw. Learn. Syst.* **2016**, *27*, 2. [CrossRef]
18. Lin, F.; Wai, R.; Chen, M. Wavelet neural network control for linear ultrasonic motor drive via adaptive sliding-mode technique. *IEEE Trans. Ultrason. Ferroelectr. Freq. Control* **2003**, *50*, 686–698. [CrossRef]
19. Zhang, J.; Walter, G.G.; Miao, Y.; Lee, W.N.W. Wavelet neural networks for function learning. *IEEE Trans. Signal Process.* **1995**, *43*, 1485–1496. [CrossRef]
20. Chen, C.F.; Hsiao, C.H. Wavelet approach to optimizing dynamic systems. *IEEE Trans. Signal Process.* **1995**, *43*, 1485–1496. [CrossRef]
21. Gao, A.; Zhang, F.; Fu, Z.; Zhang, Z.; Li, H. The SOC estimation and simulation of power battery based on self-recurrent wavelet neural network. *Chin. Autom. Congr.* **2017**, 4247–4252. [CrossRef]
22. Rafiei, M.; Niknam, T.; Aghaei, J.; Shafie-khah, M.; Catalão, J.P.S. Probabilistic Load Forecasting using an Improved Wavelet Neural Network Trained by Generalized Extreme Learning Machine. *IEEE Trans. Smart Grid* **2018**, *9*, 6961–6971. [CrossRef]
23. Sheng, L.; Xiaojie, G.; Lanyong, Z. Robust Adaptive Backstepping Sliding Mode Control for Six-Phase Permanent Magnet Synchronous Motor Using Recurrent Wavelet Fuzzy Neural Network. *IEEE Access* **2017**, *5*, 14502–14515. [CrossRef]
24. Xiao, Q.; Ge, G.; Wang, J. The Neural Network Adaptive Filter Model Based on Wavelet Transform. In Proceedings of the 2009 Ninth International Conference on Hybrid Intelligent Systems, Shenyang, China, 12–14 August 2009; pp. 529–534. [CrossRef]
25. Khan, M.A.; Uddin, M.N.; Rahman, M.A. A Novel Wavelet-Neural-Network-Based Robust Controller for IPM Motor Drives. *IEEE Trans. Appl.* **2013**, *49*, 2341–2351. [CrossRef]
26. Liang, J.; Chen, H. Development of a Piezoelectric-Actuated Drop-On Demand Droplet Generator using Adaptive Wavelet Neural Network Control Scheme. In Proceedings of the 2013 IEEE International Conference on Mechatronics and Automation, Takamatsu, Japan, 4–7 August 2013; pp. 382–388. [CrossRef]
27. Li, Z.; Ruan, Y. A novel control method based on wavelet neural networks for vector control of induction motor drives. In Proceedings of the International Conference on Wavelet Analysis and Pattern Recognition, Hong Kong, China, 30–31 August 2008; pp. 1–6. [CrossRef]
28. Sharma, M.; Verma, A. Adaptive Observer Based Tracking Control for a Class of Uncertain Nonlinear Systems with Delayed States and Input Using Self Recurrent Wavelet Neural Network. In Proceedings of the 2nd International Conference on Advances in Computing, Control, and Telecommunication Technologies, Jakarta, Indonesia, 203 December 2010; pp. 27–31. [CrossRef]
29. El-Sousy, F.F.M.; Abuhasel, K.A. Self-organizing recurrent fuzzy wavelet neural network-based mixed H2/H∞ adaptive tracking control for uncertain two-axis motion control system. *IEEE Ind. App. Soc. Ann. Meet.* **2015**, 1–14. [CrossRef]
30. Gao, W.; Guo, Z. Research of recurrent wavelet neural network speed controller based on chaotic series adaptive PSO. In Proceedings of the 3rd International Conference on Information Management (ICIM), Chengdu, China, 21–23 April 2017; pp. 470–475. [CrossRef]
31. Knypiński, Ł.; Kuroczycki, S.; Márquez, F.P.G. Minimization of Torque Ripple in the Brushless DC Motor Using Constrained Cuckoo Search Algorithm. *Electronics* **2021**, *10*, 2299. [CrossRef]
32. Tarczewski, T.; Grzesiak, L.M. Artificial bee colony based auto- tuning of PMSM state feedback speed controller. In Proceedings of the 2016 IEEE International Power Electronics and Motion Control Conference, Varna, Bulgaria, 5–28 September 2016; pp. 1155–1160. [CrossRef]
33. Zhao, J.; Lin, M.; Xu, D.; Hao, L.; Zhang, W. Vector control of a hybrid axial field flux-switching permanent magnet machine based on particle swarm optimization. *IEEE Trans. Magn.* **2015**, *51*, 1–4. [CrossRef]
34. Tarczewski, T.; Grzesiak, L.M. An application of novel nature-inspired optimization algorithms to auto-tuning state feedback speed controller for PMSM. *IEEE Trans. Ind. Appl.* **2018**, *54*, 2913–2925. [CrossRef]
35. Hannan, M.A.; Ali, J.A.; Mohamed, A.; Hussain, A. Optimization techniques to enhance the performance of induction motor drives: A review. *Renew. Sustain. Energy Rev.* **2018**, *81*, 1611–1626. [CrossRef]
36. Xu, L.; Wang, H.; Lin, W.; Gulliver, T.A.; Le, K.N. GWO-BP Neural Network Based OP Performance Prediction for Mobile Multiuser Communication Networks. *IEEE Access* **2019**, *7*, 152690–152700. [CrossRef]
37. Jaiswal, K.; Mittal, H.; Kukreja, S. Randomized grey wolf optimizer (RGWO) with randomly weighted coefficients. In Proceedings of the 2017 Tenth International Conference on Contemporary Computing, Noida, India, 10–12 August 2017; pp. 1–3. [CrossRef]
38. GU, W.; Zhou, B. Improved grey wolf optimization based on the Quantum-behaved mechanism. In Proceedings of the 2019 IEEE 4th Advanced Information Technology, Electronic and Automation Control Conference, Chengdu, China, 20–22 December 2019; pp. 1537–1540. [CrossRef]
39. Emary, E.; Zawbaa, H.M.; Hassanien, A.E. Binary grey wolf optimization approaches for feature selection. *Neurocomputing* **2016**, *172*, 371–381. [CrossRef]
40. Mirjalili, S.; Saremi, S.; Mirjalili, S.M.; Coelho, L.S. Multi-objective grey wolf optimizer: A novel algorithm for multi-criterion optimization. *Expert Syst. Appl.* **2016**, *47*, 106–119. [CrossRef]
41. Knypiński, Ł. Modified grey wolf method for optimization of PM motors. *ITM Web Conf.* **2019**, *28*. [CrossRef]

42. Kamiński, M.; Szabat, K. Adaptive Control Structure with Neural Data Processing Applied for Electrical Drive with Elastic Shaft. *Energies* **2021**, *14*, 3389. [CrossRef]
43. Szczepanski, R.; Kaminski, M.; Tarczewski, T. Auto-Tuning Process of State Feedback Speed Controller Applied for Two-Mass System. *Energies* **2020**, *13*, 3067. [CrossRef]
44. Szabat, K.; Wróbel, K.; Dróżdż, K.; Janiszewski, D.; Pajchrowski, T.; Wójcik, A. A Fuzzy Unscented Kalman Filter in the Adaptive Control System of a Drive System with a Flexible Joint. *Energies* **2020**, *13*, 2056. [CrossRef]
45. Vašak, M.; Perić, N.; Szabat, K.; Cychowski, M. Patched LQR control for robust protection of multi-mass electrical drives with constraints. In Proceedings of the IEEE International Symposium on Industrial Electronics, Bari, Italy, 4–7 July 2010; pp. 3153–3158. [CrossRef]
46. Tang, Y.; Sun, W.; Wang, Y.; Zhai, X. Using Recurrent Fuzzy Wavelet Neural Network to Control AC Servo System. In Proceedings of the IEEE 5th International Power Electronics and Motion Control Conference, Shanghai, China, 14–16 August 2006; Volume 2, pp. 1–4. [CrossRef]
47. Song, J.; Shi, H. Dynamic system modeling based on wavelet recurrent fuzzy neural network. *Intern. Conf. Nat. Comput.* **2011**, *2*, 766–770. [CrossRef]
48. Liu, W.Y.; Gao, Q.W.; Zhang, Y. A novel wind turbine de-noising method based on the Genetic Algorithm optimal Mexican hat wavelet. In Proceedings of the 2016 13th International Conference on Ubiquitous Robots and Ambient Intelligence, Xi'an, China, 19–22 August 2016; pp. 1003–1006. [CrossRef]
49. Karnavas, Y.L.; Chasiotis, I.D. PMDC coreless micro-motor parameters estimation through Grey Wolf Optimizer. In Proceedings of the International Conference on Electrical Machines, Lausanne, Switzerland, 4–7 September 2016; pp. 865–870. [CrossRef]
50. Kaminski, M. Neural Network Training Using Particle Swarm Optimization—A Case Study. In Proceedings of the 24th International Conference on Methods and Models in Automation and Robotics, Międzyzdroje, Poland, 26–29 August 2019; pp. 115–120. [CrossRef]
51. Seizović, A.; Vojvodić, N.; Ristić, L.; Bebić, M. Energy efficient control of variable-speed induction motor drives based on Particle Swarm Optimization. In Proceedings of the International Symposium on Industrial Electronics and Applications, Kristiansand, Norwa, 9–13 November 2020; pp. 1–6. [CrossRef]

electronics

MDPI

Article

Pipeline Leak Detection and Estimation Using Fuzzy PID Observer

Raheleh Jafari [1], Sina Razvarz [2], Cristóbal Vargas-Jarillo [2], Alexander Gegov [3,4,*] and Farzad Arabikhan [3]

[1] School of Design, University of Leeds, Leeds LS2 9JT, UK; r.jafari@leeds.ac.uk
[2] Departamento de Control Automatico, CINVESTAV-IPN (National Polytechnic Institute), Mexico City 07360, Mexico; srazvarz@ctrl.cinvestav.mx (S.R.); cvargas@ctrl.cinvestav.mx (C.V.-J.)
[3] School of Computing, University of Portsmouth, Portsmouth PO13HE, UK; farzad.arabikhan@port.ac.uk
[4] English Language Faculty of Engineering, Technical University of Sofia, 1756 Sofia, Bulgaria
* Correspondence: alexander.gegov@port.ac.uk

Abstract: A pipe is a ubiquitous product in the industries that is used to convey liquids, gases, or solids suspended in a liquid, e.g., a slurry, from one location to another. Both internal and external cracking can result in structural failure of the industrial piping system and possibly decrease the service life of the equipment. The chaos and complexity associated with the uncertain behaviour inherent in pipeline systems lead to difficulty in detection and localisation of leaks in real time. The timely detection of leakage is important in order to reduce the loss rate and serious environmental consequences. The objective of this paper is to propose a new leak detection method based on an autoregressive with exogenous input (ARX) Laguerre fuzzy proportional-integral-derivative (PID) observation system. The objective of this paper is to propose a new leak detection method based on an autoregressive with exogenous input (ARX) Laguerre fuzzy proportional-integral-derivative (PID) observation system. In this work, the ARX–Laguerre model has been used to generate better performance in the presence of uncertainty. According to the results, the proposed technique can detect leaks accurately and effectively.

Keywords: autoregressive with exogenous input Laguerre (ARX–Laguerre); fuzzy; pipeline; PID; controller; PID observer

1. Introduction

Pipelines are the safest way for transporting crude oil, petroleum products, and natural gas over long distances. Pipelines deliver clear benefits in supporting economic growth as they provide a cheaper means to transport. However, oil and gas pipelines may be significantly damaged due to internal and external defects (e.g., corrosion, dents, gouges, weld defects). Construction and operational defects of pipes can pose major risks to supplies. Pipeline safety is possible using inspection and monitoring techniques which can be either internal or external in nature.

Over the last few years, a number of technologies have been reported to monitor pipelines such as acoustic emission [1–3], fibre optic sensor [4,5], digital signal processing, and mass–volume balance [6]. In [7], a real-time transient modelling method has been utilised for leakage detection and localization in the pipeline systems. In [8], an extended version of a real-time transient modelling method to estimate two leaks simultaneously in a piping system is proposed. The acoustic pulse reflectometry method has been used successfully to identify damage in pipelines utilising the time domain [9].

In [10], the cepstrum analysis technique is utilised to identify leaks in pipes. In [11], a new method based on auxiliary mass spatial probing by the stationary wavelet transform is suggested to detect damage in beams. Artificial intelligence with fuzzy logic has become the most effective approach, which attracts many investigators to deeply research it [12–16]. It has been successfully used for leak detection. In [17], a low-cost wireless sensor system is introduced to detect of leaks in metallic piping systems. In [18,19], a neural network technique was utilized to detect the leak in a pipeline and has provided promising results. In [20], an artificial neural network was utilized to detect the leak in a pipeline such that the sound noise data were gathered through several microphones placed within a specific distance from the damaged part. The fast Fourier transform algorithm has been performed on data and supplied to a feed-forward network for making a final decision. In [11,21], a neural network technique was used for pattern recognition in oil pipe networks.

Various researchers have used observational approaches for fault diagnosis in pipes that are based on different algorithms [22–24]. The authors in [25] focused on leakage reconstruction in pipe systems utilising sliding mode observer. The authors in [26–28] focused on leakage reconstruction in pipe systems utilising a PID (proportional-integral-derivative) model and observer. In [29], a fuzzy PI observer was used to detect leaks in pipeline. In [30], a leak inspection device consisting of an adaptive Luenberger-type observer based upon a set of two-coupled partial differential equations governing the flow dynamics is proposed. To improve the input and output performance of ARX, in [26,31], the Laguerre method is applied to ARX to filter the input and output. In [27,29], a fuzzy PID observation method using the ARX–Laguerre technique is used for diagnosing fault in pipe.

The object of this paper is to develop a new technique based on autoregressive with exogenous input Laguerre (ARX–Laguerre) fuzzy PID to detect leaks in a pipe. For this aim, in the first step, the ARX–Laguerre technique is used for pipeline modelling. In the second step, the PID observer based on the ARX–Laguerre model is designed to detect leakage in the presence of uncertainties. The numerical results demonstrate that the proposed technique detects and estimates leaks accurately. The remainder part of this paper is organized as follows: in Section 2, the pipeline model equations are described using the momentum and continuity equations. The pipeline model equations based on the ARX–Laguerre technique are given in the Section 3. The proposed new technique based on ARX–Laguerre fuzzy PID observer to detect and locate leaks in a pipe is given in Section 4. The algorithm and simulation results analysis is given in Section 5. Moreover, in this section, the proposed method is compared with some other existing methods to illustrate its value. Finally, conclusions are given.

2. Pipeline Modelling

Here, we do not consider convective speed changes and compressibility effects in process lines. The mass flow rate (m), the length of the pipe (Γ), the flow in a pipe system (Φ), the inlet pressure ($\wp_i$), and outlet pressure ($\wp_o$) at pipeline are assumed to be computable. Furthermore, the area of cross section (a) is fixed along the pipe. The suggested pipeline architecture is illustrated in Figure 1.

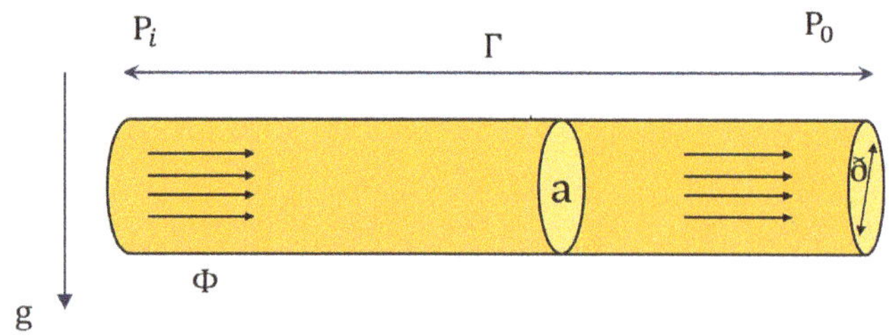

Figure 1. The suggested pipeline architecture.

The differential equation describing the dynamic behaviour of a fluid in a duct is based on the mass, momentum, and the conservation of energy [32]. Newton's second law of motion, when implemented to a control volume, generated the following momentum equation [32,33]:

$$\frac{\partial v}{\partial t} + \frac{1}{\rho}\frac{\partial \wp}{\partial x} + \frac{\Im}{2\eth}v^2 = 0 \tag{1}$$

If we substitute $\upsilon = \frac{\Phi}{a}$ as well as $\wp = \rho g \mathcal{H}$ in (1) the resulting momentum equation will be:

$$\frac{\partial \Phi}{a \partial t} + g \frac{\partial}{\partial x} \mathcal{H} + \frac{\Im \Phi^2}{2 \eth a^2} = 0 \tag{2}$$

Thus,

$$\frac{\partial \Phi}{\partial t} + a g \frac{\partial}{\partial x} \mathcal{H} + \frac{\Im \Phi^2}{2 \eth a} = 0 \tag{3}$$

in which $\mathcal{H}$ represents the pressure head, Φ the rate of flow in a pipe, x the length of pipe, t time steps, g the gravity, a the pipe cross-sectional area, $\eth$ the inside diameter of the pipe, and $\Im$ the pipe friction factor.

Coefficient of friction is typically assumed to be constant. In general, it was found to be a function of the Reynolds number (Re) and the pipe material roughness coefficient (e). The Swamee–Jain equation can be used to describe the friction factor for a pipe of circular section $(\eth)$ as follows [34,35]:

$$\Im = \left(\frac{0.5}{\ln\left[0.27\left(\frac{e}{\eth}\right) + 5.74 \frac{1}{Re^{0.9}}\right]} \right)^2 \tag{4}$$

where $\Im$ is the pipe friction factor, $\eth$ is the inside diameter of the pipe and the pipe material roughness coefficient (e)

Reynolds number equation is determined via the following equation [36]:

$$Re = 4 \frac{\rho \Phi}{\pi \eth \mu} = \frac{\rho \upsilon \eth}{\mu} \tag{5}$$

in which ρ represents the fluid density, and μ the viscosity of the flowing fluid. For $10^{-8} < \frac{e}{\eth} < 0.01$ as well as $5000 < Re < 10^8$ are provably correct.

$$\frac{\partial \wp}{\partial t} + \rho a^2 \frac{\partial \upsilon}{\partial x} = 0 \tag{6}$$

After applying the overall mass balance as well as the Reynolds transport theorem to the control volume the continuity equation will be obtained:

$$\frac{\partial \wp}{\partial t} + \rho a^2 \frac{\partial \upsilon}{\partial x} = 0 \tag{7}$$

The following equation can be acquired if we substitute the pressure head $(\mathcal{H})$ as well as the flow rate (Φ) in Equation (7):

$$\frac{\partial \mathcal{H}}{\partial t} + \frac{a^2}{g a} \frac{\partial \Phi}{\partial x} = 0 \tag{8}$$

in which a represents the speed of the wave inside a fluid filled elastic duct. The wave velocity depends on the elastic properties of the fluid and pipe. The pressure head $(\mathcal{H})$ and flow rate (Φ) change as functions of position and time, $\mathcal{H}(x,t)$ and $\Phi(x,t)$, respectively, so that $x \in [0, \Gamma]$, where Γ represents the length of the duct.

Now we can create a model of the pipe applying Equations (3) and (8). These equations need to be solved; however, coming to analytical solutions is not easy. Because of this, different methods need to be used to solve these equations such as characteristics and finite difference approaches [37]. Here, the finite difference approach is implemented such that Equations (3) and (8) are discretized to obtain a system of ordinary differential equations. The considered finite difference approach discretizes the whole pipe into N smaller sections [37,38]. Finite difference technique with a fixed step size Δs is, historically, the most popular time-stepping approach. Here, we consider finite difference method because it is an easy-to-use approach and is specially designed and applied for nonlinear observer models. In this study we define it as follows:

$$\begin{aligned} \frac{\partial\Phi(s_{i-1},t)}{\partial s} &\approx \frac{\Delta\Phi(s_{i-1},t)}{\Delta s} \approx \frac{\Phi_i-\Phi_{i-1}}{\Delta s} \\ \frac{\partial\mathscr{H}(s_{i-1},t)}{\partial s} &\approx \frac{\Delta\mathscr{H}(s_{i-1},t)}{\Delta s} \approx \frac{\mathscr{H}_i-\mathscr{H}_{i-1}}{\Delta s} \end{aligned} \tag{9}$$

$\forall i = 1, \cdots, n$, in which n represents the number of points of the grid, and $\Delta s = s_{i+1} - s_i$ represents the size of the i-section between the two successive grid points. The computational domain $s \in [0,\Gamma]$ is divided up into three smaller domains, $\{s_k\} := \{0, s_{leak}, \Gamma\}$, so that s_{leak} indicates the location of leak; see Figure 2. The leak flow rate can be measured by $\Phi_{leak} = C_d a_{leak}\sqrt{2g}\sqrt{\mathscr{H}(s_{leak}, t)}$, such that C_d represents efflux coefficient, and a_{leak} the cross-sectional area along the leak path. The leak flow rate can be calculated by $\Phi_{leak} = \Lambda\sqrt{\mathscr{H}(s_{leak}, t)}$, in which $\Lambda = C_d a_{leak}\sqrt{2g}$. The behaviour of a dynamic pipeline network can be described by an ordinary differential equation system:

$$\begin{aligned} \dot{\Phi}_1 &= \frac{ga}{s}(\mathscr{H}_1 - \mathscr{H}_2) - \frac{\Im\Phi_1{}^2}{2\eth a} \\ \dot{\mathscr{H}}_{leak} &= \frac{c^2}{gas}(\Phi_1 - \Phi_2 - \Lambda\sqrt{\mathscr{H}_{leak}}) \\ \dot{\Phi}_2 &= \frac{ga}{\Gamma - s}(\mathscr{H}_2 - \mathscr{H}_3) - \frac{\Im\Phi_2^2}{2\eth a} \end{aligned} \tag{10}$$

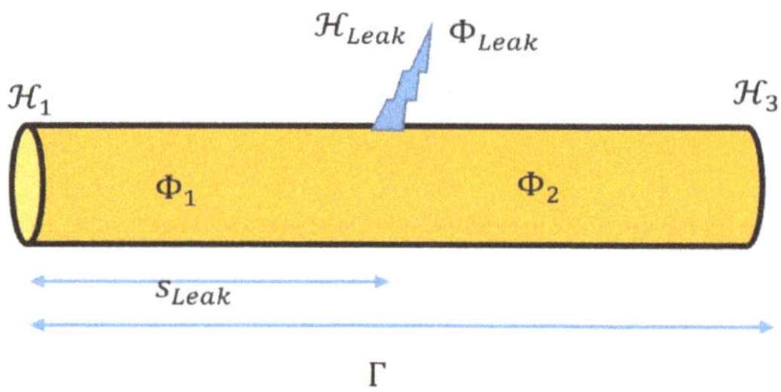

Figure 2. The suggested pipeline architecture.

Suppose that both inlet and outlet pressures, $\mathscr{H}_1$ and $\mathscr{H}_3$, respectively, are known and have been defined using external means such as a pump. The pressure $\mathscr{H}_2$ and the inlet and outlet flow rate (Φ_1 and Φ_2, respectively) of the leakage point are considered to be variables. From the continuity equation we can write:

$$\Phi_1 = \Phi_{leak} + \Phi_2 \tag{11}$$

3. Pipeline Modelling Based on the ARX–Laguerre Technique

For many years, pipelines played a huge role in oil and gas industries, as they significantly reduce transport costs. Leakage inspection in transmission pipelines is crucially significant for safe operation. In general, there are various fault detection methods, each with different potentials; however, the selection of proper leak detection technique is difficult. This is particularly important when they deal with various types of uncertain conditions. To deal with this problem, we introduce a fuzzy ARX–Laguerre PID observer in Section 4. First, in this study, the ARX–Laguerre technique is used for pipeline modelling. In the second step, the PID observer based on the ARX–Laguerre model is designed to detect leakage in the presence of uncertainties. The proposed model-based ARX–Laguerre orthonormal method is represented by developing its coefficients associated to the flow input and flow output, Fourier coefficients, and Laguerre-based orthonormal function, as follows [23,39]:

$$M_0(s) = \sum_0^{i_a} \lambda_{n.a}\left(\sum_{j=1}^{\infty} \ell_a * M_0(s)\right).x_{n.M_0}(s) + \sum_0^{i_b} \lambda_{n.b}\left(\sum_{j=1}^{\infty} \ell_b * M_i(s)\right).x_{n.M_i}(s) \tag{12}$$

in which $M_0(s)$, $(\lambda_{n.a}$ *and* $\lambda_{n.b})$, (i_a, i_b) (ℓ_a, ℓ_b),$*$, $M_i(s)$, $x_{n.M_0}(s)$, and $x_{n.M_i}(s)$ represent the pipe outflow, Fourier coefficients, the order of the system, Laguerre orthonormal function, convolution product, pipe inflow, exhaust filter, and entrance filter, respectively. By expanding the ARX model on Laguerre orthonormal bases, the following state-space model can be obtained:

$$\begin{cases} M(s+1) = \left[AM(s) + B_y(y(s) + \alpha_s(k)) + B_u(u(s) + a_p(s))\right] \\ y(s) = (S)^T M(s) + B_s\alpha_s(s), \end{cases} \tag{13}$$

in which $M(s), y(s)$, $u(s)$, $\alpha_p(s)$, and $\alpha_s(s)$ represent the state vector, calculated output, control input, pump defect, and sensor defect, respectively. A, B_y, B_u, and B_s, as well as S, represent matrices of coefficients.

4. ARX–Laguerre Fuzzy PID Observation Technique

In this section, the ARX–Laguerre fuzzy PID observation system is proposed to detect and estimate a leak in pipelines.

4.1. Modelling of Dynamic System by ARX–Laguerre

Let us consider the linear ARX state space model with disturbances illustrated by the following equation to formulate the dynamic fault detection problem:

$$\begin{cases} M(s+1) = \left[A\ M(s) + B_u(u(s) + \alpha_p(s))\right] \\ y(s) = (S)^T M(s) + B_s\alpha_s(s), \end{cases} \tag{14}$$

We define the ARX model on Laguerre base as follows [31,40]:

$$\begin{gathered} y(k) = \sum_{0}^{N_a-1} S_{(n,p)} x_{(n,y)}(s) + \sum_{0}^{N_b-1} S_{(n,b)} x_{(n,u)}(s) \\ X(k) = \left[\begin{array}{cc} x_{(n,u)}(s) & x_{(n,y)}(s) \end{array}\right] \\ x_{(n,y)}(s) = L_n^a(k, \xi_p) * y(s) \\ x_{(n,u)}(s) = L_n^b(k, \xi_b) * u(s) \end{gathered} \tag{15}$$

in which $y(k)$, $u(k)$, $\left(K_{(n,p)}, K_{(n,s)}\right)$, (N_a, N_b), $x_{(n,y)}(s)$, $x_{(n,u)}(s)$, and $\left(L_n^a(s, \xi_a), L_n^b(s, \xi_b)\right)$ represent the pipe outflow, pipe inflow, Fourier coefficients, exhaust filter, entrance filter, and Laguerre orthonormal function, respectively.

Using Equation (16) the following state-space model can be obtained in the presence of failures of the pump and sensor as well as disturbances:

$$\begin{cases} M_p(s+1) = \left[AM_p(s) + B_y(y_p(s) + \alpha_s(s)) + B_u(u(s) + \alpha_p(s))\right] \\ y(s) = (S)^T M_p(s) + B_s\alpha_s(s), \end{cases} \tag{16}$$

The fault of the pump is calculated using the following formula:

$$\begin{gathered} e_y(s) = y_p(s) - y(s) \\ e_M(s) = \left[\begin{array}{c} x_{p(n,u+\alpha_p)}(s) - x_{(n,u)}(s) \\ x_{p(n,y_a)}(s) - x_{(n,y)}(s) \end{array}\right] \end{gathered} \tag{17}$$

such that

$$x_{a(n,u+\alpha_p)}(s) \neq M_{(n,u)}(s) \rightarrow M_p(s) \neq M(s) \rightarrow y_p(s) \neq y(s) \rightarrow e_y(s) \neq 0 \tag{18}$$

The fault of the sensor is calculated using the following formula.

$$e_y(s) = y_p(s) - y(s)$$
$$e_M(s) = \begin{bmatrix} M_{p(n,u)}(k) - M_{(n,u)}(s) \\ M_{p(n,y_p+\alpha_s)}(k) - M_{(n,y)}(s) \end{bmatrix} \quad (19)$$

such that

$$M_{p(n,y_p+\alpha_s)}(s) \neq x_{(n,y)}(s) \to M_p(s) \neq M(s) \to y_p(s) \neq y(s) \to e_y(S) \neq 0. \quad (20)$$

4.2. Fault Diagnosis

In this study, the ARX–Laguerre fuzzy PID observation system is proposed to identify pump and sensor defects in pipes. We define the proposed technique by the following formulas in the presence of failures of the pump and sensor in the pipe:

$$\begin{cases} \hat{M}(s+1) = A\hat{M}(s) + B_y(\hat{y}(s) + \hat{\alpha}_s(s)) + B_y(u(s) + \hat{\alpha}_p(s)) + K_p e(s) \\ e_s(s) = (q_s(s) - \hat{q}_s(s)) \\ e_p(s) = (w_p(s) - \hat{w}_p(s)) \\ \hat{\alpha}_p(s+1) = \hat{\alpha}_p(s) + K_{ip} e_p(s) + K_{d_p}(e_p(s+1) + e_p(s) + e_p(s-1)) \\ \hat{\alpha}_s(s+1) = \hat{\alpha}_s(s) + K_{is} e_s(s) + K_{d_s}(e_s(s+1) + e_s(s) + e_s(s-1)) \\ \hat{y}(s+1) = (S)^T \hat{M}(s+1) + \beta_s \hat{\alpha}_s(s) \end{cases} \quad (21)$$

where $\hat{M}(s)$ represents the state vector, $\alpha_p(s)$ pump defect, $\alpha_s(s)$ sensor defect, and $\hat{y}(s)$ the output of the system, and A, B_y, B_u, and B_s, as well as S, represent matrices of coefficients. In accordance with Equation (21), in this paper, we particularly study three main cases and types of faults in pipe.

Case 1: In case $\alpha_p \neq 0$, $\alpha_s = 0$, and $\hat{\alpha}_p(s) \neq \alpha_p(s)$, we have:

$$\begin{gathered} (y(s+1) - \hat{y}(s+1) \neq 0) \,\&\, (M(s+1) - \hat{M}(s+1)) \neq 0 \Longrightarrow \\ \begin{bmatrix} M_1^T(s+1) & M_2^T(s+1) \end{bmatrix}^T - \begin{bmatrix} \hat{M}_1^T(s+1) & \hat{M}_{2,\alpha_p}^T(s+1) \end{bmatrix}^T \neq 0 \Longrightarrow \\ \begin{cases} M_{(n,u)}(s) - \hat{M}_{(n,u+\alpha_p)}(s) \neq 0 \\ M_{(n,y)}(s) - \hat{M}_{(n,y)}(s) \neq 0 \end{cases} \end{gathered} \quad (22)$$

In case $\alpha_p \neq 0$, $\alpha_s = 0$, and $\hat{\alpha}_p(s) = \alpha_p(s)$, we have:

$$\begin{gathered} (y(s+1) - \hat{y}(s+1) = 0) \,\&\, (M(s+1) - \hat{M}(s+1)) \neq 0 \Longrightarrow \\ \begin{bmatrix} M_1^T(s+1) & M_2^T(s+1) \end{bmatrix}^T - \begin{bmatrix} \hat{M}_1^T(s+1) & \hat{M}_{2,\alpha_p}^T(s+1) \end{bmatrix}^T \neq 0 \Longrightarrow \\ \begin{cases} M_{(n,u)}(s) - \hat{M}_{(n,u+\alpha_p)}(s) \neq 0 \\ M_{(n,y)}(s) - \hat{M}_{(n,y)}(s) = 0 \end{cases} \end{gathered} \quad (23)$$

In accordance with Equations (22) and (23), in case the error related to ARX–Laguerre fuzzy PID technique is close to zero, the detection rate of defect is very high.

The following formula can be defined for fault in the pump:

$$\hat{\alpha}_p = \alpha_q \to q_p - \hat{q}_p \cong 0 \,\&\, w - \hat{w} \neq 0 \to r = w - \hat{w} \quad (24)$$

Case 2: In case $\alpha_s \neq 0$, $\alpha_p = 0$, and $\hat{\alpha}_s(s) \neq \alpha_s(s)$, we have:

$$\begin{gathered} (y(s+1) - \hat{y}(s+1) \neq 0) \,\&\, (M(s+1) - \hat{M}(s+1)) \neq 0 \Longrightarrow \\ \begin{bmatrix} M_1^T(s+1) & M_2^T(s+1) \end{bmatrix}^T - \begin{bmatrix} \hat{M}_1^T(s+1) & \hat{M}_{2,\alpha_p}^T(s+1) \end{bmatrix}^T \neq 0 \Longrightarrow \\ \begin{cases} M_{(n,u)}(s) - \hat{M}_{(n,u)}(s) \neq 0 \\ M_{(n,y)}(s) - \hat{M}_{(n,y+\alpha_s)}(s) \neq 0 \end{cases} \end{gathered} \quad (25)$$

In case $\alpha_s \neq 0,\ \alpha_p = 0$, and $\hat{\alpha}_s(s) = \alpha_s(s)$, we have:

$$\begin{gathered}(y(s+1) - \hat{y}(s+1) = 0) \,\&\, (M(s+1) - \hat{M}(s+1)) \neq 0 \implies \\ \left[\begin{array}{cc} M_1^T(s+1) & M_2^T(s+1) \end{array}\right]^T - \left[\begin{array}{cc} \hat{M}_1^T(s+1) & \hat{M}_{2,\alpha_p}^T(s+1) \end{array}\right]^T \neq 0 \implies \\ \begin{cases} M_{(n,u)}(s) - \hat{M}_{(n,u)}(s) = 0 \\ x_{(n,y)}(s) - \hat{x}_{(n,y+\alpha_s)}(s) \neq 0 \end{cases}\end{gathered} \tag{26}$$

In accordance with Equations (25) and (26), the ARX–Laguerre fuzzy PID has a significant influence on the efficiency of sensor defect detection in a duct.

The following formula can be defined for fault in sensor:

$$\hat{\alpha}_s = \alpha_s \to w - \hat{w} \cong 0 \,\&\, q_p - \hat{q}_p \neq 0 \to r = q_p - \hat{q}_p \tag{27}$$

Case 3: In case $\alpha_s \neq 0,\ \alpha_p = 0,\ \hat{\alpha}_s(s) \neq \alpha_s(s)$, and $\hat{\alpha}_p(s) \neq \alpha_p(s)$ we have:

$$\begin{gathered}(y(s+1) - \hat{y}(s+1) \neq 0) \,\&\, (M(s+1) - \hat{M}(s+1)) \neq 0 \implies \\ \left[\begin{array}{cc} M_1^T(s+1) & M_2^T(s+1) \end{array}\right]^T - \left[\begin{array}{cc} \hat{M}_{1,\alpha_s}^T(s+1) & \hat{M}_2^T(s+1) \end{array}\right]^T \neq 0 \implies \\ \begin{cases} M_{(n,u)}(s) - \hat{M}_{(n,u+\alpha_p)}(s) \neq 0 \\ M_{(n,y)}(s) - \hat{M}_{(n,y+\alpha_s)}(s) \neq 0 \end{cases}\end{gathered} \tag{28}$$

In case $\alpha_s \neq 0,\ \alpha_p = 0$, and $\hat{\alpha}_s(s) = \alpha_s(s)$, we have:

$$\begin{gathered}(y(s+1) - \hat{y}(s+1) \neq 0) \,\&\, (M(s+1) - \hat{M}(s+1)) \neq 0 \implies \\ \left[\begin{array}{cc} M_1^T(s+1) & M_2^T(s+1) \end{array}\right]^T - \left[\begin{array}{cc} \hat{M}_1^T(s+1) & \hat{M}_{2,\alpha_p}^T(s+1) \end{array}\right]^T \neq 0 \implies \\ \begin{cases} M_{(n,u)}(s) - \hat{M}_{(n,u+\alpha_p)}(s) \neq 0 \\ M_{(n,y)}(s) - \hat{M}_{(n,y+\alpha_s)}(s) \neq 0 \end{cases}\end{gathered} \tag{29}$$

In accordance with Equation (29), in case the pipe includes sensor and pump failures, the signals received from pump and joint variable can identify the defects. Signal sensor and pump faults are:

$$\hat{\alpha}_p = \alpha_p \,\&\, \hat{\alpha}_s = \alpha_s \to r_1 = w - \hat{w} \gg 0 \,\&\, r_2 = q_p - \hat{q}_p \gg 0 \tag{30}$$

To increase the signal estimation accuracy and to modify the performance of fault estimation of the ARX–Laguerre PID technique, optimal fuzzy observer coefficients, K_{p_p}, K_{i_p}, K_{d_p}, K_{p_s}, K_{i_s} and K_{d_s}, are applied, which are defined as follows:

$$\begin{gathered} K_{i_p} = \frac{K_{pp}}{T_{ip}},\ K_{d_p} = K_{p_p}.T_{d_p} \\ K_{i_s} = \frac{K_{ps}}{T_{i_s}},\ K_{d_s} = K_{p_s}.T_{d_s} \end{gathered} \tag{31}$$

where T_{i_p}, T_{i_s}, T_{d_p}, and T_{d_s}, represent the integral gain for pump failure, the integral gain for sensor failure, the derivative gain for pump failure, and the derivative gain for sensor failure, respectively. Following Equation (29), we have:

$$\begin{gathered} \beta_p = \frac{T_{ip}}{T_{i_p}},\ K_{ip} = \frac{(K_{pp})^2}{\beta_p K_{d_p}} \\ \beta_s = \frac{T_{i_s}}{T_{i_s}},\ K_{i_s} = \frac{(K_{ps})^2}{\beta_s K_{d_s}} \end{gathered} \tag{32}$$

Normalization of the above equation can be performed by the formula described below:

$$\begin{array}{l} K'_{p_p} = \frac{K_{p_p} - K_{p_p(min)}}{K_{p_p(max)} - K_{p_p(min)}} \in [0,1],\ K'_{p_p} = \frac{K_{d_p} - K_{d_p(min)}}{K_{p_p(max)} - K_{p_p(min)}} \in [0,1], 2 \le \beta_p \le 5 \\ K'_{p_s} = \frac{K_{p_s} - K_{p_s(min)}}{K_{p_s(max)} - K_{p_s(min)}} \in [0,1],\ K'_{d_s} = \frac{K_{d_s} - K_{d_s(min)}}{K_{d_s(max)} - K_{d_s(min)}} \in [0,1], 2 \le \beta_s \le 5 \end{array} \tag{33}$$

such that $\beta = \frac{\sum_i \alpha(x_i) \cdot x_i}{\sum_i \alpha(x_i)}$ represents a membership function.

5. Simulation Results

In this section, we evaluate our proposed technique on a pipe model under the leak condition in the presence of failures of the pump and sensor in the pipe. In order to check the efficiency of the proposed ARX–Laguerre fuzzy PID observation technique for fault detection in the pipe, we consider two cases, pipe with fault and under no-fault conditions.

Pipe under no-fault condition. In this case, the duct functions under optimal circumstances and performs well. The input–output signals of the pipe model in a healthy state can be computed as follows:

$$\begin{array}{l} r(w) = w - \hat{w} \rightarrow r(w) = w - \left(w_{Observer} + \alpha_p\right) \rightarrow r(w) = w - \left(w_{Observer} + 0\right) \cong 0 \\ r(\phi) = \phi - \hat{\phi} \rightarrow r(\phi) = \phi - \left(\phi_{Observer} + \alpha_s\right) \rightarrow r(\phi) = \phi - \left(\phi_{Observer} + 0\right) \cong 0 \end{array} \tag{34}$$

The sensor signal for the pipe under no-fault condition and no noise impact is shown in Figure 3. The pump signal for the pipe under no-fault condition and no noise impact is shown in Figure 4.

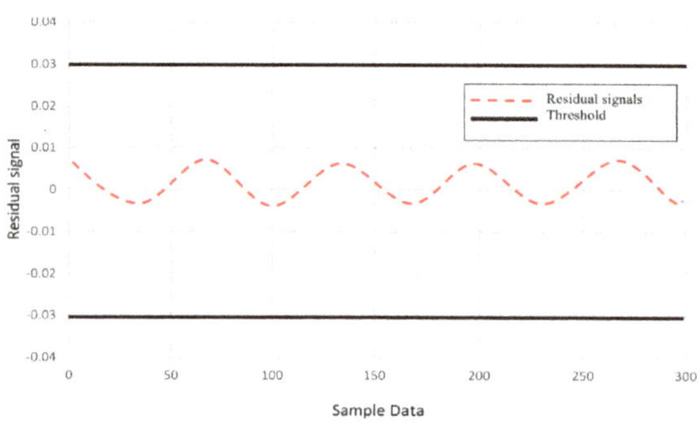

Figure 3. The sensor signal for the pipe under no-fault condition.

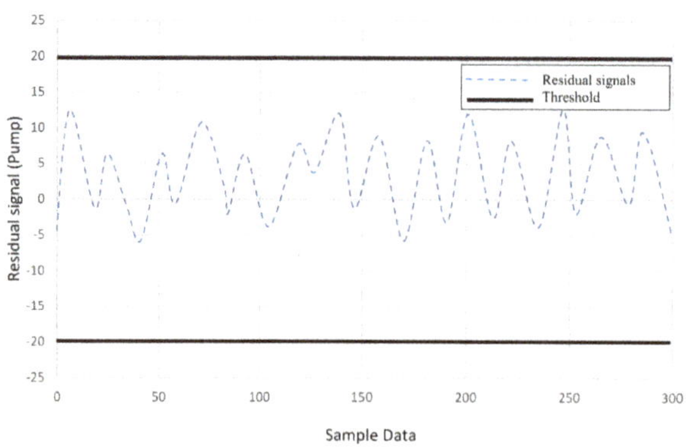

Figure 4. The pump signal for the pipe under no-fault condition.

For a healthy system, the pump and sensor faults can be described as follows:

$$\begin{aligned} Fault_{pump} &= \alpha_p(t - t_0) = \begin{cases} 0, & t < t_p \\ \alpha_p, & t > t_p \end{cases} \\ Fault_{sensor} &= \alpha_s(t - t_0) = \begin{cases} 0, & t < t_s \\ \alpha_s, & t > t_s \end{cases} \end{aligned} \tag{35}$$

The effectiveness of the proposed technique for fault estimation under no-fault condition is shown Figure 5. As can be observed from Figure 5, the proposed method is more effective than the ARX–Laguerre PI observer [41] and the adaptive fuzzy observer [42]. The error between the predicted output and the expected output based on the proposed technique under no-fault condition is shown in Figure 6. It can be seen that the proposed method yields more accurate results compared with ARX–Laguerre PI observer [41] and the adaptive fuzzy observer [42].

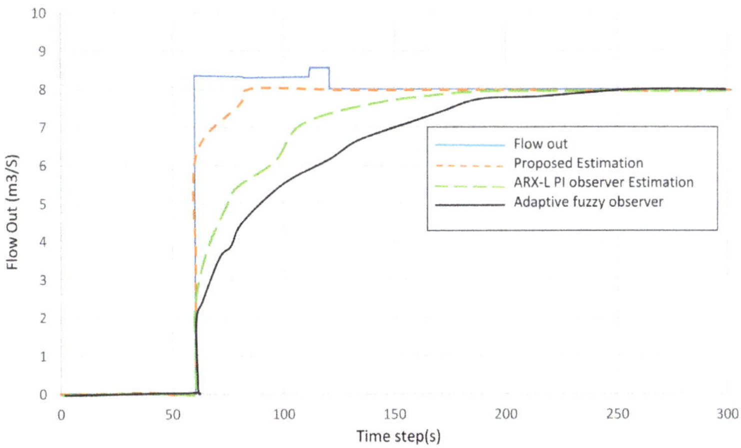

Figure 5. The effectiveness of the proposed technique for fault estimation under no-fault condition.

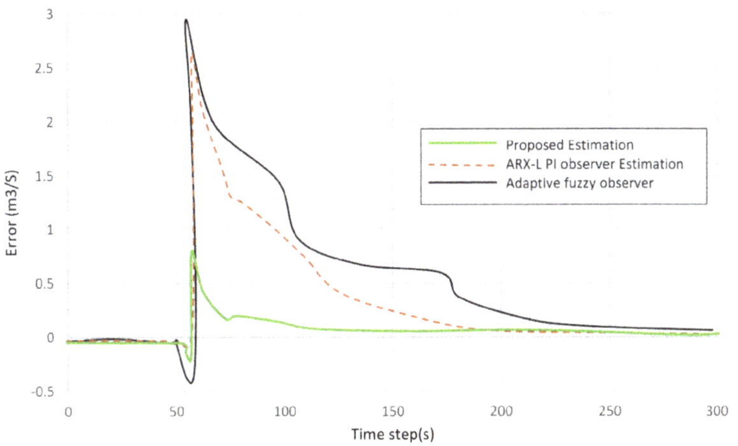

Figure 6. The error between the predicted output and the expected output based on the proposed technique under no-fault condition.

Pipe under fault condition. In this case, the duct functions under faulty circumstances. The duct has two kinds of defects simultaneously, the sensor defect and the pump defect.

The input output signals from sensor and pump in the pipe with a fault state can be computed as follows:

$$\begin{aligned} r(w) &= w - \hat{w} \rightarrow r(w) = w - \left(w_{Observer} + \alpha_p\right) \gg 0 \\ r(\phi) &= \phi - \hat{\phi} \rightarrow r(\phi) = \phi - \left(\phi_{Observer} + \alpha_s\right) \gg 0 \end{aligned} \tag{36}$$

where

$$\begin{aligned} w_{1\alpha_p}(m) &= \begin{cases} 55, & 10 \leq t \leq 25 \\ 0, & otherwise \end{cases} \\ \phi_{1\alpha_s}(m) &= \begin{cases} 0.6, & 10 \leq t \leq 25 \\ 0, & otherwise \end{cases} \end{aligned} \tag{37}$$

The pump signal for the pipe under fault condition and no noise impact is shown in Figure 7. The sensor signal for the pipe under fault condition is shown in Figure 8.

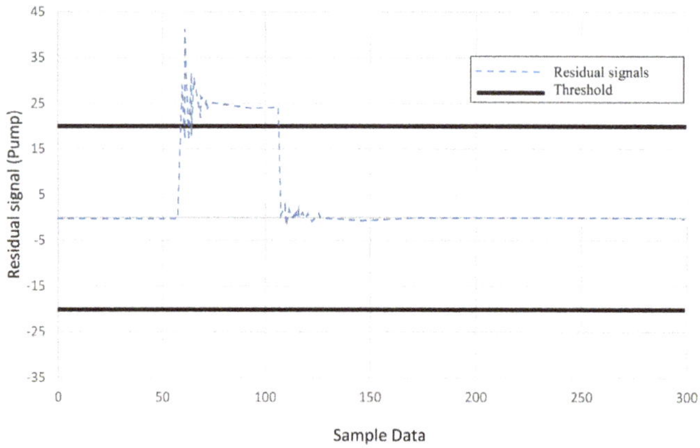

Figure 7. The pump signal for the pipe under fault condition.

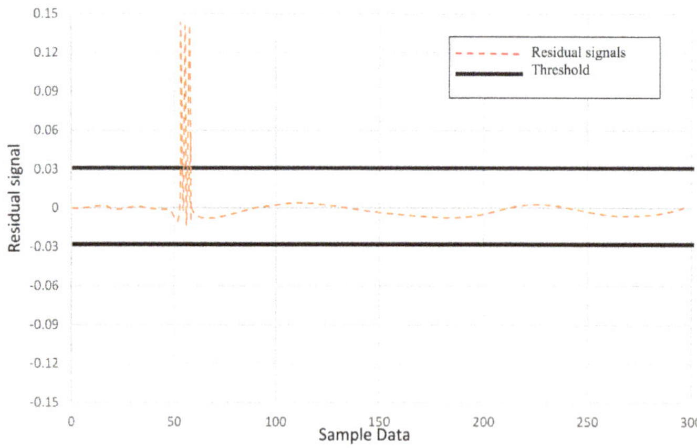

Figure 8. The sensor signal for the pipe under fault condition.

The effectiveness of the proposed technique for fault estimation under fault condition is shown Figure 9. As can be observed from Figure 9, the proposed method is more effective than the ARX–Laguerre PI observer [41] and the adaptive fuzzy observer [42]. The error between the predicted output and the expected output based on the proposed technique under fault condition is shown in Figure 10. It can be seen that the proposed method yields more accurate results compared with ARX–Laguerre PI observer [41] and the adaptive fuzzy observer [42]. Furthermore, the delay for the proposed method to fault detection in both Figures 9 and 10 is less than the other methods.

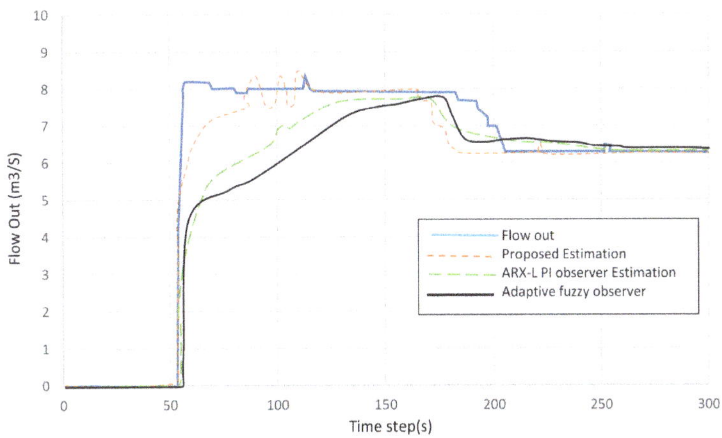

Figure 9. The effectiveness of the proposed technique for fault estimation under fault condition.

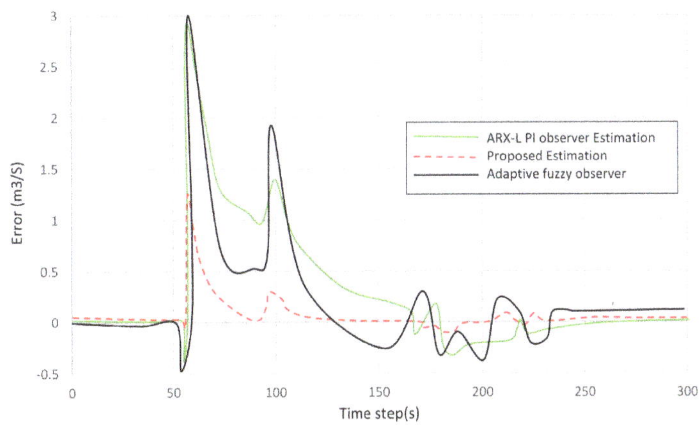

Figure 10. The error between the predicted output and the expected output based on the proposed technique under fault condition.

The effectiveness of the proposed technique for fault estimation at leakage point is shown in Figure 11. It can be seen from this figure that our proposed method detects fault in less time in comparison with ARX–Laguerre PI observer [41] and the adaptive fuzzy observer [42].

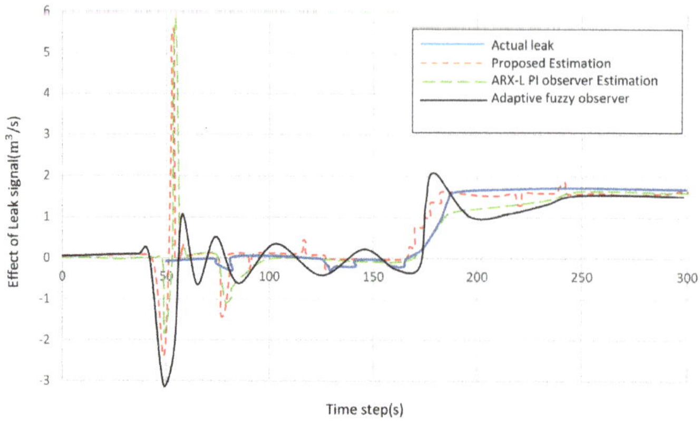

Figure 11. The effectiveness of the proposed technique for fault estimation at leakage point in pipe.

6. Conclusions

The task of precise defect detection in the pipeline system is a formidable challenge due to the uncertainties in leak signal. To better deal with uncertainties in the leak signal, in this paper, an ARX–Laguerre PID-observer is introduced to perform fault diagnosis in the pipeline system. First, in this study, the ARX–Laguerre technique was used for pipeline modelling. In the second step, the PID observer based on the ARX–Laguerre model was designed to detect leakage in the presence of uncertainties. The performance of the proposed algorithm was tested in numerical simulations. According to the results, the proposed technique can accurately locate the leakage point. Despite the high accuracy of the proposed fault diagnosis method, it has a disadvantage of large extensive computation. In the future, the proposed observation method will be used to enhance the performance of fault diagnosis when the uncertainties are in the form of Z-numbers.

Author Contributions: Conceptualization, R.J., S.R., C.V.-J., A.G. and F.A.; methodology, R.J., S.R., C.V.-J., A.G. and F.A.; software, S.R.; validation S.R.; formal analysis, R.J. and S.R.; investigation, R.J. and S.R.; resources, R.J., S.R., C.V.-J., A.G. and F.A.; writing—original draft preparation, R.J., S.R., C.V.-J., A.G. and F.A.; writing—review and editing, R.J., S.R., C.V.-J., A.G. and F.A. All authors have read and agreed to the published version of the manuscript.

Funding: This research received no external funding.

Institutional Review Board Statement: Not applicable.

Informed Consent Statement: Not applicable.

Data Availability Statement: Not applicable.

Conflicts of Interest: The authors declare no conflict of interest.

References

1. Meng, L.; Yuxing, L.; Wuchang, W.; Juntao, F. Experimental study on leak detection and location for gas pipeline based on acoustic method. *J. Loss Prev. Process Ind.* **2012**, *25*, 90–102. [CrossRef]
2. Jin, H.; Zhang, L.; Liang, W.; Ding, Q. Integrated leakage detection and localization model for gas pipelines based on the acoustic wave method. *J. Loss Prev. Process Ind.* **2014**, *27*, 74–88. [CrossRef]
3. Mahmutoglu, Y.; Turk, K. A passive acoustic based system to locate leak hole in underwater natural gas pipelines. *Digital Signal Process.* **2018**, *76*, 59–65. [CrossRef]
4. Lim, K.; Wong, L.; Chiu, W.K.; Kodikara, J. Distributed fiber optic sensors for monitoring pressure and stiffness changes in out-of-round pipes. *Struct. Control Health Monitor.* **2016**, *23*, 303–314. [CrossRef]
5. Jia, Z.; Ren, L.; Li, H.; Sun, W. Pipeline leak localization based on FBG hoop strain sensors combined with BP neural network. *Appl. Sci.* **2018**, *8*, 146. [CrossRef]
6. Wan, J.; Yu, Y.; Wu, Y.; Feng, R.; Yu, N. Hierarchical leak detection and localization method in natural gas pipeline monitoring sensor networks. *Sensors* **2012**, *12*, 189–214. [CrossRef]

7. Billmann, L.; Isermann, R. Leak detection methods for pipelines. *IFAC Proc. Vol.* **1984**, *17*, 1813–1818. [CrossRef]
8. Verde, C. Minimal order nonlinear observer for leak detection. *J. Dyn. Syst. Meas. Control* **2004**, *126*, 467–472. [CrossRef]
9. Sharp, D.; Campbell, D. Leak detection in pipes using acoustic pulse reflectometry. *Acta Acust. United Acust.* **1997**, *83*, 560–566.
10. Taghvaei, M.; Beck, S.; Staszewski, W. Leak detection in pipelines using cepstrum analysis. *Measur. Sci. Technol.* **2006**, *17*, 367. [CrossRef]
11. Zhao, J.; Li, D.; Qi, H.; Sun, F.; An, R. The fault diagnosis method of pipeline leakage based on neural network. In Proceedings of the 2010 International Conference on Computer, Mechatronics, Control and Electronic Engineering, Changchun, China, 24–26 August 2010; Volume 1, pp. 322–325.
12. Jafari, R.; Razvarz, S.; Gegov, A. Applications of Z-Numbers and Neural Networks in Engineering. In *Science and Information Conference*; Springer: Berlin/Heidelberg, Germany, 2020; pp. 12–25.
13. Jafari, R.; Razvarz, S.; Gegov, A. End-to-end memory networks: A survey. In *Science and Information Conference*; Springer: Berlin/Heidelberg, Germany, 2020; pp. 291–300.
14. Jafari, R.; Razvarz, S.; Gegov, A. A novel technique for solving fully fuzzy nonlinear systems based on neural networks. *Vietnam J. Comput. Sci.* **2020**, *7*, 93–107. [CrossRef]
15. Jafari, R.; Contreras, M.A.; Yu, W.; Gegov, A. Applications of Fuzzy Logic, Artificial Neural Network and Neuro-Fuzzy in Industrial Engineering. In *Latin American Symposium on Industrial and Robotic Systems*; Springer: Berlin/Heidelberg, Germany, 2019; pp. 9–14.
16. Razvarz, S.; Hernández-Rodríguez, F.; Jafari, R.; Gegov, A. Foundation of Z-Numbers and Engineering Applications. In *Latin American Symposium on Industrial and Robotic Systems*; Springer: Berlin/Heidelberg, Germany, 2019; pp. 15–24.
17. Christos, S.C.; Fotis, G.; Nektarios, G.; Dimitris, R.; Areti, P.; Dimitrios, S. Autonomous low-cost Wireless Sensor platform for Leakage Detection in Oil and Gas Pipes. In Proceedings of the 2021 10th International Conference on Modern Circuits and Systems Technologies (MOCAST), Thessaloniki, Greece, 5–7 July 2021; pp. 1–4.
18. Belsito, S.; Lombardi, P.; Andreussi, P.; Banerjee, S. Leak detection in liquefied gas pipelines by artificial neural networks. *AIChE J.* **1998**, *44*, 2675–2688. [CrossRef]
19. Ferraz, I.M.N.; Garcia, A.C.; Bernardini, F.V.C. Artificial neural networks ensemble used for pipeline leak detection systems. *Int. Pipeline Conf.* **2008**, *48579*, 739–747.
20. Shibata, A.; Konishi, M.; Abe, Y.; Hasegawa, R.; Watanabe, M.; Kamijo, H. Neuro based classification of gas leakage sounds in pipeline. In Proceedings of the 2009 International Conference on Networking, Sensing and Control, Okayama, Japan, 26–29 March 2009; pp. 298–302.
21. Kim, K.-H.; Lee, H.-S.; Jeong, H.-M.; Kim, H.-S.; Park, J.-H. A Study on Fault Diagnosis of Boiler Tube Leakage based on Neural Network using Data Mining Technique in the Thermal Power Plant. *Trans. Korean Inst. Electr. Eng.* **2017**, *66*, 1445–1453.
22. Gao, Z.; Cecati, C.; Ding, S.X. A survey of fault diagnosis and fault-tolerant techniques—Part I: Fault diagnosis with model-based and signal-based approaches. *IEEE Trans. Ind. Electron.* **2015**, *62*, 3757–3767. [CrossRef]
23. Piltan, F.; Kim, J.-M. Bearing fault diagnosis by a robust higher-order super-twisting sliding mode observer. *Sensors* **2018**, *18*, 1128. [CrossRef]
24. Gao, Z.; Ding, S.X.; Cecati, C. Real-time fault diagnosis and fault-tolerant control. *IEEE Trans. Ind. Electron.* **2015**, *62*, 3752–3756. [CrossRef]
25. Angulo, M.T.; Verde, C. Second-order sliding mode algorithms for the reconstruction of leaks. In Proceedings of the 2013 Conference on Control and Fault-Tolerant Systems (SysTol), Nice, France, 9–11 October 2013; pp. 566–571.
26. Wu, Q.; Saif, M. Robust fault diagnosis for a satellite large angle attitude system using an iterative neuron PID (INPID) observer. In Proceedings of the 2006 American Control Conference, Minneapolis, MN, USA, 14–16 June 2006; p. 6.
27. Piltan, F.; Sohaib, M.; Kim, J.-M. Fault diagnosis of a robot manipulator based on an ARX-laguerre fuzzy PID observer. In Proceedings of the International Conference on Robot Intelligence Technology and Applications, Daejeon, Korea, 16–17 December 2017; pp. 393–407.
28. Wu, A.-G.; Duan, G.-R.; Fu, Y.-M. Generalized PID observer design for descriptor linear systems. *IEEE Trans. Syst. Man Cybern. Part B (Cybern.)* **2007**, *37*, 1390–1395. [CrossRef]
29. Piltan, F.; Kim, J.-M. Pipeline Leak Detection and Estimation Using Fuzzy-Based PI Observer. In Proceedings of the International Conference on Intelligent and Fuzzy Systems, Istanbul, Turkey, 21–23 July 2019; pp. 1122–1129.
30. Aamo, O.M.; Smyshlyaev, A.; Krstic, M.; Foss, B.A. Output feedback boundary control of a Ginzburg–Landau model of vortex shedding. *IEEE Trans. Autom. Control* **2007**, *52*, 742–748. [CrossRef]
31. Bouzrara, K.; Garna, T.; Ragot, J.; Messaoud, H. Online identification of the ARX model expansion on Laguerre orthonormal bases with filters on model input and output. *Int. J. Control* **2013**, *86*, 369–385. [CrossRef]
32. Cebeci, T.; Bradshaw, P. *Momentum Transfer in Boundary Layers*; McGraw-Hill Book Co.: New York, NY, USA, 1977.
33. Hafeez, H.Y.; Ndikilar, C.E. 4.1 The continuity equation. In *Applications of Heat, Mass and Fluid Boundary Layers*; Woodhead Publishing: Sawston, UK, 2020; p. 67.
34. Swamee, P.K.; Swamee, N. Full-range pipe-flow equations. *J. Hydraul. Res.* **2007**, *45*, 841–843. [CrossRef]
35. Assunção, G.S.C.; Marcelin, D.; Filho, J.C.v.; Schiozer, D.J.; de Castro, M.S. Friction Factor Equations Accuracy for Single and Two-Phase Flows. In *International Conference on Offshore Mechanics and Arctic Engineering*; American Society of Mechanical Engineers: New York, NY, USA, 2020; Volume 84430, p. V011T11A043.

36. Rott, N. Note on the history of the Reynolds number. *Annu. Rev. Fluid Mech.* **1990**, *22*, 1–12. [CrossRef]
37. Tomé, M.; Mangiavacchi, N.; Cuminato, J.; Castelo, A.; McKee, S. A finite difference technique for simulating unsteady viscoelastic free surface flows. *J. Non-Newton. Fluid Mech.* **2002**, *106*, 61–106. [CrossRef]
38. Wang, X.; Wildman, R.A.; Weile, D.S.; Monk, P. A finite difference delay modeling approach to the discretization of the time domain integral equations of electromagnetics. *IEEE Trans. Antennas Propag.* **2008**, *56*, 2442–2452. [CrossRef]
39. Piltan, F.; Kim, J.-M. Advanced fuzzy-based leak detection and size estimation for pipelines. *J. Intell. Fuzzy Syst.* **2020**, *38*, 947–961. [CrossRef]
40. Kim, J.H.; Kim, K.S.; Sim, M.S.; Han, K.H.; Ko, B.S. An application of fuzzy logic to control the refrigerant distribution for the multi-type air conditioner. In Proceedings of the FUZZ-IEEE'99. 1999 IEEE International Fuzzy Systems. Conference Proceedings (Cat. No. 99CH36315), Seoul, Korea, 22–25 August 1999; Volume 3, pp. 1350–1354.
41. Najeh, T.; Njima, C.B.; Garna, T.; Ragot, J. Input fault detection and estimation using PI observer based on the ARX-Laguerre model. *Int. J. Adv. Manuf. Technol.* **2017**, *90*, 1317–1336. [CrossRef]
42. Tong, S.; Li, Y.; Li, Y.; Liu, Y. Observer-based adaptive fuzzy backstepping control for a class of stochastic nonlinear strict-feedback systems. *IEEE Trans. Syst. Man Cybern. Part B (Cybern.)* **2011**, *41*, 1693–1704. [CrossRef]

electronics

MDPI

Article

Benchmarking GHG Emissions Forecasting Models for Global Climate Policy

Cristiana Tudor [1,*] and Robert Sova [2]

1 International Business and Economics Department, Bucharest University of Economic Studies, 010374 Bucharest, Romania

2 Department of Management Information Systems, The Bucharest University of Economic Studies, 010374 Bucharest, Romania; robert.sova@ase.ro

* Correspondence: cristiana.tudor@net.ase.ro; Tel.: +40-723-254-342

Abstract: Climate change and pollution fighting have become prominent global concerns in the twenty-first century. In this context, accurate estimates for polluting emissions and their evolution are critical for robust policy-making processes and ultimately for solving stringent global climate challenges. As such, the primary objective of this study is to produce more accurate forecasts of greenhouse gas (GHG) emissions. This in turn contributes to the timely evaluation of the progress achieved towards meeting global climate goals set by international agendas and also acts as an early-warning system. We forecast the evolution of GHG emissions in 12 top polluting economies by using data for the 1970–2018 period and employing six econometric and machine-learning models (the exponential smoothing state-space model (ETS), the Holt–Winters model (HW), the TBATS model, the ARIMA model, the structural time series model (STS), and the neural network autoregression model (NNAR)), along with a naive model. A battery of robustness checks is performed. Results confirm a priori expectations and consistently indicate that the neural network autoregression model (NNAR) presents the best out-of-sample forecasting performance for GHG emissions at different forecasting horizons by reporting the lowest average RMSE (root mean square error) and MASE (mean absolute scaled error) within the array of predictive models. Predictions made by the NNAR model for the year 2030 indicate that total GHG emissions are projected to increase by 3.67% on average among the world's 12 most polluting countries until 2030. Only four top polluters will record decreases in total GHG emissions values in the coming decades (i.e., Canada, the Russian Federation, the US, and China), although their emission levels will remain in the upper decile. Emission increases in a handful of developing economies will see significant growth rates (a 22.75% increase in GHG total emissions in Brazil, a 15.75% increase in Indonesia, and 7.45% in India) that are expected to offset the modest decreases in GHG emissions projected for the four countries. Our findings, therefore, suggest that the world's top polluters cannot meet assumed pollution reduction targets in the form of NDCs under the Paris agreement. Results thus highlight the necessity for more impactful policies and measures to bring the set targets within reach.

Keywords: GHG emissions; automated forecasting; neural network autoregression model (NNAR); GHG emissions prediction; Paris agreement

1. Introduction

Along with climate change, air pollution is one of the most serious environmental hazards to human health, estimated to cause 7 million premature deaths per year [1]. The economic consequences of air pollution are dire, as estimates indicate $5 trillion in welfare losses and 225 billion in lost income [2,3].

Air pollution includes greenhouse gas (GHG) emissions that warm the earth's surface and atmosphere [4]. GHG refer to the sum of seven gases that have direct effects on climate change: carbon dioxide (CO_2), methane (CH4), nitrous oxide (N2O), chlorofluorocarbons (CFCs), hydrofluorocarbons (HFCs), perfluorocarbons (PFCs), sulfur hexafluoride (SF6), and nitrogen trifluoride (NF3) [5].

Understanding the urgency of more vigorous climate combat, decisive steps have been taken at the global level. The United Nations Framework Convention on Climate Change (UNFCCC) adopted the Kyoto Protocol (1997) and the Paris Agreement (2015) [6]. The Paris Agreement, signed in December 2015, gathered all signatory countries under a common goal toward making significant efforts to tackle climate change and air pollution [7,8]. The Paris Agreement is meant to improve upon and replace the Kyoto Protocol, an earlier international treaty designed to curb the release of GHG, whose effectiveness has been heavily criticized because the world's two top carbon dioxide-emitting countries, China and the United States, chose not to be part of the agreement [9]. In contrast, the 2015 Paris agreement has been signed by nearly every country in the world (together responsible for more than 90 percent of global emissions), with 190 of the signatory countries (including the US and China) going further and having underlined their support with formal approval. As such, while before the Paris Conference the signatory countries submitted carbon reduction targets (i.e., "intended nationally determined contributions" or INDCs), these targets subsequently became "nationally determined contributions" or NDCs after the formal approval of the agreement [10]. Hence, the Paris Agreement and the attainment of long-term climate targets are built around these NDCs representing each country's efforts to cut national emissions and adapt to climate change consequences. Given the heterogeneity in circumstances, resources, and capabilities, the agreement was developed so that each country establishes their own commitments in terms of how much they can contribute to the 2030 Agenda. However, almost all submitted NDCs contain a target to reduce polluting emissions by a specific percentage over a specified period, in most cases, the first established deadline being 2030. However, while signatory parties are legally required to establish an NDC under the Paris agreement and to take actions to accomplish it, the NDC itself is not legally binding or enforceable pledge [11].

Considering the GHG emission mitigation targets that most world countries have set for 2030 and/or 2050 under the Paris agreement, the total GHG emissions were expected to decline significantly in the aftermath of its adoption and to continue a decreasing trend over the next decades. However, the vast majority of world economies are yet to deliver on their pledges [12].

Data employed in our study backs this finding. Figure 1 shows that on average total GHG emissions have continued to increase after 2015, although there is high heterogeneity across countries at the world level when it comes to their contribution to world pollution. Figure 2 highlights that only a handful of countries significantly contributed to world pollution over the 1970–2018 period. Specifically, the main culprits reflected in Figure 2 are the US, with a mean annual value for total GHG emissions measured in kt of CO_2 equal to 6,134,747 over the 49-year period, closely followed by China with 5,439,570 kt average annual GHG over the same period and at some distance by the Russian Federation, which registered 2,635,846 kt average annual GHG emissions. The rhythm of emissions growth has also been heterogenic at the world level over the past decades, as our study will further reflect. Overall, global greenhouse gas emissions have risen considerably since 1970, showing a 67.31% increase by 2018 (when total GHG emissions in kt of CO_2 equivalent at world level registered a mean value of 254,047.3) relative to their 1970 levels (mean value of 151,837.9 kt of CO_2 equivalent). This translates into an increase of 102,209.4 kt CO_2 in absolute terms over the 1970–2018. Over the entire 49-year period, interim short-term reversals followed economic contractions, with a sharper decrease during the 1990s economic recession caused by the Gulf War and subsequent oil price shocks.

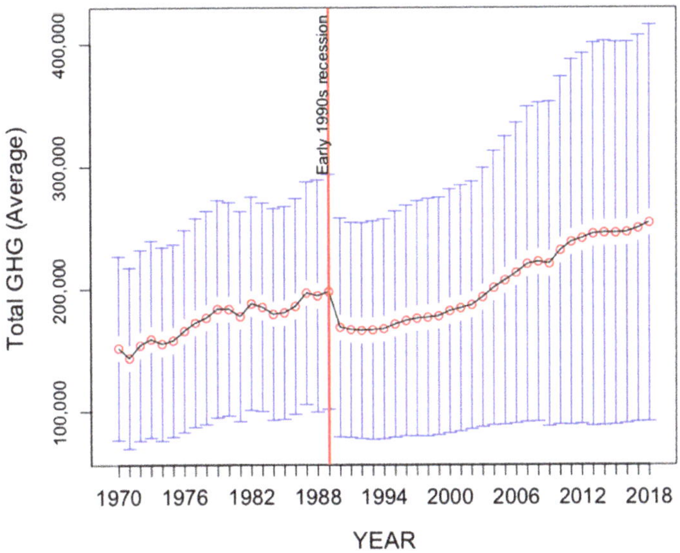

Figure 1. Historical trend of mean GHG emissions in 175 countries (1970–2018).

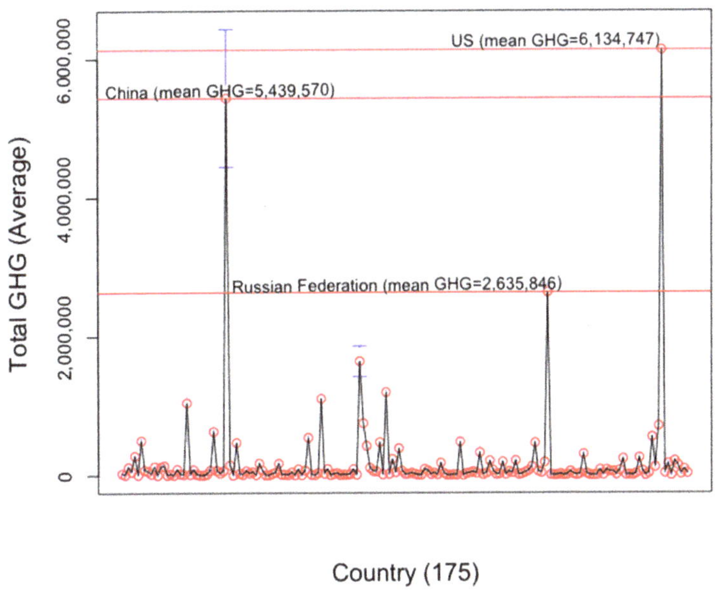

Figure 2. Mean GHG emissions per country over 1970–2018 (175 countries).

This incongruence between policy targets and the current reality is particularly worrying given that top polluters continue to show significant increases in total GHG emissions and highlights the necessity of more impactful policies and measures to bring the set targets within reach. Consequently, accurate and robust forecasts for polluting emissions are needed for an effective and efficient policy-making process. The issue is timely, as countries must juggle post-pandemic recovery and bend the emission trends [13]. However, the task is particularly challenging, as the world should halve annual greenhouse gas emissions in the next eight years to keep global warming below 1.5 °C this century, and thus meet the aspirational goal of the Paris Agreement [14]. Other studies report the need for a cut of total GHG emissions by 7.6 percent each year between 2020 and 2030 to stay on track toward the 1.5 °C temperature goal of the Paris Agreement [15]. Current statistics show a rapid recovery of economic activity and increasing emissions as energy demand soars [16].

Unsurprisingly, polluting emissions have steadily drawn the attention of academics and policymakers over the past decades, and national and international agencies increasingly employ forecasts of polluting emissions in their policy-making process. Consequently, producing accurate estimates for GHG emissions and their evolution is critical for robust policy-making processes and ultimately for solving global climate challenges [17]. This in turn is an important motivator for this study, which intends to identify the over-performing predictive model in terms of forecasting accuracy for total GHG emissions and subsequently apply it for producing forecasts for GHG emissions in top-emitting countries over long forecasting horizons, covering the first benchmark set for individual pledges within the Paris agreement, i.e., 2030.

Unlike most studies in the existing literature that investigate driving factors for polluting emissions, we take a univariate approach. This further brings two important advantages. First, it eliminates the challenge of identifying the right mix of macroeconomic, social, and financial variables that are potential impact factors for polluting emissions, and thus eliminates the risk of model misspecification, with further gains in terms of increasing estimation efficiency. Second, and most importantly, our approach allows us to produce forecasts for a validated leading indicator, independent of other variables.

Considering the above considerations, this study makes several contributions to the extant literature, as follows.

First, we employ a wider variety of candidate predictive models, including econometric and machine-learning methods, and perform a battery of robustness checks to assure that the best-performing out-of-sample forecasting model is identified. As we are more concerned with prediction accuracy than in-sample information, and in light of the previous literature, we a-priori expect machine learning methods to over-perform.

Secondly, we use a more relevant metric for air pollution, GHG emissions, instead of CO_2 emissions that are usually employed in previous studies. Consequently, by including a more accurate indicator of air pollution (i.e., CO_2 emissions account for approximately 76 percent of total GHG emissions, according to the Center for Climate and Energy Solutions [18], estimation results are more relevant for policymakers. To this end, this study uses data for the 1970–2018 period provided by the World Development Indicators (WDI) database of the World Bank.

Thirdly, unlike most of the aforementioned previous studies that focus only on a single country or cover at most a handful of economies, this study includes the 12 most polluting countries in the world, which are responsible together for around 75% of total GHG emissions at world level. This contributes to assuring the robustness of the forecasting method and further increases the relevance of results for policymakers.

Results of this study confirm prior expectations and find that overall on average, the neural network autoregression model (NNAR) presents the best out-of-sample forecasting performance for GHG emissions over a long forecasting horizon by reporting the lowest average RMSE within the array of predictive models. Results further show that the world's top polluters will not meet assumed GHG emissions' reduction targets under the Paris agreement, and thus more impactful policies and measures are needed to bring the set goals within reach.

The remainder of the paper is organized as follows. The next section gives an overview of the related literature. Next, Section 3 explains the data and methodology employed in the empirical investigation, while Section 4 presents and discusses the estimation results and the performed robustness checks. Finally, Section 5 concludes the study.

2. Literature Review

The environmental Kuznets curve (EKC) theory [19,20] states that pollution rises with the economic expansion until a certain level of wealth is achieved, at which point emissions begin to decline, implying an inverted U-shaped link between environmental degradation and income [21]. Overall, mixed results were obtained from previous research that looked at the presence of the EKC in different countries and across different time periods [22]. As a result, the topic of how economic growth and environmental quality are related (i.e., the form of the environmental Kuznets curve) continues to be contentious [23]. As such, on one hand, the EKG hypothesis has been validated empirically by numerous studies (among others, [6,24–26]). However, on the other hand, a bidirectional causality has also been repeatedly encountered [27], thus suggesting that emissions can also be a leading indicator of growth.

Moreover, besides its proven impact on economic growth, air pollution has a substantial influence on public health [28]. Hence, previous studies confirmed that polluting emissions are also a leading indicator for various health variables [29] and for mortality [30,31]. These effects have been found in both long-term studies, which have followed cohorts of exposed individuals over time, and in studies that connect day-to-day fluctuations in air pollution and health [32]. Moreover, there is mounting evidence that indoor air pollution is a severe concern to human health in addition to ambient air quality, particularly in low-income nations where biomass fuels are still used as an energy source [33]. All these findings further highlight the importance of combating climate change.

As such, given its validated role as an impact factor for important socio-economic variables, the primary objective of this study is to produce more accurate forecasts of GHG emissions. This in turn contributes to the timely evaluation of the progress achieved toward meeting global climate goals set by international agendas and also acts as an early-warning system when projections show that the state of affairs does not reflect policy statements and formal pledges are not followed by concrete measures and results. Hence, results of this study are also important for policymakers to incorporate forecasts of polluting emissions in their policy-making process.

However, time series analysis and forecasting remain challenging tasks [34], and air pollution prediction is no exception [35]. Broadly, based on the work of [36] prediction models pertain to two main cultures or schools of thought [37], each with its benefits and drawbacks [38]: (i) econometrics, or statistical methods, a category that covers many familiar models [39], and (ii) machine learning (self-learning systems, capable of learning from data to improve their performance). Their two common goals, information, and predictability [40] are differently prioritized, with statistical methods focusing on inference, whereas machine-learning techniques concentrate on prediction [41]. As the British statistician George Box has famously put it: "All models are wrong, but some are useful." Consequently, the aim in time-series forecasting should be to identify the best predictive model within a pool of candidates and employ it to produce forecasts for the series of interest. This study does not deviate from this goal. Previous studies that attempt to model and forecast univariate polluting emission time series (most often CO_2) primarily employ statistical methods, including the logistic equation [42], the ARIMA [43], and the ARIMA, Holt–Winters, exponential smoothing, and singular spectrum analysis (SSA) [44]. In the second category, we encounter among others [45] that use extreme learning machines based on particle swarm optimization to predict CO_2 emissions in Hebei, ref. [46] that use an artificial neural network (ANN) to predict carbon emission intensity for Australia, Brazil, China, India, and the USA, and [47], which employ a neural network model for forecasting the CO_2 emission produced by the cereal sector in a southern Italy region. Overall, previous studies confirm that nonlinear models can capture the nonlinear pattern of real-world data, and thus overcome the limitation of linear models, improving their prediction performance [48]. Additionally, artificial neural networks (ANN) are found to be useful in time series modeling where past values of a variable of interest are used to determine its future values [49].

In this study, we attempt to forecast the evolution of GHG emissions by employing six candidate models belonging to both the aforementioned categories. As such, we estimate the innovations state-space models for exponential smoothing (ETS), the Holt–Winters (HW) model, the autoregressive integrated moving average (ARIMA) model, the trigonometric ETS state-space model with Box-Cox transformation, ARMA errors, trend and seasonal components (TBATS) model, the structural time series model (STS) and the neural network autoregression (NNAR) model. Additionally, a naive model is also employed for comparative purposes.

Similar approaches in the literature, but with application on other time series, include the study by [50], which estimate and report the forecasting performance of nine models for the price of gold, concluding that on average, the exponential smoothing model is providing the best forecasts in terms of the lowest root mean squared error. Similarly, ref. [51] uses seven automated forecasting techniques, including statistical and machine learning models, for explaining and predicting the evolution of CO_2 emissions in Bahrain and identify the NNAR model to provide the most accurate out-of-sample forecasts. More recently, ref. [34] also predicted the evolution of Bahrain's CO_2 emissions by employing a neural network time series nonlinear autoregressive model, the Gaussian process regression model, and Holt's method, to agree that the NNAR model is outperforming the other candidates. Ref. [52] also employs four of the techniques applied in this investigation (i.e., ARIMA, ETS, NNAR, and TBATS) along with their feasible hybrid combinations to forecast the second wave of COVID-19 hospitalizations in Italy, concluding that the best single models were NNAR and ARIMA, and that the best hybrid models always included a NNAR process. Finally, ref. [53] employ statistical and deep learning methods to forecast long-term pollution trends for the two categories of particulate matter (PM) in a major city in eastern India, i.e., Kolkata. They conclude that statistical methods (i.e., auto-regressive (AR), seasonal auto-regressive integrated moving average (SARIMA) and Holt–Winters) outperform deep learning methods for their data. However, they argue that the results might be due to the limited data available, and that with a higher quantity of data and higher frequency and forecasting horizon, deep-learning models would out-perform.

All of these works bring important results for the global climate fight related literature. However, most of these works have a narrow interest (i.e., most are single-country studies, as seen above) and most importantly, they do not strongly defend their results robustness. The vast majority stops at evaluating the predictive ability of alternative models by reporting various forecasting accuracy metrics. [34] employs the root mean square errors (RMSE) to this end, whereas [53] estimate both RMSE and MAE, and [52] reports MAE, MAPE, MASE, and RMSE metrics. Nonetheless, except [51] that reports the KSPA test, other studies do not estimate and present statistical tests for multiple forecast comparisons and thus, do not investigate the hypothesis whether forecasts are significantly different, defending their results. Additionally, none of these previous works have re-estimated the models by employing an alternative forecasting technique (i.e., recursive window, changing window length, various time series slitting rules, etc.).

In this study, results' robustness is assured firstly by employing out-of-sample forecasting on a holdout sample of observations and investigating the accuracy of several forecasting methods in comparative perspective, then by reassessing the predictive ability of candidate models via the recursive window forecasting technique, and finally by performing all estimations for 12 different top polluting countries, responsible for around $\frac{3}{4}$ of total GHG emissions at world level. Moreover, applying the Kolmogorov–Smirnov (KS) predictive accuracy test (KSPA) proposed by [54] and the Diebold–Mariano (DM) test introduced by [55] and developed by [56] further contributes to testing the over-performance of the best predictive model and assures our results' robustness.

Additionally, a further advantage of our approach consists in the fact that the employment of standard econometric methods together with machine-learning techniques in estimations and predictions allows comparison with previous results from the literature.

3. Materials and Methods

3.1. Data

3.1.1. Database

This study uses annual data on total GHG emissions measured in kt of CO_2 for the period 31 December 1970–31 December 2018, thus covering a total of 49 years. The source of data is the World Development Indicators (WDI) database of the World Bank (Data source: https://data.worldbank.org/indicator/EN.ATM.GHGT.KT.CE, accessed on 8 November 2021).

In the first stage, GHG data were extracted from the WDI for all countries included in the database, thus resulting in a sample of 205 individual economies. Then, we have removed countries for which data were unavailable over the entire period, resulting in the final sample of 175 countries and 8575 annual observations included in the analysis.

An exploratory analysis aimed at uncovering the state of affairs was subsequently performed.

3.1.2. GHG Emissions by Country, Top Polluters and Historical Trends

Table 1 reflects the top 20 GHG emitters in the world in the most recent year of available data, i.e., 2018.

Table 1. Greenhouse Gas Emissions by Top Emitters, 2018 and emission trends (1970–2018).

Country	GHG Emissions 2018 (Total, kt of CO_2)	Region	Income Category	% Change (Relative to 2015)	% Change (Relative to 1970)
China	12,355,240	East Asia & Pacific	Upper middle	4.18	559.31
United States	6,023,620	North America	High income	0.33	11.54
India	3,374,990	South Asia	Lower middle	10.16	352.11
Russian Federation	2,543,400	Europe & Central Asia	Upper middle	2.73	13.50
Japan	1,186,770	East Asia & Pacific	High income	−6.19	26.10
Brazil	1,032,640	Latin America & Caribbean	Upper middle	−4.62	−18.11
Indonesia	969,580	East Asia & Pacific	Lower middle	13.80	185.44
Iran, Islamic Rep.	828,280	Middle East & North Africa	Upper middle	5.31	484.04
Germany	806,090	Europe & Central Asia	High income	−4.88	−37.35
Canada	724,930	North America	High income	2.40	46.46
Korea, Rep.	718,880	East Asia & Pacific	High income	4.82	711.00
Mexico	679,880	Latin America & Caribbean	Upper middle	1.46	222.91
Australia	615,380	East Asia & Pacific	High income	3.50	92.89
Turkey	502,520	Europe & Central Asia	Upper middle	15.83	432.17
United Kingdom	452,080	Europe & Central Asia	High income	−9.17	−46.15
Pakistan	431,220	South Asia	Lower middle	17.89	394.90
France	423,350	Europe & Central Asia	High income	−1.58	−31.11
Thailand	416,950	East Asia & Pacific	Upper middle	6.15	280.61
Italy	399,600	Europe & Central Asia	High income	−3.98	2.92
Poland	389,650	Europe & Central Asia	High income	6.39	−16.42
			Average (top 20 polluters)	3.23%	183.34%
			Average (175 countries)	3.4%	67%

As of 2018, the world's top greenhouse gas (GHG) emitters in absolute terms are China, the United States, India, the Russian Federation, Japan, and Brazil. The 20 top polluters reflected in Table 1 belong to all income categories, among which 50% are high-income countries, 35% are upper-middle-income countries, and 15% lower-middle-income economies (i.e., India, Indonesia, and Pakistan). This confirms that high polluting emissions are a problem across the development divide [57]. The rhythm of GHG emissions growth is highest in Korea, with an alarming 711% increase over 1970–2018, followed by China with 559% and Iran with 484% over the same period. Only five of the world's top polluters (i.e., Brazil, Germany, UK, France, and Poland) register a decrease in emissions since 1970, with overall modest decreasing rates (emissions have fallen the most in the UK, with a negative evolution of −46%). As such, although these (mostly) developed countries have shown a downward trend in overall emissions, their levels remain in the upper decile as of 2018 (for Brazil, Germany, UK, France), while Poland is on the 8th decile in rank of the world countries with most GHG emissions in 2018. Over the 49-year period, the top 20 world polluters recorded an enormous 183.34% of GHG emissions growth, whereas the world average (including the top polluters) is 67% over the same period, as shown in Figure 1. The disparities in emissions growth are also reflected in Figure 3.

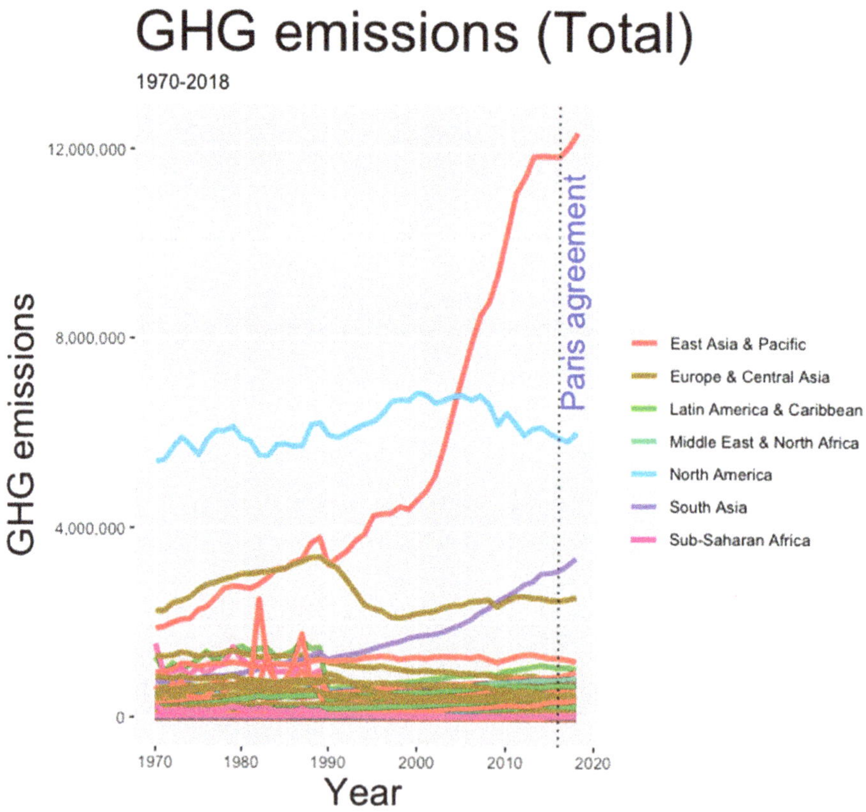

Figure 3. Historical trends of greenhouse gas emissions.

Equally troublesome, only six countries have actually reduced their GHG emissions in the aftermath of the Paris agreement (i.e., Japan, Brazil, Germany, UK, France, and Italy). All other top polluters continue to register increases in emissions since 2015, with Pakistan, Turkey, and Indonesia showing the highest growth levels.

Figure 4 confirms that a small handful of nations account for the majority of global greenhouse gas emissions. On an absolute basis, China, the United States, and India are the three largest emitters.

Together, they account for 48% of 2018 global GHG emissions. The 12 most polluting countries produce overall around three quarters of total GHG emissions at the world level, while the other 163 countries included in the analysis are responsible together for 26% of total greenhouse gas emissions in 2018. This underlines that a minority of countries create a global problem with systemic consequences. This in turn further motivates us to focus on the 12 top emitting countries in our investigation.

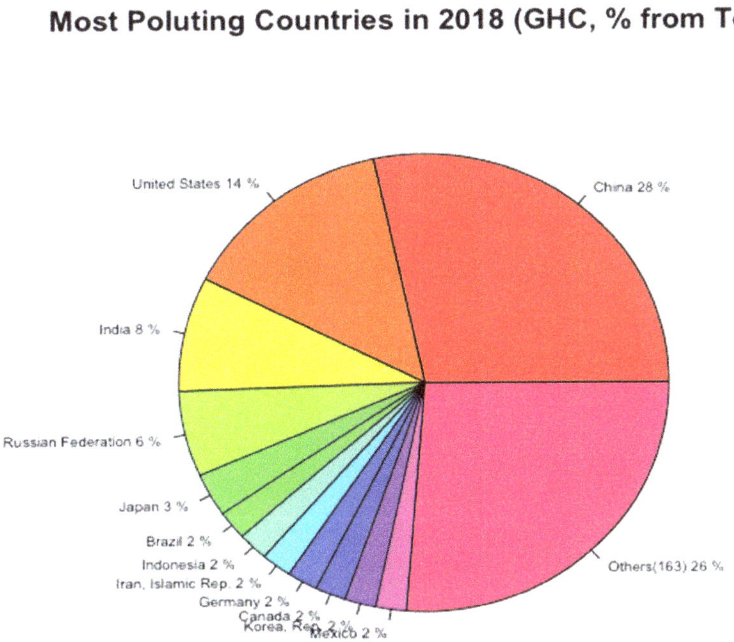

Figure 4. Contribution of world top polluters to total GHG emission (2018).

3.2. Method

Firstly, Appendix A presents the notations and definitions that are employed in the empirical investigations.

3.2.1. Forecasting Technique

This study implements a holdout technique to compare and select an optimal model for forecasting GHG emissions in 12 countries. This technique requires the division of the historical data series of length Ni, $i \in \{1, \ldots, 12\}$ in two subsets corresponding to a training (or fit) period and a test period. For our purposes, the data up until 2013 (i.e., approximately 90% of observations) are used in-sample for model training and validation whilst the period covering 2014–2018 (i.e., 10% of observations) is set aside for testing the out-of-sample forecasting accuracy of the predictive models. The last observation in the training interval Si is thus the forecasting origin (here, GHG emissions in 2013), whereas the period that is predicted (here, 2014–2018) represents the forecasting horizon or lead-time, equal to Ni-Si [58]. Figure 5 depicts the holdout forecasting technique employed in this study.

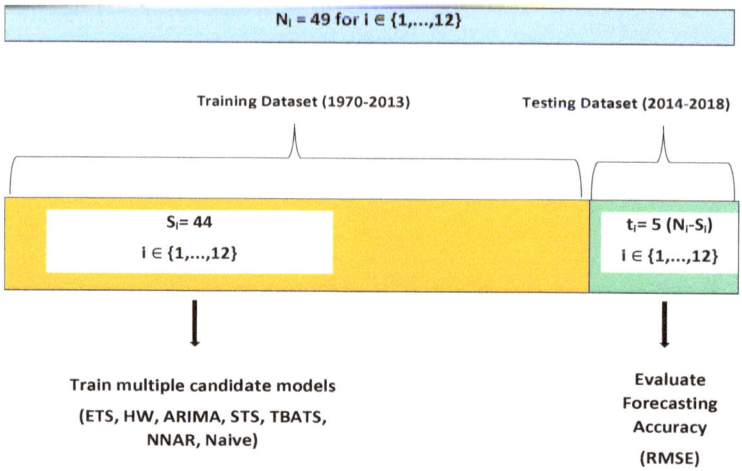

Figure 5. The holdout forecasting with training/test sets.

As most NDCs under the Paris agreement specify the year 2030 as the first deadline for emissions reduction, we are particularly concerned with identifying the best predictive model within a pool of seven candidates and subsequently using it for providing h = 12 steps ahead forecasts for GHG emissions in the 12 top polluting countries, thus including this first deadline in the forecasting horizon.

R software is employed to implement the method and estimate the predictive models via automatic forecasting algorithms, mainly included in the "forecast" package [59] and the "stats" package [60].

3.2.2. Robustness Checks

Forecasting accuracy: The forecasting accuracy of all candidate models for each of the 12 series is assessed through estimating the root mean squared error (RMSE), as in [44,55]. This accuracy metric brings the valuable benefit of being directly interpretable in terms of measurement units. RMSE represents the square root of the mean square error, and thus is estimated by taking the differences between each point forecast and corresponding observed value within the lead time, squaring it, and averaging it, as in Equation (1):

$$\text{RMSE} = \sqrt{\frac{1}{N}\sum_{i=1}^{N}(y_i - \hat{y}_l)^2} \quad (1)$$

RMSE, as many other Goodness-of-Fit (GoF) metrics, is referred to as scale-dependent [61]. Within the scale-dependent category of GoFs, RMSE, and the mean absolute error (MAE) emerged as the most popular. However, RMSE carries some benefits relative to MAE and is usually the recommended metric [62], although it cannot be used to measure out-of-sample forecast accuracy at a single forecast horizon [63] when multiple series of different measurement unit are analyzed. To solve this issue, ref. [63] proposed a new GoF metric, MASE (the mean absolute scaled error), thus a scale free error metric, which we also report in this study for robustness checks purposes. MASE is thus estimated by taking the MAE and dividing it by the MAE of an in-sample naive benchmark, as in Equation (2).

$$\text{MASE} = \frac{\text{MAE}}{\text{MAE}_{\text{in-sample,naive}}} = \frac{1}{n}\sum_{i=1}^{n}|y_i - \hat{y}_l| \quad (2)$$

The MASE metric is symmetrical and resistant to outliers, and values larger than 1 imply that the predictions are, on average, poorer than the naïve model's in-sample one-step forecasts [63]. The MASE would only be infinite or undefined if all historical observations were equal or if all of the actual values throughout the in-sample period were zeros [64].

The recursive window forecasting technique: To further assure the robustness of our results, all estimations for the 12 time series are repeated by implementing one of the most popular techniques for cross-validation, a fixed-length rolling-window forecasting technique.

As such, the dataset covers the training period set for the first S observations (i.e., 44 years) in the sample, and a testing period of length N-S, where N is the total number of observations for each country, i.e., 49. For each year n in the testing interval [S+1:N], or here [2014:2018], the GHG emissions are predicted after the candidate models have been fit on the recursive window of S past observations. This sequence is repeated recursively over the lead-time, and consequently a total of N-S iterations (5) are performed for each of the 12 time series. Figure 6 illustrates this process applied for the current investigation.

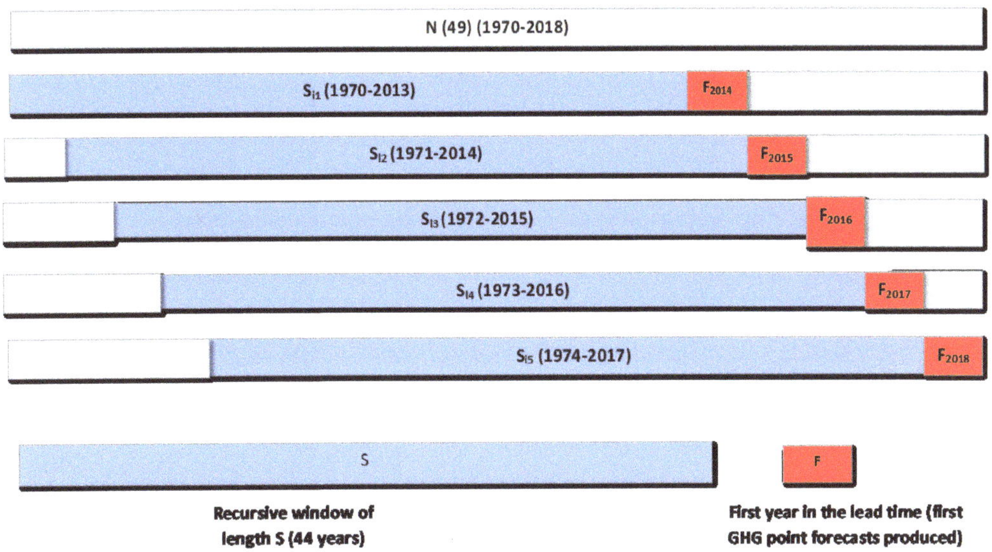

Figure 6. The fixed-length recursive window out-of-sample forecasting technique.

3.2.3. The Predictive Models

Exponential Smoothing State Space Model (ETS): [65] extended the Exponential Smoothing (ES) classical method and developed the exponential smoothing state space (ETS) model. The basic ETS model contains two equations, respectively a forecast equation and a smoothing equation, which are integrated into an innovation state space model. The estimation of the ETS model is fully automated through the "forecast" package in R and, together with ARIMA models, is the base model for the most popular automatic forecasting algorithms [66]. In this study, the system is instructed to automatically select the error, type, and season, and to apply the corrected Akaike information criterion (AICc) for model selection. Hence, following the terminology of [59,65], we specify the three-character string identifying method as (Z,Z,Z).

The Holt–Winters Model (HW): The HW model was introduced in the late 1950s and early 1960s by [67,68]. It applies three exponential smoothing formulae to the time series: to the mean, trend, and each seasonal sub-series, respectively [69]. In this study, the estimation of the HW model for the 12 time series is automated through the "HoltWinters" function included in the "stats" package in R software. It computes Holt–Winters filtering of a given time series, and identifies unknown parameters by minimizing the squared prediction error.

TBATS Model (Exponential Smoothing State Space Model with Box-Cox Transformation, ARMA Errors, Trend, and Seasonal Components): The TBATS model, which is capable of handling multiple and complex seasonality has been introduced by [70]. The TBATS model is fit for the 12 time series through the "forecast" package in R. The fitted model is identified as TBATS (*omega*, *phi*, $<m_1,k_1>$, . . . ,

$s m_J, k_J >$), where *omega* is the Box-Cox parameter and *phi* is the damping parameter, $m_1, \ldots, m_J$ reflect the seasonal periods, and $k_1, \ldots, k_J$ are the corresponding number of Fourier terms used for each seasonality. The Box-Cox parameter, the trend and the damping parameters are automatically selected in our estimations by AIC.

ARIMA: ARIMA models constitute a popular statistical technique for time series forecasting that is capable of describing the autocorrelations in the data. This study applies the automatic ARIMA methodology provided through the "auto.arima function" within the "forecast" package for the R software. As in [66], the function uses unit root tests, minimization of the AICc and MLE to return the best ARIMA model, through a step-wise automated procedure.

Structural Time Series Models (STS): Structural time series models are (linear Gaussian) state-space models for (univariate) time series based on a decomposition of the series into a number of components [71]. STS models can be easily implemented in R through the function "StructTS" in the "stats" package, as in [72]. This is automatically realized in this study for the 12 GHG time series by maximum likelihood.

Neural network autoregression model (NNAR): The main predictive model of interest in this study is NNAR, which provides the adaptability advantage by learning from the provided inputs and training itself to optimize weights. Generally, a neural network autoregression model (NNAR) uses p lagged values of the time series as inputs to a neural network with k hidden nodes, for forecasting the output y(t). The model is thus usually specified as NNAR(p,k), and the hidden nodes are nonlinear functions of the original provided inputs. The functions that are applied at the nodes of the hidden layers are called activation functions. A more complex specification is needed when the data is seasonal, and thus the model in this case is written as NNAR(p,P,k), where P is the number of seasonal lags.

Figure 7 reflects the general structure of a neural network autoregression model, with its three main layers: the first layer of the autoregressive neural network receives the lagged values of the series (here GHG emissions) as inputs, then a linear combination of the weighted inputs are fed forward to the hidden layer or layers of the network, and finally a nonlinear activation function modifies the result from the hidden layer nodes which is then passed to the last output layer that contains a single node representing the predicted value.

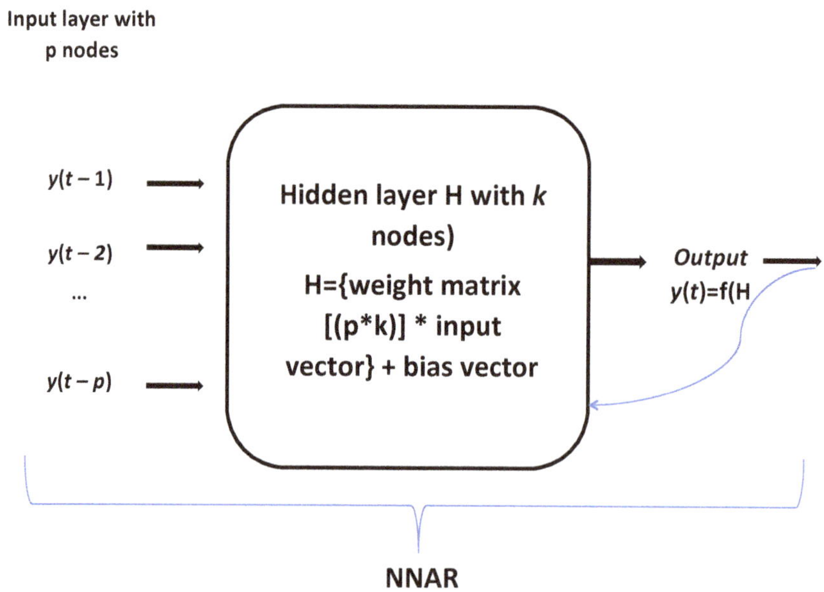

Figure 7. General structure of the nonlinear autoregressive neural network (NNAR) with one hidden layer.

In equation format, the NNAR model depicted in Figure 7 can be expressed as:

$$Y = f(H) = f(W * X + B), X = [y(t-1), y(t-2), \ldots, y(t-p)] \quad (3)$$

where Y is the output vector, f is the activation function, H is the vector of nodes in the hidden layer, W represents the weight matrix between the input and the hidden layers, X is the vector of inputs, and B is a bias vector.

In this study, the "nnetar" function within the R software "forecast" package is used to automatically fit multilayer feed-forward neural networks with a single hidden layer, k nodes and p lagged inputs, by automatically selecting parameters p and P through AIC. The algorithm is also instructed to make 25 repetitions and to estimate the number of hidden notes as $k = (p + P + 1)/2$ (rounded to the nearest integer). As the initial weights at the input layer take random values and are subsequently updated using the observed data, we follow best practices and train the network 25 times using different random starting weights, and then average the results. Based on previous results (i.e., [51]), we expect NNAR models to out-perform other candidates in terms of forecasting accuracy when applied for GHG emissions series.

3.2.4. The Conceptual Framework

For a clearer view of the implemented method, Figure 8 reflects the consecutive steps that have been taken to estimate the alternative models and produce out-of-sample forecasts.

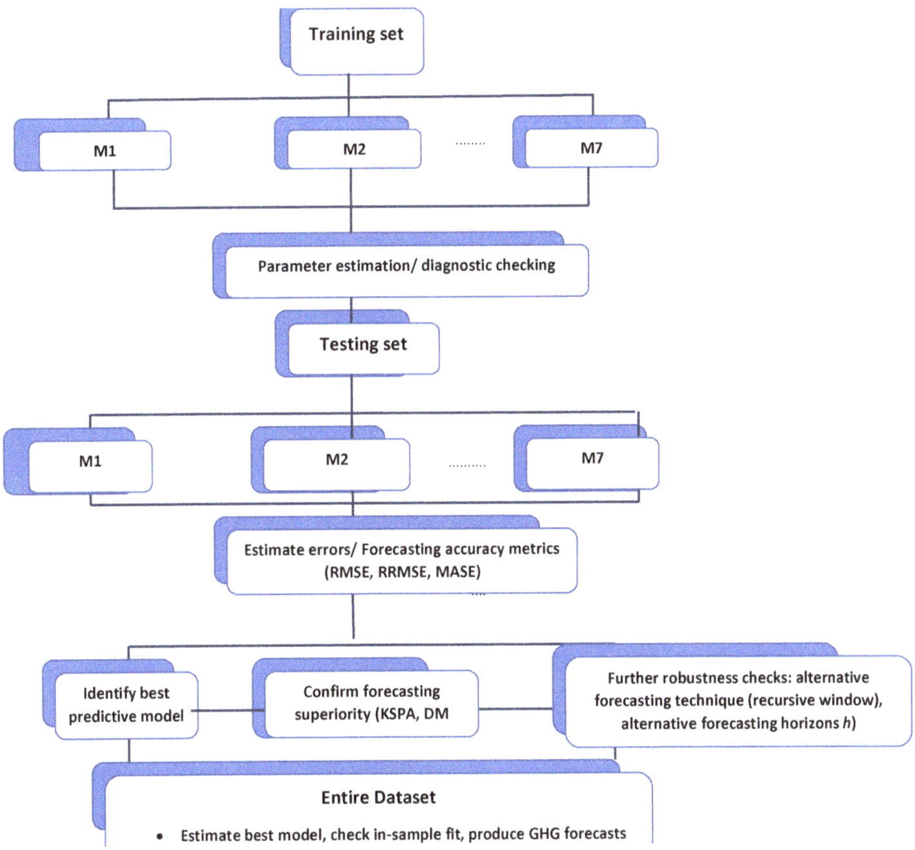

Figure 8. Sequential steps of the forecasting procedure.

Next, Figure 9 puts together all building blocks of the research and gives an overview of the work conducted.

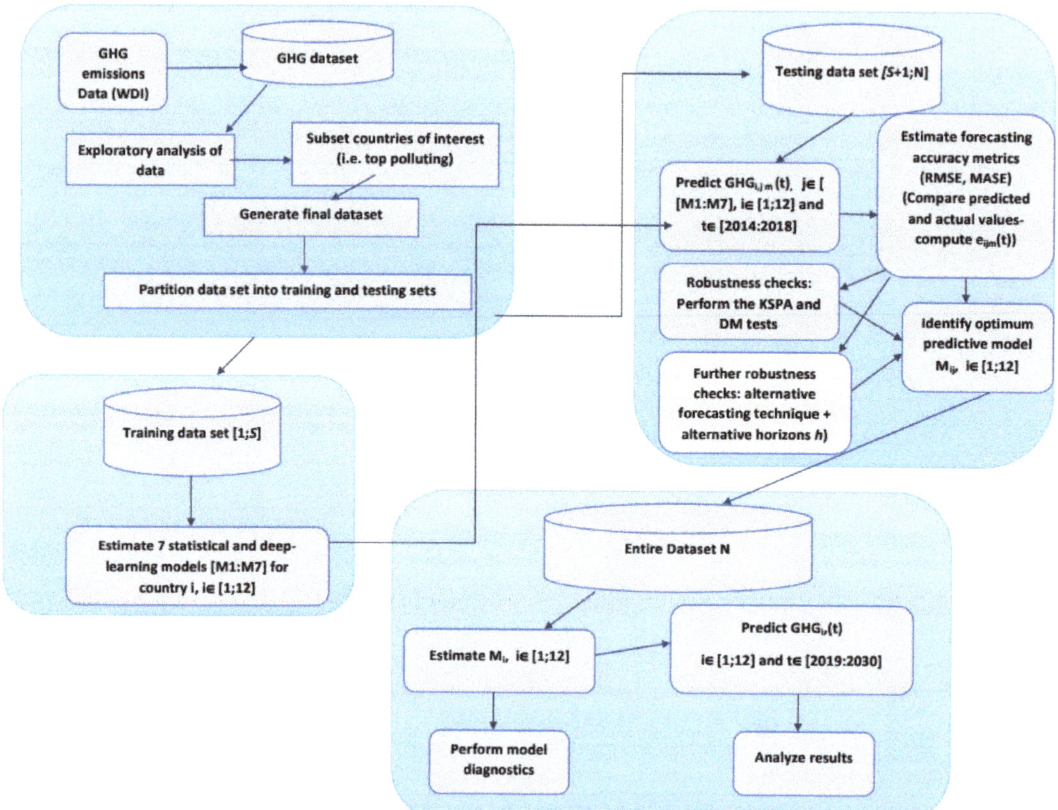

Figure 9. The conceptual framework of the study.

4. Results and Discussion

4.1. Empirical Results

Table 2 reports the RMSE for out-of-sample forecasting results at a horizon of h = 5 steps ahead (covering the data test period, or 2014–2018) for the models described above, along with a "naive" forecasting model, which predicts a flat line equal to the last observation in the training set. Although no single model can provide the best forecast for GHG emissions at a horizon of five years, the NNAR is over-performing within the pool of seven competing models. The same conclusion is extracted from estimations of the second estimated GoF metric, MASE, which is reported in Appendix C. The overall scoring given by the two metrics is identical. Consequently, when a decision should be made about relying on a single predictive model for GHG emissions at the selected forecasting horizon, NNAR emerges as the optimal choice. The STS comes in second in terms of the lowest RMSE, at a significant distance, while other models are not able to provide competitive forecasts for the evolution of GHG emissions in the 12 top polluting countries considered in this study.

Table 2. Forecasting accuracy (RMSE for out-of-sample forecasting at h = 5).

	NNAR	ETS	ARIMA	STS	H-W	BATS/TBATS	Naive
China	**241,141.3**	1578,920.1	1,500,806.5	1,511,817.9	1,622,516.1	1,646,765.7	392,357.5
United States	**145,181.9**	153,472.8	16,6416.3	196,148.3	255,999.2	175,472.4	165,455.0
India	58,230.5	76,108.4	54,133.7	**42,551.3**	269,141.0	45,626.0	310,503.0
Russian Federation	**32,264.24**	57,429.15	43,193.64	54,974.53	66,939.67	52,285.81	62,813.95
Japan	**51,971.29**	74,274.37	89,904.26	98,164.92	94,184.98	94,746.37	53,984.63
Brazil	50,432.98	34,096.97	43,155.88	**24,167.78**	114,618.17	75,126.30	43,755.23
Indonesia	106,501.64	121,314.90	137,564.51	**59,337.21**	438,966.52	123,244.94	130,566.57
Iran, Islamic Rep.	**8763.64**	22,545.14	45,868.70	23,366.34	17,374.46	35,536.55	32,180.85
Germany	**15,978.24**	50,292.81	22,668.79	25,631.45	27,811.22	41,023.36	50,293.06
Canada	21,034.85	18,123.81	**10,440.79**	31,330.76	32,214.06	15,313.01	28,000.70
Korea, Rep.	**15,875.00**	23,220.19	20,179.04	23,187.95	45,057.87	27,507.61	26,638.77
Mexico	**10,752.22**	16,296.63	17,818.57	16,413.70	14,488.03	15,481.74	23,683.56
Score *	8	0	1	3	0	0	0
Score (%) **	66.67%	0%	8.33%	25.00%	0%	0%	0%
Rank	1	4–7	3	2	4–7	4–7	4–7

Notes: * Score indicates the number of times the model outperforms the other candidate models in term of forecasting accuracy; ** Score (%) indicates the percentage of outperformance (out of 12 iterations, or countries); Bold values underline the minimum RMSE across the seven candidate predictive models for each country.

Table 3 reports the relative root mean squared error (RRMSE) results for the out-of-sample forecasts, where the best performing forecasting model (i.e., NNAR) acts as a benchmark. Hence, the forecasting performance of the neural network model is found to be 28% better than the ETS forecast, 19% better than the ARIMA model, 14% better than STS, 54% better than Holt–Winters, 31% better than TBATS, and 37% better than the naive model for forecasting GHG emissions in the 12 top polluters.

Table 3. RRMSE for out-of-sample forecasts of GHC emissions at h = 5 (O = M1/M2).

	NNAR/ETS	NNAR/ARIMA	NNAR/STS	NNAR/H-W	NNAR/TBATS	NNAR/Naive
China	0.15	0.16	0.16	0.15	0.15	0.61
United States	0.95	0.87	0.74	0.57	0.83	0.88
India	0.77	1.08	1.37	0.22	1.28	0.19
Russian Federation	0.56	0.75	0.59	0.48	0.62	0.51
Japan	0.70	0.58	0.53	0.55	0.55	0.96
Brazil	1.48	1.17	2.09	0.44	0.67	1.15
Indonesia	0.88	0.77	1.79	0.24	0.86	0.82
Iran, Islamic Rep.	0.39	0.19	0.38	0.50	0.25	0.27
Germany	0.32	0.70	0.62	0.57	0.39	0.32
Canada	1.16	2.01	0.67	0.65	1.37	0.75
Korea, Rep.	0.68	0.79	0.68	0.35	0.58	0.60
Mexico	0.66	0.60	0.66	0.74	0.69	0.45
Average	0.72	0.81	0.86	0.46	0.69	0.63
Score	10	9	9	12	10	11

Appendix B presents the graphical representation of the forecasting performance, showing the NNAR model's fit to the real test set data for the 12 countries. It can be seen that the NNAR model (despite its nonlinear nature) fails to precisely follow the complex real data dynamics behavior (due to real data highly nonlinear characteristics) and in some instances (i.e., particularly for Brazil, Indonesia, and Canada) is not able to accurately predict the trend over the testing interval.

Subsequently, applying the Kolmogorov–Smirnov (KS) Predictive Accuracy test (KSPA) proposed by [54] and also the Diebold-Mariano (DM) test introduced by [55] and developed by [56] further tests the over-performance of NNAR and contributes to assuring the robustness of results. The test identifies significant differences between forecasts produced by NNAR and the second-best performing model in each of the cases where NNAR emerged as the optimal model. In instances where NNAR is not found to over-perform, the KSPA/DM tests are applied to identify the differences between forecasts from NNAR and the specific optimal predictive model. As such, the forecast errors from NNAR and competing forecasting models are introduced as inputs into the two-sided KSPA/DM tests, which are then estimated to identify a statistically significant difference in the distribution of forecasts errors from the two models.

Table 4 reports the results of the predictive accuracy tests for each pair of competing models and each country, considering NNAR as the benchmark. When the two-sided predictive accuracy tests statistic are significant at 1%, we can reject the null hypothesis and accept the alternate, thus confirming that the forecast errors from NNAR and the other candidate model do not share the same distribution. The KSPA and DM tests confirm for the vast majority of countries that the NNAR forecasting technique provides superior forecasts in comparison to its competitor (the only exceptions are encountered for estimations in the US and Germany). These findings align with those of [51]. In the instances when NNAR is not the optimal model in terms of forecasting accuracies, the predictive accuracy tests generally do not confirm the superiority of the competing model (i.e., for India, Brazil, Indonesia, and Canada).

Table 4. Results of the KSPA and DM tests (*p*-values).

Country	KPSA (*p*-Value)	DM (*p*-Value)
China	0.07937 ***	0.04076 **
United States	0.1871	0.2182
India	1	0.4692
Russian Federation	0.07937 ***	0.0569 ***
Japan	0.0235 **	0.0455 **
Brazil	1	0.1265
Indonesia	0.3571	0.4517
Iran, Islamic Rep.	0.0793 ***	0.0571 ***
Germany	0.3571	0.2092
Canada	0.8730	0.1067
Korea, Rep.	0.002057 *	0.03032 **
Mexico	0.0524 ***	0.0493 **

Note: * indicates a statistically significant difference between the distribution of forecast errors from the best and second best performing models based on the two-sided HS test at a 1% significance level; ** denotes significance at 5%; *** denotes significance at 10%.

Table 5 confirms the superiority of NNAR throughout further robustness checks, including re-estimation at a forecasting horizon of 3 years and also re-estimation by employing the recursive window forecasting technique, while holding h = 5.

Table 5. Robustness checks: RMSE score of candidate models for holdout out-of-sample forecasting at h = 3 and RMSE for recursive window forecasting at h = 5.

	NNAR	ETS	ARIMA	STS	H-W	TBATS	Naive
Score (h = 3, holdout)/Rank	8/1	0	1/3	3/2	0	0	0
Score (h = 5, recursive window)	10/1	0	2/2	0	0	0	0

In the last stage of this investigation, the over-performing predictive model (i.e., NNAR) is fitted to the entire dataset and further employed to produce point forecasts for GHG emissions in the 12 countries for the 2019–2030 period (i.e., h = 12). We should also mention that the in-sample fit has been verified by estimating the Ljung-Box test to check the residuals for any significant evidence of non-zero correlations at lags 1–20. Test results confirm that all models are correctly specified. We thus confidently proceed with a discussion of forecasting results.

Table 6 contains the point forecasts in absolute terms, whereas Table 7 reflects the percentage change relative to the last year with available data within the dataset (i.e., 2018). On average, results indicate a continuation of the current increasing trend of GHG emissions produced by top polluting countries' in the next decade. Therefore, the NNAR model predicts that top polluters countries will see an overall increase of 3.67% in GHG emissions relative to 2018 levels, although significant disparities are identified among individual countries. Thus, in relative terms, the projections translate into a 22.75% increase for Brazil, a 15.75% increase for Indonesia, and 7.45% for India. The only countries that are projected to decrease polluting emissions are Canada (−5.57%), Russian Federation (−3.01%), the US (−0.76%), and China (−0.89%), although total GHG emissions remain in the upper decile and fall well behind set pledges.

Table 6. Total GHG emissions in top polluting countries, kt of CO_2 tons (forecasted values for 2019–2030).

Year	Point Forecast * China	Point Forecast US	Point Forecast India	Point Forecast Russian Federation
2019	12,309,920	6,016,766	3,431,213	2,557,312
2020	12,283,414	6,010,620	3,476,984	2,543,205
2021	12,267,808	6,005,139	3,513,591	2,513,877
2022	12,258,584	6,000,273	3,542,441	2,483,813
2023	12,253,120	5,995,972	3,564,909	2,462,427
2024	12,249,879	5,992,186	3,582,242	2,451,886
2025	12,247,954	5,988,863	3,595,515	2,449,864
2026	12,246,812	5,985,956	3,605,621	2,452,769
2027	12,246,133	5,983,420	3,613,282	2,457,491
2028	12,245,729	5,981,212	3,619,069	2,461,957
2029	12,245,489	5,979,295	3,623,431	2,465,131
2030	12,245,347	5,977,633	3,626,711	2,466,778
	Point Forecast Japan	**Point Forecast Brazil**	**Point Forecast Indonesia**	**Point Forecast Iran**
2019	1,192,158	1,076,958	1,076,732	823,679.7
2020	1,196,957	1,121,942	1,209,626	820,617.5
2021	1,201,228	1,163,625	1,307,557	818,561.4
2022	1,205,024	1,198,314	1,221,594	817,172.9
2023	1,208,393	1,224,208	1,235,139	816,231.7
2024	1,211,380	1,241,788	1,472,859	815,592.0

Table 6. *Cont.*

Year	Point Forecast * China	Point Forecast US	Point Forecast India	Point Forecast Russian Federation
2025	1,214,023	1,252,892	1,462,027	815,156.5
2026	1,216,360	1,259,567	1,380,622	814,859.6
2027	1,218,422	1,263,456	1,391,117	814,657.1
2028	1,220,240	1,265,679	1,339,545	814,518.9
2029	1,221,841	1,266,936	1,253,736	814,424.5
2030	1,223,250	1,267,643	1,119,400	814,360.0
	Point Forecast Germany	**Point Forecast Canada**	**Point Forecast Korea**	**Point Forecast Mexico**
2019	818,123.0	685,765.5	719,072.9	682,001.7
2020	825,845.8	684,968.0	719,233.5	683,925.4
2021	830,972.1	684,929.4	719,367.3	685,666.7
2022	834,448.5	684,927.5	719,478.7	687,240.6
2023	836,839.9	684,927.4	719,571.4	688,661.3
2024	838,500.6	684,927.4	719,648.6	689,942.2
2025	839,661.5	684,927.4	719,712.9	691,095.8
2026	840,476.8	684,927.4	719,766.4	692,133.6
2027	841,051.1	684,927.4	719,810.9	693,066.5
2028	841,456.6	684,927.4	719,848.0	693,904.4
2029	841,743.4	684,927.4	719,878.8	694,656.3
2030	841,946.4	684,927.4	719,904.5	695,330.8

* all numbers represent total GHG emissions measured in kt of CO_2.

Table 7. Predicted change in GHG emissions in top polluting countries over 2019–2030.

Country	GHG %
China	−0.89
United States	−0.76
India	7.45
Russian Federation	−3.01
Japan	3.07
Brazil	22.75
Indonesia	15.75
Iran, Islamic Rep.	−1.68
Germany	4.45
Canada	−5.52
Korea, Rep.	0.14
Mexico	2.27
Average growth of GHG until 2030	**3.67%**

4.2. Discussion of Results

Among all tested models for predicting GHG emissions in the 12 top polluters, the neural network autoregressive model has illustrated the best forecasting performance. This in line with [34,51] who reach the same conclusion from forecasting a similar time series (i.e., CO_2 emissions) in a single country, and support those of [49], thus confirming that artificial neural networks (ANN) are useful in time series modeling when past values of a variable are used as inputs to explain its future values.

Consequently, similar to the approaches of the aforementioned studies, we issue forecasted values for total GHG emissions in the 12 countries by using the neural network time series nonlinear autoregressive model (NNAR). Overall, we find that both the recent evolution of total GHG emissions in top polluting countries and also future projections of emissions fall significantly below what is needed to achieve set climate goals. Emissions have seen massive increases in Korea, China, and Iran over the 1970–2018 period, due to the rapid economic growth, poverty eradication, and substantial integration into global value chains that characterized these economies over the period [73–76]. However, GHG emissions are projected to increase most in Brazil, Indonesia, and India over the 2019–2030 interval. Our findings conform to those that emerge from a recent study of the International Energy Agency [16], which shows that polluting emissions have increased in 2020 as economic activity increased toward the middle of the year, but deviate from the projections of the European Environment Agency [13] concerning the EU country included in the study (i.e., Germany).

However, whereas emissions have continued to increase since 2015 (recording an overall 3.4% increase at the world level and 3.23% increase among the global top 20 polluters), the Paris Agreement requires yearly cuts of almost 8% on average at world level to reach the global warming threshold of 1.5 degrees Celsius [15]. Moreover, ref. [77] find that emissions reductions about 80% more ambitious than those in the Paris Agreement are required to stay within the 2 degrees target, thus highlighting that set global warming targets are even more out-of-reach than previously considered. Ref. [78] also confirm that the current commitments are inadequate to meet temperature targets. Projections of future GHG emissions that emerge from our study confirm that no country is expected to meet its NDCs under the Paris agreement, which in turn are nonetheless inadequate in the context of limiting global warming. Given this finding, and considering the catastrophic impact of pollution on public health variables [28,29], including mortality rate [30,31], the current trend is particularly troublesome, and significant efforts should be directed toward its reversal.

Our findings further highlight that more impactful policies are needed to successfully combat global pollution. Considering previous results in the literature that indicate a negative relationship between renewable energy and polluting emissions [79–85]), we argue that countries, especially top GHG emitters, should use the recovery funds available in the aftermath of the global COVID-19 pandemic and prioritize sustainable energy policies. This is also in line with the conclusion of [21].

Moreover, given that the bulk of global greenhouse gas emissions has historically come from a few countries, and that this situation is expected to continue for the foreseeable future, the logical solution should be to encourage particular nations in implementing specific GHG reduction targets, rather than issuing global policies that cover the entire spectrum of economies. Consequently, the small number of nations that causes a global problem with systemic effects, in particular, must issue and implement ambitious low-carbon policies. We take a similar view to [86], who suggest that although average global reductions are expected, advanced economies should contribute more in terms of emissions reduction, considering their historical contribution to world pollution.

5. Conclusions

Greenhouse gas emissions (GHG) have risen significantly for the past 49 years at the world level. However, enormous disparities are encountered among individual countries, both in terms of absolute GHG emissions values and in terms of their rhythm of growth over the 1970–2018 period. On an absolute basis, China, the United States, and India are the three largest emitters. Together, they account for 48% of 2018 global GHG emissions. The 12 most polluting countries produce overall around three quarters of total GHG emissions at the world level, while the other 163 countries included in the analysis are responsible together for 26% of total greenhouse gas emissions in 2018. This underlines that a minority of countries create a global problem with systemic consequences and further motivates our focus on the 12 top emitting countries in our investigation.

The primary objective of this study is thus is to produce more accurate forecasts of GHG emissions. This in turn contributes to the timely evaluation of the progress achieved towards meeting global climate goals set by international agendas and also acts as an early-warning system when projections show that the state of affairs does not reflect policy statements and formal pledges are not followed by concrete measures and results. Results of this study are also important for policymakers that incorporate forecasts of polluting emissions in their policy-making process. A policy can only be efficient if it is developed based on robust input elements. Consequently, an accurate estimation of GHG emissions in top polluting countries is not only paramount for an effective policy-making process in the climate combat arena but will also play a vital role in planning economic developments over the long run. The issue is timely, as countries have to pursue post-pandemic economic recovery while bending the emissions trend.

As such, this paper attempts to forecast the evolution of GHG emissions in the world top polluters by employing seven statistical and machine learning methods, such as the exponential smoothing state-space model (ETS), the Holt–Winters model, the TBATS model, ARIMA, the structural time series model (STS), and the neural network time series forecasting method (NNAR). A naive model is also estimated and serves for comparative purposes. In particular, the study takes a univariate approach that offers the important advantage of producing forecasts for a validated leading indicator independent of other variables, aside from increasing efficiency. The results demonstrate that the best single model in terms of forecasting accuracy for GHG emissions is NNAR, and this finding resists a battery of robustness checks (including re-estimations at different forecasting horizons and re-estimation by implementing a recursive window forecasting technique). Consequently, the NNAR model is further employed to produce GHG emissions point forecasts for the 12 top polluting countries until 2030, i.e., until the first benchmark under the Paris agreement.

Although total GHG emissions were expected to decline sharply in the aftermath of the 2015 Paris agreement and to continue a decreasing trend over the next decades, empirical results indicate that top polluters will see an overall increase of 3.67% in GHG emissions relative to their 2018 levels. However, significant disparities remain among individual countries. Projections from the NNAR model at the 2030 forecasting horizon point to a 22.75% increase in GHG total emissions in Brazil, a 15.75% increase in Indonesia, and 7.45% in India. Decreases in GHG total emissions are expected in Canada (−5.57%), the Russian Federation (−3.01%), the US (−0.76%), and China (−0.89%), although they remain in the upper decile. More importantly, GHG projected levels fall well behind set pledges for all top polluting countries and none of the 12 sample economies is expected to meet its NDCs under the Paris agreement.

Overall, this study makes several important contributions to the extant literature, as follows: (i) it employs a wider variety of candidate predictive models for polluting emissions, including econometric and machine-learning methods, and also performs a battery of robustness checks to defend its findings; (ii) it employs a more accurate indicator for air pollution, thus increasing the relevancy of its results; (iii) it focuses on the 12 most polluting countries that are together responsible for around 75% of total GHG emissions at world level, thus further increasing the relevancy of the findings relative to single-country/narrower studies.

We conclude that country-specific policies would be more efficient to tackle global pollution than the global approach that is currently being implemented. In addition, a country-specific approach is only fair, given the enormous historical disparities in terms of individual countries' contributions to world pollution, which are expected to persist. Moreover, public policies and the recovery funds directed toward post-pandemic economic recovery should target sustainable energy production and consumption, which in turn mitigate polluting emissions.

Author Contributions: Conceptualization, C.T. and R.S.; methodology, C.T.; software, C.T. and R.S.; validation, C.T. and R.S.; formal analysis, C.T.; investigation, C.T.; data curation, C.T.; writing—original draft preparation, C.T.; writing—review and editing, C.T.; visualization, C.T.; supervision, C.T.; project administration, C.T. All authors have read and agreed to the published version of the manuscript.

Funding: This research received no external funding.

Data Availability Statement: Data is publicly available from the World Bank's Development Indicators (WDI) database.

Conflicts of Interest: The author declares no conflict of interest.

Appendix A

Table A1. Variables' notations and definitions.

Variable	Definition
$Y_i(t)$	real GHG time series data for 12 countries, $i = 1 \ldots 12$ and $t = 1, \ldots, 49$.
N	the length of each time series, i.e., 49 (annual data over 1970–2018 for each of the 12 countries, $i = 1 \ldots 12$)
S	S_i is the last observation in the training interval for each time series i, $i = 1 \ldots 12$, and represents the forecasting origin
Training data set	[1;S]
Testing data set	[S + 1:N]
$\{y_1, \ldots, y_S\}$	the observations in the training data set
$\{y_{S+1}, y_{S+2}, \ldots, y_N\}$	the observations in the test data set
$\hat{y}_i(t) = y_{ijm}(t)$	the 84 (i.e., 7 × 12) forecasted time series from the seven models for each country over the testing period, i.e., $y_{ijm}(t)$, $i = 1 \ldots 12$, $t = S + 1, \ldots, 49$, j = {M1, M2, ..., M7}, m-model
M_j, $j = \{M_1, M_2, \ldots, M_7\}$	The 7 predictive models: 1. the exponential smoothing state-space model (ETS), 2. the Holt-Winters Model (HW), 3. the TBATS model, 4. the ARIMA model, 5. the structural time series model (STS), 6. the neural network autoregression model (NNAR)), 7. the naive model
Naive model	A naive forecast is the most recently observed value, such that the *k*-step-ahead naive forecast ($F_{i,t+k}$) equals the observed value for country i at time *t*: $F_i(t+k) = y_i(t)$
$e_{ijm}(t)$	The 84 vectors of forecast errors representing the difference between an observed value and its point forecast over the testing period for each country, such as: $e_{ijm}(t) = y_i(t) - \hat{y}_i(t)$, $i = 1 \ldots 12$, $t = S + 1, \ldots, 49$, and j = {M1, M2, ..., M7}

Appendix B. NNAR Fit to the Test Set Data for the 12 Countries

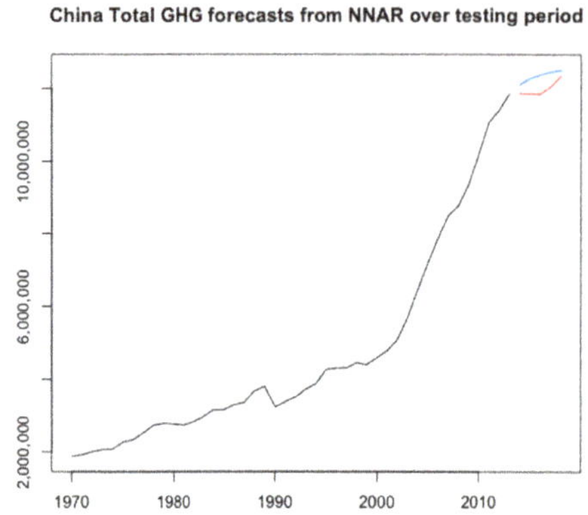

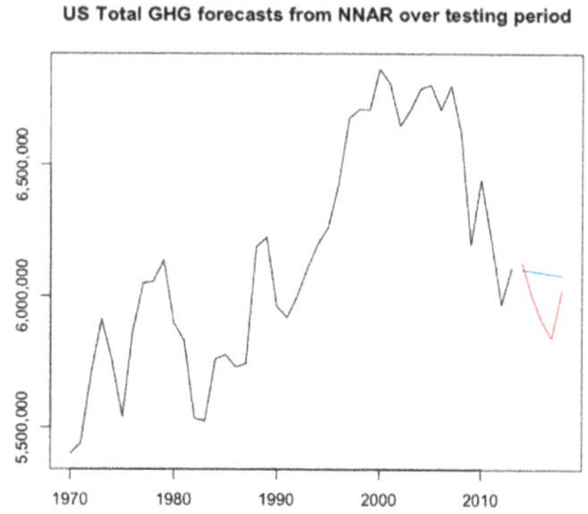

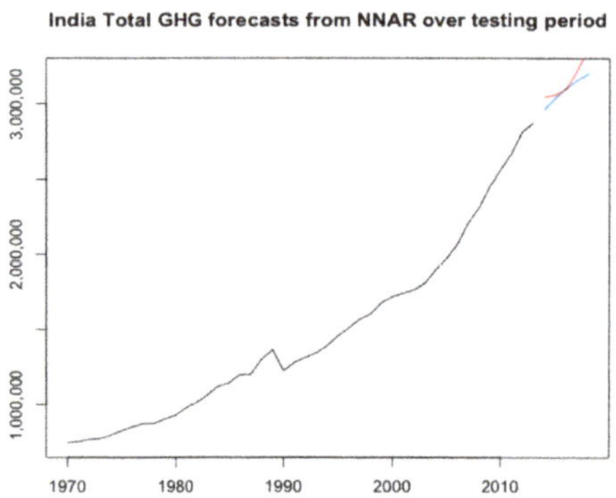

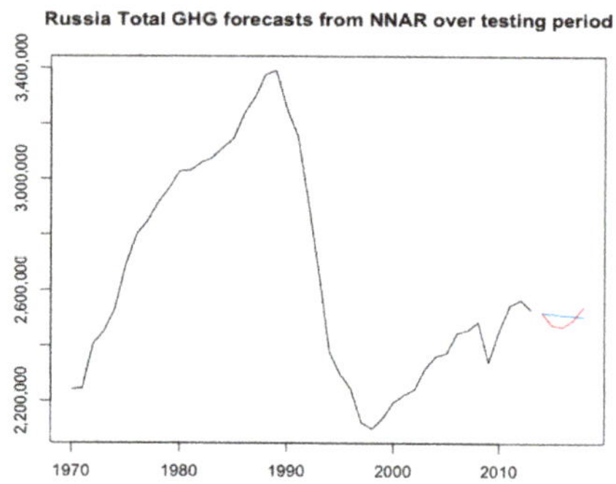

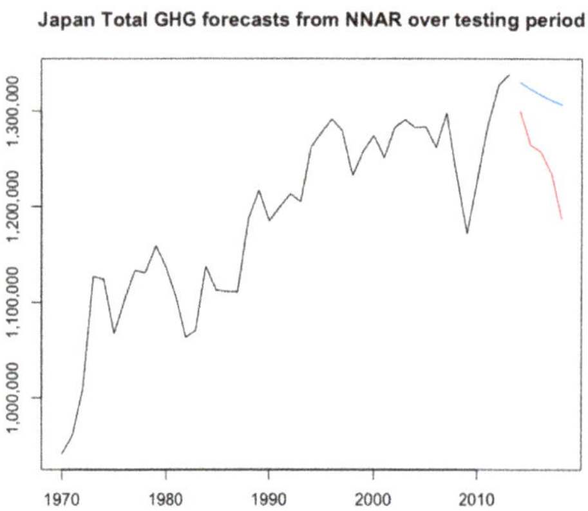

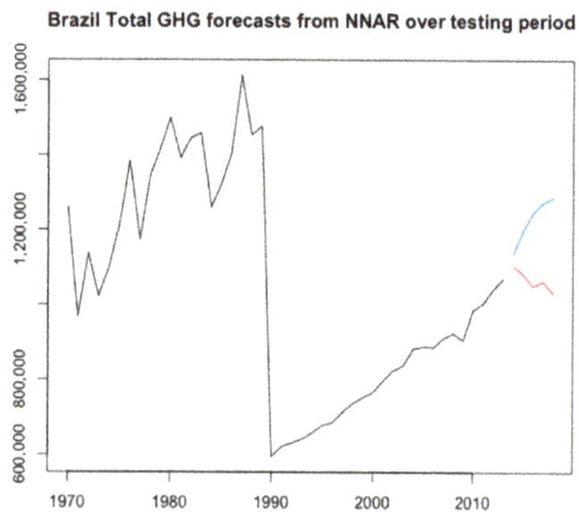

Figure A1. *Cont.*

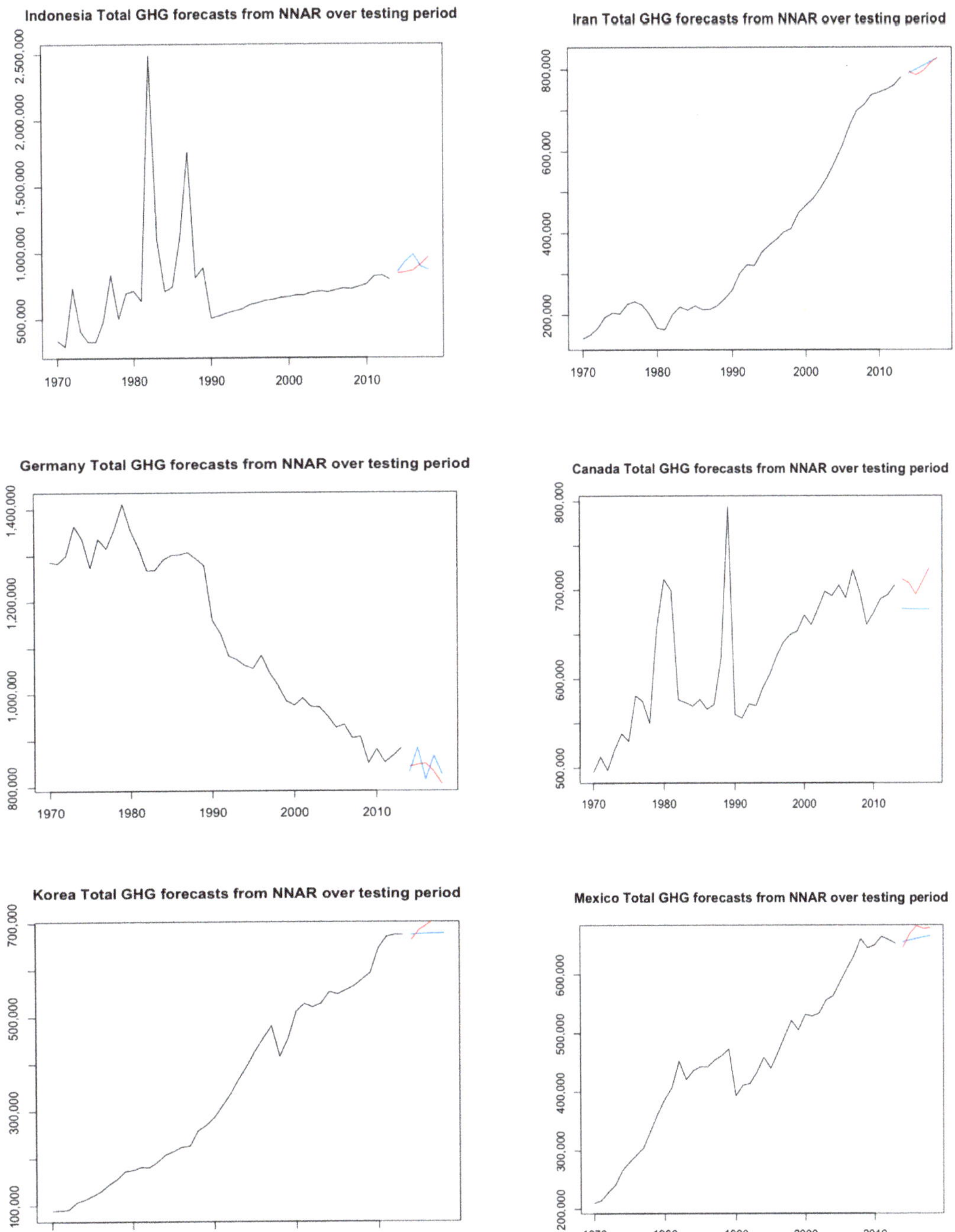

Figure A1. Countries (Predicted Line in Blue versus Real Time Evolution in Red).

Appendix C. Forecasting Accuracy (MASE for Out-of-Sample Forecasting at h = 5)

Table A2. Forecasting Accuracy (MASE for Out-of-Sample Forecasting at h = 5).

	NNAR	ETS	ARIMA	STS	H-W	BATS/TBATS
China	**0.55**	3.45	1.33	2.43	3.95	4.67
United States	**0.84**	0.95	0.98	1.22	1.33	1.03
India	1.04	1.20	0.88	**0.69**	4.24	0.81
Russian Federation	**0.36**	0.45	0.38	0.47	0.95	0.36
Japan	**0.94**	1.64	2.24	3.78	3.08	3.05
Brazil	1.07	0.25	1.27	**0.22**	1.85	1.67
Indonesia	0.32	0.33	0.60	**0.23**	1.27	0.47
Iran, Islamic Rep.	**0.36**	1.15	2.05	1.38	0.94	1.52
Germany	**0.45**	1.74	0.72	0.74	1.73	1.73
Canada	0.50	0.39	**0.29**	0.98	1.03	0.30
Korea, Rep.	**0.75**	1.48	1.20	1.31	1.87	1.42
Mexico	**0.49**	0.77	1.15	0.90	0.61	0.75
Score *	8	0	1	3	0	0
Score (%) **	66.67%	0%	8.33%	25.00%	0%	0%
Rank	1	4–7	3	2	4–7	4–7

Notes: * Score indicates the number of times the model outperforms the other candidate models in term of forecasting accuracy; ** Score (%) indicates the percentage of outperformance (out of 12 iterations, or countries); Bold values underline the minimum MASE across the seven candidate predictive models for each country.

References

1. World Health Organization (WHO). New WHO Global Air Quality Guidelines Aim to Save Millions of Lives from Air Pollution. 2021. Available online: https://www.who.int/news/item/22-09-2021-new-who-global-air-quality-guidelines-aim-to-save-millions-of-lives-from-air-pollution (accessed on 25 October 2021).
2. World Meteorological Organization (WMO). Global Air Quality Forecasting and Information System (GAFIS). 2020. Available online: https://community.wmo.int/activity-areas/gaw/science-for-services/gafis (accessed on 5 October 2021).
3. World Bank, Institute for Health Metrics and Evaluation. *The Cost of Air Pollution: Strengthening the Economic Case for Action*; World Bank: Washington, DC, USA, 2016.
4. Ramanathan, V.; Feng, Y. Air pollution, greenhouse gases and climate change: Global and regional perspectives. *Atmos. Environ.* **2009**, *43*, 37–50. [CrossRef]
5. Organisation for Economic Co-Operation and Development. Air and GHG Emissions. 2020. Available online: https://data.oecd.org/air/air-and-ghg-emissions.htm (accessed on 5 October 2021).
6. Lazar, D.; Minea, A.; Purcel, A.A. Pollution and economic growth: Evidence from Central and Eastern European countries. *Energy Econ.* **2019**, *81*, 1121–1131. [CrossRef]
7. Crippa, M.; Guizzardi, D.; Solazzo, E.; Muntean, M.; Schaaf, E.; Monforti-Ferrario, F.; Banja, M.; Olivier, J.; Grassi, G.; Rossi, S.; et al. *GHG Emissions of All World Countries, EUR 30831 EN*; Publications Office of the European Union: Luxembourg, 2021; ISBN 978-92-76-41547-3. JRC126363. [CrossRef]
8. United Nations Framework Convention on Climate Change (UNFCCC). The Paris Agreement. 2021. Available online: https://unfccc.int/process-and-meetings/the-paris-agreement/the-paris-agreement (accessed on 10 November 2021).
9. Deutsche Welle. Tackling Climate Change from Kyoto to Paris and Beyond. 2020. Available online: https://www.dw.com/en/kyoto-protocol-climate-treaty/a-52375473 (accessed on 8 December 2021).
10. United Nations Climate Change. Nationally Determined Contributions (NDCs). 2021. Available online: https://unfccc.int/process-and-meetings/the-paris-agreement/nationally-determined-contributions-ndcs/nationally-determined-contributions-ndcs (accessed on 7 December 2021).
11. United Nations Framework Convention on Climate Change (UNFCCC). Nationally Determined Contributions under the Paris Agreement. 2021. Available online: https://unfccc.int/sites/default/files/resource/cma2021_08_adv_1.pdf (accessed on 10 November 2021).
12. Scientific American. Global CO_2 Emissions Rise after Paris Climate Agreement Signed. 2018. Available online: https://www.scientificamerican.com/article/global-co2-emissions-rise-after-paris-climate-agreement-signed/ (accessed on 7 December 2021).

13. European Environment Agency (EEA). Total Greenhouse Gas Emission Trends and Projections in Europe. 2021. Available online: https://www.eea.europa.eu/ims/total-greenhouse-gas-emission-trends (accessed on 15 November 2021).
14. UN Environment Programme. Emissions Gap Report 2021. 2021. Available online: https://www.unep.org/resources/emissions-gap-report-2021 (accessed on 5 October 2021).
15. United Nations Climate Change. Cut Global Emissions by 7.6 Percent Every Year for Next Decade to Meet 1.5 °C Paris Target—UN Report. 2019. Available online: https://unfccc.int/news/cut-global-emissions-by-76-percent-every-year-for-next-decade-to-meet-15degc-paris-target-un-report (accessed on 6 December 2021).
16. International Energy Agency (IEA). Global Energy Review: CO_2 Emissions in 2020. 2021. Available online: https://www.iea.org/articles/global-energy-review-co2-emissions-in-2020 (accessed on 15 November 2021).
17. Wen, L.; Yuan, X. Forecasting CO_2 emissions in Chinas commercial department, through BP neural network based on random forest and PSO. *Sci. Total Environ.* **2020**, *718*, 137194. [CrossRef]
18. Center for Climate and Energy Solutions. Global Emissions. 2021. Available online: https://www.c2es.org/content/international-emissions/ (accessed on 25 October 2021).
19. Grossman, G.M.; Krueger, A.B. *Environmental impacts of a North American free trade agreement, NBER Working Paper No. 3914*; National Bureau of Economic Research (NBER): Palo Alto, CA, USA; Cambridge, MA, USA, 1991. [CrossRef]
20. Panayotou, T. *Empirical Tests and Policy Analysis of Environmental Degradation at Different Stages of Economic Development (No. 992927783402676)*; International Labour Organization: Geneva, Switzerland, 1993.
21. Tudor, C.; Sova, R. On the Impact of GDP per Capita, Carbon Intensity and Innovation for Renewable Energy Consumption: Worldwide Evidence. *Energies* **2021**, *14*, 6254. [CrossRef]
22. Dinda, S. Environmental Kuznets curve hypothesis: A survey. *Ecol. Econ.* **2004**, *49*, 431–455. [CrossRef]
23. Kijima, M.; Nishide, K.; Ohyama, A. Economic models for the environmental Kuznets curve: A survey. *J. Econ. Dyn. Control* **2010**, *34*, 1187–1201. [CrossRef]
24. Kong, Y.; Khan, R. To examine environmental pollution by economic growth and their impact in an environmental Kuznets curve (EKC) among developed and developing countries. *PLoS ONE* **2019**, *14*, e0209532. [CrossRef]
25. Sarkodie, S.A. The invisible hand and EKC hypothesis: What are the drivers of environmental degradation and pollution in Africa? *Environ. Sci. Pollut. Res.* **2018**, *25*, 21993–22022. [CrossRef] [PubMed]
26. Armeanu, D.; Vintilă, G.; Andrei, J.V.; Gherghina, Ş.C.; Drăgoi, M.C.; Teodor, C. Exploring the link between environmental pollution and economic growth in EU-28 countries: Is there an environmental Kuznets curve? *PLoS ONE* **2018**, *13*, e0195708. [CrossRef] [PubMed]
27. Mardani, A.; Streimikiene, D.; Cavallaro, F.; Loganathan, N.; Khoshnoudi, M. Carbon dioxide (CO_2) emissions and economic growth: A systematic review of two decades of research from 1995 to 2017. *Sci. Total Environ.* **2019**, *649*, 31–49. [CrossRef] [PubMed]
28. *Air Pollution and Health*; Ayres, J.G.; Maynard, R.L.; Richards, R.J. (Eds.) World Scientific: Singapore, 2006; Volume 3.
29. Kampa, M.; Castanas, E. Human health effects of air pollution. *Environ. Pollut.* **2008**, *151*, 362–367. [CrossRef]
30. Anderson, H.R. Air pollution and mortality: A history. *Atmos. Environ.* **2009**, *43*, 142–152. [CrossRef]
31. Di, Q.; Wang, Y.; Zanobetti, A.; Wang, Y.; Koutrakis, P.; Choirat, C.; Dominici, F.; Schwartz, J.D. Air pollution and mortality in the Medicare population. *N. Engl. J. Med.* **2017**, *376*, 2513–2522. [CrossRef]
32. Brunekreef, B.; Holgate, S.T. Air pollution and health. *Lancet* **2002**, *360*, 1233–1242. [CrossRef]
33. Mannucci, P.M.; Franchini, M. Health effects of ambient air pollution in developing countries. *Int. J. Environ. Res. Public Health* **2017**, *14*, 1048. [CrossRef] [PubMed]
34. Qader, M.R.; Khan, S.; Kamal, M.; Usman, M.; Haseeb, M. Forecasting carbon emissions due to electricity power generation in Bahrain. *Environ. Sci. Pollut. Res.* **2021**, in press. [CrossRef] [PubMed]
35. Mahajan, S.; Chen, L.J.; Tsai, T.C. An empirical study of PM2.5 forecasting using neural network. In Proceedings of the 2017 IEEE SmartWorld, Ubiquitous Intelligence & Computing, Advanced & Trusted Computed, Scalable Computing & Communications, Cloud & Big Data Computing, Internet of People and Smart City Innovation (SmartWorld/SCALCOM/UIC/ATC/CBDCom/IOP/SCI), San Francisco, CA, USA, 4–8 August 2017; IEEE: San Francisco, CA, USA, 2017; pp. 1–7.
36. Breiman, L. Statistical modeling: The two cultures (with comments and a rejoinder by the author). *Stat. Sci.* **2001**, *16*, 199–231. [CrossRef]
37. Charpentier, A.; Flachaire, E.; Ly, A. Econometrics and machine learning. *Econ. Et Stat.* **2018**, *505*, 147–169. [CrossRef]
38. Miller, A.C.; Foti, N.J.; Fox, E.B. Breiman's Two Cultures: You Don't Have to Choose Sides. *Obs. Stud.* **2021**, *7*, 161–169. [CrossRef]
39. Bristone, M.; Prasad, R.; Abubakar, A.A. CPPCNDL: Crude oil price prediction using complex network and deep learning algorithms. *Petroleum* **2019**, *6*, 353–361. [CrossRef]
40. Koehrsen, W. Thoughts on the Two Cultures of Statistical Modeling. 2019. Available online: https://towardsdatascience.com/thoughts-on-the-two-cultures-of-statistical-modeling-72d75a9e06c2 (accessed on 7 November 2021).
41. IJ, H. Statistics versus machine learning. *Nat. Methods* **2018**, *15*, 233.
42. Meng, M.; Niu, D. Modeling CO_2 emissions from fossil fuel combustion using the logistic equation. *Energy* **2011**, *36*, 3355–3359. [CrossRef]
43. Malik, A.; Hussain, E.; Baig, S.; Khokhar, M.F. Forecasting CO_2 emissions from energy consumption in Pakistan under different scenarios: The China–Pakistan economic corridor. *Greenh. Gases Sci. Technol.* **2020**, *10*, 380–389. [CrossRef]

44. Silva, E.S. A combination forecast for energy-related CO_2 emissions in the United States. *Int. J. Energy Stat.* **2013**, *1*, 269–279. [CrossRef]
45. Sun, W.; Wang, C.; Zhang, C. Factor analysis and forecasting of CO_2 emissions in Hebei, using extreme learning machine based on particle swarm optimization. *J. Clean. Prod.* **2017**, *162*, 1095–1101. [CrossRef]
46. Acheampong, A.O.; Boateng, E.B. Modelling carbon emission intensity: Application of artificial neural network. *J. Clean. Prod.* **2019**, *225*, 833–856. [CrossRef]
47. Gallo, C.; Conto, F.; Fiore, M. A neural network model for forecasting CO_2 emission. *AGRIS On-Line Pap. Econ. Inform.* **2014**, *6*, 31–36.
48. Kheirkhah, A.; Azadeh, A.; Saberi, M.; Azaron, A.; Shakouri, H. Improved estimation of electricity demand function by using of artificial neural network, principal component analysis and data envelopment analysis. *Comput. Ind. Eng.* **2013**, *64*, 425–441. [CrossRef]
49. Rather, A.M.; Agarwal, A.; Sastry, V.N. Recurrent neural network and a hybrid model for prediction of stock returns. *Expert Syst. Appl.* **2015**, *42*, 3234–3241. [CrossRef]
50. Hassani, H.; Silva, E.S.; Gupta, R.; Segnon, M.K. Forecasting the price of gold. *Appl. Econ.* **2015**, *47*, 4141–4152. [CrossRef]
51. Tudor, C. Predicting the evolution of CO_2 emissions in Bahrain with automated forecasting methods. *Sustainability* **2016**, *8*, 923. [CrossRef]
52. Perone, G. Comparison of ARIMA, ETS, NNAR, TBATS and hybrid models to forecast the second wave of COVID-19 hospitalizations in Italy. *Eur. J. Health Econ.* **2021**, in press. [CrossRef]
53. Nath, P.; Saha, P.; Middya, A.I.; Roy, S. Long-term time-series pollution forecast using statistical and deep learning methods. *Neural Comput. Appl.* **2021**, *33*, 1–20. [CrossRef] [PubMed]
54. Hassani, H.; Silva, E.S. A Kolmogorov-Smirnov Based Test for Comparing the Predictive Accuracy of Two Sets of Forecasts. *Econometrics* **2015**, *3*, 590–609. [CrossRef]
55. Diebold, F.X.; Mariano, R.S. Comparing predictive accuracy. *J. Bus. Econ. Stat.* **1995**, *13*, 253–263.
56. Harvey, D.; Leybourne, S.; Newbold, P. Testing the equality of prediction mean squared errors. *Int. J. Forecast.* **1997**, *13*, 281–291. [CrossRef]
57. United Nations Conference on Trade and Development (UNCTAD). Carbon Emissions Anywhere Threaten Development Everywhere. 2021. Available online: https://unctad.org/news/carbon-emissions-anywhere-threaten-development-everywhere (accessed on 8 December 2021.).
58. Tashman, L.J. Out-of-sample tests of forecasting accuracy: An analysis and review. *Int. J. Forecast.* **2000**, *16*, 437–450. [CrossRef]
59. Hyndman, R.J.; Khandakar, Y. Automatic time series forecasting: The forecast package for R. *J. Stat. Softw.* **2008**, *27*, 1–22. [CrossRef]
60. R Core Team. *R: A Language and Environment for Statistical Computing*; R Foundation for Statistical Computing: Vienna, Austria, 2013; ISBN 3-900051-07-0. Available online: http://www.R.-project.org/ (accessed on 5 October 2021).
61. Hyndman, R. Another Look at Forecast Accuracy Metrics for Intermittent Demand. *Foresight Int. J. Appl. Forecast.* **2006**, *4*, 43–46.
62. Chai, T.; Draxler, R.R. Root Mean Square Error (RMSE) or Mean Absolute Error (MAE)?—Arguments against Avoiding RMSE in the Literature. *Geosci. Model Dev.* **2014**, *7*, 1247–1250. [CrossRef]
63. Hyndman, R.J.; Koehler, A.B. Another look at measures of forecast accuracy. *Int. J. Forecast.* **2006**, *22*, 679–688. [CrossRef]
64. Kim, S.; Kim, H. A New Metric of Absolute Percentage Error for Intermittent Demand Forecasts. *Int. J. Forecast.* **2016**, *32*, 669–679. [CrossRef]
65. Hyndman, R.J.; Koehler, A.B.; Snyder, R.D.; Grose, S. A state space framework for automatic forecasting using exponential smoothing methods. *Int. J. Forecast.* **2002**, *18*, 439–454. [CrossRef]
66. Hyndman, R.J.; Athanasopoulos, G. *Forecasting: Principles and Practice*; OTexts: Melbourne, Australia, 2018; Available online: OTexts.com/fpp2 (accessed on 8 December 2021).
67. Holt, C.C. *Forecasting Seasonals and Trends by Exponentially Weighted Moving Averages, ONR Research Memorandum*; Carnegie Institute of Technology: Pittsburgh, PA, USA, 1957; p. 52.
68. Winters, P.R. Forecasting sales by exponentially weighted moving averages. *Manag. Sci.* **1960**, *6*, 324–342. [CrossRef]
69. Chatfield, C. The Holt–Winters Forecasting Procedure. *Appl. Stat.* **1978**, *27*, 264–279. [CrossRef]
70. De Livera, A.M.; Hyndman, R.J.; Snyder, R.D. Forecasting time series with complex seasonal patterns using exponential smoothing. *J. Am. Stat. Assoc.* **2011**, *106*, 1513–1527. [CrossRef]
71. Petris, G.; Petrone, S. State space models in R. *J. Stat. Softw.* **2011**, *41*, 1–25. [CrossRef]
72. Ripley, B.D. Time Series in R 1.5.0. *R News* **2011**, *2*, 2–7.
73. Lee, H.; Lee, M.; Park, D. Growth Policy and Inequality in Developing Asia: Lesson from Korea. ERIA Discussion Paper Series. 2012. Available online: http://eria.org/ERIA-DP-2012-12.Pdf (accessed on 7 December 2021).
74. Frederick, S.; Bamber, P.; Brun, L.; Cho, J.; Gereffi, G.; Lee, J. *Korea in Global Value Chains: Pathways for Industrial Transformation. Joint Project Between GVCC and KIET*; Duke GVC Center: Durham, NC, USA, 2017.
75. Organisation for Economic Co-operation and Development (OECD). *Perspectives on Global Development 2019: Rethinking Development Strategies*; OECD Publishing: Paris, France, 2018. [CrossRef]
76. World Bank. The World Bank in Republic of Korea. 2021. Available online: https://www.worldbank.org/en/country/korea/overview#1 (accessed on 8 December 2021).

77. Liu, P.R.; Raftery, A.E. Country-based rate of emissions reductions should increase by 80% beyond nationally determined contributions to meet the 2 C target. *Commun. Earth Environ.* **2021**, *2*, 1–10. [CrossRef]
78. Mills-Novoa, M.; Liverman, D.M. Nationally determined contributions: Material climate commitments and discursive positioning in the NDCs. *Wiley Interdiscip. Rev. Clim. Chang.* **2019**, *10*, e589. [CrossRef]
79. Shafiei, S.; Salim, R.A. Non-renewable and renewable energy consumption and CO_2 emissions in OECD countries: A comparative analysis. *Energy Policy* **2014**, *66*, 547–556. [CrossRef]
80. Bilgili, F.; Koçak, E.; Bulut, Ü. The dynamic impact of renewable energy consumption on CO_2 emissions: A revisited Environmental Kuznets Curve approach. *Renew. Sustain. Energy Rev.* **2016**, *54*, 838–845. [CrossRef]
81. Lee, J.W. Long-run dynamics of renewable energy consumption on carbon emissions and economic growth in the European Union. *Int. J. Sustain. Dev. World Ecol.* **2019**, *26*, 69–78. [CrossRef]
82. Jebli, M.B.; Farhani, S.; Guesmi, K. Renewable energy, CO_2 emissions and value added: Empirical evidence from countries with different income levels. *Struct. Chang. Econ. Dyn.* **2020**, *53*, 402–410. [CrossRef]
83. Koengkan, M.; Santiago, J.A.F.R. The relationship between CO_2 emissions, renewable and non-renewable energy consumption, economic growth, and urbanisation in the Southern Common Market. *J. Environ. Econ. Policy* **2020**, *9*, 383–401. [CrossRef]
84. Usman, M.; Kousar, R.; Yaseen, M.R.; Makhdum, M.S.A. An empirical nexus between economic growth, energy utilization, trade policy, and ecological footprint: A continent-wise comparison in upper-middle-income countries. *Environ. Sci. Pollut. Res.* **2020**, *27*, 38995–39018. [CrossRef] [PubMed]
85. Wolde-Rufael, Y.; Weldemeskel, E.M. Environmental policy stringency, renewable energy consumption and CO_2 emissions: Panel cointegration analysis for BRIICTS countries. *Int. J. Green Energy* **2020**, *17*, 568–582. [CrossRef]
86. Heil, M.T.; Wodon, Q.T. Inequality in CO_2 emissions between poor and rich countries. *J. Environ. Dev.* **1997**, *6*, 426–452. [CrossRef]

electronics

MDPI

Article

A Wavenet-Based Virtual Sensor for PM_{10} Monitoring

Claudio Carnevale *, Enrico Turrini, Roberta Zeziola, Elena De Angelis and Marialuisa Volta

Department of Mechanical and Industrial Engineering, University of Brescia, I-25123 Brescia, Italy; enrico.turrini@unibs.it (E.T.); r.zeziola001@unibs.it (R.Z.); e.deangelis@unibs.it (E.D.A.); marialuisa.volta@unibs.it (M.V.)

* Correspondence: claudio.carnevale@unibs.it

Abstract: In this work, a virtual sensor for PM_{10} concentration monitoring is presented. The sensor is based on wavenet models and uses daily mean NO_2 concentration and meteorological variables (wind speed and rainfall) as input. The methodology has been applied to the reconstruction of PM_{10} levels measured from 14 monitoring stations in Lombardy region (Italy). This region, usually affected by high levels of PM_{10}, is a challenging benchmarking area for the implemented sensors. Neverthless, the performances are good with relatively low bias and high correlation.

Keywords: virtual sensors; wavenet; air quality

1. Introduction

Exposure to high levels of particulate matter (PM_{10}) is a big social problem [1] due to its impacts on human health, with effects including pulmonary and cardio-vascular diseases [2,3]. One of the main challenges in decision making related to PM_{10} control is that, usually, win–win solutions that also consider other pollutants, such as nitrogen oxides (NO_2) and ozone (O_3), are complex to identify and implement [4–7]. For this reason, having detailed information about the level of all of the significant air pollutants over a certain area is a key issue in decision-making processes. In this context, the use of integrated information coming from regional networks and novel/private networks supported by low-cost technology [8,9] has become more and more important, which has been mainly due to the fact that they can provide suitable information for chemical transport models (CTMs), allowing them to compute concentrations far away from the official monitoring network stations [10–12].

In principle, four main techniques for the measurement of PM_{10} are presented in literature [13]: (1) gravimetric analysis of pumped and filtered particles; (2) tapering element oscillating microbalance (TEOM); (3) beta-attenuation; (4) light scattering. The first three of these techniques are quite expensive, so their use is limited to regional authorities, private companies and research groups [13]. Light scattering, instead, is a relatively low-cost technique, but it is often affected by consistent biases [14].

The objective of this work is to evaluate the possibility of implementing a virtual sensor for PM_{10} daily mean concentration starting from the data measured by sensors detecting other pollutants and meteorological variables. In particular, the virtual sensors applied in this work are based on NO_2 daily mean concentration and meteorological variables, such as wind speed, rainfall, relative humidity and temperature.

As indicated by the name, virtual sensors can be broadly described as a software that allows us to compute the value of a certain variable without direct measurement considering measurements that are physically/chemically related to the variable that should be reproduced [15]. They assume a key role when it is not possible to place a physical sensor due to any kind of limitations (e.g., unreachable position, high cost). There are two possible approaches to virtual sensor implementation:

1. Data-driven: in this approach, time series of input and output variables are collected from direct measurement and are used to compute a mathematical, approximated relationship between the measured variables' and sensors' output [16];
2. Deterministic: in this approach, the (eventually approximated) physical/chemical relationships among input and output variables are used to compute the unmeasured variable through the virtual sensor [17].

This work presents a data-driven approach based on wavenet models to implement a PM_{10} virtual sensor using NO_2 and meteorological variables. All these variables are strictly related to the phenomena involved in the formation and accumulation of PM_{10} in atmosphere; their choice is due to the presence in the literature of low-cost sensors with performances that are adequate [18] enough to identify a virtual sensor, therefore allowing the definition of a low-cost PM_{10} measuring network. Wavenets are data-driven models resulting from the integration of wavelet theory and neural network models [19]. Their main applications are related to sound management/filtering [20], even if their nonlinear function approximation (and thus forecasting) properties have been applied with good results also in other fields such as energy systems [19,21]. These approximation properties make them suitable for environmental monitoring and forecasting applications, but still, there is no literature related to their application to reproduce PM_{10} or other air quality pollutants. Therefore, since artificial neural networks are widely used in this field [4,22,23], wavenets could also be useful for the definition of a PM_{10} virtual sensor. The paper is organized in two main parts, a methodological one (Section 2) where the basics of the artificial neural network, wavelet theory and wavenets are introduced and a second part presenting the evaluation of the results on a test case.

2. Materials and Methods

In this section, the theoretical framework used to derive a virtual air quality sensor based on wavenets [24] is presented.

2.1. Artificial Neural Networks

Artificial Neural Networks (ANNs) are functions approximating human brain behavior, considered as a network of smaller units, called neurons, representing the information processing unit (Figure 1).

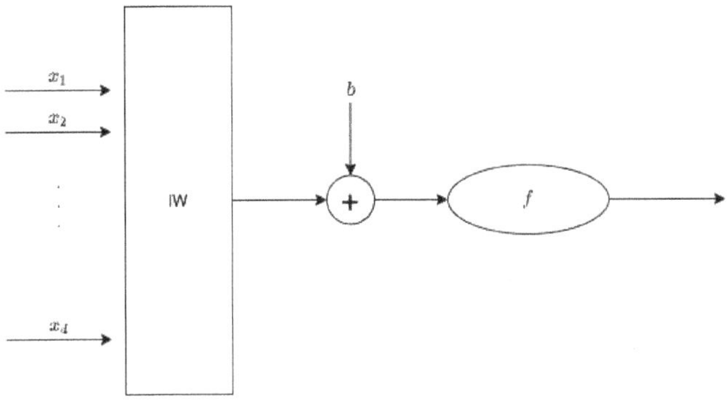

Figure 1. Typical neuron model.

Each input x_i of the network is multiplied by a corresponding weight w_i, analogous to a synaptic force; then all the weighted inputs are added together, including also a bias b term in order to compute the activation level x of the neuron. The output signal $y(x)$ is usually a nonlinear function $f(x)$ of the activation level. Hence, the typical neuron model is represented as (1):

$$y(x) = f\left(\sum_{i=1}^{d} x_i \times w_i + b\right) \quad (1)$$

where d is the length of the input vector.

The approximation capacity of a single neuron is quite limited; to overcome this, they are collected in layers sharing the same input. The final structure of a neural network is obtained by connecting several layers, as in the case of the two-layer feedforward neural network in Figure 2.

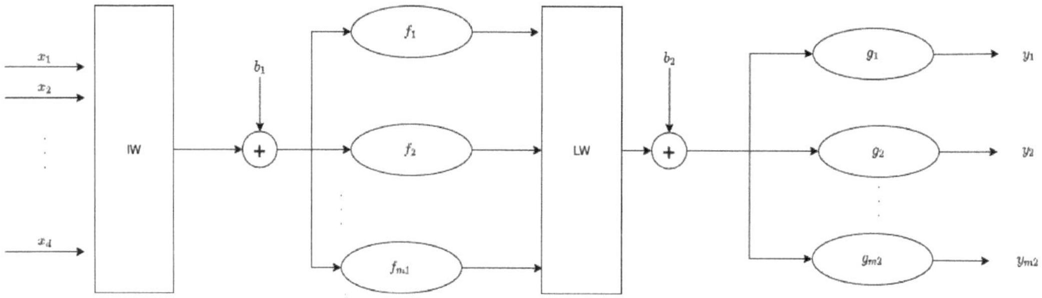

Figure 2. Two-layer feedforward neural network structure.

In this case, the output $y(x)$ can be computed as:

$$y(x) = g(LW \times f(IW \times x + b_1) + b_2) \quad (2)$$

where $y(x) \in \mathbb{R}^{m2}$ is the output of the network, $x \in \mathbb{R}^d$ is its input vector, $f : \mathbb{R}^d \to \mathbb{R}^{m1}$ and $g : \mathbb{R}^{m1} \to \mathbb{R}^{m2}$ are the activation functions of the hidden and output layers, respectively, and, finally, $m1$ and $m2$ are the lengths of the activation function output and the neural network output. The bias terms $b_1, b_2 \in \mathbb{R}^{m1}$ and the weight matrices $IW \in \mathbb{R}^{m1\times d}$ and $LW \in \mathbb{R}^{m2\times m1}$ are computed during the training phase. Even if the number of layers of an artificial neural network can be higher than 2, following the proof of the Cybenko approximation theorem, and in order to limit the complexity of the network, in real applications only a two layers neural network is used [25].

2.2. Wavelets and Wavenet Models

Wavelets are a family of orthonormal basis functions that can be used to perform transformations among spaces. Their use ranges from function approximation to audio compression [26–28]. The wavelet approximation theory is strictly related to multi-resolution analysis [26]. In this context, a function $h(x)$ can be approximated using the so-called wavelet (mother) and scaling (father) functions, as:

$$h(x) = \sum_k c_{j_0}(k)\phi_{j_0,k}(x) + \sum_{j=j_0}^{\infty}\sum_k d_j(k)\psi_{j,k}(x) \quad (3)$$

where:

- $c_{j_0}(k)$ are the scaling coefficients;
- $d_j(k)$ are the details (wavelet) coefficient;
- $\phi_{j_0,k}(x)$ is the selected scaling (father) function family;
- $\psi_{j,k}(x)$ is the selected wavelet (mother) function family.

The computation of the scaling and wavelet coefficient is strongly connected to the selected wavelet family (considered as the couple wavelet/scaling functions). Up to now, a number of different functions has been considered and are currently used. More details about wavelet transformation can be found in [26–28].

Wavenets (wavelet networks) [24] can be considered as a one hidden layer network with wavelets as activation functions. In particular, the wavenet output $Y(x)$ for an input $x \in \mathbb{R}^d$ can be computed as:

$$\begin{aligned} Y(x) = & WN(x) = (x-r)G+ \\ & + \sum_{i=1}^{n_s} a_{s\_i}\phi(b_{s\_i}((x-r)Q - c_{s\_i})+ \\ & + \sum_{j=1}^{n_w} a_{w\_j}\psi(b_{w\_j}((x-r)Q - c_{s\_j}) \end{aligned} \tag{4}$$

where $\phi(z) = e^{-0.5z \cdot z'}$, $z = b_{s\_i}((x-r)Q - c_{s\_i}$ is the scaling function, $\psi(t) = (m - t \cdot t')e^{-0.5t \cdot t'}$, $t = b_{w\_j}((x-r)Q - c_{s\_j})$ is the wavelet function, $x \in \mathbb{R}^{1 \times d}$ is the row vector input of the wavenet, $a_{s\_i}, b_{s\_i}, a_{w\_i}, b_{w\_i}, r \in \mathbb{R}^{1 \times d}$, $G \in \mathbb{R}^{d \times 1}$ and $Q \in \mathbb{R}^{d \times d}$ are the parameters to be computed during the training.

The comparison between Equations (2) and (4) shows that the wavenet can be considered as a neural network with the function:

$$f(\cdot) = \begin{bmatrix} \phi(\cdot) \\ \psi(\cdot) \end{bmatrix} \tag{5}$$

as the activation function of the hidden layer.

When the phenomena to model with the wavenet is dynamical, the wavenet is feeded by an input vector $x(t)$ that is the output of a time delay phase:

$$x(t) = \begin{bmatrix} u_1(t) \\ u_1(t-1) \\ \ldots \\ u_1(t-n_1) \\ \ldots \\ u_m(t) \\ u_m(t-1) \\ \ldots \\ u_m(t-n_m) \end{bmatrix} \tag{6}$$

where $u_1 \ldots u_m$ are the variables selected to compute the output $y(t)$ of the overall system. In this work, since the PM_{10} formation, accumulation and removal are clearly dynamical processes, the system structure presented in Figure 3 is used.

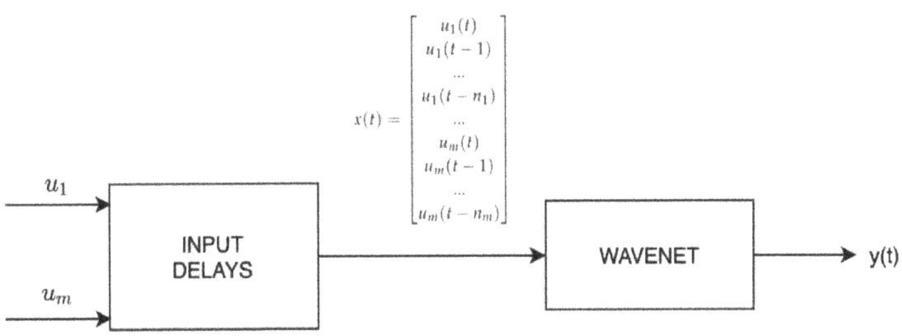

Figure 3. Wavenet structure.

3. Results and Discussion

3.1. Case Study and Dataset Definition

The aim of this work is the definition of a virtual sensor to compute PM_{10} daily average concentrations starting from the measured data of daily average NO_2 concentration and the measured values of two meteorological variables: average daily wind speed WS, total daily rainfall RF, average daily relative humidity RH and average daily temperature T. The selection of NO_2 as the input variable is due to the fact that its levels are strongly related to PM_{10} ones, as they shared some emission drivers (i.e., road traffic, domestic heating) and chemical paths (i.e., formation of secondary inorganic aerosol starting from the ammonium nitrates). On the other hand, the selected meteorological variables can be related to general deposition or dispersion conditions (mainly rainfall and wind speed) or to the formation of secondary aerosol by condensation. Thus, the $Y(x)$ in Equation (4) is the dailyPM_{10} concentration computed by the model, which is referred to as n$P\hat{M}_{10}(x)$ from now on. Moreover, the input x of the wavenet function is time dependent, so $x = x(t)$, and it includes both NO_2 concentrations and meteorological variables for the day t and the previous days, as in:

$$x(t) = \begin{bmatrix} NO_2(t) \\ NO_2(t-1) \\ \dots \\ NO_2(t-n_{NO_2}) \\ \dots \\ WS(t) \\ WS(t-1) \\ \dots \\ WS(t-n_{WS}) \\ \dots \\ RF(t) \\ RF(t-1) \\ \dots \\ RF(t-n_{RF}) \\ \dots \\ RH(t) \\ RH(t-1) \\ \dots \\ RH(t-n_{RH}) \\ \dots \\ T(t) \\ T(t-1) \\ \dots \\ T(t-n_T) \end{bmatrix} \quad (7)$$

In order to test the presented methodology, a series of models has been trained and validated to reproduce the PM_{10} daily mean concentrations starting from different input measured by the Lombardy region monitoring network. The work has been tested using data measured by 14 monitoring stations belonging to the Lombardy region (Italy) monitoring network (Figure 4).

More in detail, the data from year 2019 have been used ($365 \times 14 = 5110$ available raw data tuples). The performance evaluation for the different models has been performed using a leave-p-out approach with $p = 4$. Following this approach, 100 tests have been performed for each model configuration, with 10 stations being used for the identification, and the data for $p = 4$ being randomly selected as stations queued in order to define the metastation used for the validation.

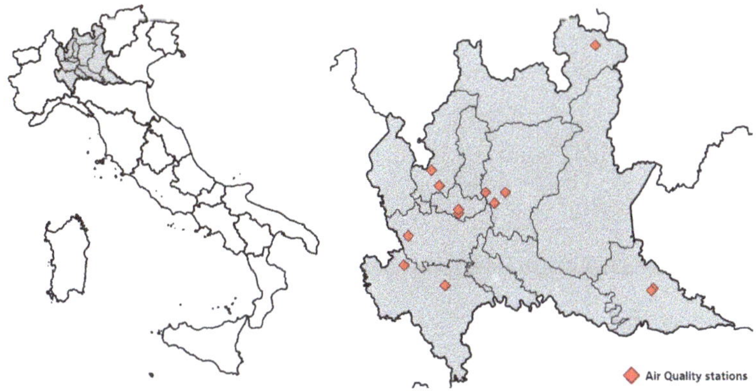

Figure 4. Domain and measuring stations.

3.2. Configuration Tests

In order to evaluate the capability of the methodology presented in Section 2 to compute PM_{10} concentrations, all the possible configurations among the input variables have been considered, and the relative models $PM_{10} = WN(x)$ trained.

In principle, the different configurations can be grouped into three categories:

- Configurations including only NO_2 concentration as input;
- Configurations including only meteorological variables as input;
- Configurations including both NO_2 concentrations and meteorological variables as input.

For each test, an analysis of the memory of the systems, i.e., an evaluation of the performances of varying n_{NO_2}, n_{WS}, n_{RF}, n_{RH} and n_T, has been performed. On the basis of the knowledge of the phenomena related to the formation of PM_{10} in atmosphere, a maximum value of 5 days can be considered for these parameters. Each model has been evaluated on the basis of the following three different statistical indexes:

- Normalized Root Mean Squared Deviation:

$$NRMSD = \frac{\sqrt{\frac{\sum_{t=1}^{T}(PM_{10}(t)-\hat{PM}_{10}(t))^2}{n}}}{PM_{10}^{max}-PM_{10}^{min}}$$

- Root Mean Squared Error

$$RMSE = \sqrt{\frac{\sum_{t=1}^{T}(PM_{10}(t)-\hat{PM}_{10}(t))^2}{T}}$$

- Correlation Coefficient

$$Correlation = \frac{\sum_{t=1}^{T}(PM_{10}(t)-\mu_{PM_{10}})(\hat{PM}_{10}(t)-\mu_{\hat{PM}_{10}})}{\sqrt{\sum_{t=1}^{T}(PM_{10}(t)-\mu_{PM_{10}})^2}\cdot\sqrt{\sum_{t=1}^{T}(\hat{PM}_{10}(t)-\mu_{\hat{PM}_{10}})^2}}$$

where $\hat{PM}_{10}(t)$ and $PM_{10}(t)$ are, respectively, the t-th values of the model output and of the validation dataset, and $\mu_{\hat{PM}_{10}}$ and $\mu_{PM_{10}}$ are their mean values. From the huge set of performed tests, only the best-performing ones are presented in this context, in particular for the combination of multiple input.

3.3. Validation Results

3.3.1. Models with NO_2 as Input

This first class of models includes only NO_2 daily mean concentrations as input. This is due to the fact that PM_{10} and NO_2

concentrations are generated by several common emitting activities (i.e., road transport) and that the secondary inorganic fraction of PM_{10} is composed, in part, of nitrates, in particular ammonia nitrate, whose formation depends on the NO_2 concentration in atmosphere. Table 1 highlights that the performances are quite good in terms of correlation, with values around 0.74, and acceptable in terms of root mean square error, with a normalised root mean standard deviation (allowing one to compare the root mean square error with respect to the overall variability of the output time series) around 0.1.

From these results, it is clear that an increase in the memory of the system does not lead to significant impacts on the performances and on the behavior of the model. The negligible increase in performances for the test with $n_{NO_2} = 4$ does not justify the increasing number of parameters. Table 2 shows the performances for the same configurations for the part of the time series where PM_{10} concentrations higher than 30 $\mu g/m^3$ have been measured. The table states that the model has strong difficulties in reproducing high concentrations, as highlighted by the strong decrease in statistical indexes.

3.3.2. Models with Meteorological Variables as Input

The second class of models considers only the meteorological variables as input. These tests allow an assessment of the relative "importance" between meteorology and NO_2 concentration for the computation of PM_{10} levels. Tables 3 and 4 show poor performances, with the limited exception of the cases with temperature T as input. Thus, the performances suggest that the meteorological conditions alone are not enough to estimate PM_{10} concentrations, and, so, they may be at best used to increase the performances in addition to the NO_2 concentrations.

Table 1. NO_2 input configuration performances.

	$x = \{NO_2\}$
	$n_{NO_2} = 1$
correlation	0.723
RMSE	10.896
NRMSD	0.1101
	$n_{NO_2} = 2$
correlation	0.722
RMSE	10.927
NRMSD	0.1104
	$n_{NO_2} = 3$
correlation	0.732
RMSE	10.764
NRMSD	0.1087
	$n_{NO_2} = 4$
correlation	0.733
RMSE	10.743
NRMSD	0.1085
	$n_{NO_2} = 5$
correlation	0.742
RMSE	10.575
NRMSD	0.1068

Table 2. NO_2 input configuration performances for $PM_{10} > 30\ \mu g/m^3$.

	$x = \{NO_2\}$
	$n_{NO_2} = 1$
correlation	0.39
RMSE	11.531
NRMSD	0.1696
	$n_{NO_2} = 2$
correlation	0.39
RMSE	11.481
NRMSD	0.1688
	$n_{NO_2} = 3$
correlation	0.41
RMSE	11.390
NRMSD	0.1675
	$n_{NO_2} = 4$
correlation	0.40
RMSE	11.412
NRMSD	0.1678
	$n_{NO_2} = 5$
correlation	0.40
RMSE	11.444
NRMSD	0.1683

Table 3. Meteorological input configuration performances.

	$x = \{WS\}$	$x = \{RF\}$	$x = \{RH\}$	$x = \{T\}$	$x = \{RH, T\}$
	$n_{WS} = 1$	$n_{RF} = 1$	$n_{RH} = 1$	$n_T = 1$	$n_{RH,T} = 1$
correlation	0.33	0.10	0.150	0.461	0.47
RMSE	16.733	16.622	16.380	14.807	14.736
NRMSD	0.1690	0.1679	0.1655	0.1496	0.1488
	$n_{WS} = 2$	$n_{RF} = 2$	$n_{RH} = 2$	$n_T = 2$	$n_{RH,T} = 2$
correlation	0.37	0.18	0.185	0.494	0.50
RMSE	16.723	16.486	16.132	14.551	14.469
NRMSD	0.1689	0.1665	0.1630	0.1470	0.1462
	$n_{WS} = 3$	$n_{RF} = 3$	$n_{RH} = 3$	$n_T = 3$	$n_{RH,T} = 3$
correlation	0.37	0.23	0.171	0.503	0.52
RMSE	16.899	16.283	16.176	14.467	14.385
NRMSD	0.1707	0.1644	0.1634	0.1461	0.1453
	$n_{WS} = 4$	$n_{RF} = 4$	$n_{RH} = 4$	$n_T = 4$	$n_{RH,T} = 4$
correlation	0.38	0.27	0.190	0.513	0.513
RMSE	16.912	15.9010	16.085	14.347	14.474
NRMSD	0.1708	0.1606	0.1625	0.1449	0.1462
	$n_{WS} = 5$	$n_{RF} = 5$	$n_{RH} = 5$	$n_T = 5$	$n_{RH,T} = 5$
correlation	0.339	0.30	0.183	0.514	0.52
RMSE	16.846	15.730	16.126	14.348	14.419
NRMSD	0.1701	0.1588	0.1629	0.1449	0.1456

Table 4. Meteorological input configuration performances for $PM_{10} > 30$ µg/m^3.

	$x = \{WS\}$	$x = \{RF\}$	$x = \{RH\}$	$x = \{T\}$	$x = \{RH, T\}$
	$n_{WS} = 1$	$n_{RF} = 1$	$n_{RH} = 1$	$n_T = 1$	$n_{UT} = 1$
correlation	0.19	0.079	0.15	0.35	0.32
RMSE	12.711	12.517	12.296	11.732	11.889
NRMSD	0.1869	0.1841	0.1808	0.1725	0.1748
	$n_{WS} = 2$	$n_{RF} = 2$	$n_{RH} = 2$	$n_T = 2$	$n_{UT} = 2$
correlation	0.196	0.153	0.18	0.40	0.43
RMSE	12.862	12.425	12.231	11.411	11.263
NRMSD	0.1891	0.1827	0.1799	0.1678	0.1656
	$n_{WS} = 3$	$n_{RF} = 3$	$n_{RH} = 3$	$n_T = 3$	$n_{UT} = 3$
correlation	0.185	0.212	0.20	0.43	0.40
RMSE	12.935	12.272	12.193	11.220	11.536
NRMSD	0.1902	0.1805	0.1793	0.1650	0.1696
	$n_{WS} = 4$	$n_{RF} = 4$	$n_{RH} = 4$	$n_T = 4$	$n_{UT} = 4$
correlation	0.24	0.210	0.17	0.44	0.42
RMSE	12.926	12.272	12.284	11.190	11.388
NRMSD	0.1901	0.1805	0.1806	0.1646	0.1675
	$n_{WS} = 5$	$n_{RF} = 5$	$n_{RH} = 5$	$n_T = 5$	$n_{UT} = 5$
correlation	0.192	0.220	0.20	0.44	0.45
RMSE	12.979	12.244	12.178	11.164	11.193
NRMSD	0.1909	0.1801	0.1791	0.1642	0.1646

3.3.3. Models with NO_2 and Meteorological Variables as Input

The last class of models considers both the meteorological variables and the NO_2 daily mean concentration as input in order to evaluate if the joint use of these information sources leads to an increase in the performances. Table 5 presents the results with NO_2 concentrations coupled to a meteorological variable at a certain time. The performances are in line with that of the models with only NO_2 as an input. Moreover, the combined use of more than one meteorological variable did not lead to a consistent increase in performance (Tables 6–8). The only slight improvement can be seen for high concentrations when the temperature is used as input (Tables 9–12), but also, in this case, the performances seem not to be good enough (correlation coefficient close to 0.52) in the preproduction of the peaks. These results suggest that, to reproduce mean PM_{10} levels in this domain, only the NO_2 concentrations should used, thus relying on cheaper sensors. Nevertheless, a bond in the performances exists, which did not allow the reconstruction of peak concentrations.

Table 5. NO_2 and one meteorological variable input configuration performance.

	$x = \{NO_2, WS\}$	$x = \{NO_2, RF\}$	$x = \{NO_2, RH\}$	$x = \{NO_2, T\}$
	$n_{NO_2,WS} = 1$	$n_{NO_2,RF} = 1$	$n_{NO_2,RH} = 1$	$n_{NO_2,T} = 1$
correlation	0.69	0.72	0.71	0.72
RMSE	11.285	10.987	10.969	10.808
NRMSD	0.1139	0.1109	0.1108	0.1092
	$n_{NO_2,WS} = 2$	$n_{NO_2,RF} = 2$	$n_{NO_2,RH} = 2$	$n_{NO_2,T} = 2$
correlation	0.70	0.73	0.72	0.73
RMSE	11.207	10.796	10.916	10.672
NRMSD	0.1132	0.1090	0.1103	0.1078
	$n_{NO_2,WS} = 3$	$n_{NO_2,RF} = 3$	$n_{NO_2,RH} = 3$	$n_{NO_2,T} = 3$
correlation	0.71	0.73	0.72	0.73
RMSE	11.042	10.735	10.890	10.669
NRMSD	0.1115	0.1084	0.1100	0.1078
	$n_{NO_2,WS} = 4$	$n_{NO_2,RF} = 4$	$n_{NO_2,RH} = 4$	$n_{NO_2,T} = 4$
correlation	0.71	0.731	0.72	0.74
RMSE	11.007	10.670	10.906	10.543
NRMSD	0.1111	0.1077	0.1102	0.1065
	$n_{NO_2,WS} = 5$	$n_{NO_2,RF} = 5$	$n_{NO_2,RH} = 5$	$n_{NO_2,T} = 5$
correlation	0.711	0.741	0.71	0.73
RMSE	10.950	10.500	10.954	10.716
NRMSD	0.1106	0.1060	0.1106	0.1082

Table 6. NO_2 and two meteorological variable input best configuration performances.

	$x = \{NO_2, WS, RF\}$	$x = \{NO_2, RH, T\}$	$x = \{NO_2, WS, T\}$	$x = \{NO_2, RF, RH\}$	$x = \{NO_2, RF, T\}$
	$n_{NO_2,WS,RF} = 1$	$n_{NO_2,RH,T} = 1$	$n_{NO_2,WS,T} = 1$	$n_{NO_2,RF,RH} = 1$	$n_{NO_2,RF,T} = 1$
correlation	0.70	0.72	0.70	0.72	0.73
RMSE	11.132	10.859	11.103	10.870	10.768
NRMSD	0.1124	0.1097	0.1122	0.1098	0.1088
	$n_{NO_2,WS,RF} = 2$	$n_{NO_2,RH,T} = 2$	$n_{NO_2,WS,T} = 2$	$n_{NO_2,RF,RH} = 2$	$n_{NO_2,RF,T} = 2$
correlation	0.72	0.73	0.69	0.725	0.73
RMSE	10.844	10.743	11.385	10.748	10.725
NRMSD	0.1095	0.1085	0.1150	0.1086	0.1083
	$n_{NO_2,WS,RF} = 3$	$n_{NO_2,RH,T} = 3$	$n_{NO_2,WS,T} = 3$	$n_{NO_2,RF,RH} = 3$	$n_{NO_2,RF,T} = 3$
correlation	0.711	0.73	0.72	0.72	0.73
RMSE	10.945	10.690	10.945	10.837	10.690
NRMSD	0.1105	0.1080	0.1106	0.1095	0.1080
	$n_{NO_2,WS,RF} = 4$	$n_{NO_2,RH,T} = 4$	$n_{NO_2,WS,T} = 4$	$n_{NO_2,RF,RH} = 4$	$n_{NO_2,RF,T} = 4$
correlation	0.72	0.72	0.73	0.71	0.73
RMSE	10.803	10.849	10.823	10.965	10.752
NRMSD	0.1091	0.1096	0.1093	0.1108	0.1086
	$n_{NO_2,WS,RF} = 5$	$n_{NO_2,RH,T} = 5$	$n_{NO_2,WS,T} = 5$	$n_{NO_2,RF,RH} = 5$	$n_{NO_2,RF,T} = 5$
correlation	0.731	0.72	0.72	0.70	0.71
RMSE	10.62	10.880	10.918	11.109	11.032
NRMSD	0.1072	0.1099	0.1103	0.1122	0.1114

Table 7. NO_2 and three meteorological variable input configuration performances.

	$x = \{NO_2, RF, RH, T\}$	$x = \{NO_2, WS, RF, RH\}$	$x = \{NO_2, WS, RF, T\}$
	$n_{NO_2,RF,RH,T} = 1$	$n_{NO_2,WS,RF,RH} = 1$	$n_{NO_2,WS,RF,T} = 1$
correlation	0.72	0.692	0.71
RMSE	10.841	11.241	10.992
NRMSD	0.1095	0.1135	0.1110
	$n_{NO_2,RF,RH,T} = 2$	$n_{NO_2,WS,RF,RH} = 2$	$n_{NO_2,WS,RF,T} = 2$
correlation	0.72	0.72	0.71
RMSE	10.826	10.868	11.064
NRMSD	0.1094	0.1098	0.1118
	$n_{NO_2,RF,RH,T} = 3$	$n_{NO_2,WS,RF,RH} = 3$	$n_{NO_2,WS,RF,T} = 3$
correlation	0.72	0.703	0.72
RMSE	10.869	11.084	10.916
NRMSD	0.1097	0.1119	0.1098
	$n_{NO_2,RF,RH,T} = 4$	$n_{NO_2,WS,RF,RH} = 4$	$n_{NO_2,WS,RF,T} = 4$
correlation	0.70	0.71	0.721
RMSE	11.098	10.032	11.163
NRMSD	0.1121	0.1114	0.1128
	$n_{NO_2,RF,RH,T} = 5$	$n_{NO_2,WS,RF,RH} = 5$	$n_{NO_2,WS,RF,T} = 5$
correlation	0.69	0.70	0.714
RMSE	11.324	11.207	11.071
NRMSD	0.1144	0.1132	0.1118

Table 8. NO_2 and four meteorological variable input configuration performances.

	$x = \{NO_2, WS, RF, RH, T\}$
	$n_{NO_2,WS,RF,RH,T} = 1$
correlation	0.70
RMSE	11.046
NRMSD	0.1116
	$n_{NO_2,WS,RF,U,T} = 2$
correlation	0.72
RMSE	10.926
NRMSD	0.1104
	$n_{NO_2,WS,RF,U,T} = 3$
correlation	0.73
RMSE	10.788
NRMSD	0.1090
	$n_{NO_2,WS,RF,U,T} = 4$
correlation	0.71
RMSE	11.632
NRMSD	0.1127
	$n_{NO_2,WS,RF,U,T} = 5$
correlation	0.71
RMSE	11.297
NRMSD	0.1141

Table 9. NO_2 one meteorological variable input configuration performance for $PM_{10} > 30$ µg/m^3.

	$x = \{NO_2, WS\}$	$x = \{NO_2, RF\}$	$x = \{NO_2, RH\}$	$x = \{NO_2, T\}$
	$n_{NO_2,WS} = 1$	$n_{NO_2,RF} = 1$	$n_{NO_2,RH} = 1$	$n_{NO_2,T} = 1$
correlation	0.381	0.39	0.392	0.39
RMSE	12.176	11.492	11.474	11.445
NRMSD	0.1791	0.1690	0.1687	0.1683
	$n_{NO_2,WS} = 2$	$n_{NO_2,RF} = 2$	$n_{NO_2,RH} = 2$	$n_{NO_2,T} = 2$
correlation	0.39	0.401	0.422	0.49
RMSE	11.970	11.456	11.280	10.817
NRMSD	0.1760	0.1685	0.1659	0.1591
	$n_{NO_2,WS} = 3$	$n_{NO_2,RF} = 3$	$n_{NO_2,RH} = 3$	$n_{NO_2,T} = 3$
correlation	0.382	0.413	0.406	0.50
RMSE	12.086	11.384	11.467	10.744
NRMSD	0.1777	0.1674	0.1686	0.1580
	$n_{NO_2,WS} = 4$	$n_{NO_2,RF} = 4$	$n_{NO_2,RH} = 4$	$n_{NO_2,T} = 4$
correlation	0.40	0.405	0.395	0.51
RMSE	11.938	11.438	11.553	10.671
NRMSD	0.1756	0.1682	0.1699	0.1569
	$n_{NO_2,WS} = 5$	$n_{NO_2,RF} = 5$	$n_{NO_2,RH} = 5$	$n_{NO_2,T} = 5$
correlation	0.40	0.425	0.402	0.52
RMSE	11.855	11.311	11.498	10.570
NRMSD	0.1743	0.1663	0.1691	0.1554

Table 10. NO_2 and two meteorological variable input best configuration performances for $PM_{10} > 30$ µg/m^3.

	$x = \{NO_2, WS, RF\}$	$x = \{NO_2, RH, T\}$	$x = \{NO_2, WS, T\}$	$x = \{NO_2, RF, RH\}$	$x = \{NO_2, RF, T\}$
	$n_{NO_2,WS,RF} = 1$	$n_{NO_2,U,T} = 1$	$n_{NO_2,WS,T} = 1$	$n_{NO_2,RF,U} = 1$	$n_{NO_2,RF,T} = 1$
correlation	0.394	0.42	0.45	0.394	0.44
RMSE	12.058	11.246	11.445	11.458	11.160
NRMSD	0.1773	0.1654	0.1683	0.1685	0.1641
	$n_{NO_2,WS} = 2$	$n_{NO_2,U,T} = 2$	$n_{NO_2,WS,T} = 2$	$n_{NO_2,RF,U} = 2$	$n_{NO_2,RF,T} = 2$
correlation	0.39	0.503	0.47	0.414	0.485
RMSE	11.970	10.750	11.367	11.364	10.832
NRMSD	0.1760	0.1581	0.1672	0.1671	0.1593
	$n_{NO_2,WS} = 3$	$n_{NO_2,U,T} = 3$	$n_{NO_2,WS,T} = 3$	$n_{NO_2,RF,U} = 3$	$n_{NO_2,RF,T} = 3$
correlation	0.382	0.49	0.47	0.40	0.49
RMSE	12.086	10.895	11.237	11.575	10.825
NRMSD	0.1777	0.1602	0.1652	0.1702	0.1592
	$n_{NO_2,WS} = 4$	$n_{NO_2,U,T} = 4$	$n_{NO_2,WS,T} = 4$	$n_{NO_2,RF,U} = 4$	$n_{NO_2,RF,T} = 4$
correlation	0.40	0.50	0.51	0.40	0.51
RMSE	11.938	10.919	10.839	11.658	10.667
NRMSD	0.1756	0.1606	0.1594	0.1714	0.1569
	$n_{NO_2,WS} = 5$	$n_{NO_2,U,T} = 5$	$n_{NO_2,WS,T} = 5$	$n_{NO_2,RF,U} = 5$	$n_{NO_2,RF,T} = 5$
correlation	0.40	0.514	0.52	0.40	0.49
RMSE	11.855	10.707	10.703	11.632	10.856
NRMSD	0.1743	0.1575	0.1574	0.1711	0.1597

Table 11. NO_2 and three meteorological variable input configuration performances for $PM_{10} > 30\ \mu g/m^3$.

	$x = \{NO_2, RF, RH, T\}$	$x = \{NO_2, WS, RF, RH\}$	$x = \{NO_2, WS, RF, T\}$
	$n_{NO_2,RF,RH,T} = 1$	$n_{NO_2,WS,RF,RH} = 1$	$n_{NO_2,WS,RF,T} = 1$
correlation	0.430	0.390	0.436
RMSE	11.201	11.660	11.444
NRMSD	0.1647	0.1715	0.1683
	$n_{NO_2,RF,RH,T} = 2$	$n_{NO_2,WS,RF,RH} = 2$	$n_{NO_2,WS,RF,T} = 2$
correlation	0.503	0.407	0.462
RMSE	10.720	11.863	11.275
NRMSD	0.1576	0.1744	0.1658
	$n_{NO_2,RF,RH,T} = 3$	$n_{NO_2,WS,RF,RH} = 3$	$n_{NO_2,WS,RF,T} = 3$
correlation	0.49	0.381	0.478
RMSE	10.945	12.103	11.063
NRMSD	0.1610	0.1780	0.1627
	$n_{NO_2,RF,RH,T} = 4$	$n_{NO_2,WS,RF,RH} = 4$	$n_{NO_2,WS,RF,T} = 4$
correlation	0.503	0.396	0.498
RMSE	10.892	12.077	10.846
NRMSD	0.1602	0.1776	0.1595
	$n_{NO_2,RF,RH,T} = 5$	$n_{NO_2,WS,RF,RH} = 5$	$n_{NO_2,WS,RF,T} = 5$
correlation	0.511	0.399	0.518
RMSE	10.756	11.953	10.678
NRMSD	0.1582	0.1758	0.1570

Table 12. NO_2 and four meteorological variable input configuration performances for $PM_{10} > 30\ \mu g/m^3$.

	$x = \{NO_2, WS, RF, RH, T\}$
	$n_{NO_2,WS,RF,RH,T} = 1$
correlation	0.425
RMSE	11.484
NRMSD	0.1689
	$n_{NO_2,WS,RF,RH,T} = 2$
correlation	0.494
RMSE	11.067
NRMSD	0.1627
	$n_{NO_2,WS,RF,RH,T} = 3$
correlation	0.484
RMSE	11.191
NRMSD	0.1646
	$n_{NO_2,WS,RF,RH,T} = 4$
correlation	0.492
RMSE	11.107
NRMSD	0.1633
	$n_{NO_2,WS,RF,RH,T} = 5$
correlation	0.522
RMSE	10.875
NRMSD	0.1599

3.4. Comparison to State-of-the-Art Models

In this section, the comparison of the wavenet approach used in this work with two different state-of-the-art models is presented. The two models are a (1) K-nearest neighbors (KNN) and an (2) artificial neural network-based model, which are often used in this context to capture the dynamic of the PM_{10} [29]. The comparison (Table 13) shows how the performances of the best-identified wavenet are strongly better than that of the KNN model and very similar (slightly better for high orders) to that of the ANN ones. Moreover, it has to be stressed how the best model for the wavenet approach ensures these performances with limited complexity and with a limited number of variables (only NO_2 concentration) with respect to the other approaches.

Figures 5–7 present the time series plots for the best configuration of wavenet, artificial neural network and KNN models, respectively. As expected, the behaviour of the wavenet and ANN models is very similar, with the first models showing slightly better performances for the low value close to the sample n. 800. In general, the KNN model reproduces higher value but, as also stated by the lower values of correlation coefficient, the time series rarely follows the value and the gradient of the measured values.

Table 13. Best configuration performances.

	WT ($x = \{NO_2\}$)	**ANN** ($x = \{NO_2, RF\}$)	**KNN** ($x = \{NO_2, WS, RF, U\}$)
	$n_{NO_2} = 1$	$n_{NO_2,RF} = 1$	$n_{NO_2,WS,RF,U} = 1$
correlation	0.723	0.72	0.523
RMSE	10.896	10.940	14.860
NRMSD	0.1101	0.1105	0.1501
	$n_{NO_2} = 2$	$n_{NO_2,RF} = 2$	$n_{NO_2,WS,RF,U} = 2$
correlation	0.722	0.732	0.581
RMSE	10.927	10.651	14.082
NRMSD	0.1104	0.1076	0.1422
	$n_{NO_2} = 3$	$n_{NO_2,RF} = 3$	$n_{NO_2,WS,RF,U} = 3$
correlation	0.732	0.72	0.59
RMSE	10.764	10.877	13.904
NRMSD	0.1087	0.1099	0.1404
	$n_{NO_2} = 4$	$n_{NO_2,RF} = 4$	$n_{NO_2,WS,RF,U} = 4$
correlation	0.733	0.713	0.61
RMSE	10.743	10.909	13.628
NRMSD	0.1085	0.1102	0.1377
	$n_{NO_2} = 5$	$n_{NO_2,RF} = 5$	$n_{NO_2,WS,RF,U} = 5$
correlation	0.742	0.73	0.634
RMSE	10.575	10.675	13.435
NRMSD	0.1068	0.1078	0.1357

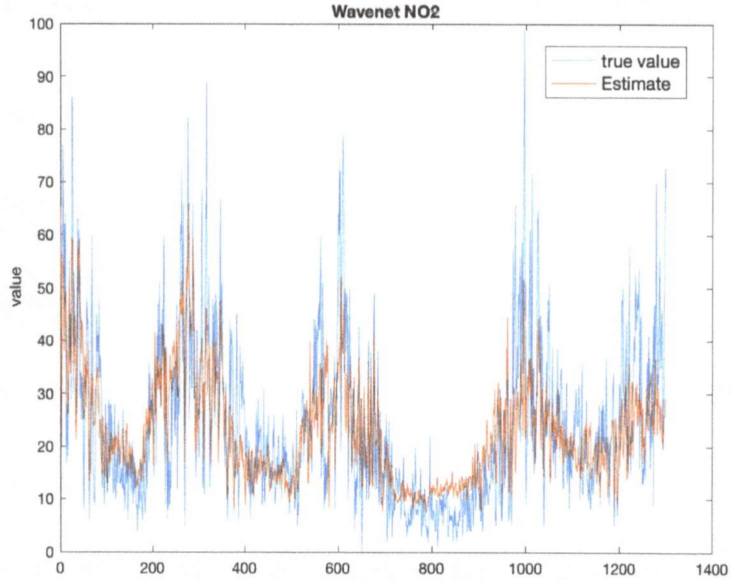

Figure 5. Time series comparison between the measured values (blue) and the best wavenet model output ($n_{NO_2} = 5$, red).

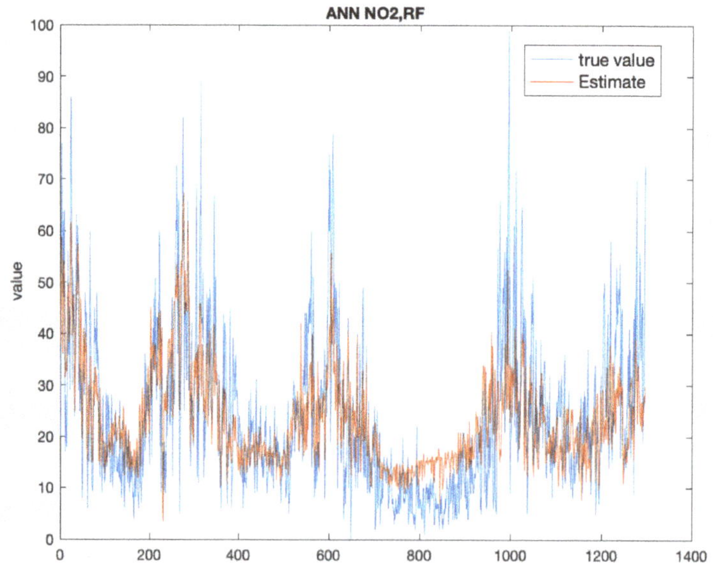

Figure 6. Time series comparison between the measured values (blue) and the best neural network model output ($n_{NO_2,RF} = 2$, red).

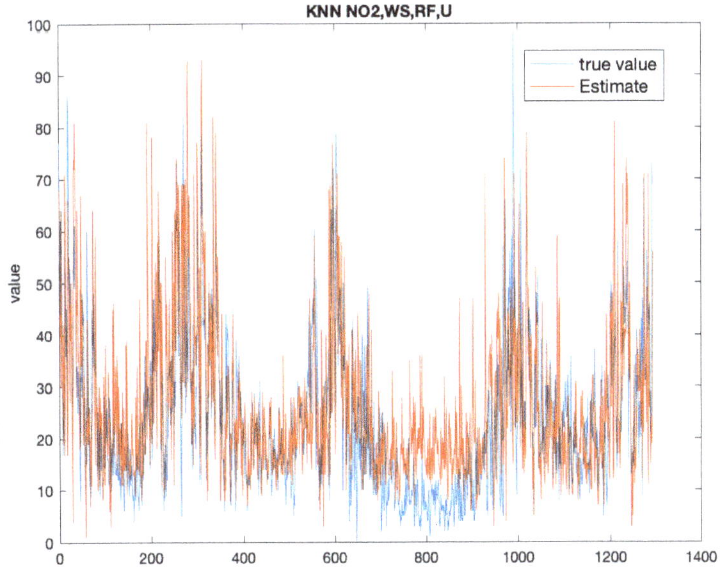

Figure 7. Time series comparison between the measured values (blue) and the best KNN model output ($n_{NO_2,RF} = 5$, red).

4. Conclusions

In this work, a data-driven, wavenet-based virtual sensor for PM_{10} daily mean concentration is presented and evaluated. Different model configurations have been tested and evaluated. The methodology has been applied to data measured by the Lombardy regional monitoring network. The results show good agreement between the output of the virtual sensor and the measured data used for validation when the daily mean NO_2 concentration is used as input—in particular, around the mean concentration values. Therefore, the models fail to reproduce the peak concentrations, and this behaviour will not change even if other inputs, such as meteorological data, are used. Nevertheless, the performances show that this approach can be used to produce supporting information to integrate the regional monitoring network that can be made available through app/web services due to a relatively fast computation.

Author Contributions: Conceptualization, C.C., E.T., R.Z.; software, C.C., R.Z.; validation, C.C., E.D.A., M.V.; funding acquisition, M.V. All authors have read and agreed to the published version of the manuscript.

Funding: This research received no external funding.

Conflicts of Interest: The authors declare no conflict of interest.

References

1. Landrigan, P.; Fuller, R.; Acosta, N.; Adeyi, O.; Arnold, R.; Basu, N.; Baldé, A.; Bertollini, R.; Bose-O'Reilly, S.; Boufford, J.; et al. The Lancet Commission on pollution and health. *Lancet* **2018**, *391*, 462–512. [CrossRef]
2. Pope, C., III; Dockery, D.; Spengler, J.; Raizenne, M. Respiratory health and PM_{10} pollution: A daily time series analysis. *Am. Rev. Respir. Dis.* **1991**, *144*, 668–674. [CrossRef]
3. Pope, C., III; Dockery, D. Acute health effects of PM_{10} pollution on symptomatic and asymptomatic children. *Am. Rev. Respir. Dis.* **1992**, *145*, 1123–1128. [CrossRef] [PubMed]
4. Turrini, E.; Carnevale, C.; Finzi, G.; Volta, M. A non-linear optimization programming model for air quality planning including co-benefits for GHG emissions. *Sci. Total Environ.* **2018**, *621*, 980–989. [CrossRef]
5. Carnevale, C.; Ferrari, F.; Guariso, G.; Maffeis, G.; Turrini, E.; Volta, M. Assessing the Economic and Environmental Sustainability of a Regional Air Quality Plan. *Sustainability* **2018**, *10*, 3568. [CrossRef]
6. Gimez Vilchez, J.; Julea, A.; Peduzzi, E.; Pisoni, E.; Krause, J.; Siskos, P.; Thiel, C. Modelling the impacts of EU countries electric car deployment plans on atmospheric emissions and concentrations. *Eur. Transp. Res. Rev.* **2019**, *11*, 40. [CrossRef]

7. Relvas, H.; Miranda, A.; Carnevale, C.; Maffeis, G.; Turrini, E.; Volta, M. Optimal air quality policies and health: A multi-objective nonlinear approach. *Environ. Sci. Pollut. Res.* **2017**, *24*, 13687–13699. [CrossRef]
8. Marques, G.; Pires, I.M.; Miranda, N.; Pitarma, R. Air Quality Monitoring Using Assistive Robots for Ambient Assisted Living and Enhanced Living Environments through Internet of Things. *Electronics* **2019**, *8*, 1375. [CrossRef]
9. Arroyo, P.; Lozano, J.; Suárez, J. Evolution of Wireless Sensor Network for Air Quality Measurements. *Electronics* **2018**, *7*, 342. [CrossRef]
10. Carnevale, C.; Finzi, G.; Pederzoli, A.; Pisoni, E.; Thunis, P.; Turrini, E.; Volta, M. A methodology for the evaluation of re-analyzed PM10 concentration fields: A case study over the PO Valley. *Air Qual. Atmos. Health* **2015**, *8*, 533–544. [CrossRef]
11. Candiani, G.; Carnevale, C.; Finzi, G.; Pisoni, E.; Volta, M. A comparison of reanalysis techniques: Applying optimal interpolation and Ensemble Kalman Filtering to improve air quality monitoring at mesoscale. *Sci. Total Environ.* **2013**, *458–460*, 7–14. [CrossRef]
12. Carnevale, C.; Finzi, G.; Pederzoli, A.; Turrini, E.; Volta, M.; Ferrari, F.; Gianfreda, R.; Maffeis, G. Impact of pollutant emission reductions on summertime aerosol feedbacks: A case study over the PO valley. *Atmos. Environ.* **2015**, *122*, 41–57. [CrossRef]
13. Winkel, A.; Llorens Rubio, J.; Huis in't Veld, J.W.; Vonk, J.; Ogink, N.W. Equivalence testing of filter-based, beta-attenuation, TEOM, and light-scattering devices for measurement of PM10 concentration in animal houses. *J. Aerosol. Sci.* **2015**, *80*, 11–26. [CrossRef]
14. Costa, A.; Guarino, M. Definition of yearly emission factor of dust and greenhouse gases through continuous measurements in swine husbandry. *Atmos. Environ.* **2009**, *43*, 1548–1556. [CrossRef]
15. Pathak, D.; Halale, V.P. An Introductory Approach to Virtual Sensors and Its Modelling Techniques. *Sci. Eng. Res.* **2016**, *7*, 461–464.
16. Sun, S.; He, Y.; Zhou, S.D.; Yue, Z.J. A Data-Driven Response Virtual Sensor Technique with Partial Vibration Measurements Using Convolutional Neural Network. *Sensors* **2017**, *17*, 2888. [CrossRef]
17. Kuo, S.; Zhou, M. Virtual sensing techniques and their applications. In Proceedings of the International Conference on Networking, Sensing and Control, Okayama, Japan, 26–29 March 2009; pp. 31–39
18. Rai, A.C.; Kumar, P.; Pilla, F.; Skouloudis, A.N.; Sabatino, S.D.; Ratti, C.; Yasar, A.; Rickerby, D. End-user perspective of low-cost sensors for outdoor air pollution monitoring. *Sci. Total Environ.* **2017**, *607–608*, 691–705. [CrossRef]
19. Saljooghi, S.; Hezarkarkhani, A. Comparison of WAVENET and ANN for predicting the porosity obtained from well log data. *J. Petrol. Sci. Eng.* **2014**, *123*, 172–182. [CrossRef]
20. van den Oord, A.; Dieleman, S.; Zen, H.; Simonyan, K.; Vinyals, O.; Graves, A.; Kalchbrenner, N.; Senior, A.; Kavukcuoglu, K. WaveNet: A Generative Model for Raw Audio. *arXiv* **2016**, arXiv:1609.03499.
21. Saljooghi, S.; Hezarkarkhani, A. A new approach to improve permeability prediction of petroleum reservois using neural network adaptive wavelet (Wavenet). *J. Petrol. Sci. Eng.* **2015**, *123*, 851–861. [CrossRef]
22. Carnevale, C.; Angelis, E.; Finzi, G.; Turrini, E.; Volta, M. Application of data fusion techniques to improve air quality forecast: A case study in the Northern Italy. *Atmosphere* **2020**, *11*, 244. [CrossRef]
23. Carnevale, C.; De Angelis, E.; Tagliani, F.; Turrini, E.; Volta, M. A short-term air quality control for PM_{10} levels. *Electronics* **2020**, *9*, 1409. [CrossRef]
24. Sujatha, P. *Vibration and Acoustics: Measurement and Signal Analysis*; McGraw-Hill Education: Gautam Buddha Nagar, India, 2010.
25. Cybenko, G. Approximation by Superposition of a Sigmoidal Function. *Math. Control Signals Syst.* **1989**, *2*, 303–314. [CrossRef]
26. Mallat, S. A Theory for Multiresolution Signal Decomposition The Wavelet Representation. *IEEE Trans. Pattern Anal. Mach. Intell.* **1989**, *11*, 674–693. [CrossRef]
27. Zakeri, V.; Naghavi, V.; Safavi, A. Developing real-time wave-net models for non-linear time-varying experimental processes. *Comput. Chem. Eng.* **2009**, *33*, 1379–1385. [CrossRef]
28. Postalcioglu, S.; Erkan, K.; Bolat, E.D. Comparison of Wavenet and Neuralnet for System Modeling. In *Knowledge-Based Intelligent Information and Engineering Systems*; Khosla, R., Howlett, R.J., Jain, L.C., Eds.; Springer: Berlin/Heidelberg, Germany, 2005; pp. 100–107.
29. Carnevale, C.; Finzi, G.; Guariso, G.; Pisoni, E.; Volta, M. Surrogate models to compute optimal air quality planning policies at a regional scale. *Environ. Model. Softw.* **2012**, *34*, 44–50. [CrossRef]

electronics

MDPI

Article

Dimensioning an FPGA for Real-Time Implementation of State of the Art Neural Network-Based HPA Predistorter

Abdelhamid Louliej [1], Younes Jabrane [2], Víctor P. Gil Jiménez [3,*] and Frédéric Guilloud [4]

1 SHTC Team, Ibn Zohr University, Agadir 80000, Morocco; a.louliej@uca.ac.ma
2 MSC Lab, Cadi Ayyad University, Marrakech 40000, Morocco; y.jabrane@uca.ma
3 Department of Signal Theory and Communications, University Carlos III de Madrid, 28911 Leganés, Madrid, Spain
4 IMT Atlantique, Lab-STICC, UMR CNRS 6285, F-29238 Brest, France; frederic.guilloud@imt-atlantique.fr
* Correspondence: vgil@tsc.uc3m.es; Tel.: +34-916-245-973

Abstract: Orthogonal Frequency Division Multiplexing (OFDM) is one of the key modulations for current and novel broadband communications standards. For example, Multi-band Orthogonal Frequency Division Multiplexing (MB-OFDM) is an excellent choice for the ECMA-368 Ultra Wideband (UWB) wireless communication standard. Nevertheless, the high Peak to Average Power Ratio (PAPR) of MB-OFDM UWB signals reduces the power efficiency of the key element in mobile devices, the High Power Amplifier (HPA), due to non-linear distortion, known as the non-linear saturation of the HPA. In order to deal with this limiting problem, a new and efficient pre-distorter scheme using a Neural Networks (NN) is proposed and also implemented on Field Programmable Gate Array (FPGA). This solution based on the pre-distortion concept of HPA non-linearities offers a good trade-off between complexity and performance. Some tests and validation have been conducted on the two types of HPA: Travelling Wave Tube Amplifiers (TWTA) and Solid State Power Amplifiers (SSPA). The results show that the proposed pre-distorter design presents low complexity and low error rate. Indeed, the implemented architecture uses 10% of DSP (Digital Signal Processing) blocks and 1% of LUTs (Look up Table) in case of SSPA, whereas it only uses 1% of LUTs in case of TWTA. In addition, it allows us to conclude that advanced machine learning techniques can be efficiently implemented in hardware with the adequate design.

Keywords: ECMA-368; MB-OFDM; HPA; PAPR; pre-distortion; neural networks; FPGA

1. Introduction

Ultra Wideband (UWB) technology has been deployed for broadband wired and wireless communications since in February 2002, the implementation of a regulation gave authorization on the use of UWB technology for telecommunications consumer in the United States by the Federal Communications Commission (FCC). Once the frequency band of 7.5 GHz not subject to licensing (FCC 02-48) has been allotted, the FCC welcomed the very high data rate (beyond Gbps) wireless communications. UWB was basically linked to waveforms without carriers (carrier-free) built from very short pulses [1,2]. In this way, a simple approved definition considered that these signals having a fractional bandwidth $FB \geq 0.25$ with a frequency bandwidth $\geq$500 MHz can be considered UWB [2].

OFDM is a modulation technology that guarantees an orthogonality in the frequency domain since it uses the sinusoidal basis function [3]. Then, a cyclic prefix or zero padding is added to each symbol, which makes it possible to avoid the inter-symbol interference (ISI) due to the multipath channel. However, if the orthogonality between the sub-carriers is lost, it results in inter-carrier-interference (ICI), and thus OFDM system performances is degraded. In order to decrease the impact of these problems, a new Multi-band Orthogonal Frequency Division Modulation (MB-OFDM) system has been proposed in

[4]. To make wireless connectivity possible between devices within the personal area network. At the same time, it is important to undergo the European Conformity (CE) and the multimedia industry current needs in the field of wireless personal area network (WPAN) with very high data-rates or for their use in future Wireless Universal Serial Bus (WUSB/IEEE 1394) [5], different standards have been implemented: Multi-band OFDM Alliance (MBOA), Wimedia and ECMA-368 [6]. In this paper, the ECMA-368 Standard is used. It points out the MB-OFDM scheme to transmit information for a wireless personal area network, however identically to all OFDM based communications systems, the ECMA-368 undergoes the large Peak to Average Power Ratio (PAPR), this drawback reduces the High Power Amplifier (HPA) efficiency at the transmitter.

In the ECMA-368 system, very efficient amplifiers are used, mainly of two different types, namely, Traveling Wave Tube Amplifiers (TWTA) and Solid State Power Amplifiers (SSPA). Unfortunately, these amplifiers are highly non-linear and thus, in order to avoid the distortion of the signal, large back-offs are needed. As result, the efficiency is substantially reduced. This phenomenon leads to the in-band distortion, which increases the bit error rate (BER) [7] and the out-band spectral re-growthwhich also increases adjacent channel interference. Numerous methods have been proposed to overcome the high PAPR problem in OFDM signals [8,9]. Among these techniques, the HPA pre-distorter [10] is one of the most promising ones because it avoids the increase on transmit energy, it does not need side information which reduces efficiency, it is only needed to be applied at the transmitter, which eases the implementation, and it does not increase the BER, among other advantages.

It should be noted that most of the results and designing parameters in this paper can also be extended to other OFDM standards [11–14].

TWTA and SSPA are the most efficient amplifiers, and are the two main amplifier choices for space-based RF communications. TWTA and SSPA are generally more advantageous for higher power and higher frequencies, at a reduced size, cost, and with improved thermal performance. Unfortunately, these amplifiers are highly non-linear [15], hence, a large back-off [16] is needed to mitigate the signal distortion. As outcome, the efficiency is substantially reduced.

To run off a large back-off, several techniques were used to reduce the power envelope fluctuations (PAPR) [8,17]. However, the non-linearity of HPA [18] still provoke a signal distortion, compromising the system performance. These non-linearity can be identified in the amplitude with the Amplitude Modulation/Amplitude Modulation (AM/AM), and in the phase with the Amplitude Modulation/Phase Modulation (AM/PM) functions [19]. In addition, those techniques, as indicated earlier, increase transmission power due to the expansion on the transmitted constellation.

In order to overcome this problem, we can pre-distort the signal before the HPA like to linearize the HPA, i.e., to linearize the AM/AM and AM/PM characteristics of the HPA. In order to better understand the effect and issues with AM/AM and AM/PM distortion, please see [20] and the references therein.

Artificial NNs are being successfully applied through a wide range of complex computational problems [21,22]. Among the different NN architectures [23], Multilayer Perceptron (MLP) is the most used one. It connects a set of input data to an appropriate output's set by using a supervised training techniques. In this paper, we developed a very simple pre-distorter architecture based on two MLPs for, respectively, AM/AM and AM/PM conversions. Then, two HPA models, namely, TWTA and SSPA [24] have been tested. Finally, the implementation of the proposal on FPGA is described and analyzed showing that it is well suited to future wireless communications systems [25].

The remainder of this paper is organized as follows. Section 2 describes the NN models for HPA pre-distortion. Section 3 presents the implementation of our proposed design on FPGA. Then, results are detailed in Section 4. Finally, Section 5 summarizes the conclusion of the paper.

2. NN Models for HPA Pre-Distortion

First, in this section, the signal model and the NN design are described and analyzed.

2.1. Transmitted Signal

The transmitted radio frequency ECMA-368 signal can be mathematically described as [6]

$$x(t) = \Re\left\{ \sum_{n=0}^{N_{pq}-1} S_n(t - nT_{SYM}) \exp(j2\pi\mathcal{F}q(n)t) \right\} \quad (1)$$

where $\Re\{.\}$ stands for the real part of the signal, T_{SYM} is the symbol duration , N_{pq} is the number of symbols that every packet has, $\mathcal{F}$ is the center frequency, and $q(n)$ is a the mapping function of the nth symbol to the appropriate frequency.

Once the signal has been described, the pre-distortion scheme and the proposal will be presented. It should be highlighted that, although this paper uses the ECMA-368 standard for describing the signal and obtaining the results, all the recommendations and analysis can be easily extrapolated to other MB-OFDM or even OFDM system or standard, which makes the contribution of this paper very valuable.

2.2. HPA Pre-Distortion Concept

The model for a HPA can be characterized by the AM/AM and the AM/PM distortion, as it can be seen in Figure 1. The output $y(t)$ of the non-linear amplifiers TWTA and SSPA corresponding to $x(t)$ input, is expressed as

$$y(t) = AM(|x(t)|)e^{j[PM(|x(t)|)+\phi(x(t))]} \quad (2)$$

where $AM(.)$ and $PM(.)$ are, respectively, the AM/AM and AM/PM distortion functions. According to Saleh's model [26], the AM/AM and AM/PM conversions can be written as

$$AM(|x(t)|) = \frac{\alpha_{||}|x(t)|}{(1 + \beta_{||}|x(t)|^2)} \quad (3)$$

$$PM(|x(t)|) = \frac{\alpha_{PM}|x(t)|^2}{(1 + \beta_{PM}|x(t)|^2)} \quad (4)$$

where $\alpha_{||}$ is the small signal gain, $A_{sat} = \frac{1}{\sqrt{\beta_{||}}}$ is the input saturation voltage of TWTA or SSPA, and $A_{max} = \frac{\alpha_{||}}{2\sqrt{\beta_{||}}} = \frac{\alpha_{||}A_{sat}}{2}$ is the maximum output amplitude.

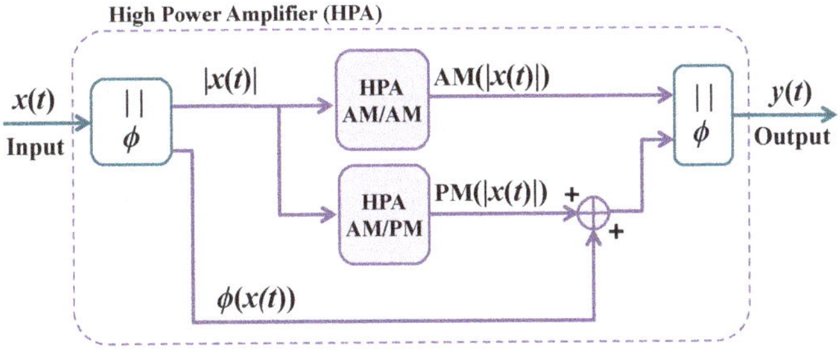

Figure 1. HPA's operating principle.

The modified Rapp model [27] is used instead for the SSPA case. Where, the AM/AM and AM/PM conversions is given as

$$AM'(|x(t)|) = g\frac{|x(t)|}{(1 + (\frac{g|x(t)|}{A_{sat}})^{2s})^{\frac{1}{2s}}} \quad (5)$$

$$PM'(|x(t)|) = \frac{\alpha|x(t)|^{c_1}}{(1+(\frac{|x(t)|}{\beta})^{c_2})} \quad (6)$$

where g is the small gain signal, s is a smoothness factor parameter, A_{sat} is the saturation level with a similar meaning as in the TWTA, and parameters α, β, c_1 and c_2 are adjusted to match the amplifier's characteristics.

A common parameter in HPA is the Input Back Off (*IBO*), which is defined as

$$IBO = 10\log_{10}\frac{P_{sat}}{P_{avg}} \quad (7)$$

where the P_{sat} represents the saturation input power and P_{avg} denotes the average input power. The *IBO* accounts for how much power need to be reduced to obtain a low level of distortion output signal, and it is usually understood as a loss in link budget analysis. A summary of these operating principle is illustrated in Figure 1.

The concept of pre-distortion is to compensate the AM/AM and AM/PM distortion with an inverse non-linearity. With the formulated AM/AM and AM/PM pre-distortion functions, the amplifier input can be re-written as

$$y(t) = AM^{-1}(|x(t)|)e^{j[PM^{-1}(|x(t)|)+\phi(x(t))]} \quad (8)$$

where $AM^{-1}(|x(t)|)$ and $PM^{-1}(x(t))$ are the AM/AM and the AM/PM pre-distorter functions, respectively. The pre-distorter output can be expressed as

$$z(t) = AM^{-1}(|y(t)|)e^{j[PM^{-1}(|y(t)|)+\phi(y(t))]} \quad (9)$$

It should be highlighted here that, although these pre-distortion schemes allow the use of lower *IBO* than other techniques, we still need an *IBO* to absorb the near-flat part of the curve due to the hard saturation in AM/AM characteristic (see Figure 2). In the case of the amplifiers in Figure 2, it should be around 4 dB of *IBO* for the SSPA (worst case), around 2 dB for TWT2 and 1 dB for TWTA1, while other techniques would probably need an *IBO* of around 8-10 dB. Of course, it will depend on the specific HPA characteristics and the hard saturation point. Since a minimum *IBO* is needed, the dynamic range of the HPA is reduced. However, the higher the *IBO* the lower the dynamic range. Thus, with pre-distortion techniques, since the *IBO* can be lowered, so the the dynamic range can be larger than with other techniques.

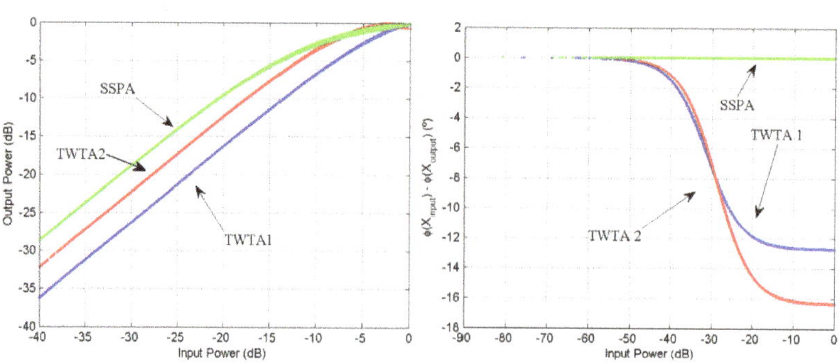

Figure 2. HPA non-linear response for amplitude (**left**) and phase (**right**). TWTA1: $\alpha_{||} = 2, \beta_{||} = 1, \alpha_{PM} = 4, \beta_{PM} = 9$, TWTA2: $\alpha_{||} = 3, \beta_{||} = 2, \alpha_{PM} = 2, \beta_{PM} = 7$, SSPA: NEC GaAs [10].

2.3. NN Pre-Distorter Architecture

The main idea behind the concept of pre-distortion is the aim of introducing inverse nonlinearities that can compensate the AM/AM and AM/PM distortion of the HPA.

In order to ease the design of the predistorter and to accelerate the identification, two MLP NN are proposed for $AM^{-1}(|x(t)|)$ and $PM^{-1}(|x(t)|)$. The first one synthesizes the AM/AM pre-distortion function while the second one synthesizes the AM/PM pre-distortion function.

Each MLP NN is off-line trained using the levenberg-marquardt algorithm [28]. Once it is already trained, it is ready for the continuous and real-time operation. The maximum number of epochs = 1000, and the mean squared error (MSE) is fixed to be less than or equal to 1E-6. The off-line training process is depicted in Figure 3 and is processed according to the following steps:

1. Decompose the original signal $x(t)$ into magnitude $|x(t)|$ and phase angle $\phi(x(t))$.
2. Apply the HPA AM/AM conversion function to the original magnitude $|x(t)|$ to obtain HPA magnitude $AM(|x(t)|)$.
3. Apply the HPA AM/PM conversion function to the original magnitude $|x(t)|$ to obtain HPA phase angle $PM(|x(t)|)$.
4. Train the NN AM/AM pre-distorter model using magnitudes $[|x(t)|, AM(|x(t)|)]$ to synthesize the AM^{-1} pre-distorter function.
5. Calculate the difference between the HPA AM/PM output and original phase angle $(PM(|x(t)|) - \phi(x(t)))$.
6. Train the NN AM/PM pre-distorter model using the original magnitude $(|x(t)|)$ and $PM(|x(t)|) - \phi(x(t))$.
7. Finally, using NN models, the pre-distorters magnitude $(AM^{-1}(|x(t)|))$ and phase angle $(PM^{-1}(|x(t)|))$ signals are generated.

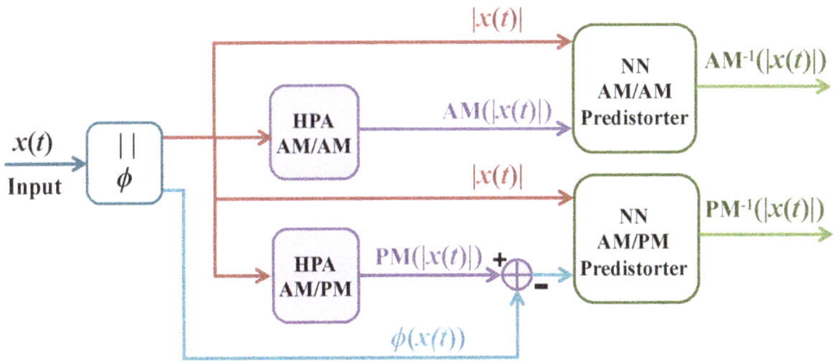

Figure 3. Pre-distorter training phase.

Following off-line training, both NN models are used before the high-power amplifier, as shown in Figure 4. We would like to highlight that the examples of amplifiers used in this paper are only meant to obtain results and validate the performance of the proposed pre-distorter scheme. Once trained with the specific amplifier response, the NN models are able to pre-distort the input signal adequately.

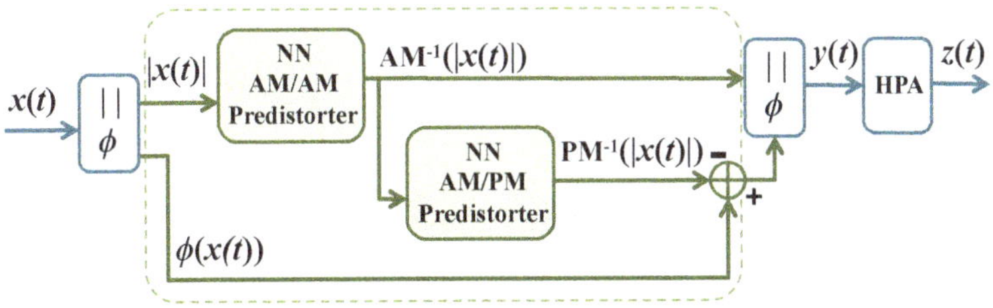

Figure 4. Pre-distorter architecture.

It is worth noting that the amplifier 's response can vary during the time. However, if the NNs have been trained with enough data and possibilities, the NNs will be able to follow these changes real time even if the amplifier changes its behavior. Obviously, there is a limitation on the possible changes, but it is robust enough for normal operation.

Going deep into the NN architecture of each MLP pre-distorter used, in Figures 3 and 4 consists in 3 layers as illustrated in Figure 5.

- The input layer: receives the input signal of the system.
- The hidden layer includes:
    - $n = 4$ neurons adopting triangular basis (**tribas**) function in case of TWTA.
    - $n = 2$ neurons with radial basis (**radbas**) function in case of SSPA.
- The output layer: with a single neuron using a linear activation function.

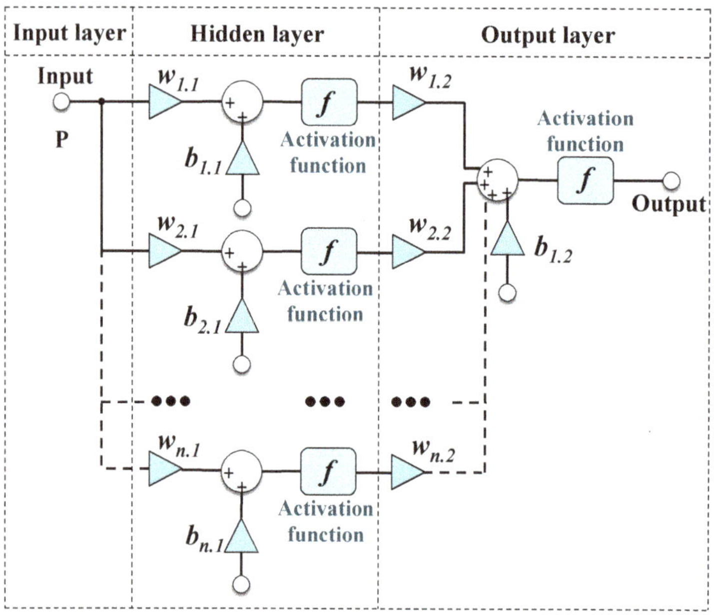

Figure 5. Multilayer perceptrons neural networks pre-distorter.

Mathematically each neuron output can be expressed as

$$y = f(u),\ u = \sum_{i=1}^{L} W_i P_i + b \tag{10}$$

where P is an input vector $P = (P_1, P_2, P_3 \ldots, P_i)^T$, W is set of synaptic connections also known as the set of weights $W = (W_1, W_2, W_3 \ldots, W_i)^T$ these weights multiply the input to get WP and b is the added bias to WP. For the MLP NN hidden layer, $L = 1$ is the number of inputs of each neuron, $f(u) = \textbf{tribas}(u)$ is a **tribas** function (TWTA) and $f(u) = e^{(-u^2)}$ is a radial basis function (SSPA) while for the MLP NN output layer $L = 4$ in case of TWTA, $L = 2$ in case of SSPA and $f(u) = u$ is a linear function.

Since **radbas** function uses an exponential calculation, in [29,30], authors proposed a new approximation to express the exponential function using Taylor series. It has been shown that it consumes less FPGA resources and does not require any memory blocks. In fact, in this paper, this approximation for the SSPA predistorter is adopted.

3. FPGA Implementation

To implement the proposed NN pre-distorters, an FPGA has been used for the benefits they offer [31,32]. Indeed an FPGA enables a higher sampling frequency, tolerates higher data rates and provides real-time processing [33]. Since the training of the NN pre-distorters is carried out off-line, only the real-time part, i.e., their layers, will be implemented on an FPGA, without the need of implementing the learning algorithm.

Figures 6 and 7 represent the architecture of a neural networks, of the AM/AM pre-distorter for TWTA and SSPA, respectively, implemented using Xilinx system generator [34]. To achieve the proposed implementations signed fixed-point representation has been adopted, allowing a better computational speed and minimal resources consumption at expenses of a reduced degradation. The number of bits has been optimized to obtain the best trade-off between speed, space and degradation. Each sample is encoded on 16 bits: 5 bits are reserved for the integer part, 10 bits for the fractional part and one bit of sign. It should be noted that the number of bits at the transmitter side is not usually a problem and it is fixed to the maximum number of bits at Digital to Analog Converter (DAC) to maximize the dynamic range of the transmitted signal. It is worth noting that for AM/PM pre-distorter, the same NN architecture implementation is adopted, the difference is that the weights and bias take a different values, for TWTA and SSPA, respectively. It should be noted that complex multipliers are needed to operate in the output layer, which corresponds to a four real-valued multipliers pipe-line architecture in the implementation as a trade-off between complexity, efficiency and resources.

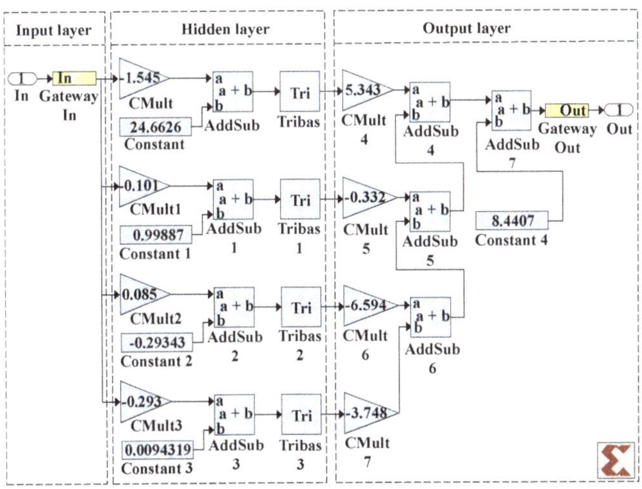

Figure 6. Implementation for NN AM/AM TWTA pre-distorter.

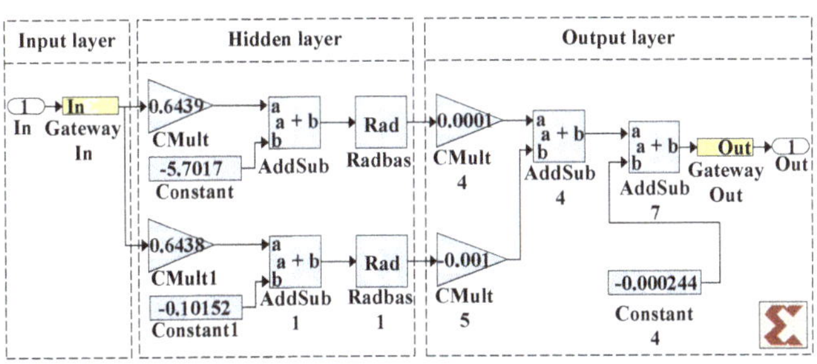

Figure 7. Implementation for NN AM/AM SSPA pre-distorter.

Figure 8 represents the Register Transfer Level (RTL) schematic of Figures 6 and 7, while Figures 9 and 10 represent a zoom on both entities AM/AM and AM/PM of Figure 8.

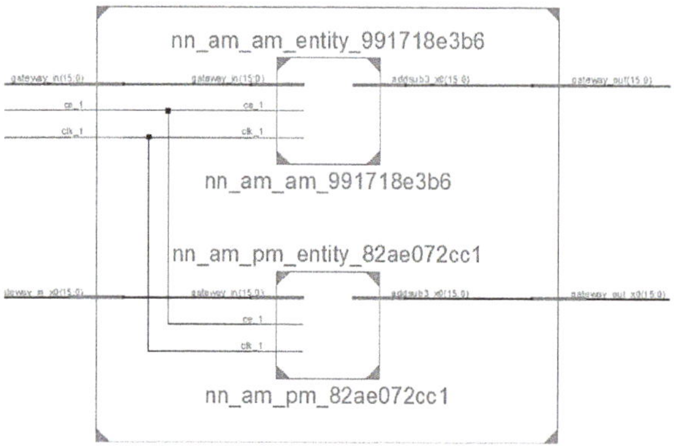

Figure 8. RTL Schematic for NN TWTA and SSPA pre-distorters.

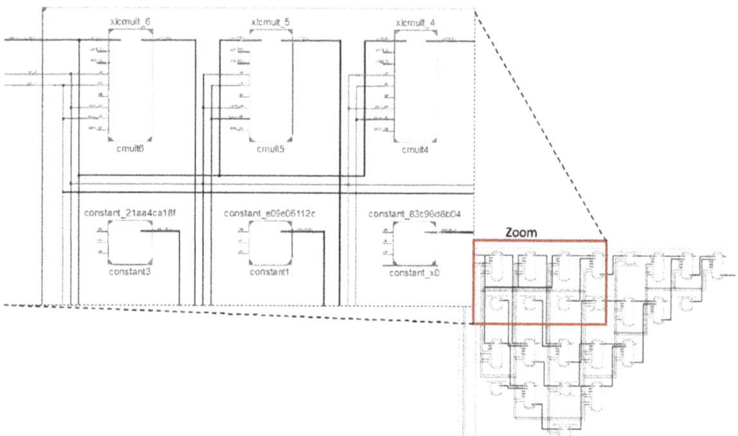

Figure 9. A zoom on NN AM/AM entity.

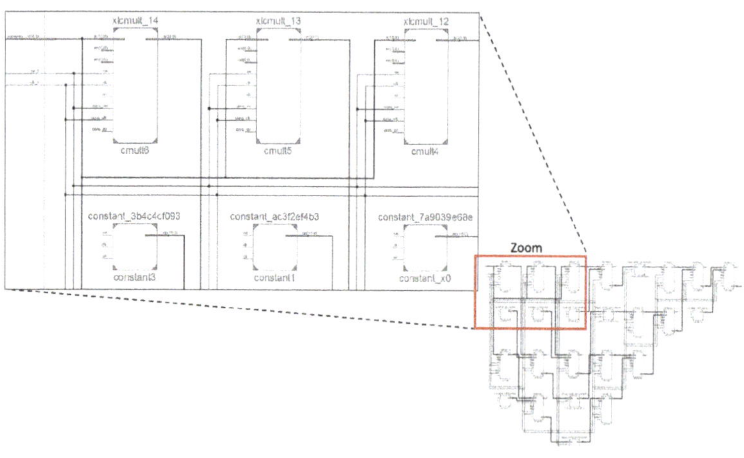

Figure 10. A zoom on NN AM/PM entity.

4. Results

The TWTA has been used with $\alpha_{||} = 2, \beta_{||} = 1, \alpha_{PM} = 4$ and $\beta_{PM} = 9$ [10], while the SSPA used is the NEC GaAs Power Amplifier used for standardization with parameters: $g = 19$, $A_{sat} = 1.4$, $s = 0.81$, $\alpha = -48000$, $\beta = 0.123$, $c_1 = 3.8$ and $c_2 = 3.7$ [10].

To evaluate the performance of our implementation, several metrics have been used, namely: the FPGA resources consumption, the bit error rate and finally the power spectral density.

Table 1 shows the consumed resources on virtex-4, virtex-5 and virtex-6 FPGAs. The table also shows the maximum frequency supported (it is worth noting that the maximum frequency stands for the maximum throughput supported by the designs).

Table 1. Resources consumption.

Solutions	FPGA	DSP Blocks	LUTs	Max Freq (MHz)
TWTA predistorter	Virtex-6 xc6vlx130	0 (0%)	1560 (1%)	492
	Virtex-5 xc5vlx110	0 (0%)	1611 (2%)	425
	Virtex-4 xc4vlx100	0 (0%)	1796 (1%)	344
SSPA predistorter	Virtex-6 xc6vlx130	52 (10%)	2744 (1%)	200
	Virtex-5 xc5vlx110	52 (81%)	2805 (4%)	157
	Virtex-4 xc4vlx100	78 (81%)	3285 (3%)	122

From Table 1, it can be concluded that the TWTA pre-distorter is faster and less resources consuming than the SSPA. This can be justified by the use of radial basis function based on exponential function approximation, leading to slower and more complex calculation. Since the HPA is usually imposed by the application, we need to guarantee that both design can be efficiently implemented.

Table 2 and Figure 11 show the power consumption for TWTA and SSPA pre-distorters. It is worth noting that the TWTA pre-distorter consumes less power than the SSPA pre-distorter. It can also be seen in Figure 11 that the novel FPGA architectures (Spartan) are more efficient than older ones, and our proposal can better exploit the optimization characteristics on these devices. It is especially relevant that in Spartan 6 boards, the power consumption of our proposal could even be neglected, which is a relevant contribution in this context. The power estimation has been obtained with Xilinx Power Analyzer, using Simulation Activity Files (SAIF or VCD) for accurate power analysis, which guarantees enough accuracy on the results.

Table 2. Power consumption.

Device	Virtex5 5vfx100t	Virtex6 6vcx130t	Virtex6 6vcx130tL	Virtex4 4vfx100	Spartan3 XC3S 4000	Spartan6 XC6SLX 100	Spartan6 XC6SLX 100 L
SSPA power consumption (W)	1.97	1.343	0.932	0.944	0.564	0.198	0.134
TWTA power consumption (W)	1.66	1.23	0.83	0.84	0.272	0.081	0.058

The proposed MLP NNs have been simulated and implemented on FPGA, following ECMA-368 standard. If nothing is indicated in other sense, the IBO has been fixed to 2 dB, a very optimistic value for realistic systems. Figure 12 shows the transmitted constellation after the TWTA and SSPA without the pre-distortion (warped constellation), and when using our proposal (close to the original constellation). It can be seen that, even in this taught conditions, the proposed design is able to work properly.

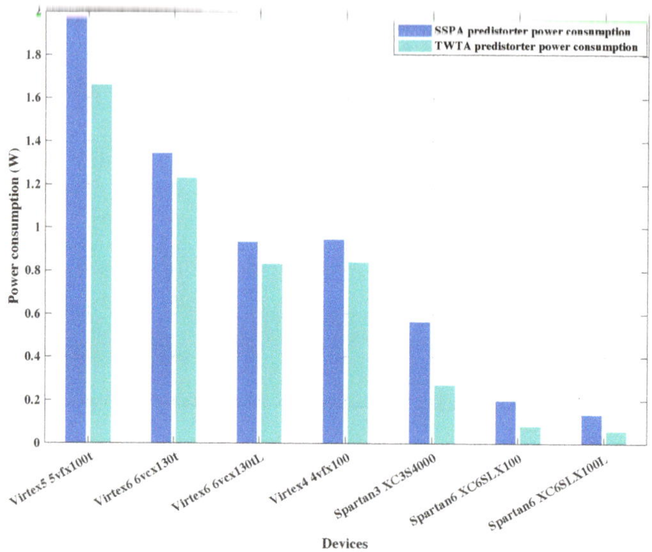

Figure 11. Power consumption For both SSPA and TWTA pre-distorter implementation.

In Figure 12, it can be concluded that using the proposed NN pre-distorters, the constellation is like the original signal without distortion, which will greatly improve the bit error rate.

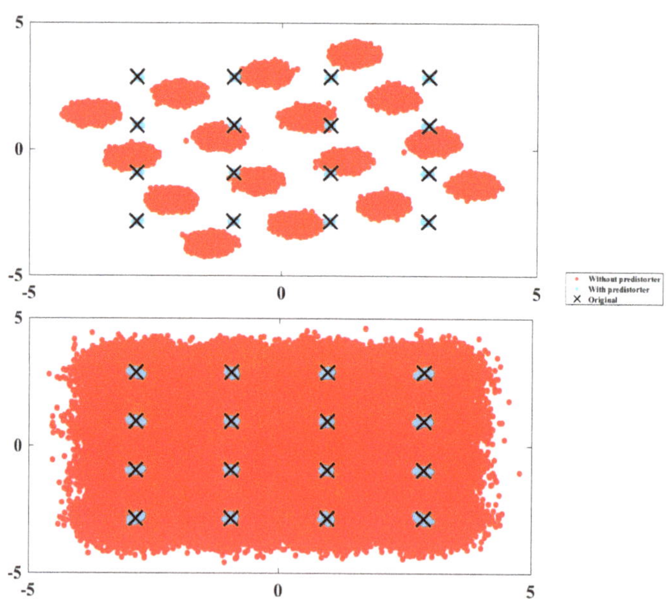

Figure 12. DCM Constellation—Before and after NN pre-distorters for TWTA (**up**) and SSPA (**down**), mean input power = 22.5 dBm.

To make sure that our implementation for both designs does not affect the performance of the ECMA-368 wireless communication system, the Bit Error Rate (BER) is also obtained and analyzed for different standard channels CM1, CM2, CM3 and CM4. In order to do so, a JTAG hardware co-simulation [35] is used to accelerate the simulation of the whole implemented designs on the FPGA platform. In Figure 13, only the proposed NNs has been implemented on the hardware while the rest is simulated by software. The software transmits a data frame to the hardware at each clock cycle for processing. For a fast transmission, both software and hardware communicate through a JTAG or Ethernet cable.

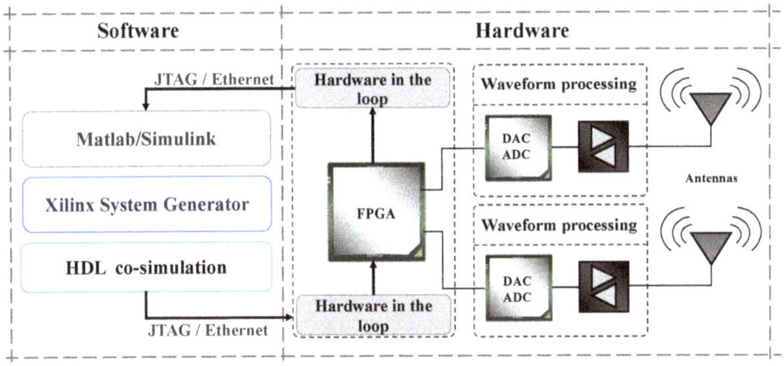

Figure 13. Co-simulation platform.

As shown in Figures 14–17 the system performance does not undergo any degradation for both TWTA and SSPA pre-distorters for different channels CM1, CM2, CM3 and CM4 with respect to the ECMA-368 standard. The mean input power to generate these figures was 22.5 dBm. The transmit power was kept constant and we varied the noise power. The input power saturation of the HPA was 30 dBm. As it can be observed in the figures, the degradation is lower than 0.4 dB for lower data rates and less than 0.1 dB for higher data rates. These results shows a twofold conclusion. First, the optimization carried out in terms of number of bits works because the degradation is very low. Second, it is possible to implement a real-time high data rate pre-distorter using FPGA. It can be seen that even at very high data rate of nearly 500 Mbs the system is working properly.

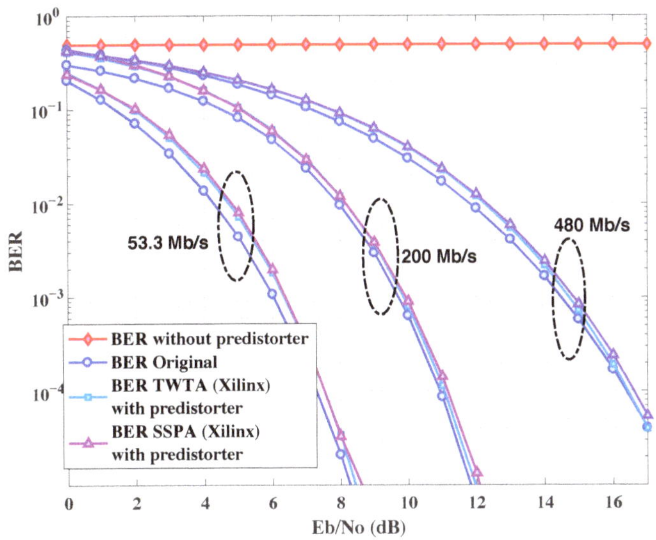

Figure 14. Bit Error Rate without and with NN pre-distorter for CM1.

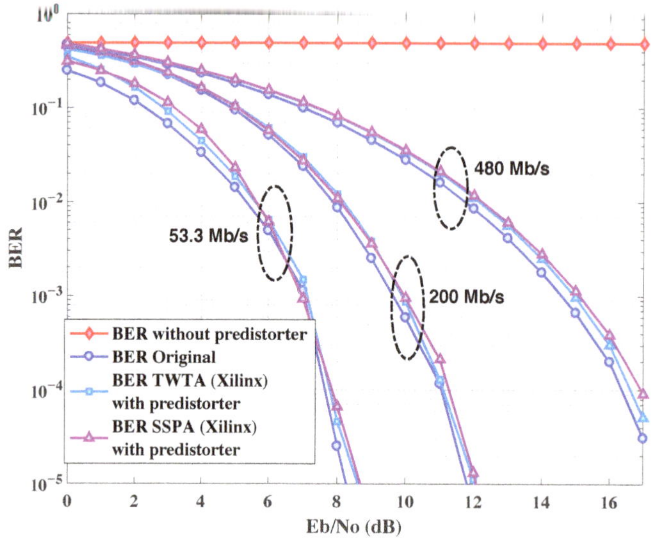

Figure 15. Bit Error Rate without and with NN pre-distorter for CM2.

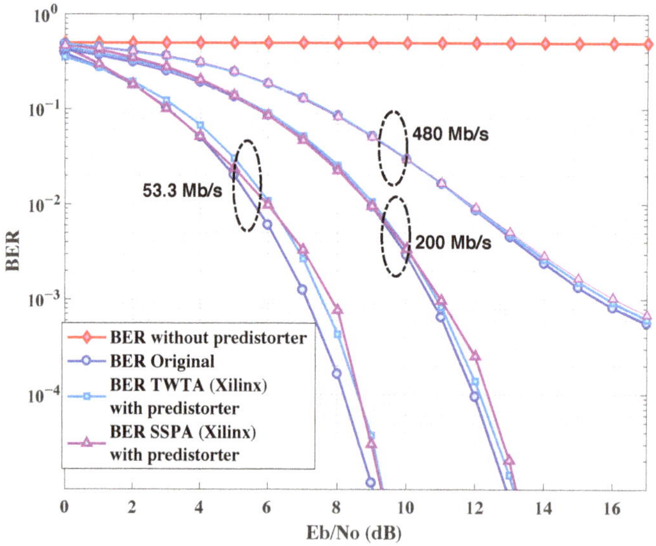

Figure 16. Bit Error Rate without and with NN pre-distorter for CM3.

In Figure 18, the power spectral density (PSD) of HPA output signal with and without NN pre-distorters is shown. It can be observed that by using our proposals, the PSD regrowth is negligible. In fact, it is about 5 dB for the TWTA, whereas it is 7 dB for the SSPA, which is very reduced compared to the original signal.

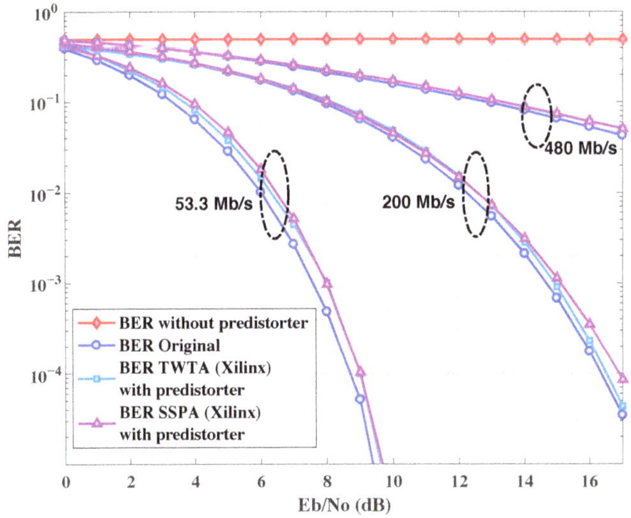

Figure 17. Bit Error Rate without and with NN predistorter for CM4.

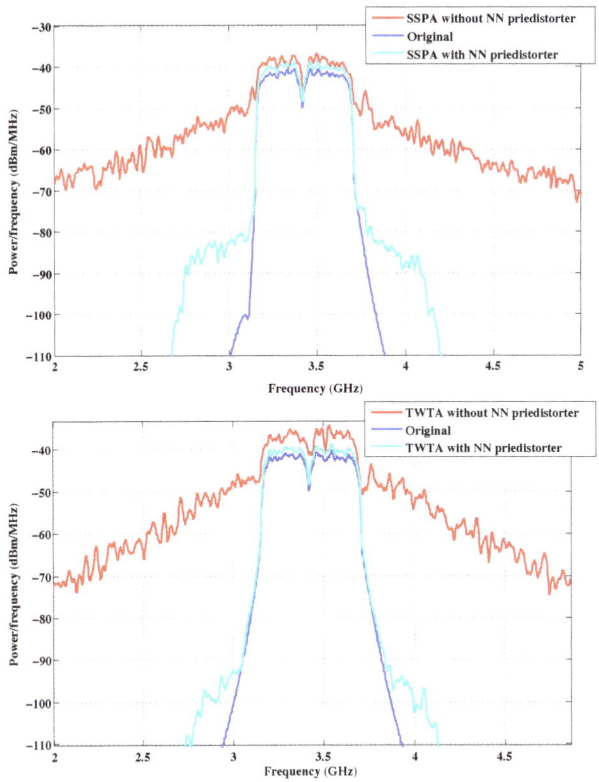

Figure 18. Power Spectral Density: without NN pre-distorter and with implemented NN pre-distorter on Xilinx for both TWTA and SSPA.

5. Conclusions

In this paper, a novel and efficient architectures for HPA non-linearity pre-distortion have been designed, optimized and implemented on FPGA. Then, it has been tested by using two types of HPA: TWTA and SSPA. To evaluate the performance of our implemented designs, three metrics were used: resource consumption, bit error rate and power spectral density. By using the proposed pre-distorters, the modulation constellation is not modified with respect to the original while respecting the demodulation slicer. In addition, a low consumption of resources is used, about 1% in case of TWTA, which makes it feasible to be implemented with the rest of ECMA-368 transmission chain on the same FPGA. In order to make sure that our implementations do not degrade the performance of the proposed wireless communication system standard, we carried out a bit error rate simulation and plotted the power spectral density. The results show that the system does not undergo any BER degradation for both TWTA and SSPA pre-distorters, with a negligible PSD regrowth. For future works, this proposal can be of interest in 5G and beyond communication systems.

Author Contributions: This work is developed in contribution of all authors including simulation, designing, implementation and validation. All authors have read and agreed to the published version of the manuscript.

Funding: This work was partly funded by projects TERESA-ADA (TEC2017-90093-C3-2-R) (MINECO/AEI/FEDER, UE) and MFOC (Madrid Flight on Chip—Innovation Cooperative Projects Comunidad of Madrid—HUBS 2018/MadridFlightOnChip).

Institutional Review Board Statement: Not applicable.

Informed Consent Statement: Not applicable.

Data Availability Statement: Not applicable.

Conflicts of Interest: The authors declare no conflict of interest. The funding sponsors had no role in the design of this research, in the analyses, interpretation data and decision to publish the results.

References

1. Ghavami, M.; Michael, L.B.; Haruyama, S.; Kohno, R. A novel uwb pulse shape modulation system. *Springer Wirel. Pers. Commun.* **2002**, *23*, 105–120. [CrossRef]
2. FCC. FCC 01-382 Public Safety Application and Broadband Internet Access among Uses Envisioned by FCC Authorization of Ultra Wideband Technology. 2002. Available online: https://www.naic.edu/~phil/rfi/fccactions (accessed on 24 June 2018).
3. Rahman, M.; NaghshvarianJahromi, M.; Mirjavadi, S.S.; Hamouda, M.A. Bandwidth Enhancement and Frequency Scanning Array Antenna Using Novel UWB Filter Integration Technique for OFDM UWB Radar Applications in Wireless Vital Signs Monitoring. *Sensors* **2018**, *18*, 3155. [CrossRef] [PubMed]
4. Foerster, J.; Li, Q. *UWB Channel Modeling Contribution From Intel Research and Development*; IEEE P802.15 Wireless Personal Area Networks; Intel Research and Development: Hillsboro, OR, USA, 2002.
5. IEEE. *1394-2008—IEEE Standard for a High-Performance Serial Bus*; IEEE Computer Society: New York, NY, USA, 2008; pp. 1–954. [CrossRef]
6. ECMA-368. *High Rate Ultra Wideband PHY and MAC Standard*, 3rd ed.; ECMA International: Geneva, Switzerland, 2008.
7. Ryu, H.S.; Lee, J.S.; Kang, G.C. BER Analysis of Dual-Carrier Modulation (DCM) over Rayleigh Fading Channel. In Proceedings of the International Congress on Ultra Modern Telecommunications and Control Systems, Moscow, Russia, 18–20 October 2010. [CrossRef]
8. Krongold, B.S.; Jones, L.D. PAR reduction in OFDM via active constellation extension. *IEEE Trans. Broadcast.* **2003**, *49*, 525–533. [CrossRef]
9. Louliej, A.; Jabrane, Y.; Said, B.A.E.; Ouahman, A.A. Reduction of Power Fluctuation in ECMA-368 Ultra Wideband Communication Systems Using Multilayer Perceptron Neural Networks. *Wirel. Pers. Commun.* **2013**, *72*, 1565–1583. [CrossRef]
10. Jimenez, V.P.G.; Jabrane, Y.; Armada, A.G.; Said, B.A.E.; Ouahman, A.A. High Power Amplifier Pre-Distorter Based on Neural-Fuzzy Systems for OFDM Signals. *IEEE Trans. Broadcast.* **2011**, *57*, 149–158. [CrossRef]
11. Schulze, H.; Luders, C. *Theory and Applications of OFDM and CDMA: Wideband Wireless Communications*; John Wiley & Sons Ltd.: Chichester, UK, 2005. [CrossRef]
12. Couasnon, T.D.; Monnier, R.; Rault, J.B. OFDM for digital TV broadcasting. *Signal Process.* **1994**, *39*, 1–32. [CrossRef]
13. Bingham, A.C.J. Multicarrier modulation for data transmission: An idea whose time has come. *IEEE Comm. Mag.* **1990**, *28*, 5–14. [CrossRef]
14. Arrano, H.F.; Azurdia-Meza, A.C. OFDM: Today and in the future of next generation wireless communications. In Proceedings of the 2016 IEEE Central America and Panama Student Conference (CONESCAPAN), Guatemala City, Guatemala, 27–30 September 2016. [CrossRef]

15. Jayati, A.E.; Suryani, T. Nonlinear Distortion Cancellation using Predistorter in MIMO-GFDM Systems. *Electronics* **2019**, *8*, 620. [CrossRef]
16. Kenneth, Y.J. *Satellite Communications Network Design and Analysis*; Artech House: Norwood, MA, USA, 2011.
17. Jayalath, A.D.S.; Tellambura, C. SLM and PTS peak-power reduction of OFDM signals without side information. *IEEE Trans Wirel Commun.* **2005**, *4*, 2006–2013. [CrossRef]
18. Rudiakova, A.N.; Krizhanovski, V. *Advanced Design Techniques for RF Power Amplifiers*; Springer: Dordrecht, The Netherlands, 2006.
19. Nam, H.; Sim, T.; Kim, J. A 2.4 GHz 20 W 8-channel RF Source Module with Solid-State Power Amplifiers for Plasma Generators. *Electronics* **2020**, *9*, 1378. [CrossRef]
20. Fernando, X.N.; Sesay, A.B. Adaptive Asymmetric Linearization of Microwave Fiber Optic Links for Wireless Access. *IEEE Trans. Veh. Technol.* **2002**, *51*, 1576–1596. [CrossRef]
21. Matta, M.; Cardarilli, G.C.; Nunzio, L.D.; Fazzolari, R.; Giardino, D.; Nannarelli, A.; Re, M.; Spanò, S. A reinforcement learning-based QAM/PSK symbol synchronizer. *IEEE Access* **2019**, *7*, 124147–124157. [CrossRef]
22. Zhang, M.; Liu, Z.; Li, L.; Wang, H. Enhanced Efficiency BPSK Demodulator Based on One-Dimensional Convolutional Neural Network. *IEEE Access* **2018**, *6*, 26939–26948. [CrossRef]
23. Dash, R.N.; Subudhi, B.; Das, S. A comparison between MLP NN and RBF NN techniques for the detection of stator inter-turn fault of an induction motor. In Proceedings of the 2010 International Conference on Industrial Electronics, Control and Robotics, Rourkela, India, 27–29 December 2010; pp. 251–256. [CrossRef]
24. Lohmeyer, W.Q.; Aniceto, R.J.; Cahoy, L.K. Communication satellite power amplifiers: Current and future SSPA and TWTA technologies. *Int. J. Satell Commun. Netw.* **2016**, *34*, 95–113. [CrossRef]
25. Vihriala, J.; Ermolova, N.; Lahetkangas, E.; Tirkkonen, O.; Pajukoski, K. On the Waveforms for 5G Mobile Broadband Communications. In Proceedings of the 2015 IEEE 81st Vehicular Technology Conference (VTC Spring), Glasgow, UK, 11–14 May 2015. [CrossRef]
26. Saleh, A.A.M. Frequency-independent and frequency-dependent nonlinear models of TWT amplifiers. *IEEE Trans. Commun.* **1981**, *29*, 1715–1720. [CrossRef]
27. Honkanen, M.; Haggman, S.G. New aspects on nonlinear power amplifier modeling in radio communication system simulations. In Proceedings of the 8th International Symposium on Personal, Indoor and Mobile Radio Communications-PIMRC'97, Helsinki, Finland, 1–4 September 1997; pp. 844–848. [CrossRef]
28. Marquardt, D.W. An algorithm for least-squares estimation of nonlinear parameters. *J Soc. Indust. Appl. Math.* **1963**, *11*, 431–441. [CrossRef]
29. Louliej, A.; Jabrane, Y.; Zhu, W.P. Design and FPGA implementation of a new approximation for PAPR reduction. *AEU Int. J. Electron. Commun.* **2018**, *94*, 253–261. [CrossRef]
30. Louliej, A.; Jabrane, Y.; Jiménez, V.P.G.; Armada, A.G. Practical Guidelines for Approaching the Implementation of Neural Networks on FPGA for PAPR reduction in Vehicular Networks. *Sensors* **2019**, *19*, 116. [CrossRef] [PubMed]
31. Liu, Y.; Shen, Y.; Li, L.; Wang, H. FPGA implementation of a BPSK 1D-CNN demodulator. *Appl. Sci.* **2018**, *8*, 441. [CrossRef]
32. Shirvaikar, M.; Bushnaq, T. A comparison between DSP and FPGA platforms for real-time imaging applications. In *Real-Time Image and Video Processing 2009*; IS&T/SPIE Electronic Imaging: San Jose, CA, USA, 2009; Volume 7244, pp. 1–10. [CrossRef]
33. Duren, R.; Stevenson, J.; Thompson, M. A comparison of FPGA and DSP development environments and performance for acoustic array processings. In Proceedings of the 2007 50th Midwest Symposium on Circuits and Systems, Montreal, QC, Canada, 5–8 August 2007; pp. 1177–1180. [CrossRef]
34. Xilinx. *Model-Based DSP Design Using System Generator*, v2019.2 ed.; Vivado Design Suite User Guide; Xilinx Inc.: San Jose, CA, USA, 2016.
35. Delva, J.; Chirila-Rus, A.; Chan, B.; Seng, S. *Using System Generator for Systematic Hdl Design, Verification, and Validation*, v1.0 ed.; Xilinx, Inc.: San Jose, CA, USA, 2008.

electronics

MDPI

Article

A Control-Oriented ANFIS Model of Evaporator in a 1-kWe Organic Rankine Cycle Prototype

Hamid Enayatollahi [1], Paul Sapin [2], Chinedu K. Unamba [2], Peter Fussey [1], Christos N. Markides [2] and Bao Kha Nguyen [1,*]

[1] Department of Engineering and Design, University of Sussex, Brighton BN1 9QT, UK; h.enayatollahi@sussex.ac.uk (H.E.); p.m.fussey@sussex.ac.uk (P.F.)
[2] Clean Energy Processes (CEP) Laboratory, Department of Chemical Engineering, Imperial College London, London SW7 2AZ, UK; p.sapin@imperial.ac.uk (P.S.); chinedu.unamba13@imperial.ac.uk (C.K.U.); c.markides@imperial.ac.uk (C.N.M.)
* Correspondence: b.k.nguyen@sussex.ac.uk; Tel.: +44-(0)12-7387-2869

Abstract: This paper presents a control-oriented neuro-fuzzy model of brazed-plate evaporators for use in organic Rankine cycle (ORC) engines for waste heat recovery from exhaust-gas streams of diesel engines, amongst other applications. Careful modelling of the evaporator is both crucial to assess the dynamic performance of the ORC system and challenging due to the high nonlinearity of its governing equations. The proposed adaptive neuro-fuzzy inference system (ANFIS) model consists of two separate neuro-fuzzy sub-models for predicting the evaporator output temperature and evaporating pressure. Experimental data are collected from a 1-kWe ORC prototype to train, and verify the accuracy of the ANFIS model, which benefits from the feed-forward output calculation and backpropagation capability of the neural network, while keeping the interpretability of fuzzy systems. The effect of training the models using gradient-descent least-square estimate (GD-LSE) and particle swarm optimisation (PSO) techniques is investigated, and the performance of both techniques are compared in terms of RMSEs and correlation coefficients. The simulation results indicate strong learning ability and high generalisation performance for both. Training the ANFIS models using the PSO algorithm improved the obtained test data RMSE values by 29% for the evaporator outlet temperature and by 18% for the evaporator outlet pressure. The accuracy and speed of the model illustrate its potential for real-time control purposes.

Keywords: ANFIS; dynamic modelling; evaporator; organic Rankine cycle; waste heat recovery

1. Introduction

The internal combustion (IC) engine is the main technology currently used in the transportation sector. A typical IC engine converts about 40% of the fuel combustion energy into useful work. Legislation on vehicle emission continues to become more stringent to reduce the impact of IC engines on the environment. To this end, technologies—such as gasoline direct injection (GDI) [1], turbo direct injection (TDI) [2], and fuel stratified injection (FSI) [3]—have been developed and implemented in recent years to increase the efficiency of IC engines. Despite the advantages of such technologies, the thermal efficiency of IC engines needs to be improved to meet regulatory targets such as those agreed upon at the COP21 in the legally binding Paris Agreement, which is set to reduce greenhouse gas emissions. Recently, new methods of waste heat recovery (WHR) have been explored to utilise the significant amount of energy that is released to the atmosphere from the exhaust and coolant of IC engines [4]. The objective is to convert this waste thermal energy into useful mechanical or electrical energy. Several viable WHR technologies can be used to harness this waste thermal energy, such as turbo-compound, thermoelectric generators, piezoelectric generators, and organic Rankine cycle (ORC) engines. Among them, ORC systems are the preferred method of WHR in IC engines due

 https://www.mdpi.com/journal/electronics

to their low manufacturing cost and high efficiency. WHR technologies can contribute to enhancing the overall conversion efficiency of IC engines [5–7].

ORCs are a promising WHR technology that has been widely considered in many industries due to their features such as simplicity and high efficiency. The ORC is a heat-engine thermodynamic cycle that exhibits the potential to be deployed for recovery of waste heat in IC engines, the exhaust gases of which are an unsteady heat source with fluctuating temperature and mass flow rate [8,9]. Key characteristics of the ORC engine that make it a desirable solution for waste heat recovery in IC engines include modularity, versatility, and technological maturity of components (due to the similarities with the refrigeration systems). Moreover, ORC systems are able to recover waste heat in the low- to medium-temperature range. Most current investigations on ORCs are focused on theoretical and thermodynamic analysis [10], cycle optimisation [11], techno-economic optimisation [12,13], and working fluid selection [14]. In particular, combined fluid-design optimisation studies explore the potential of novel working fluids using computer aided molecular design (CAMD) techniques [15–17]. Several studies also propose advanced off-design optimisation algorithms to maximise the performance of an ORC engine operating under variable heat-source conditions [18–21].

However, the latter are based on quasi-steady models of the ORC engine and are thus not suitable for dynamic applications. For safe and successful implementation of ORCs in the automotive industry, a reliable and precise control scheme is required to ensure the safe operation of the engine, prevent organic fluid decomposition, and reduce the risk of component damage. Furthermore, designing a reliable control algorithm for the ORC in the mobile applications depends on accurate modelling of all the components within the cycle. The heat exchanges (i.e., evaporator and condenser) are key components of the ORC system as they are responsible for a large share of the overall exergy destruction [22] (heat transfer over a finite temperature difference being irreversible by nature) and are challenging to model due to the high nonlinearity of their governing equations. In addition, the dynamic behaviour of ORC engines is governed by the large thermal inertia of the heat exchangers, in particular by that of the evaporator, which has a direct impact on the response time of an ORC engine subject to fluctuations in heat-source conditions (namely, temperature and mass flowrate). Therefore, an accurate model of the evaporator is required to capture the dynamics of the system and is of prominent importance, not only because it is necessary for cycle optimisation and working fluid selection, but also as it allows a comprehensive optimisation of the dynamic control strategy.

Evaporator models available in the literature can be categorised into three main categories, namely: finite volume (FV) models, moving boundary (MB) models, and intelligent based models such as fuzzy and neural network models [23–25]. As illustrated in Figure 1, FV models are based on a spatial discretisation of the evaporator into a finite number of equally spaced control volumes, with the thermo-physical properties of the working fluid considered constant within each control volume. For this modelling technique, a higher number of control volumes results in an increased precision but significantly increases the computational complexity. Therefore, a trade-off must be made between accuracy and processing time to select the adequate spatial resolution of FV models [26]. FV techniques are computationally expensive and are thus appropriate for performance assessment and working fluid selection, but cannot be applied to high-frequency, real-time control purposes.

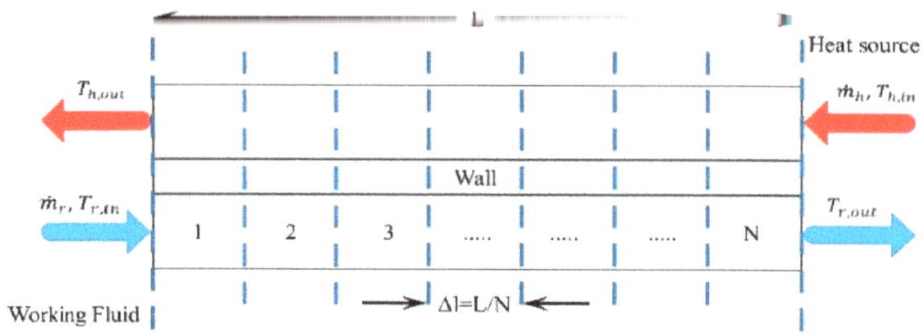

Figure 1. Discretisation of evaporator into N control volumes [27].

By contrast, MB models are control-oriented models based on a fixed spatial discretisation of the evaporator into three regions (liquid, two-phase mixture, vapour), the size of which varies with time. The MB technique results in a slight improvement in computational complexity, however, models developed by this technique cannot tolerate nonexistence of the distinct phases of the working fluid. Therefore, this technique is not suitable for situations such as start-up or shut-down because of the resulting singularity in numerical problems [23]. Evaporator fuzzy models have been developed recently to improve the real-time calculation speed of the models [24,28]; however, setting the rules for identifying the model based on the available data is a time-consuming task. Another approach for developing an agile model of the evaporator is the neuro-fuzzy technique. Neuro-fuzzy models are data-driven techniques that require training before implementation. As opposed to predictive methods, which require an iterative solution, neuro-fuzzy models are much faster and can be utilised for control purposes. Adaptive neuro-fuzzy inference system (ANFIS) is an intelligent modelling technique acquiring the modelling benefits of Sugeno fuzzy inference system and pattern recognition ability of feedforward neural network [29]. Khosravi et al. [30] used ANFIS-PSO algorithm for thermodynamic modelling of geothermal based ORC equipped with solar system. Authors, in previous studies [27,31], have developed ANFIS models based on the available data from FV evaporator models that offer reduced complexity, high accuracy and lower computational burden for prediction of the working-fluid and heat-source outlet temperatures. This paper investigates the application of neuro-fuzzy techniques for modelling a plate evaporator using time-resolved high-fidelity experimental data obtained on a 1-kWe ORC prototype.

This paper is structured as follows: Section 2 describes the layout and operation of the 1-kWe ORC testing facility. In Section 3, the architecture of the ANFIS model and the node functions within its layers are discussed for a fuzzy inference system with two inputs and one output. Two methods are introduced in Section 4 for training the ANFIS model and limitations and advantages of both methods are pointed out. In Section 5, data collection and application of the ANFIS method for modelling the evaporator outlet temperature and pressure in the testing facility are discussed. The simulation results and discussions of the study are presented in Section 6. The simulation tests are designed to evaluate the effectiveness of the proposed modelling technique. Finally, the paper closes by summarising and discussing key conclusions from this work in Section 7.

2. ORC System Layout and Test Bench Prototype

The testing facility, commissioned at the Clean Energy Processes (CEP) Laboratory at Imperial College London, comprises a rotary-vane pump, brazed-plate evaporator and condenser, and a scroll expander coupled magnetically to a generator with an adjustable resistive load. The ORC prototype is operated with R245fa as the working fluid, which can maintain above-atmospheric pressure within the condenser and prevent non-condensable air from leaking into the closed loop. The rotary-vane pump circulates the organic fluid through the cycle and allows adjustment of the flowrate. Shaft power is produced from the expansion of the high-temperature, high-pressure vapour exiting the evaporator down to the low pressure maintained in the condenser. The generator converts the expander shaft mechanical work into electrical energy, which is dissipated within a resistive load bank made of a set of adjustable resistors – with an equivalent overall resistance ranging from 10 to 60 Ω. This resistive load bank is able to dissipate safely up to 2 kW of heat without external ventilation and allows to control the torque applied to the expander shaft. The low-pressure vapour leaving the expander is then cooled down and fully condensed in the water-cooled condenser. To avoid cavitation in the pump and maintain zero subcooling at the condenser outlet, a liquid receiver is placed between the condenser and the pump. An 18-kW electric oil heater with adjustable delivery temperature is used as the heat source for the ORC prototype, thus providing a controllable stream of hot Marlotherm SM oil. A detailed piping and instrumentation diagram (P&ID) of the testing facility is shown in Figure 2 and an actual picture of the test bench is presented in Figure 3.

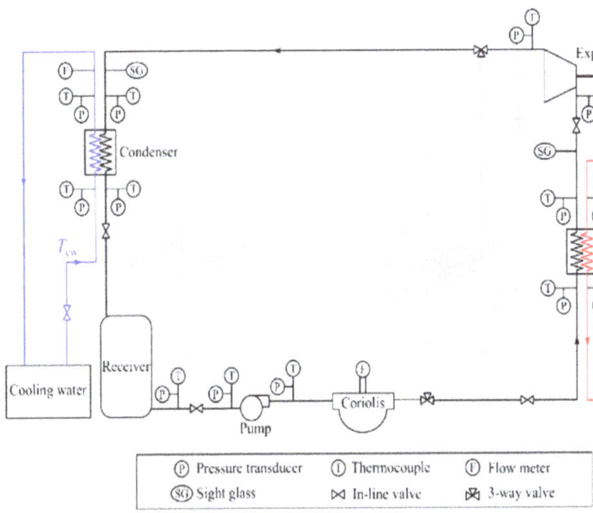

Figure 2. Piping and instrumentation diagram of ORC (organic Rankine cycle) testing facility (taken from [32]).

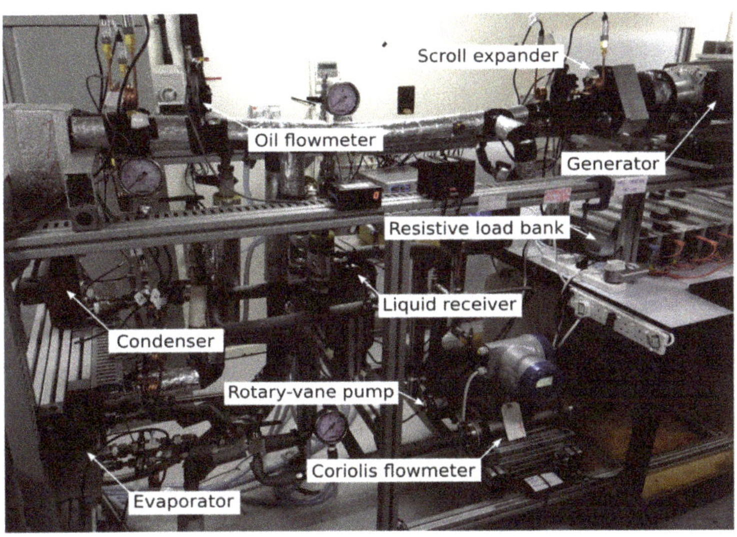

Figure 3. Experimental test facility and ORC prototype (taken from [19]).

As shown in Figure 2, pressure transducers and thermocouples (T-type) are placed at the inlet and outlet of each component to monitor the working fluid state throughout the cycle and provide high-fidelity measurements of the components and system performance. A DAQ970A data acquisition system is used to record time-resolved experimental data from the apparatus with a 1/2-Hz sampling rate. Detailed specifications of the key ORC components are listed in Table 1.

Table 1. Components specification of the ORC test prototype [32].

	Fluid Name	**Mass Flowrate**		**Temperature Range**
Heat-source thermal fluid	Marlotherm SM oil	0.01–1.4 kg/s		93–142 °C
Working fluid	R254fa	14–58 g/s		7–136 °C
Cooling fluid	Water	0.4 kg/s		18 °C
	Model	**Type**	**Area**	**Specifications**
Pump	TMFR2 (Fluid-o-Tech, Italy)	Magnet-driven rotary vane pump	-	1100–3000 RPM
Condenser	CB60-30H-F (Alfa Laval, Sweden)	Brazed-plate	1.62 m^2	-
Evaporator	B12Lx18 (SWEP, UK)	Brazed-plate	0.45 m^2	-
Expansion machine	E15H22N4.25 (Air Squared, USA)	Scroll expander	-	14.5 cm^3/rev, 1kWe
	Model			
Data acquisition system	DAQ970A (Keysight Technologies, UK)			
Pressure transducers	PXM309 (Omega Engineering, UK)			
Coriolis flowmeter	Optimass 6000 (Krohne, UK)			

3. Architecture of an Adaptive Neuro-Fuzzy Inference System (ANFIS)

ANFIS is as an advanced method widely used to model and control complex engineering systems [29]. An ANFIS network is able to extract non-linear relationships of complex multivariable problems using modelling benefits of Sugeno fuzzy inference system and pattern recognition power of feedforward neural networks by means of learning with training data. The advantage of this method compared with other similar methods, such as ANN, is the interpretability in terms of linguistic variables [33]. Because of its fuzzy logic capabilities, ANFIS models are not considered as pure black-box models, and therefore are more interpretable [33]. Moreover, ANFIS is an adequate compromise between neural network and fuzzy system providing smoothness and adaptability for the model [34]. Consequently, the model is able to handle uncertainties better and is less sensitive to noise. The ANFIS architecture comprises five layers. Each layer contains some adaptive or fixed nodes which are connected using directional links to form the network. Fixed nodes are performing a specific task while the output of adaptive nodes depends on the parameters incorporated in their node function. The learning rule specifies how these parameters should change to minimise a prescribed error function [29].

To avoid complexity, a FIS with two inputs and one output is assumed in describing the ANFIS architecture. In the rule base of FIS two TSK rules are considered as follows:

$$\begin{aligned} &\textbf{Rule 1:} && \text{if } x \text{ is } A_1 \text{ is } B_1, \text{ then}: \\ & && f_1 = p_1 x + q_1 y + r_1; \\ &\textbf{Rule 2:} && \text{if is } A_2 \text{ is } B_2, \text{ then}: \\ & && f_2 = p_2 x + q_2 y + r_2, \end{aligned} \tag{1}$$

where x and y denote the input variables and f_i is the output. A_i and B_i are demarcated over the input domain and are regarded as the fuzzy sets. p_i, q_i, and r_i are regarded as the linear polynomial parameters in the fourth layer of ANFIS network. Figure 4 represents the architecture of the ANFIS network, formed by implementing these two rules. The square and circle node symbols are deployed to illustrate the adaptive and fixed nodes, respectively. The node function for layers 1 to 5 of this architecture are as follows:

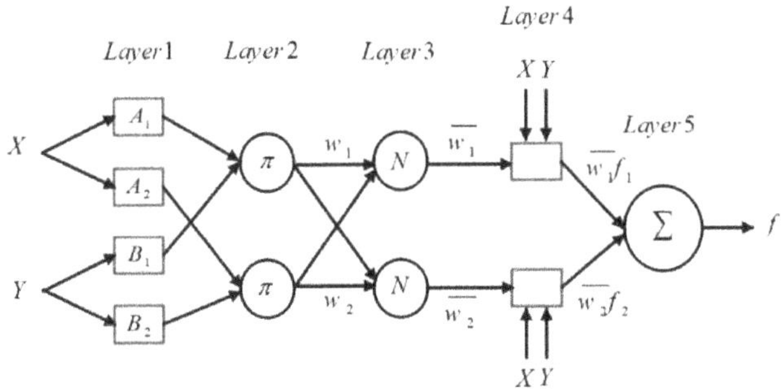

Figure 4. Architecture of adaptive neuro-fuzzy inference system (ANFIS) used to model the evaporator.

Layer 1: The nodes in the first layer of ANFIS are parameterised membership functions and the parameters set in this layer are referred to as premise parameters. These nodes are adaptive and can represent various types of membership functions such as triangular, trapezoidal, generalised bell and Gaussian. In case of the Gaussian shape membership function, the node function is

$$\begin{aligned} O_{1,\,i} &= \mu_{A_i}(x) \quad \text{for } i = 1,\, 2;\ \text{or} \\ O_{1,\,i} &= \mu_{B_{i-2}}(y) \quad \text{for } i = 3,\, 4. \end{aligned} \tag{2}$$

A and B denote the linguistic labels, x and y represent the inputs to the node i and $\mu(x)$ and $\mu(y)$ are Gaussian membership functions ranging from 0 to 1, as follows:

$$\mu(x) = \exp\left(-\frac{(C_i - x)^2}{2\sigma_i{}^2}\right), \tag{3}$$

where c_i determine the centre and σ_i represent the fuzzy set width. The training cost is determined using the number of training parameters, thus, since Gaussian membership function has only two adjustable parameters it is the most frequently used membership function in the literature [35]. In this study, Gaussian membership function is adopted for partitioning the input space because of its features such as fewer tuneable parameters and smooth representation of the domain.

Layer 2: Nodes in the second layer are fixed and labelled as π. In this layer, the output of nodes is obtained by multiplying all incoming signals. The node output ascertains the firing strength of the rules, as:

$$O_{2,i} = w_i = \mu_{A_i}(x)\mu_{B_i}(y) \quad \text{for } i = 1,\, 2. \tag{4}$$

Layer 3: The fixed nodes in this layer are labelled as N. The normalised firing strengths is obtained by dividing the firing strength of ith rule to sum of all rules firing strengths:

$$\overline{w}_i = \frac{w_i}{w_1 + w_2} \quad \text{for } i = 1,\, 2. \tag{5}$$

Layer 4: The nodes in the fourth layer have three adjustable parameters and hence are regarded as adaptive nodes. Their node function is calculated as:

$$O_{4,i} = \overline{w}_i f_i = \overline{w}_i(p_i x + q_i y + r_i)\,, \tag{6}$$

where $\overline{w}_i$ is the normalised firing strength, and p_i, q_i and r_i are referred to as consequent parameters, which are identified during the training process of the network.

Layer 5: The single node in this layer is a fixed node and is labelled as Σ. The crisp output of this layer is calculated by adding all of the incoming signals as

$$O_{5,1} = \sum_i \overline{w}_i f_i = \frac{\sum_i w_i f_i}{\sum_i w_i}. \tag{7}$$

4. Learning Algorithm of ANFIS

The aim of training the ANFIS network is to adjust the premise and consequent parameters in the adaptive nodes to minimise a performance measure known as the error function. Despite outperforming other fuzzy methods, ANFIS requires an effective learning algorithm for training the parameters of the network. In the original ANFIS paper proposed by Jang [29] a hybrid gradient descent, least square estimate (GD-LSE) method is used to identify the premise and consequent parameters of the network. In this method, because of utilising a gradient-based approach, the algorithm has a tendency to trap in local minima. Therefore, in search for a more effective training method for ANFIS, metaheuristic approaches have been investigated by researchers as an alternative for identifying the network parameters. Extensive literature review illustrates that various metaheuristic algorithms—such as PSO, GA, ABC, and their variants—have been used for training the premise and consequent parameters of the ANFIS network for a range of engineering problems. Table 2 summarises some studies which have used metaheuristic methods for training the ANFIS network.

Table 2. Summary of studies based on metaheuristic algorithms for ANFIS training.

	Premise	Consequent
Shoorehdeli, Teshnehlab [36]	AWPSO	FFRLS
Shoorehdeli, Teshnehlab [37]	AWPSO	EKF
Sargolzaei et al. [38]	PSO	PSO
Turki, Bouzaida [39]	PSO	PSO
Rini, Shamsuddin [40]	PSO	PSO
Karaboga, Kaya [41]	ABC	ABC
Soto, Melin [42]	GA	LSE
Cardenas, Garcia [43]	GA	GA

In this study, among many methods of minimising the performance measure, the particle swarm optimisation (PSO) and standard gradient descent, lest square estimate (GD-LSE) are chosen to train the ANFIS network. Moreover, their performance for matching training and test datasets is compared. The root mean square error (RMSE) is selected as the main performance indicator. The network output will better match the training target as the RMSE approaches zero.

4.1. GD-LSE Algorithm

In the architecture of the aforementioned ANFIS network, layer 1 and layer 4 contain adjustable parameters that need to be tuned for the network to match the training data. The least square estimate can be utilised to find the optimal values for the consequent parameters; however, since the premise parameters are not fixed, the search space becomes too large and it affects the convergence speed adversely. Therefore, by using a hybrid approach GD-LSE algorithm can speed up the process of training the network. The hybrid GD-LSE comprises a forward and a backward pass to train consequent and premise parameters, respectively. Table 3 illustrates this two-pass algorithm for identifying the premise and consequent parameters of the model.

Table 3. Two-pass parameter identification of the GD-LSE method.

Parameter	Forward Pass	Backward Pass
Antecedent parameters	Fixed	Gradient decent
Consequent parameters	Least square estimate	Fixed
Signals	Node outputs	Error signals

The data is presented to the network after fixing the premise parameters. The node outputs propagate forward through the network and, consequently, the network output is obtained as a linear combination of consequent parameters as:

$$f = \frac{w_1}{w_1 + w_2} f_1 + \frac{w_2}{w_1 + w_2} f_2 = \overline{w}_1 f_1 + \overline{w}_2 f_2. \tag{8}$$

Substituting the fuzzy if-then rules into Equation (8) yields:

$$f = (\overline{w}_1 x) p_1 + (\overline{w}_1 y) q_1 + (\overline{w}_1) r_1 + (\overline{w}_2 x) p_2 + (\overline{w}_2 y) q_2 + (\overline{w}_2) r_2. \tag{9}$$

Equation (9) is linear in the consequent parameters p_1, q_1, r_1, p_2, q_2 and r_2, and can thus be written as:

$$f = XW, \tag{10}$$

and, if the X matrix is invertible:

$$W = X^{-1} f. \tag{11}$$

Otherwise, W is calculated by deploying a pseudo-inverse as:

$$W = \left(X^T X\right)^{-1} X^T f, \tag{12}$$

where X^T is the transpose of X, and $\left(X^T X\right)^{-1} X^T$ is the pseudo-inverse of X if $X^T X$ is non-singular. However, $X^T X$ may become singular during the iterations that makes the problem ill-defined. Moreover, although Equation (12) is concise in notation finding the inverse of X is expensive in computation. Therefore, to overcome this issue the recursive LSE method proposed by Jang [29] can be employed as:

$$W_{i+1} = W_i + S_{i+1} x_{i+1} \left(f_{i+1}^T - x_{i+1}^T W_i \right) \qquad \text{with } i = 0,\ 1,\ \ldots,\ P-1; \tag{13}$$

$$S_{i+1} = S_i - \frac{S_i x_{i+1} x_{i+1}^T S_i}{1 + x_{i+1}^T S_i x_{i+1}}, \tag{14}$$

where S_i is the covariance matrix and least square estimate of W is equal to W_P. x_i^T is the ith row vector of matrix X and f_i^T is the ith element of f.

After identifying the consequent parameters, the output of network can be calculated and the error measure of the nth entery of the training data can be obtained as:

$$E_n = (T_n - O_n)^2 \tag{15}$$

where T_n and O_n represent the desired output and ANFIS output, respectively. Therefore, the RMSE of the whole training dataset can be computed as follows:

$$RMSE = \sqrt{\sum \frac{E_n}{n}} \tag{16}$$

In the backwards pass, the consequent parameters are fixed and the error signals propagate through the network in the reverse direction. Accordingly, using the GD algorithm, the premise parameters located in the first layer of the network are updated as:

$$c_{ij}(t+1) = c_{ij}(t) - \frac{\eta}{p} \cdot \frac{\partial E}{\partial c_{ij}}, \tag{17}$$

where, c_{ij} is the membership function's adjustable parameter and η represents the learning rate. To obtain the partial derivative, $\frac{\partial E}{\partial c_{ij}}$, the chain rule is applied as:

$$\frac{\partial E}{\partial c_{ij}} = \frac{\partial E}{\partial f} \cdot \frac{\partial f}{\partial f_i} \cdot \frac{\partial f_i}{\partial w_i} \cdot \frac{\partial w_i}{\partial \mu_{ij}} \cdot \frac{\partial \mu_{ij}}{\partial c_{ij}}. \tag{18}$$

4.2. Particle Swarm Optimisation

PSO is an iterative metaheuristic computational algorithm inspired by social behaviour of birds and fishes within a flock. This method is first proposed by Eberhart and Kennedy and is considered as one of the swarm intelligence population-based search methods that is usually exploited to solve optimisation problems [44]. In PSO algorithm, potential solutions to the optimisation problem are referred to as particles. In each iteration, the position and velocity of the particles are updated by moving them in the search domain. Each particle movement is determined using its local best position ($x_{\mathrm{P,best}}$) but is influenced by the other particles best-known position in the search-space ($x_{\mathrm{G,best}}$) as

$$v_i(k) = wv_i(k-1) + \rho_1(x_{\mathrm{P,best}} - x_i(k)) + \rho_2(x_{\mathrm{G,best}} - x_i(k)) \tag{19}$$

$$x_i(k) = x_i(k-1) + v_i(k) \tag{20}$$

where ρ_1 and ρ_2 are random variables defined as $\rho_1 = r_1c_1$ and $\rho_2 = r_2c_2$, with r_1 and $r_2 \sim U(0, 1)$. The variables c_1 and c_2 are positive acceleration constants that satisfy the condition $c_1 + c_2 \leq 4$ [45]. w is the inertial weight and is determined using the inertial weight approach (IWA) as follows [46]:

$$w = w_{\max} - \frac{w_{\max} - w_{\min}}{N_{\mathrm{itr,max}}} N_{\mathrm{itr}} \tag{21}$$

where $w_{\max}$ and $w_{\min}$ are the initial and final weights, respectively, N_{itr} is the current iteration number, and $N_{\mathrm{itr,max}}$ denotes the maximum number of iterations.

In the original GD-LSE method proposed by Jang [29], convergence of parameters is dependent on their initial value. Since this method is a gradient based approach the convergence speed of the algorithm is quite slow, especially for problems with a large set of variables. Furthermore, setting the best learning rate in the backpropagation algorithm is not an easy task and requires trial and error.

The PSO algorithm does not use the gradient of the optimisation problem as opposed to the classic optimisation methods such as GD-LSE. Therefore, it does not require the optimisation problem to be differentiable, however it cannot guarantee convergence to an optimal solution. Moreover, for a determined size of network, training ANFIS using the PSO algorithm is favourable as it is less computationally expensive [37].

5. Data Collection and Model Implementation

In this experiment, for modelling the evaporator, a set of 756 input-output data pairs are collected from the ORC testing facility by varying the heat source mass flow rate and temperature and working fluid mass flow rate. For the heat source, the mass flow rate and temperature of the supplied Marlotherm SM oil stream is altered using the electric heater in the range of 0.01 to 1.37 kg/s and 93 to 142 °C, respectively. Mass flow rate of the working fluid is also altered in the range of 14.4 to 57.8 g/s by manually changing the pump speed. Four separate multi-input single-output sub-models are trained for prediction of evaporator output temperature ($T_{\mathrm{r,out}}$) and evaporator output pressure ($P_{\mathrm{r,out}}$). The inputs to sub-models are identical and consist of mass flow rate of heat source ($\dot{m}_{\mathrm{h}}$), temperature of heat source (T_{h}) and mass flow rate of the working fluid ($\dot{m}_{\mathrm{r}}$). The recorded outputs for the sub-models are the evaporator outlet temperature ($T_{\mathrm{r,out}}$) and evaporator outlet pressure ($P_{\mathrm{r,out}}$). For evaluating the models, the data set is randomly divided to two subsets of training data set and test data set. The ANFIS network is optimised using the training data set whereas the test data set which is deployed for evaluating the model. In sub-models, 70% of data points are used for training the network and the remaining data points are deployed to test the constructed network. Among the available methods of clustering, fuzzy c-means (FCM) algorithm, due to its high flexibility is used for clustering the input space and generating the base FIS. The GD-LSE and PSO techniques are applied as the learning algorithm to optimise the base FIS. The training parameters for all four sub-models are listed in Table 4. The performance of both training methods is compared in terms of the RMSE and linear correlation coefficient (R) for both sub-models.

Table 4. Summary of R coefficients obtained for the evaporator outlet temperature sub-model.

Parameters	GD-LSE ANFIS Model for $T_{r,out}$	GD-LSE ANFIS Model for $P_{r,out}$	PSO ANFIS Model for $T_{r,out}$	PSO ANFIS Model for $P_{r,out}$
Training dataset samples	529 × 4	529 × 4	529 × 4	529 × 4
Test dataset samples	227 × 4	227 × 4	227 × 4	227 × 4
Clustering method	FCM	FCM	FCM	FCM
Membership functions	Gaussian	Gaussian	Gaussian	Gaussian
Number of clusters	8 × 3	8 × 3	8 × 3	8 × 3
Number of epochs	1000	1000	-	-
Number of linear parameters	32	32	32	32
Number of nonlinear parameters	48	48	48	48
Total number of parameters	80	80	80	80
Number of fuzzy rules	8	8	8	8
Maximum iteration	-	-	1000	1000
Population size	-	-	80	80
Inertial weight	-	-	1	1
Personal learning coefficient (C_1)	-	-	1	1
Global learning coefficient (C_2)	-	-	2	2

6. Results and Discussion

Two neuro-fuzzy models of evaporator are developed to predict the evaporator outlet temperature and evaporator outlet pressure in a 1-kWe ORC test rig. Figure 5 represents the comparison between evaporator outlet temperature prediction in the models trained using GD-LSE and PSO techniques. As illustrated in Figure 5, for the training dataset, RMSE of 3.5 and 2.4 achieved for GD-LSE and PSO, respectively. Furthermore, to evaluate the generalisation ability of the models, an unseen test dataset is applied to the models. For the test dataset, the obtained RMSEs are equal to 3.4 and 2.4 in the model trained using GD-LSE method and PSO technique, respectively. Comparison of RMSE for the evaporator outlet temperature models clearly indicates the models trained using the PSO algorithm have higher accuracies. For the training dataset, training the network using the PSO algorithm results in reduction of RMSE by 29% as compared to the GD-LSE algorithm. Similarly, for the test dataset, the RMSE reduced by 29% for the model trained using the PSO algorithm which indicates higher accuracy of this model as compared to the model trained using the GD-LSE algorithm.

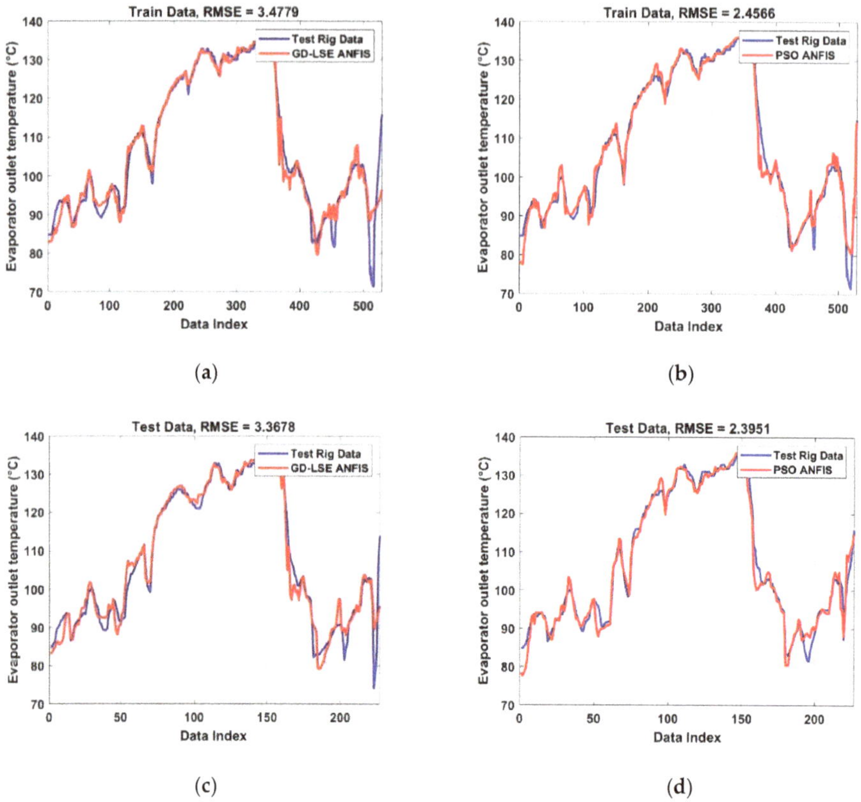

Figure 5. Comparison of GD-LSE ANFIS and PSO ANFIS model predictions of the evaporator outlet temperature, $T_{r,out}$, using training and test data: (**a**) training data (GD-LSE); (**b**) training data (PSO); (**c**) test data (GD-LSE); and (**d**) test data (PSO).

Furthermore, regression plots are shown in Figure 6, to illustrate the deviation of the predicted evaporator outlet temperatures from the experimentally obtained evaporator outlet temperatures. The linear correlation coefficient (R) for both GD-LSE and PSO models are listed in Table 5. Comparison of the R values indicate an acceptable fit for training and test data for both models. However, the R coefficients in the PSO model are closer to one, which imply better fit and greater generalisation ability of the model optimised by the PSO method. For the training and test datasets, the R coefficients improved 1.1% and 0.9%, respectively, by deploying the PSO method for training.

Table 5. Summary of R coefficients obtained for the evaporator outlet temperature sub-model.

Training Method	Training Data	Test Data
GD-LSE	0.98	0.98
PSO	0.99	0.99

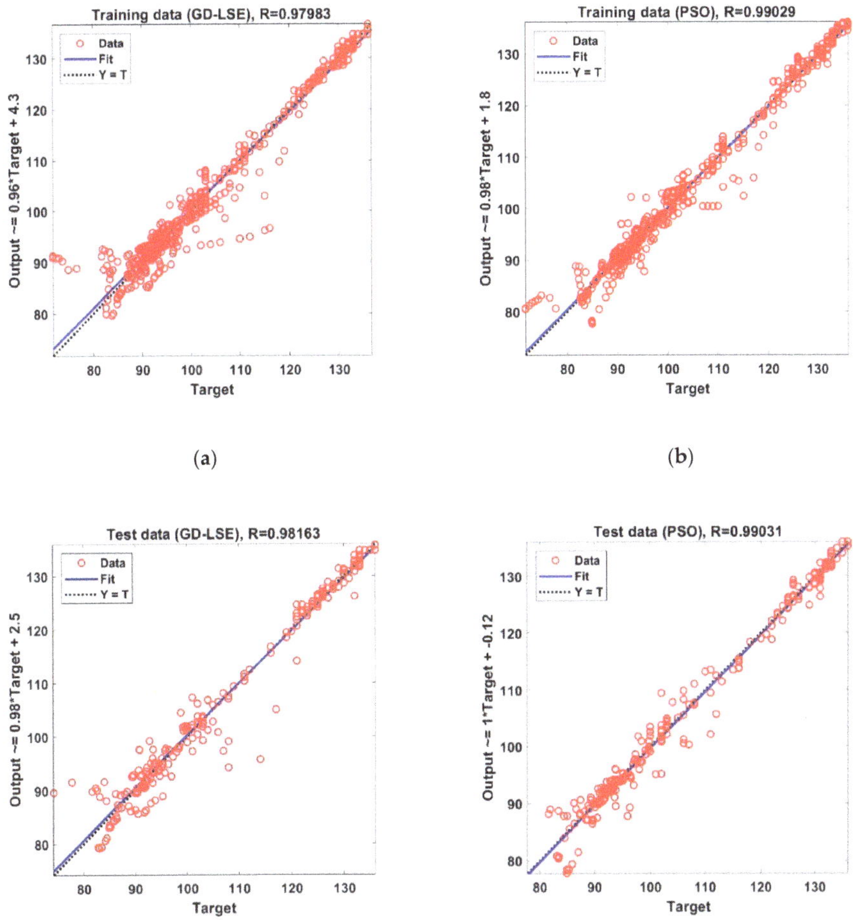

(a) (b)

(c) (d)

Figure 6. Comparison of regression plots between GD-LSE ANFIS and PSO ANFIS models for prediction of evaporator outlet temperature, $T_{r,out}$, using the training and test data: (**a**) training data (GD-LSE); (**b**) training data (PSO); (**c**) test data (GD-LSE); and (**d**) test data (PSO).

ANFIS model is applied to predict evaporator outlet pressure. The new sub-model is trained by deploying the GD-LSE technique and PSO technique. Comparison of the obtained RMSE values from both training and test dataset is presented in Figure 7. For the training dataset RMSE of 0.42 and 0.35 are achieved from the models trained using GD-LSE technique and PSO technique, respectively. The obtained RMSE for the unseen test data is 0.45 for the PSO ANFIS model and 0.54 for the GD-LSE model. It can be inferred that the evaporator outlet pressure results achieved from the PSO ANFIS model have a better compliance with the experimental data as evaluated against the model trained by the GD-LSE technique. For the training data, deploying the PSO algorithm to train the neuro fuzzy model results in 15% improvement in the RMSE as compared with the GD-LSE method. Moreover, for the test data the RMSE of the model trained using the PSO technique enhanced by 18%, which illustrates better generalisation ability in prediction of the evaporator outlet pressure.

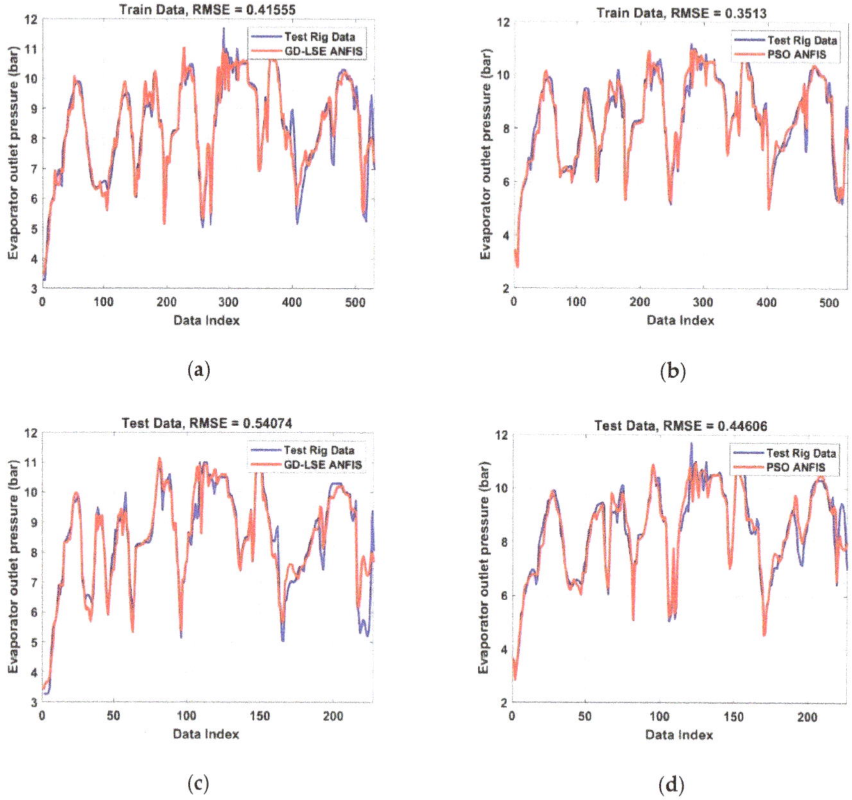

Figure 7. Comparison of GD-LSE ANFIS and PSO ANFIS model predictions of the evaporator outlet pressure, $P_{r,out}$, using training and test data: (**a**) training data (GD-LSE); (**b**) training data (PSO); (**c**) test data (GD-LSE); and (**d**) test data (PSO).

Similarly, to examine the accuracy of the models, comparison of the regression plots for the models trained by GD-LSE and PSO methods are shown in Figure 8. The R coefficient for the training and test data sets in both models are close to one, which indicates the agreement between the predictions from the models and the experimentally measured evaporator outlet pressures. The obtained linear correlation coefficients are listed in Table 6. The R values achieved for the training and test data sets are higher in the PSO model. Furthermore, the highest obtained accuracy is for the refrigerant output pressure model optimised using PSO algorithm with the linear correlation coefficient of 0.98 for the training dataset, and 0.96 for the test dataset. These two sub-models for the evaporator outlet temperature and evaporator outlet pressure can be used to identify the phase of the working medium instantaneously. Therefore, in the application of the ORC for recovery of the wasted heat in IC engines, this neuro-fuzzy model can be deployed to design an accurate control system to ensure the system safety and prevent decomposition of the working fluid by adjusting the pump speed.

Table 6. Summary of R coefficients obtained for the evaporator outlet pressure sub-model.

Training Method	Training Data	Test Data
GD-LSE	0.96	0.95
PSO	0.98	0.96

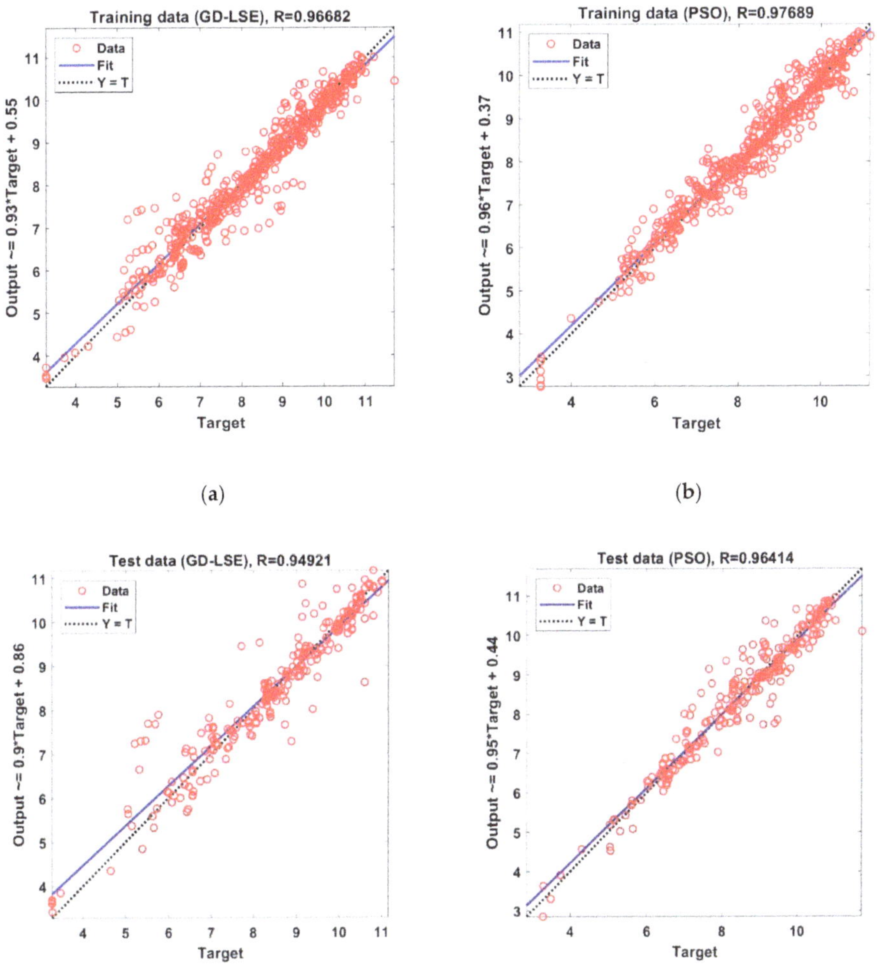

Figure 8. Comparison of regression plots between GD-LSE ANFIS and PSO ANFIS model predictions of the evaporator outlet pressure, $P_{r,out}$, using training and test data: (**a**) training data (GD-LSE); (**b**) training data (PSO); (**c**) test data (GD-LSE); and (**d**) test data (PSO).

The neuro-fuzzy models developed to predict the evaporator outlet temperature and evaporator outlet pressure are very agile due to the modelling benefits of fuzzy systems. Compared to the conventional models of evaporator such as FV and MB models, the neuro-fuzzy models do not require numerical solution of governing differential equations, and therefore, are computationally less expensive. The accuracy and speed of the neuro-fuzzy evaporator models illustrate its potential for real-time control purposes.

7. Conclusions

In this study, GD-LSE and PSO algorithms have been to train two neuro-fuzzy models for prediction of the evaporator outlet temperature and pressure of a 1-kWe ORC prototype. As system safety is vital in ORC applications for the recovery of waste heat from the exhaust gases of IC engines, accurate modelling of the evaporator outlet temperature, and pressure plays a pivotal role in the design of suitable control systems. Comparisons of experimentally gathered data and predictions from the neuro-fuzzy models reveal an acceptable accuracy in predicting the evaporator outlet temperature and pressure.

Based on the obtained results the main findings from this study are as follows:

- The neuro-fuzzy models offer reduced complexity, high accuracy and lower computational burden for prediction of the evaporator outlet temperature and pressure.
- The models developed by using neuro-fuzzy technique can be deployed for real-time control of ORC in various applications.
- Compared to the models trained using the GD-LSE algorithm, the models trained using the population-based PSO algorithm obtained better accuracy in terms of RMSEs and R coefficients for the training and test datasets. For the evaporator outlet temperature, a 29% improvement in the RMSE was achieved for both the training and test data. Furthermore, the evaporator outlet pressure RMSE improved by 15% and 18% for the training and test data, respectively, by using the PSO algorithm.
- The effort to identify the model parameters reduced substantially in the ANFIS models as opposed to the conventional non-adaptive methods of fuzzy system tuning.

Author Contributions: H.E.: conceptualization, methodology, experimentation, validation and writing; P.S.: methodology, experimentation, review and editing; C.K.U.: experimentation; P.F.: supervision; C.N.M.: supervision and review; B.K.N.: supervision and review. All authors have read and agreed to the published version of the manuscript.

Funding: This work was supported by the Department of Engineering, School of Engineering and Informatics, University of Sussex, UK. This work was also supported by the UK Engineering and Physical Sciences Research Council (EPSRC) [grant numbers EP/P004709/1, and EP/R045518/1].

Data Availability Statement: The data presented in this study are available on request from the first author.

Conflicts of Interest: The authors declare no conflict of interest.

Nomenclature

ABC	artificial bee colony
ANFIS	adaptive network-based fuzzy inference system
AWPSO	adaptive weighted particle swarm optimisation
EKF	extended Kalman filter
FFRLS	forgetting factor recursive least squares
FSI	fuel stratified injection
FV	finite volume
GA	genetic algorithm
GD	gradient descent
GDI	gasoline direct injection
HDDE	heavy-duty diesel engine
ICE	internal combustion engine
IWA	inertial weight approach
KW	kilowatt
LSE	least square estimate
MB	moving boundary
ORC	organic Rankine cycle
PSO	particle swarm optimisation
RMSE	root mean square error
SRC	steam Rankine cycle
TDI	turbo direct injection
TES	thermal energy storage
TP	two-phase region
TP-V	two-phase and vapour region
WHR	waste heat recovery

Greek letters	
η	learning rate
μ	membership function
ρ	random variable
σ	fuzzy set width
Variables	
A, B	linguistic variables
c	fuzzy set centre
C	acceleration constant
L	length of evaporator
$\dot{m}$	mass flow rate
N	number of control volumes
P	pressure
p, q, r	consequent parameters
T	temperature
W	inertial weight
Subscripts	
ev	evaporator
G	global
h	heat source
in	inlet
itr	iteration
out	outlet
P	personal
r	refrigerant

References

1. Saliba, G.; Saleh, R.; Zhao, Y.; Presto, A.A.; Lambe, A.T.; Frodin, B.; Sardar, S.; Maldonado, H.; Maddox, C.; May, A.A.; et al. Comparison of gasoline direct-injection (GDI) and port fuel injection (PFI) vehicle emissions: Emission certification standards, cold-start, secondary organic aerosol formation potential, and potential climate impacts. *Environ. Sci. Technol.* **2017**, *51*, 6542–6552. [CrossRef]
2. Lecointe, B.; Monnier, G. Downsizing a gasoline engine using turbocharging with direct injection. *SAE Tech. Paper Ser.* **2003**, *1*, 542. [CrossRef]
3. Ciatti, S.; Johnson, M.; Das Adhikary, B.; Reitz, R.D.; Knock, A. Efficiency and emissions performance of multizone stratified compression ignition using different octane fuels. *SAE Tech. Paper Ser.* **2013**, *1*, 263. [CrossRef]
4. Armstead, J.R.; Miers, S.A. Review of waste heat recovery mechanisms for internal combustion engines. *J. Therm. Sci. Eng. Appl.* **2013**, *6*, 014001. [CrossRef]
5. Sprouse, C.; Depcik, C. Review of organic Rankine cycles for internal combustion engine exhaust waste heat recovery. *Appl. Therm. Eng.* **2013**, *51*, 711–722. [CrossRef]
6. Yang, K.; Zhang, H.; Song, S.; Zhang, J.; Wu, Y.; Zhang, Y.; Wang, H.; Chang, Y.; Bei, C. Performance analysis of the vehicle diesel engine-ORC combined system based on a screw expander. *Energies* **2014**, *7*, 3400–3419. [CrossRef]
7. Katsanos, C.; Hountalas, D.; Pariotis, E. Thermodynamic analysis of a Rankine cycle applied on a diesel truck engine using steam and organic medium. *Energy Convers. Manag.* **2012**, *60*, 68–76. [CrossRef]
8. Freymann, -I.H.R.; Strobl, D.-I.W.; Obieglo, S.T.A. The turbosteamer: A system introducing the principle of cogeneration in automotive applications. *MTZ Worldw.* **2008**, *69*, 20–27. [CrossRef]
9. Enayatollahi, H.; Fussey, P.; Nguyen, B. Control of organic Rankine cycle, a neuro-fuzzy approach. *Control. Eng. Pract.* **2021**, *109*, 104728. [CrossRef]
10. Yu, G.; Shu, G.; Tian, H.; Wei, H.; Liu, L. Simulation and thermodynamic analysis of a bottoming organic Rankine cycle (ORC) of diesel engine (DE). *Energy* **2013**, *51*, 281–290. [CrossRef]
11. Dai, Y.; Wang, J.; Gao, L. Parametric optimization and comparative study of organic Rankine cycle (ORC) for low grade waste heat recovery. *Energy Convers. Manag.* **2009**, *50*, 576–582. [CrossRef]
12. Le Brun, N.; Simpson, M.; Acha, S.; Shah, N.; Markides, C.N. Techno-economic potential of low-temperature, jacket-water heat recovery from stationary internal combustion engines with organic Rankine cycles: A cross-sector food-retail study. *Appl. Energy* **2020**, *274*, 115260. [CrossRef]
13. Simpson, M.C.; Chatzopoulou, M.A.; Oyewunmi, O.A.; Le Brun, N.; Sapin, P.; Markides, C.N. Technoeconomic analysis of internal combustion engine–organic Rankine cycle systems for combined heat and power in energy-intensive buildings. *Appl. Energy* **2019**, *253*, 113462. [CrossRef]
14. Wang, E.; Zhang, H.; Fan, B.; Ouyang, M.; Zhao, Y.; Mu, Q. Study of working fluid selection of organic Rankine cycle (ORC) for engine waste heat recovery. *Energy* **2011**, *36*, 3406–3418. [CrossRef]

15. van Kleef, L.M.; Oyewunmi, O.; Markides, C.N. Multi-objective thermo-economic optimization of organic Rankine cycle (ORC) power systems in waste-heat recovery applications using computer-aided molecular design techniques. *Appl. Energy* **2019**, *251*, 112513. [CrossRef]
16. Oyewunmi, O.; Taleb, A.I.; Haslam, A.J.; Markides, C.N. On the use of SAFT-VR Mie for assessing large-glide fluorocarbon working-fluid mixtures in organic Rankine cycles. *Appl. Energy* **2016**, *163*, 263–282. [CrossRef]
17. White, M.; Oyewunmi, O.; Chatzopoulou, M.; Pantaleo, A.; Haslam, A.; Markides, C. Computer-aided working-fluid design, thermodynamic optimisation and thermoeconomic assessment of ORC systems for waste-heat recovery. *Energy* **2018**, *161*, 1181–1198. [CrossRef]
18. Chatzopoulou, M.A.; Lecompte, S.; De Paepe, M.; Markides, C.N. Off-design optimisation of organic Rankine cycle (ORC) engines with different heat exchangers and volumetric expanders in waste heat recovery applications. *Appl. Energy* **2019**, *253*, 113442. [CrossRef]
19. Schuster, S.; Markides, C.N.; White, A.J. Design and off-design optimisation of an organic Rankine cycle (ORC) system with an integrated radial turbine model. *Appl. Therm. Eng.* **2020**, *174*, 115192. [CrossRef]
20. Van Erdeweghe, S.; Van Bael, J.; Laenen, B.; D'Haeseleer, W. Design and off-design optimization procedure for low-temperature geothermal organic Rankine cycles. *Appl. Energy* **2019**, *242*, 716–731. [CrossRef]
21. Chatzopoulou, M.A.; Simpson, M.; Sapin, P.; Markides, C.N. Off-design optimisation of organic Rankine cycle (ORC) engines with piston expanders for medium-scale combined heat and power applications. *Appl. Energy* **2019**, *238*, 1211–1236. [CrossRef]
22. Freeman, J.; Hellgardt, K.; Markides, C.N. An assessment of solar-powered organic Rankine cycle systems for combined heating and power in UK domestic applications. *Appl. Energy* **2015**, *138*, 605–620. [CrossRef]
23. Wei, D.; Lu, X.; Lu, Z.; Gu, J. Dynamic modeling and simulation of an Organic Rankine Cycle (ORC) system for waste heat recovery. *Appl. Therm. Eng.* **2008**, *28*, 1216–1224. [CrossRef]
24. Chowdhury, J.I.; Nguyen, B.K.; Thornhill, D. Modelling of evaporator in waste heat recovery system using finite volume method and fuzzy technique. *Energies* **2015**, *8*, 14078–14097. [CrossRef]
25. Horst, T.A.; Rottengruber, H.-S.; Seifert, M.; Ringler, J. Dynamic heat exchanger model for performance prediction and control system design of automotive waste heat recovery systems. *Appl. Energy* **2013**, *105*, 293–303. [CrossRef]
26. Desideri, A.; Dechesne, B.; Wronski, J.; Broek, M.V.D.; Gusev, S.; Lemort, V.; Quoilin, S. Comparison of moving boundary and finite-volume heat exchanger models in the Modelica language. *Energies* **2016**, *9*, 339. [CrossRef]
27. Enayatollahi, H.; Fussey, P.; Nguyen, B.K. Modelling evaporator in organic Rankine cycle using hybrid GD-LSE ANFIS and PSO ANFIS techniques. *Therm. Sci. Eng. Prog.* **2020**, *19*, 100570. [CrossRef]
28. Chowdhury, J.I.; Nguyen, B.K.; Thornhill, D.; Hu, Y.; Soulatiantork, P.; Balta-Ozkan, N.; Varga, L. Fuzzy nonlinear dynamic evaporator model in supercritical organic Rankine cycle waste heat recovery systems. *Energies* **2018**, *11*, 901. [CrossRef]
29. Jang, J.-S. ANFIS: Adaptive-network-based fuzzy inference system. *IEEE Trans. Syst. Man Cybern.* **1993**, *23*, 665–685. [CrossRef]
30. Khosravi, A.; Syri, S.; Zhao, X.; Assad, M.E.H. An artificial intelligence approach for thermodynamic modeling of geothermal based-organic Rankine cycle equipped with solar system. *Geothermics* **2019**, *80*, 138–154. [CrossRef]
31. Enayatollahi, H.; Fussey, P.; Nguyen, B.K. A neuro-fuzzy model of evaporator in organic Rankine cycle. In Proceedings of the 5th World Congress on Mechanical, Chemical, and Material Engineering 2019, Lisbon, Portugal, 15–17 August 2019.
32. Unamba, C.K.; Sapin, P.; Li, X.; Song, J.; Wang, K.; Shu, G.; Tian, H.; Markides, C.N. Operational optimisation of a non-recuperative 1-kWe organic Rankine cycle engine prototype. *Appl. Sci.* **2019**, *9*, 3024. [CrossRef]
33. Kharb, R.K.; Shimi, S.; Chatterji, S.; Ansari, F. modeling of solar PV module and maximum power point tracking using ANFIS. *Renew. Sustain. Energy Rev.* **2014**, *33*, 602–612. [CrossRef]
34. Esen, H.; Inalli, M.; Sengur, A.; Esen, M. Predicting performance of a ground-source heat pump system using fuzzy weighted pre-processing-based ANFIS. *Build. Environ.* **2008**, *43*, 2178–2187. [CrossRef]
35. Awadallah, M.A.; Bayoumi, E.H.; Soliman, H.M. Adaptive deadbeat controllers for brushless DC drives using PSO and ANFIS techniques. *J. Electr. Eng.* **2009**, *60*, 3–11.
36. Shoorehdeli, M.A.; Teshnehlab, M.; Sedigh, A.K.; Khanesar, M.A. Identification using ANFIS with intelligent hybrid stable learning algorithm approaches and stability analysis of training methods. *Appl. Soft Comput.* **2009**, *9*, 833–850. [CrossRef]
37. Shoorehdeli, M.A.; Teshnehlab, M.; Sedigh, A.K. Training ANFIS as an identifier with intelligent hybrid stable learning algorithm based on particle swarm optimization and extended Kalman filter. *Fuzzy Sets Syst.* **2009**, *160*, 922–948. [CrossRef]
38. Sargolzaei, A.; Faez, K.; Sargolzaei, S. A new method for Foetal Electrocardiogram extraction using Adaptive Nero-Fuzzy Interference System trained with PSO algorithm. In Proceedings of the 2011 IEEE International Conference on Electro/Information Technology, Mankato, MN, USA, 15–17 May 2011; pp. 1–5.
39. Turki, M.; Bouzaida, S.; Sakly, A.; M'Sahli, F. Adaptive control of nonlinear system using neuro-fuzzy learning by PSO algorithm. In Proceedings of the 2012 16th IEEE Mediterranean Electrotechnical Conference, Institute of Electrical and Electronics Engineers (IEEE), Hammamet, Tunisia, 25–28 March 2012; pp. 519–523.
40. Rini, D.P.; Shamsuddin, S.M.; Yuhaniz, S.S. Balanced the trade-offs problem of anfis using particle swarm optimization. *TELKOMNIKA Telecommun. Comput. Electron. Control* **2013**, *11*, 611–616. [CrossRef]
41. Karaboga, D.; Kaya, E. Training ANFIS using artificial bee colony algorithm. In *2013 IEEE INISTA*; Institute of Electrical and Electronics Engineers (IEEE): New York, NY, USA, 2013; pp. 1–5.

42. Soto, J.; Melin, P.; Castillo, O. Optimization of interval type-2 fuzzy integrators in ensembles of ANFIS models for prediction of the Mackey-Glass time series. In Proceedings of the 2014 IEEE Conference on Norbert Wiener in the 21st Century (21CW), Boston, MA, USA, 24–26 June 2014; pp. 1–8.
43. Cárdenas, J.J.; García, A.; Romeral, J.L.; Kampouropoulos, K. Evolutive ANFIS training for energy load profile forecast for an IEMS in an automated factory. *ETFA2011* **2011**, 1–8. [CrossRef]
44. Kennedy, J.; Eberhart, R. Particle swarm optimization. In Proceedings of the ICNN'95 International Conference on Neural Networks, Perth, Australia, 27 November–1 December 1995; Volume 4, pp. 1942–1948.
45. Kennedy, J. Swarm intelligence. In *Handbook of Nature-Inspired and Innovative Computing*; Springer: New York, NY, USA, 2006; pp. 187–219.
46. Kennedy, J. The behavior of particles. In *International Conference on Evolutionary Programming*; Springer: Berlin/Heidelberg, Germany, 1998; pp. 579–589.

electronics

MDPI

Article

Automatic Identification Algorithm of Equivalent Electrochemical Circuit Based on Electroscopic Impedance Data for a Lead Acid Battery

Javier Olarte [1,2,3], Jaione Martínez de Ilarduya [1], Ekaitz Zulueta [3], Raquel Ferret [2], Unai Fernández-Gámiz [3] and Jose Manuel Lopez-Guede [3,*]

1 Bcare. C/Albert Einstein 48, 01510 Miñano, Álava, Spain; jolarte@bcaremb.com (J.O.); jmartinez@bcaremb.com (J.M.d.I.)
2 Centre for Cooperative Research on Alternative Energies (CIC energiGUNE), Basque Research and Technology Alliance (BRTA), Alava Technology Park, Albert Einstein 48, 01510 Vitoria-Gasteiz, Álava, Spain; rferret@cicenergigune.com
3 UPV/EHU. C/Nieves Cano 12, 01006 Vitoria-Gasteiz, Álava, Spain; ekaitz.zulueta@ehu.eus (E.Z.); unai.fernandez@ehu.eus (U.F.-G.)
* Correspondence: jm.lopez@ehu.eus; Tel.: +34-945-297108

Abstract: Obtaining tools to analyze and predict the performance of batteries is a non-trivial challenge because it involves non-destructive evaluation procedures. At the research level, the development of sensors to allow cell-level monitoring is an innovative path, and electrochemical impedance spectrometry (*EIS*) has been identified as one of the most promising tools, as is the generation of advanced multivariable models that integrate environmental and internal-battery information. In this article, we describe an algorithm that automatically identifies a battery-equivalent electrochemical model based on electroscopic impedance data. This algorithm allows in operando monitoring of variations in the equivalent circuit parameters that will be used to further estimate variations in the state of health (SoH) and state of charge (SoC) of the battery based on a correlation with experimental aging data corresponding to states of failure or degradation. In the current work, the authors propose a two-step parameter identification algorithm. The first consists of a rough differential evolution algorithm-based identification. The second is based on the Nelder–Mead Simplex search method, which gives a fine parameter estimation. These algorithm results were compared with those of the commercially available Z-view, an equivalent circuit tool estimation that requires expert human input.

Keywords: automatic identification; electrochemical model; electrochemical impedance spectrometry (*EIS*); electric equivalent circuit (EEC); lead acid batteries

1. Introduction

Batteries fulfill a vital function in many stationary applications, so any problem in a cell or module that could destabilize its energy storage capacity represents a significant expense. For instance, solutions based on the manual measurements of the state of health of the energy storage system involves high maintenance costs. If the review frequency is low, failures are not detected in time, the battery's life expectancy is not maximized, and end-user has added expenses. In this framework, the integration of sensors at the cell level and the development and optimization of a Battery Management System (BMS) are important for creating batteries that can meet these requirements. The monitoring of the battery by the implementation of smart models and algorithms to the BMS permits the continuous collection of historical data, including the State of Charge (SoC) and State of Health (SoH), thereby minimizing battery failure. In addition, it can be identified continuously. This monitoring action would also reduce the maintenance costs associated with on-site visits. For example, the biggest challenge in lead-acid battery management is determining the health status of the battery throughout its life while optimizing operational and maintenance costs [1–7].

As the requirements of batteries increase in demand and complexity, the ability to understand, control, and predict battery performance becomes more important. It seems axiomatic that the identification and characterization of battery electrochemical models is crucial to predicting battery life and to controlling and understanding the battery itself. These models are based on interpreting electrochemical behavior with respect to a wide range of battery properties (performance, life span, and especially safety), and in this Electrochemical Impedance Spectroscopy (*EIS*) plays a remarkable role [6].

In summary, integration of smart *EIS* sensing and the extraction of key parameters produces a detailed understanding and evaluation of the battery, develops better energy management strategies, and enables smart SoC and SoH identification to improve performance. The review presented by Unguren et al. [8] includes a valuable updated comparison of the different types of models that have been used, mainly for electric mobility applications. This work focuses on the dynamic identification of electrochemical model parameters, as suggested by Kwiecien et al. [6]. The work of Lin et al. [9] includes an overview of the latest work in electric mobility, but there is still room to improve battery management algorithms, despite the enormous efforts made. Regarding possible improvements in the battery management system, thermal management is also important, as shown by the study by Jilte et al. [10]. Possibly one of the positive messages of this report is the importance of collecting as much experimental data as possible to implement incremental improvements in the models. Indeed, the more relevant models, which range from simple one-dimensional models to highly complex multi-dimensional coupled ones, as suggested by Olarte et al. [11], are be made by in operando electrochemical data, as in the case of this work.

The process of determining the SoC and SoH of batteries is challenging. Several imaginative monitoring approaches have been introduced that have generated a number of patents covering different technologies [12]. Over many years, this kind of research paid attention mainly to lead-acid technology to make it more accessible to customers. A number of advances in assessing the behavior of cell resistance upon cycling in Pb-acid batteries was made possible by the introduction of Electrochemical Impedance Spectroscopy (*EIS*), which evaluates the battery's SoC and SoH by combining a set of direct measurements, namely, resistance, current pulse quantities, *EIS*, coulomb counting, and open circuit voltage-based approximations.

Numerous studies have reported different ways to estimate SoC and SoH variables, which can be divided into different categories: direct measurements, electrical and electrochemical models, and adaptive and machine learning methods [13–16]. For example, Chaturvedi et al. reviewed different algorithms for SoC and SoH indication and commercially available Battery Management Systems and concluded that SoC and SoH identification in vehicle batteries was still not accurate enough [13].

Among direct measurements, discharge test capacities can only be done at the beginning of a battery's working life or for intermediate measurements of its SoH. However, this type of method, even if precise, cannot be incorporated into an intelligent diagnostic detection system by itself, as explained by Lukic et al. [17].

Some electrochemical models are based on coulomb counting, which can be very accurate but only if the initial input is valid, and for this high accuracy current sensors are required [18,19]. Open Circuit Voltage (OCV) measurement is used in lead-acid, lithium-ion or zinc/bromine batteries, which are based on the relation of the OCV to the SoC. The OCV is usually measured in off-line conditions, but it could be conducted on-line if the OCV is deduced from terminal voltage real values or suitable models.

Another method for making real-time predictions by interpreting parameters from the spectra is Electrochemical Impedance Spectroscopy (*EIS*). It is difficult to implement the electrochemical model because it depends on a specific technology [18], but it is expected to be very accurate. The last electrochemical model is Kalman filters, which can be implemented in all battery systems, although implementation entails a high level of difficulty.

The difficulty in determining the parameters of the *EIS* spectrum lies in the development of an adequate and advanced algorithm that allows both automatic and reliable identification. There are different techniques for identifying system parameters, and the common laboratory approach consists of measuring the impedance spectrum of a cell's frequency domain by means of a single sine-sweep signal. Then, the ECM parameters are fitted to the frequency domain. Among the authors who have developed work related to this topic, is Al Nazer et al., who presented a two-step method, although initial expert background to define the initial parameter values was necessary [20]. Nasser-Eddine et al. presented a two-step identification method combining chronopotentiometry and *EIS* [21]. Gonzalez et al. used a self-adaptive differential evolution algorithm for metal coating systems that had only been tested with experimental inputs [22]. On the other hand, the study of Alavi et al. [23] paid attention to the estimation of ECM parameters directly from data gathered in the time domain. That technique could have practical applications for parameter estimation in battery-powered vehicles. In addition, Zou et al. [24] presented a critical synopsis of fractional-order techniques for dealing with lead-acid batteries, lithium-ion batteries, and supercapacitors. In the study of Ramos et al. [25], an improvement in the gene expression programming of specific details of implementation was presented with pre-embedded knowledge to improve the efficiency of identifying circuits in impedance spectroscopy. On the other hand, a convolutional neural network (CNN) was used by Chun et al. [26] to predict or prevent problems by observing the inner states of lithium-ion batteries.

In this paper, direct measurements based on the analysis of *EIS* impedance spectra were used to determine the electric equivalent circuit (EEC) parameters. Changes or variations in value based on a correlation with experimental *EIS* data from aging batteries corresponding to known states of failure or degradation allowed the fast mapping to SoC and SoH in combination with additional historical operational data of the battery system. Regarding the *EIS* impedance measurement, different authors made comments. According to Baccouche et al. [19], this method is very reliable as it presents high accuracy; however, it could be very time consuming and hard to implement. According to Rivera-Barrera et al. [15], this estimation method is only suitable for identical charging conditions. According to Chang [14], impedance measurements are very versatile in that they give information about many parameters, such as SoC, battery degradation, and failure modes.

The main innovation of the present work consists of proposing a new model to improve the certainty of EEC parameter estimation from *EIS*. The process of identification and use of parameters is interactive, which allows for the integration of more experimental variables. As important as developing an efficient and highly accurate algorithm of battery EEC parameters may be, it must also be implemented economically in hardware integrated into an advanced Battery Management System (BMS). A valuable part of the work to be done is inspired by the guidelines defined by the European Commission [12], which shares the objective of this work, i.e., the development of economical and efficient sensors. In this manner, this work has directed efforts to implement a computationally efficient yet robust algorithm that can be used in a low-cost device. With the implementation of the present algorithm, lead-acid batteries may become zero-maintenance because the adjusted predictions of the remaining useful life (RUL) and historical data records would allow continuous improvement that would improve overall performance, cycling strategies, battery safety and operation, and maintenance costs.

The remainder of the manuscript is structured as follows: Section 2 describes the aging data and the identification methods used to characterize battery impedance. Section 3 presents the main results of the identification process setup and the set of identified parameters. Finally, the main conclusions and future directions are summarized in Section 4.

2. Aging Data and Identification Methods

2.1. Aging Tests and Electrochemical Data Logs

The work is based on the aging and measurements of four lead-acid battery models from different manufacturers. These have between 80 and 100 Ah and 12 V, with improved performance at high temperatures compared to standard lead-acid batteries. They contain an anode of metallic lead (Pb), while the cathode consists of a paste of lead oxide (PbO_2). Between the electrodes is a porous separator impregnated with an electrolyte consisting of an aqueous acid solution of H_2SO_4. First, a standard characterization is performed to extract electrical parameters as inputs for the electrochemical model to characterize the SoC at standard C-rates, such as C/10. (The C-rate is a measure that governs the current at which a battery is charged and discharged. The capacity of a rechargeable battery is commonly rated at 1 C, meaning that a 1000 mAh battery should provide a current of 1000 mA for 1 h.)

Second, aging tests were developed based on the load profile for the stationary case application. These induced accelerated aging through a number of temperature profiles and modified cycling frequencies. In both type of tests, standard and aging characterization, the testing protocol included the constant current (CC) and constant voltage (CV) charge stages. Periodic impedance measurements were taken at different SoC levels and SoH stages (in the case of accelerated tests), at $\Delta h\% = 20$. At each SoC level, a 12 h relaxation time was established before performing the impedance measurement under an excitation current of 50 mA and in a frequency range from 10 mHz to 10 kHz. From these accelerated aging tests, suitable parameters/signals from the electrochemical system were extracted for integration into the model to determine the SoH for the lead-acid batteries. This testing protocol included voltage, current, temperature, and *EIS* spectra identification at different operational conditions. Figure 1 illustrates the equivalent circuit model proposed by the authors because all experiments showed inductive behavior at high frequencies and a circular shape spectrum at medium frequencies. At low frequencies, another lager circular shape spectrum is shown. The EEC was selected to monitor variations in impedance and resistance as well as charge transfer and diffusion phenomena, to allow us to monitor or detect variations in battery failure modes. The algorithm proposed in this work can be used with other associated EECs to monitor other interpretations of the electrochemical processes and dynamics in other batteries.

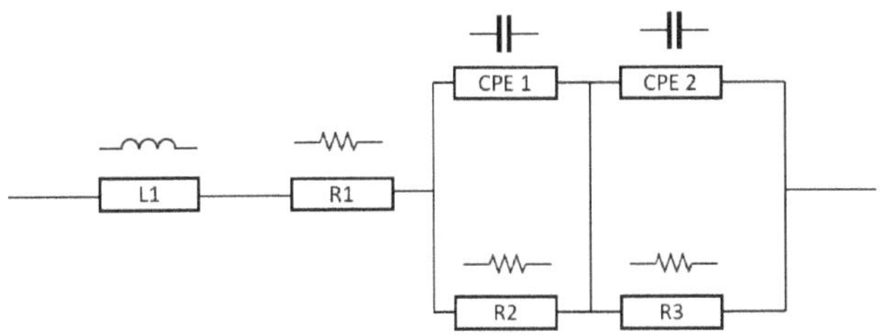

Figure 1. Equivalent *EIS* circuit model.

During both tests, electrochemical data from the *EIS* spectra and EEC parameters are recorded in logs. Specifically, this EEC is selected with constant phase elements so that the experimental data can be adjusted. Non-ideal capacitive behavior of an electrode (suppressed semi-circles on the Nyquist plot) are taken into account, and a constant phase element (*CPE*) is used (see Equation (1)), which is a capacitor with a leakage parameter of α. If the parameter is 1, the element is a pure capacitor (see Aksal et al. [1]).

$$ZCPE = \frac{1}{C(i\omega)^{\alpha}} \tag{1}$$

Using the gathered data, tendencies are analyzed, and complete electrochemical models are developed for each lead-acid battery.

2.2. Data Processing, Proposed Intelligent Identification Algorithm, and Cost Function

EIS is a faster technique for identifying the SoH and the SoC of lead-acid batteries provided that the data sets have been interpreted using a convenient EEC model. This section explains the mathematic expression of the *EIS* based on an equivalent electrical circuit from the previous section. From circuit theory, it follows that the *EIS* of the battery is given by Equation (2):

$$Z_{EIS} = Z_{R_1} + Z_{L_1} + Z_{R_2||CPE_1} + Z_{R_3||CPE_2} \quad (2)$$

Taking into account that the EEC consists of the simple electrical circuit elements *R*, *L* (and in this case constant phase elements (*CPEs*)), Equation (2) can be expressed as Equation (3):

$$Z_{R_2||CPE_1} = \frac{R_2\left(R_2C_1\omega^{\alpha_1}\cdot\left(cos\frac{\pi}{2}\alpha_1 - jsincos\frac{\pi}{2}\alpha_1\right) + 1\right)}{R_2^2C_1^2\omega^{2\alpha_1} + 2R_2C_1\omega^{\alpha_1}cos\frac{\pi}{2}\alpha_1 + 1} \quad (3)$$

The same procedure is followed for CPE_2:

$$Z_{R_3||CPE_2} = \frac{R_3\left(R_3C_2\omega^{\alpha_2}\cdot\left(cos\frac{\pi}{2}\alpha_2 - jsincos\frac{\pi}{2}\alpha_2\right) + 1\right)}{R_3^2C_2^2\omega^{2\alpha_2} + 2R_3C_3\omega^{\alpha_2}cos\frac{\pi}{2}\alpha_2 + 1} \quad (4)$$

To understand the previous equations, the following parameters need to be explained:

j = imaginary number ($j^2 = -1$)
ω = angular frequency (rad/s)
α = constant phase angle of the *CPE* (rad)
R = resistance (Ω)
C = capacitance (F)
L = inductance (H)

2.3. Proposed Intelligent Identification Algorithm

There are different types of algorithms for solving complex problems, and because of them we have a better understanding of lead-acid battery behavior such as the SoC and SoH.

Current research proposes the so-called differential evolution (DE) algorithm, which was first proposed in 1997 [27]. As is the case with Particle Swarm Optimization (PSO), DE is a noncomplex but powerful population-based stochastic search technique. As presented in Aramendia et al. [28], different agent sets are proposed by DE, and all agents follow the same procedure to improve the resulting agent set, evaluation, crossing, mutation, and selection. The three main vectors are described as follows:

- Target vector: The solution undergoing evolution used in mutation to generate a donor vector.
- Donor vector: Undergoes recombination to obtain the trial vector.
- Trial vector. An offspring formed by recombination of the donor with the target vector.

The set of variables to be optimized in this case were $R_1, L_1, R_2, C_1, \alpha_1, R_3, C_2,$ and α_2, which were real, so they were arranged or codified in a vector. The length of the resulting vectors (N) was the same as the number of variables. The nomenclature X_p^g was used to define a vector, where p indicated the individual population ($p = 1 \ldots NP$), g was the corresponding generational number, and NP is the agent number. The candidate solutions are defined in Equation (5):

$$X_p^g = \left\{x_{p,m}^1, \ldots, x_{p,m}^g\right\} \quad (5)$$

where $m = 1 \ldots n$. The DE algorithm is composed of four steps:

2.3.1. Initialization

The population was generated randomly without exceeding either the maximum or minimum limits, as described in Equation (6):

$$x_{p,m}^1 = x_m^{min} + rand(0,1)\cdot\left(x_m^{max} - x_m^{min}\right) \quad (6)$$

where $p = 1 \ldots NP$ and a uniformly distributed random variable within the range [0, 1] is represented by rand (0,1). This equation corresponded to generation 1 ($g = 1$).

2.3.2. Mutation

In the mutation operation, three random solutions (X_{r1}, X_{r2}, X_{r3}) were selected from a population of solutions. These solutions could not be identical. The donor vector was achieved with Equation (7):

$$V_p^g = X_{r3} + F\cdot(X_{r1} - X_{r2}) \quad (7)$$

where $p = 1 \ldots NP$; F is a scaling factor, a positive control parameter between (0,2) that scales the difference vector. For its target, $X_{p,\,g}$, at generation g, the associated donor vector, $V_p^g = \left\{v_{p,g}^1, \ldots, v_{p,g}^m\right\}$, can be generated.

2.3.3. Recombination

This operation increases the diversity of the population. The crossover operator generates a trial vector, $T_p^g = \left\{t_{p,g}^1, \ldots, t_{p,g}^m\right\}$, out of each target vector, $X_{p,\,g}$, and corresponding donor vector, $V_{p,\,g}$. For simpler implementation, the DE algorithm employs a binomial (uniform) crossover operator, as defined in Equation (8)

$$t_{p,m}^g = \begin{cases} v_{p,\,m}^g \; if \; rand([0,1]) < GR \\ x_{p,m}^g \; if \; any \; other \; case \end{cases} \quad (8)$$

where $m = 1 \ldots n$, $p = 1 \ldots NP$, and GR is the crossover rate, which actually is a constant defined by the user and has a value constrained by the range that controls the fraction of parameter values copied from the donor vector; $v_{p,\,m}^g$ is a variable of the donor vector, $x_{p,m}^g$ is a variable of the target vector, and $t_{p,m}^g$ is a variable of the trial vector.

2.3.4. Selection

The selection operation is determined by Equation (9):

$$X_p^{g+1} = \begin{cases} t_p^g \; if \; f\left(t_p^g\right) \leq f\left(X_p^g\right) \\ X_p^g \; otherwise \end{cases} \quad (9)$$

where $f\left(T_p^g\right)$ is the objective function value of each trial vector and is compared to that of its corresponding target vector, $f(X_p^g)$, with the current population. If the objective function value with the trial vector is less than or equal to the corresponding target vector, then the target vector will be replaced by the trial vector and enter into the next generation population. Otherwise, there will be no changes and the target vector will be kept for the next generation population. The previous three steps are repeated for an undetermined number of generations until specific termination criteria are reached.

2.4. Cost Function

As highlighted in the study of Martinez-Rico et al. [29], the optimization problem covers the objective of minimizing the loss of value. To know this loss of value, the following cost function, determined by Equation (10), is proposed:

$$J = \sum_{\mu=1}^{\mu=Nsamples} \left\| \vec{Z}_{EISexp}\left(\vec{\omega_\mu}\right) - \vec{Z}\left(\rightarrow, \vec{\omega_\mu}\right) \right\|^2 \tag{10}$$

where $\rightarrow = [R_1, L_1, R_2, C_1, \alpha_1, R_3, C_2, \alpha_2]$ and $\vec{\omega_\mu}$ = angular frequency. This angular frequency vector has 121 different frequencies, as defined by N samples.

According to Equation (10), it is possible to know the difference between the experimental values and the values of the proposed battery model, both the real and the imaginary parts. The experimental values were obtained as a function of different frequencies. Instead, the electrochemical impedance spectroscopy (*EIS*) of the model depended on several parameters, specifically the $\rightarrow$ parameters, which, as mentioned in the differential evolution algorithm part, were the ones that must be optimized to achieve the least possible loss of value.

2.5. Fine Parameter Identification Process

The Nelder–Mead Simplex method is a well-known optimization procedure. Its main disadvantage is that it must be near the optimal point because this algorithm can stop at local minima points. Nevertheless, the main advantage of this algorithm is its good convergence to a minimal point. Therefore, we combined it with DE to achieve a good set of identification parameters. This set was the initial value for the second step of parameter identification.

2.6. Test Definition

A total of 36 tests were performed over 5 months. The first was a discharge cycle test from 100 to 0% of the SoC. The exact SoCs evaluated were 100, 80, 60, 40, 20, and 0%. The battery was kept at 25 °C the whole time. Once the discharge cycle was finished, it was again charged to 100%, and the battery was kept in a floating state for a whole month. Afterwards, another discharge cycle started; therefore, the authors conducted 36 *EIS* experimental tests for each battery model after 5 months: 6 monthly tests with 6 SoCs. The tests had 121 frequencies with a logarithmic span as shown in Table 1.

Table 1. Test frequencies.

Highest Frequency	Lowest Frequency	Units
10,000	0.01	Hertz

3. Results

3.1. Identification Process Setup

The authors studied different optimization algorithms to match a parameter set-generated spectrum to the experimental spectrum. This issue was explained in Equation (10), and the corresponding frequencies are shown in Table 1. The first-step differential evolution algorithm options are included in Table 2, and the second-step Nelder–Mead Simplex algorithm options are in Table 3.

Table 2. First Step Differential Evolution algorithm options.

Agent Number	F Option	CR Option	Number of Iterations [1]
10,000	1	0.5	0.011

[1] First step's options do not change much parameter identification cost.

Table 3. Second Step Nelder–Mead Simplex algorithm options.

ρ	χ	γ	σ
1	2	0.5	0.5^2

The parameters/variables ρ and χ correspond to the reflection and expansion coefficients, respectively. The values presented in Table 3 are well-known as the best values for the Nelder–Mead Simplex method given by Lagarias et al. [30].

To improve convergence, DE algorithms were normalized between 0 and 1, and in the second step, we conducted the same normalization. The identification of parameters to set maximum and minimum normalized values is included in Table 4. These parameter set values were proposed by the experience obtained from the test data.

Table 4. Identification parameter set maximum and minimum values applied in normalization.

Identification Parameter	Maximum Value	Minimal Value	Units
R1	0.01	0.001	Ohms
R2	0.02	0.002	Ohms
R3	1	0.001	Ohms
C1	12	1	F
α_1	0.9	0.4	-
C2	300	40	F
α_2	0.8	0.4	-
L1	10^{-6}	10^{-8}	H^3

The parameters shown in Table 4 are the outputs of the proposed identification process. They had to be set to match the experimental *EIS* test data and were usually identified using commercial standard software, which needed high human expertise to obtain reliable matches with the experimental *EIS* data tests.

3.2. Identified Parameter Sets

The authors compared the cost functions obtained from DE and from DE combined with the Nelder–Mead Simplex method to improve the optimization of cost function values. $J_{DEprediction}$ is the optimization cost function value with unique DE optimization. $J_{DEoptim}$ is the two-step optimization. Figure 2 illustrates the square errors obtained from one-step DE-based identification and the two-step identification square errors. According to the results presented in Figure 2, the proposed identification improved significantly.

This optimization combined the exploration capability of DE with the fine convergence of the Nelder–Mead Simplex method as shown in Equation (11), where the improvement metric was defined. The authors compared these two methods with the mean square error. In Equation (10), the authors showed the applied metric. As the electrochemical impedance spectroscopy (*EIS*) data were complex-valued sample sets, the authors applied a complex number module to the error between the test and models data, which is the standard measurement technique for complex data. The authors reduced the ratio between the mean square errors obtained from the two-step identification and the one-step DE-based identification. The summary of all improved results is shown in Table 5.

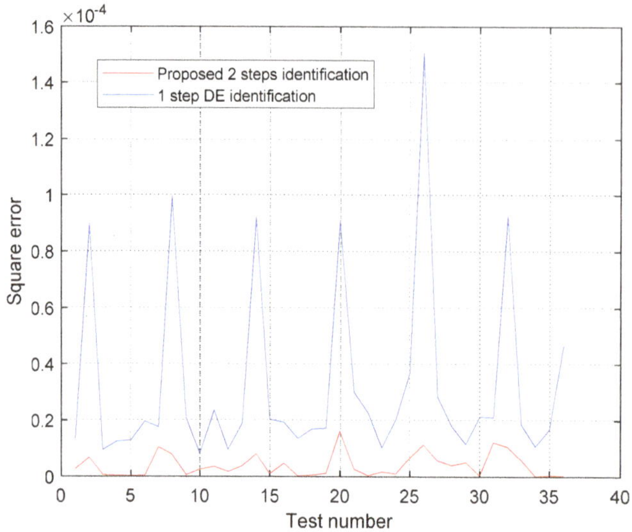

Figure 2. Square errors with proposed identification and with only DE algorithm identification.

Table 5. Mean and standard deviation improvement related to one differential evolution optimization.

Mean Improvement with Two-Step Optimization	Standard Deviation with Two-Step Optimization in %
85.1315	14.9142 [2]

[2] "In %" refers to the cost function, J, of one-step DE optimization.

In Figure 2, the x axis is the one-step DE-based identification RMSE and the two-step identification RMSE. The y axis is the test reference.

$$Improvement\ \% = 100 \cdot \frac{J_{DEprediction} - J_{DEoptim}}{J_{DEprediction}} \tag{11}$$

In Table 5, the mean and standard deviation improvement values relating to one differential evolution optimization are shown. The improvement is related to the RMSE obtained from the two-step optimization compared with the RMSE obtained by only taking into account the first-step optimization using DE.

In all tests, two-step optimization results were an improvement over one-step optimization. The first step gave a good approximation, but after a good parameter value set was proposed, the second-step optimization made a fine parameter fitting. In fact, the second algorithm had a fast convergence if it started close to the optimal solution. This second algorithm needed fewer iterations to make a fine fitting and a suitable initialization point. Consequently, the authors propose using DE to obtain a good starting point for the second optimization step.

Figure 3 shows the *EIS* experiment results. This Nyquist diagram illustrates three different regions: Region 1 has the contribution of the inductance and the ohmic resistance (L1 and R1 parameters, see Table 4) with high frequency samples; Region 2 is related to the first *CPE* parallel to the R2 identification parameter, which is usual for characterizing a circular *EIS* spectrum with these two elements; Region 3 is characterized as a larger circular spectrum, and for this reason, a characterization with a second *CPE* element parallel to R3 was made. In total, 36 experiments were carried out and all spectra showed similar behavior with these three different regions. Consequently, the equivalent circuit schema described in Figure 1 was proposed.

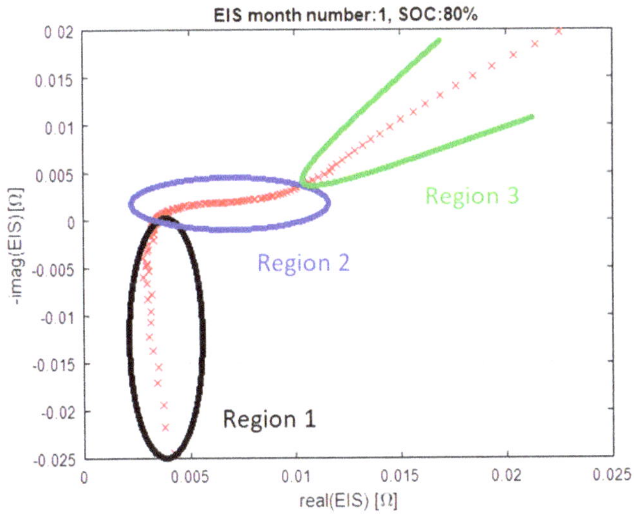

Figure 3. 80% SoC *EIS* experiment in first iteration (Pristine Battery).

Figure 4 represents the same experiment presented in Figure 3, with identification results added to the experimental samples represented by red crosses. The red line represents the DE optimization-based identification results, and the black line represents the two-step optimization-based identification results. Figure 4 shows that DE optimization gave a reasonably good parameter identification, but it was not fine enough (see red line). The parameter identification based on the two optimization steps represented by the black line gave a much better identification performance.

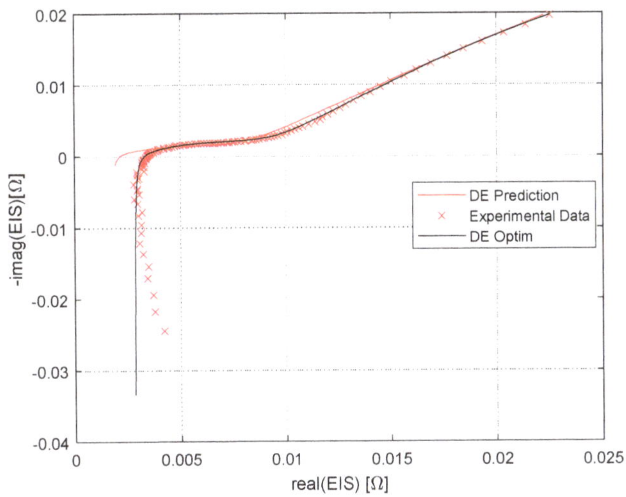

Figure 4. Comparison between one-step DE optimization-based identification result and two-step DE optimization-based identification results at 80% SoC.

In Figure 4, authors show that the two-step identification-based model (black line) showed better performance than did the one-step identification model (red line). The experimental data are identified by red crosses. The one-step identification model did not match Region 1 at all (defined in Figure 3), but the two-step identification model matched

Region 1's data very well. In Region 2, both models were good enough to match the experimental data. Finally, in Region 3, the two-step identification model matched the experimental data very well, even in the transition between Region 2 and 3; however, the transition between Regions 1 and 2 did not match the one-step identification correctly.

Note that 36 figures with experimental data were added as supplementary material. In addition, another 36 figures with graphic comparisons between the one-step DE and the combined DE–Nelder–Mead Simplex method were added. To confirm the efficiency of the identification proposed, 36 *EIS* experimental tests for each battery model were conducted after 5 months for a total of 6 monthly tests with 6 SoCs (100, 80, 60, 40, 20, and 0%). In emf format files named *OptimizationResults_month_X_SOC_Y*, the authors showed the identification results and the experimental data in X month with Y SoC. In emf format files named *month* = *X SOC* = *Y*, the authors showed only the experimental data in X month with Y SoC.

4. Conclusions

In summary, we proposed the use of an automatic algorithm to identify variations in the parameters for a given EEC. Usually, conventional identification needs expert human support to guide the identification results. The proposed algorithm allows in operando monitoring of the variation of the EEC parameters to further estimate changes or variations in the battery's state of charge (SoC) and state of health (SoH) based on a correlation with experimental aging data associated with states of failure or degradation. The authors proposed a reliable alternative for improving the parameter identification time of an *EIS*: A two-step optimization algorithm. In that way, the best characteristics of each algorithm were applied in the identification process.

Even though the proposed algorithm was shown to be robust enough, there is still room for improvement by gathering more experimental data and conducting a post-mortem analysis. These improvements will be based on the development of a complete SoH lead-acid battery supervisor that will gather both the proposed improved algorithm and the failure identification mode to apply preventive and corrective action to the complete battery system. This would not only be a significant advance in the field of predicting battery performance, but also be key to the development of remote monitoring systems.

Supplementary Materials: The following are available online at https://www.mdpi.com/2079-9292/10/11/1353/s1: The authors have added 36 figures with experimental data, 36 other figures with graphic comparisons between Differential Evolution unique step, and the combinations of Differential Evolutions with Nelder–Mead Simplex method.

Author Contributions: Conceptualization, supervision, and methodology, J.O.; optimization of algorithm proposal, implementation, and validation, E.Z.; testing and data analysis, J.M.d.I.; formal analysis, R.F.; investigation and writing—original draft, review and editing, U.F.-G. and J.M.L.-G. All authors have read and agreed to the published version of the manuscript.

Funding: Special thanks should also be expressed for the Torres Quevedo (PTQ) 2019 Aid from the State Research Agency, within the framework of the State Program for the Promotion of Talent and its Employability in R + D + i, Ref. PTQ2019-010787 /AEI/10.13039/501100011033.

Acknowledgments: The authors would like to express their gratitude to CIC energiGUNE and Bcare for the access to their facilities.

Conflicts of Interest: The authors declare no conflict of interest.

Abbreviations

Acronyms	
EIS	Electrochemical Impedance Spectroscopy
SoC	State of Charge
SoH	State of Health
RUL	Remaining Useful Lifetime
ECM	Equivalent Circuit Model
OCV	Open Circuit Voltage
CNN	Convolutional Neural Net wok
EEC	Electric Equivalent Circuit
CPE	Constant Phase Element
DE	Differential Evolution
ZCPE	Impedance Constant Phase Element
PSO	Particle Swarm Optimization
BMS	Battery Management System

Abbreviations

Greek and Other Symbols	
i	imaginary number ($i^2 = -1$)
ω	angular frequency (rad/s)
α	constant phase angle of the *CPE* (rad)
R	resistance (Ω)
C	capacitance (F)
L	inductance (H)
ρ	Reflection coefficient of Nelder–Mead algorithm
χ	Expansion coefficient of Nelder–Mead algorithm
γ	Coefficient of Nelder–Mead algorithm
σ	Coefficient of Nelder–Mead algorithm

References

1. Aksakal, C.; Şişman, A. On the Compatibility of Electric Equivalent Circuit Models for Enhanced Flooded Lead Acid Batteries Based on Electrochemical Impedance Spectroscopy. *Energies* **2018**, *11*, 118. [CrossRef]
2. Andre, D.; Appel, C.; Soczka-Guth, T.; Sauer, D.U. Advanced mathematical methods of SOC and SOH estimation for lithium-ion batteries. *J. Power Sources* **2013**, *224*, 20–27. [CrossRef]
3. Badeda, J.; Kwiecien, M.; Schulte, D.; Sauer, D.U. Battery State Estimation for Lead-Acid Batteries under Float Charge Conditions by Impedance: Benchmark of Common Detection Methods. *Appl. Sci.* **2018**, *8*, 1308. [CrossRef]
4. Culpin, B.; Rand, D. Failure modes of lead/acid batteries. *J. Power Sources* **1991**, *36*, 415–438. [CrossRef]
5. Dost, P.; Sourkounis, C. Generalized Lead-Acid based Battery Model used for a Battery Management System. *Athens J. Technol. Eng.* **2016**, *3*, 255–270. [CrossRef]
6. Kwiecien, M.; Huck, M.; Badeda, J.; Zorer, C.; Komut, K.; Yu, Q.; Sauer, D.U. Variation of Impedance in Lead-Acid Batteries in the Presence of Acid Stratification. *Appl. Sci.* **2018**, *8*, 1018. [CrossRef]
7. McKeon, B.B.; Furukawa, J.; Fenstermacher, S. Advanced Lead–Acid Batteries and the Development of Grid-Scale Energy Storage Systems. *Proc. IEEE* **2014**, *102*, 951–963. [CrossRef]
8. Ungurean, L.; Cârstoiu, G.; Micea, M.V.; Groza, V. Battery state of health estimation: A structured review of models, methods and commercial devices: Battery State of Health Estimation: A Structured Review. *Int. J. Energy Res.* **2017**, *41*, 151–181. [CrossRef]
9. Lin, Q.; Wang, J.; Xiong, R.; Shen, W.; He, H. Towards a smarter battery management system: A critical review on optimal charging methods of lithium ion batteries. *Energy* **2019**, *183*, 220–234. [CrossRef]
10. Jilte, R.; Afzal, A.; Panchal, S. A novel battery thermal management system using nano-enhanced phase change materials. *Energy* **2021**, *219*, 119564. [CrossRef]
11. Olarte, J.; Dauvergne, J.-L.; Herrán, A.; Drewett, N.; Bekaert, E.; Zulueta, E.; Ferret, R. Validation of thermal imaging as a tool for failure mode detection development. *AIMS Energy* **2019**, *7*, 646–659. [CrossRef]
12. Inventing the Sustainable Batteries of the Future. Available online: https://battery2030.eu/digitalAssets/861/c_861350-l_1-k_roadmap-23march.pdf (accessed on 5 June 2021).
13. Chaturvedi, B.K.; Neeta Khare, P.K. Fpga Design Scheme For Battery Soc & Soh Algorithms For Advanced Bms. *Int. J. Eng. Sci. Res. Technol.* **2017**, *6*, 263–277. [CrossRef]
14. Chang, W.-Y. The State of Charge Estimating Methods for Battery: A Review. *ISRN Appl. Math.* **2013**, *2013*, 1–7. [CrossRef]

15. Rivera-Barrera, J.P.; Muñoz-Galeano, N.; Maldonado, H.O.S. SoC Estimation for Lithium-ion Batteries: Review and Future Challenges. *Electron.* **2017**, *6*, 102. [CrossRef]
16. Zhang, R.; Xia, B.; Li, B.; Cao, L.; Lai, Y.; Zheng, W.; Wang, H.; Wang, W. State of the Art of Lithium-Ion Battery SOC Estimation for Electrical Vehicles. *Energies* **2018**, *11*, 1820. [CrossRef]
17. Lukic, S.M.; Cao, J.; Bansal, R.C.; Rodriguez, F.; Emadi, A. Energy Storage Systems for Automotive Applications. *IEEE Trans. Ind. Electron.* **2008**, *55*, 2258–2267. [CrossRef]
18. Piller, S.; Perrin, M.; Jossen, A. Methods for state-of-charge determination and their applications. *J. Power Sources* **2001**, *96*, 113–120. [CrossRef]
19. Baccouche, I.; Jemmali, S.; Mlayah, A.; Manai, B.; Amara NE, B. Implementation of an Improved Coulomb-Counting Algorithm Based on a Piecewise SOC-OCV Relationship for SOC Estimation of Li-Ion Battery. *Int. J. Renew. Energy Res. IJRER* March. **2018**, *8*, 10. Available online: https://www.ijrer.org/ijrer/index.php/ijrer/article/view/6686/0 (accessed on 5 June 2021).
20. Nazer, R.A.; Cattin, V.; Granjon, P.; Montaru, M. A New Optimization Algorithm for a Li-Ion Battery Equivalent Electrical Circuit Identification. In Proceedings of the 9th International Conference of Modeling, Optimization and Simulation, Bordeaux, France, 6–8 June 2012; p. 8.
21. Nasser-Eddine, A.; Huard, B.; Gabano, J.-D.; Poinot, T. A two steps method for electrochemical impedance modeling using fractional order system in time and frequency domains. *Control. Eng. Pr.* **2019**, *86*, 96–104. [CrossRef]
22. Gonzalez, F.; Greiner, D.; Mena, V.; Souto, R.M.; Santana, J.J. Fitting procedure based on Differential Evolution to evaluate impedance parameters of metal-coating systems. *Eng. Comput* **2019**, *36*, 2960–2982. [CrossRef]
23. Alavi, S.; Birkl, C.; Howey, D. Time-domain fitting of battery electrochemical impedance models. *J. Power Sources* **2015**, *288*, 345–352. [CrossRef]
24. Zou, C.; Zhang, L.; Hu, X.; Wang, Z.; Wik, T.; Pecht, M. A review of fractional-order techniques applied to lithium-ion batteries, lead-acid batteries, and supercapacitors. *J. Power Sources* **2018**, *390*, 286–296. [CrossRef]
25. Ramos, P.M.; Janeiro, F.M. Gene expression programming for automatic circuit model identification in impedance spectroscopy: Performance evaluation. *Measurement* **2013**, *46*, 4379–4387. [CrossRef]
26. Chun, H.; Kim, J.; Han, S. Parameter identification of an electrochemical lithium-ion battery model with convolutional neural network. *IFAC-PapersOnLine* **2019**, *52*, 129–134. [CrossRef]
27. Storn, R.; Price, K. Differential Evolution: A Simple and Efficient Adaptive Scheme for Global Optimization over Continuous Spaces. *J. Glob. Optim.* **1997**, *11*, 341–359. [CrossRef]
28. Aramendia, I.; Zulueta, E.; Teso-Fz-Betoño, D.; Saenz-Aguirre, A.; Fernandez-Gamiz, U. Modeling of Motorized Orthosis Control. *Appl. Sci.* **2019**, *9*, 2453. [CrossRef]
29. Martinez-Rico, J.; Zulueta, E.; Fernandez-Gamiz, U.; De Argandoña, I.R.; Armendia, M. Forecast Error Sensitivity Analysis for Bidding in Electricity Markets with a Hybrid Renewable Plant Using a Battery Energy Storage System. *Sustainability* **2020**, *12*, 3577. [CrossRef]
30. Lagarias, J.C.; Reeds, J.A.; Wright, M.H.; Wright, P.E. Convergence Properties of the Nelder–Mead Simplex Method in Low Dimensions. *SIAM J. Optim.* **1998**, *9*, 112–147. [CrossRef]

electronics

MDPI

Article

Novel Control Strategy for Enhancing Microgrid Operation Connected to Photovoltaic Generation and Energy Storage Systems

Dina Emara [1], Mohamed Ezzat [1], Almoataz Y. Abdelaziz [2], Karar Mahmoud [3,4], Matti Lehtonen [3] and Mohamed M. F. Darwish [3,5,*]

1 Department of Electrical Power and Machines, Faculty of Engineering, Ain-Shams University, Cairo 11517, Egypt; dina.essam@eng.asu.edu.eg (D.E.); moh_ezzat@eng.asu.edu.eg (M.E.)
2 Faculty of Engineering and Technology, Future University in Egypt, Cairo 11835, Egypt; almoataz.abdelaziz@fue.edu.eg
3 Department of Electrical Engineering and Automation, School of Electrical Engineering, Aalto University, FI-00076 Espoo, Finland; karar.mostafa@aalto.fi (K.M.); matti.lehtonen@aalto.fi (M.L.)
4 Department of Electrical Engineering, Faculty of Engineering, Aswan University, Aswan 81542, Egypt
5 Department of Electrical Engineering, Faculty of Engineering at Shoubra, Benha University, Cairo 11629, Egypt
* Correspondence: mohamed.m.darwish@aalto.fi or mohamed.darwish@feng.bu.edu.eg

Abstract: Recently, the penetration of energy storage systems and photovoltaics has been significantly expanded worldwide. In this regard, this paper presents the enhanced operation and control of DC microgrid systems, which are based on photovoltaic modules, battery storage systems, and DC load. DC–DC and DC–AC converters are coordinated and controlled to achieve DC voltage stability in the microgrid. To achieve such an ambitious target, the system is widely operated in two different modes: stand-alone and grid-connected modes. The novel control strategy enables maximum power generation from the photovoltaic system across different techniques for operating the microgrid. Six different cases are simulated and analyzed using the MATLAB/Simulink platform while varying irradiance levels and consequently varying photovoltaic generation. The proposed system achieves voltage and power stability at different load demands. It is illustrated that the grid-tied mode of operation regulated by voltage source converter control offers more stability than the islanded mode. In general, the proposed battery converter control introduces a stable operation and regulated DC voltage but with few voltage spikes. The merit of the integrated DC microgrid with batteries is to attain further flexibility and reliability through balancing power demand and generation. The simulation results also show the system can operate properly in normal or abnormal cases, thanks to the proposed control strategy, which can regulate the voltage stability of the DC bus in the microgrid with energy storage systems and photovoltaics.

Keywords: microgrid; photovoltaic; storage systems; control strategy; islanded mode

1. Introduction

Global warming and carbon dioxide emissions, attributed to traditionally used energy sources, have become severe issues in the world for the last few years. Hence, the improvement of renewable energy sources (RES) has gained great research interest to mitigate and reduce such risks. Some RES, such as photovoltaic cells or wind turbines, are well-developed since they are clean and cost-effective [1–3]. However, other sources such as fuel cells and biomass are still in their growth stage [4].

Microgrid systems, which are classified as AC or DC microgrids, could merge RES with household and industrial loads [5–7]. The differences between both types of microgrids as well as their advantages are deeply discussed in the literature [8,9]. In fact, power electronic devices (PED) have recently become a must in grid integration, since photovoltaic systems output DC power while wind systems' output is in the form of variable frequency/voltage AC power. Additionally, some modern electronic loads, such as computers and plug-in hybrid electric vehicles, and even traditional AC loads such as induction motors, require DC power when driven by a variable-speed drive. Consequently, DC microgrids have been proven as one of the most efficient and cost-effective systems in the integration of RES with loads, as they decrease the AC-DC and DC-AC power conversion stages compared to AC microgrids [10,11]. Machine learning and artificial intelligence have shown promising performance in different electrical engineering applications [12–16] as well as power system components, e.g., power transformers and high voltage transmission lines [17–23]. Figure 1 illustrates the microgrid components in which the load and the diesel generator along with the wind turbines are connected to the AC side. In turn, PV units and battery energy storage systems (BESS) are tied to the DC side which is connected to the AC side by DC/AC inverter.

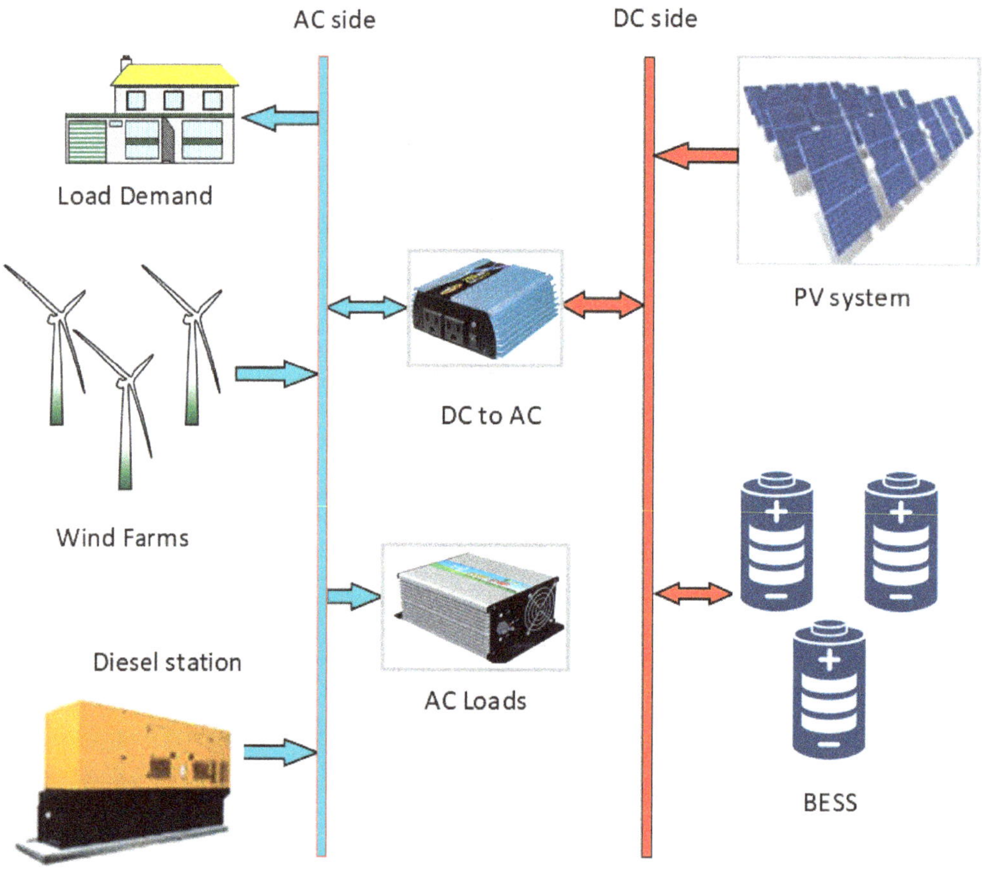

Figure 1. Schematic diagram of a microgrid system.

Among different RES merged with DC microgrids, photovoltaic (PV) cells are considered clean and scalable. PV microgrids operate in islanded mode to supply power to a small community or are tied to a grid as a distributed generator. However, a PV system is an intermittent source of energy as it depends on weather conditions and whether the sun is shining [24,25]. To overcome such drawbacks, energy storage systems (ESS) such as batteries or supercapacitors should be applied in the microgrid to attain smooth and reliable power generation from the PV system. ESS is charged during sunlight hours when PV power exceeds load demand, while during peak times, shortages of power generation, or unstable generation of PV, ESS discharge their energy [26–28]. The PV systems are widely operated in two modes of operation: stand-alone and grid-connected modes [29–33]. During the stand-alone mode, ESS compensates for the shortage of power generated by the PV modules, and if the stored power was insufficient, the system undergoes load shedding to meet the system requirements [34]. On the other hand, the utility grid manages to achieve power balance and DC voltage stability in the grid-tied mode [35]. Different strategies have been proposed for the control of DC microgrids. Standalone PV system control with a battery storage system through a bidirectional buck-boost converter is discussed in [36], with the aim of maintaining DC voltage stability. A control strategy for the integrated DC microgrid under variable load demand and different insolation levels through islanded mode and grid-connected mode is demonstrated in [37]. A hybrid AC/DC microgrid control that can manage and regulate power flow with both DC and AC buses in grid-connected and islanded modes is presented in [38]. Some limitations on battery discharge and grid power transfer are simulated in [39].

In this paper, the integration of a PV system, a battery storage system, and DC load in a DC microgrid is simulated using the Simscape power systems toolbox, MATLAB/Simulink (2018b, MathWorks Inc., Natick, MA, USA) platform. The effects of various controllers on the voltage stability of the system is observed during different solar irradiation cases, load demands, batteries, and grid power transfers. In particular, DC–DC and DC–AC converters are managed to achieve DC voltage stability in the microgrid while the system is operated in two practical modes: (1) stand-alone and (2) grid-connected. The novelty of this work is that different operating techniques of the microgrid are simulated using the traditional Direct-Quadrature (DQ) control strategy in cooperation with the voltage current controllers, where the updated voltage-oriented current control regulates DC voltage and ensures power balance between sources and load. Additionally, maximum power generation from the photovoltaic system can be attained by the novel control strategy across different techniques for operating the microgrid. The proposed battery converter control can introduce a stable operation and regulate DC voltage. The advantage of the integrated DC microgrid with batteries is that it accomplishes better flexibility and reliability while balancing power demand and generation. Accordingly, the microgrid can perform properly in both normal and sudden variation cases, thanks to the proposed control strategy that improves the voltage stability of the DC bus interconnected with energy storage systems and photovoltaics.

The rest of the paper is organized as follows: The proposed PV-based DC microgrid structure and controller modeling are analyzed in Section 2. Simulation results are presented in Section 3. Finally, the conclusions drawn from the results are presented in Section 4.

2. System Configuration and Modeling

The configuration of the proposed PV microgrid includes (1) PV arrays with the DC–DC boost converter and maximum power point tracking (MPPT), (2) a battery energy storage system (BESS) with DC–DC bidirectional buck–boost converters, (3) a voltage source converter (VSC) in the case of the grid-tied system. The utility grid is represented as the three-phase ideal voltage source. The BESS is used to maintain the power balance between PV power generation and the load demand in the islanded mode. A typical radial DC microgrid configuration is shown in Figure 2. Different microgrid structures are discussed in references [35,40,41].

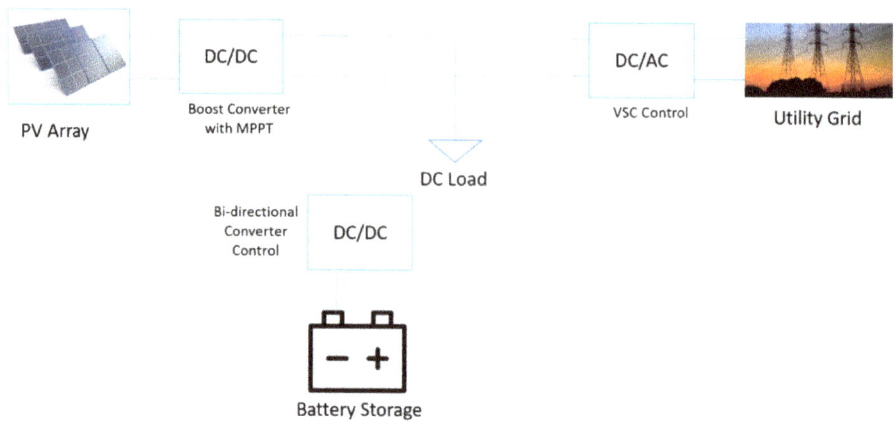

Figure 2. Typical radial DC microgrid configuration.

The PV based microgrid is controlled through a MPPT controller, a BESS local control unit that charge-discharges the battery bank based on the operation mode and a VSC controller. Table 1 introduces comparative analysis of various VSC control strategies.

Table 1. Comparative Analysis of VSC control strategies.

Control Method	Operation	Advantages	Disadvantages
Voltage Droop Control [42]	• Selects the droop parameters based on the steady-state analysis. Inner loop controls current while an outer loop regulates DC voltage.	• Reduces the effects of DC voltage disturbances.	• Reference current control could diverge in any sudden change during grid operation.
Vector Current Controller [43,44]	• Steady state operation into the d–q axis to control active power and reactive power separately.	• Fast dynamic response. • Delivers better power quality during harmonics and grid disturbances. • Can compensate grid harmonics.	• Achieves poor performance when it is applied to a DC link connected to a weak AC network.
Voltage Controller [45]	• Direct control of active power, reactive power and power angle.	• Simple and easy process.	• Active power and reactive power cannot be controlled independently. • Cannot limit the current flowing into the converter.
Proposed Voltage Oriented Control (DQ-control)	• The method is based on the transformation between stationary coordinates $\alpha\beta$ and synchronous rotating coordinates dq.	• Fast and robust. • High static performance via internal current control loop. • Advanced PWM strategies can be used.	• Coordinate transformation and PI controllers are required.

2.1. Photovoltaic System

The main source of power supply in the DC microgrid is the photovoltaic system which is controlled to operate at the maximum power point (MPP). Consequently, PV cell model representation has become an important field of study. Although there are several equivalent circuits to represent the PV array, the typical and most commonly used one is the single-diode circuit as it is characterized by its simplicity and accuracy. It is known also as the five-parameter model. The circuit shown in Figure 3 combines a photo-generated controlled current source parallel to a single diode, series resistance, and parallel resistance representing power losses [46].

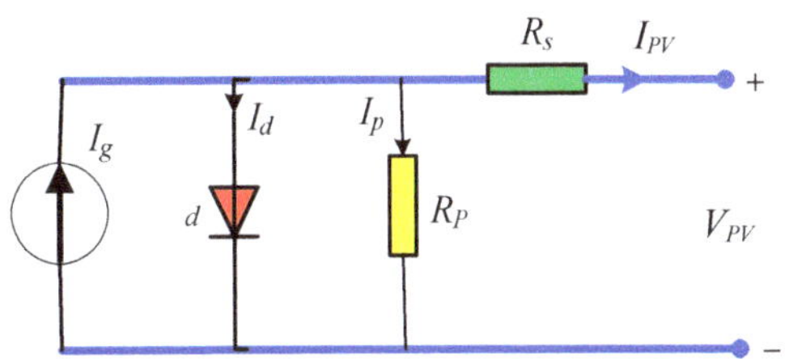

Figure 3. Equivalent circuit of PV array.

The photovoltaic cell is constructed based on P–N junctions, which are made from semiconductor materials. Silicon is dominantly used due to its abundance, non-toxicity, high and stable cell efficiencies [47]. The I–V characteristic of the solar cell is given by implicit and nonlinear equations as follows:

$$I_{PV} = I_g - I_d - \left(\frac{V_{PV} + R_s I_{PV}}{R_p}\right) \tag{1}$$

$$I_d = I_o\left[\exp\left(\frac{q(V_{PV} + R_s I_{PV})}{nKT}\right) - 1\right] \tag{2}$$

$$V_D = V_{PV} + R_s I_{PV} \tag{3}$$

In an array, PV modules are connected in series and in parallel. A group of PV cells is connected together in series to form a string, then the group of strings is connected in parallel to form an array. The current-voltage relationship of the array is affected by these connections as given by [48]:

$$I_{PV} = N_P I_g - N_P I_d - \left(\frac{V_{PV} + \frac{N_s}{N_p} R_s I_{PV}}{\frac{N_s}{N_p} R_p}\right) \tag{4}$$

$$I_d = I_o\left[\exp\left(\frac{q(V_{PV} + \frac{N_s}{N_p} R_s I_{PV})}{N_s nKT}\right) - 1\right] \tag{5}$$

where q is the electronic charge, K is the Boltzmann constant, n is the ideality factor, T is the cell temperature, I_g represents a current source created by sunlight known as a photocurrent, i.e., irradiance current, I_o is the diode saturation current, R_S is the series resistance, R_P is the shunt resistance, N_s is the number of cells connected in series in the array, N_p is the number of strings in parallel, I_{PV} and V_{PV} are the current and voltage outputs of the PV array, respectively.

PV systems deliver varying power depending on solar temperature and irradiation. As a result, MPPT should take place to optimize the power that can be delivered by PV cells. MPP differs according to light intensity and cell temperature and isn't a particular operating point on the P–V curve. Hence, a control technique is applied to the PV array with a boost converter to control its duty cycle to drive the system to operate at its optimal value [49].

There are various methods to implement MPPT tracking [50]. The most common methods are incremental conductance (IC) and perturb and observe (P&O). The IC technique has the advantage of a fast response to changes in irradiation and temperature. Moreover, it can determine when MPPT reaches the MPP during these changes while P&O oscillates around the MPP [51,52]. IC is implemented based on the study of the P–V curve; the MPP is reached when $dP/dV = 0$. The equations of the IC method are [53]:

$$P = VI \tag{6}$$

$$\frac{\partial P}{\partial V} = I\frac{\partial V}{\partial V} + V\frac{\partial I}{\partial V} = I + V\frac{\partial I}{\partial V} \tag{7}$$

$$\frac{dI}{dV} = \frac{-I}{V} \quad at\ MPP \tag{8}$$

$$\frac{dI}{dV} > \frac{-I}{V} \quad Left\ of\ MPP \tag{9}$$

$$\frac{dI}{dV} < \frac{-I}{V} \quad Right\ of\ MPP \tag{10}$$

As shown in the previous equations, the output incremental conductance equals the negative of the instantaneous output conductance at the *MPP* in the IC method. MPPT controls the duty cycle of the DC–DC boost converter to reach the condition ($dI/dV = -I/V$). The flow chart of IC MPPT in Figure 4 shows the algorithm. If (9) is satisfied, the duty cycle of the converter needs to be increased in order to increase the operating voltage to attain MPP, and vice versa if (10) is satisfied.

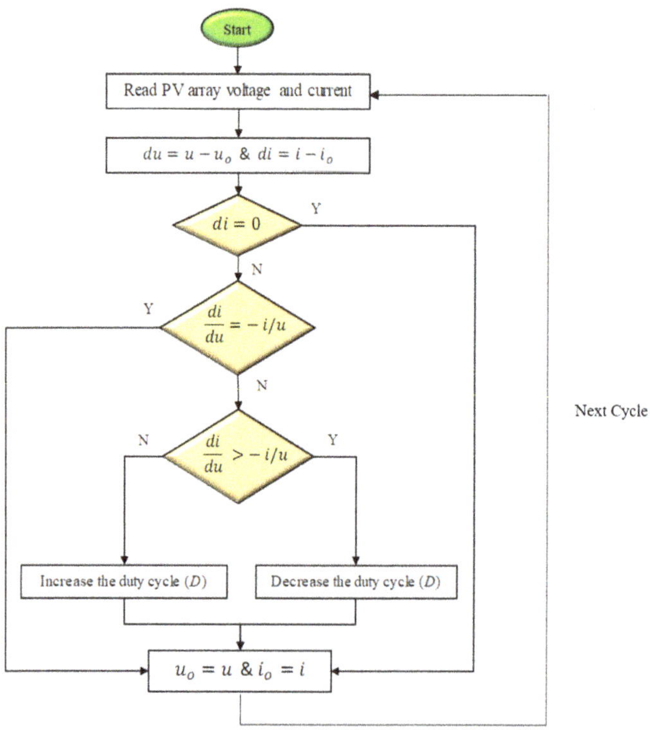

Figure 4. Flow chart of incremental conductance MPPT.

2.2. Battery Energy Storage System

Solar power generation may exceed or fall behind load demand. In addition, intermittency of PV power leads to the need for ESS to store the surplus power, supply power when there are deficits, and maintain grid stability during fluctuations resulting from changes in weather conditions like cloud shadows on the PV array. The storage module consists of a Lithium-ion battery bank and a bidirectional DC–DC buck–boost converter. Lithium-ion batteries have high energy capacity, low maintenance needs, and a robust life cycle. The control of the bidirectional buck–boost converter regulates charging and discharging of the BESS based on DC bus voltage, so the control is designed in bus monitoring (BM) mode [54]. The battery model shown in Figure 5 can be modeled through a general dynamic model that can be described by the equations [55]:

$$V_{batt} = E_g - i_{batt}R_{batt} \tag{11}$$

$$E_g = E_{go} - K\frac{Q}{Q - \int i_{batt}dt} + Ae^{B\int i_{batt}dt} \tag{12}$$

where,

E_g = no-load voltage (V)
E_{go} = battery constant voltage (V)
K = polarization voltage (V)
Q = maximum battery capacity (Ah)
$\int i_{batt}dt$ = actual battery charge (Ah)
A = exponential zone amplitude (V)
B = exponential zone time constant inverse (Ah)−1
V_{batt} = battery output voltage (V)
R_{batt} = internal resistance (resistance that the battery opposes to the flow of energy) (Ω)
i_{batt} = battery current (A)

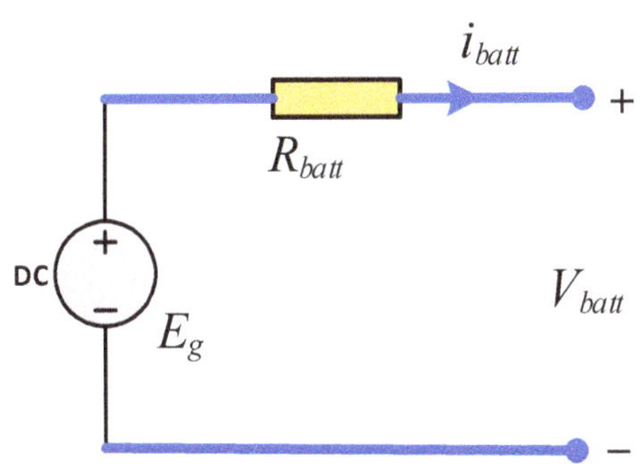

Figure 5. Equivalent circuit of battery.

The storage local control unit adjusts battery current to control charge and discharge of the battery by providing duty cycle to the converter as introduced in Figure 6. Hence, DC bus voltage remains stable.

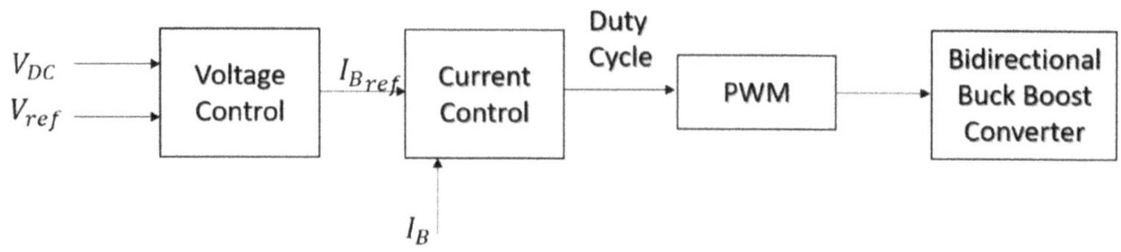

Figure 6. Battery local control.

2.3. Grid and Voltage Source Converter

The grid circuit is composed of a three-phase AC voltage source, an inductive-capacitive-inductive (LCL) filter which is responsible for reducing voltage and current switching harmonics, and a converter. Although the capacitive–inductive–capacitive (CLC) filter has the merits of reduced cost and size, it is commonly used with low current equipment. The used filter in the architecture is LCL, which has better capability in reducing total harmonic distortion compared to other filters, limits higher frequency current inflow, keeps the current harmonics in and around the operating frequency within the restricted limits, and could be designed to have a high dynamic response to meet the fast dynamics in power grids existing in Egypt. VSC is controlled to maintain the stability of the system and DC bus. A grid-connected VSC Control loop is used to adjust the DC voltage and generate pulse width modulation signals as shown in Figure 7 [56].

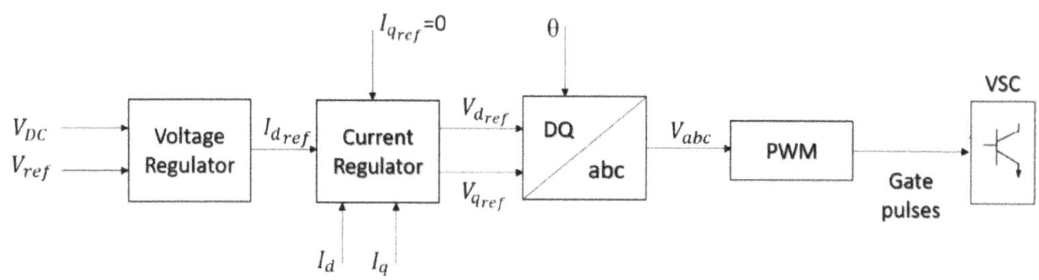

Figure 7. VSC voltage and current control.

The control strategy used with the VSC is vector control, also known as voltage-oriented control. This scheme is characterized by its high dynamic performance. There are two control loops, the outer loop is the voltage control loop for regulating the DC voltage, and the inner one is the current control loop which regulates direct axis current I_d and quadrature axis current I_q. VSC can control active and reactive powers independently. The direct axis component is responsible for controlling DC link voltage since the output from the outer voltage control loop is $I_{d\,ref}$. However, the quadrature axis component is responsible for controlling the reactive power transfer where I_q is set to zero, as there is no reactive power. The outputs of the current control loop, $V_{d\,ref}$ and $V_{q\,ref}$, are converted to a three-phase voltage reference, then the pulse width modulator (PWM) generates gate pulses to control the converter so that DC voltage is regulated [57].

3. Results and Discussions

The integration of PV microgrids with battery storage is simulated using the MATLAB/Simulink platform. The parameters of the microgrid, PV array, battery, and DC load are provided in Table 2. The PV array in the grid-tied DC microgrid is composed of 47 parallel strings each consists of 10 series modules. PV systems have higher capital costs per unit and much lower operating costs than traditional fossil-based electrical resources. However, progress in the PV industry continues, with reasonable scope for further cost reductions in the near future. As a result, PV panels can be manufactured at lower costs and can generate energy at higher efficiencies, reducing production costs per watt. The simulation sampling time is 10 μs, which is suitable to the switching frequency of the control components, so as to increase the accuracy of the controlling devices. Note that sampling time and hence sampling frequency is suitable for the switching frequency of the control components. Additionally, digital signal processors (DSP) that are used in power system applications in Egypt have switching frequency ranges from 70 to 160 kHz. The used time step in the model is variable. PWM is of an asymmetrical type. First, the microgrid is tested at constant load demand through different PV irradiance in different cases. Then, it is tested for different load demands.

Table 2. Parameters of DC microgrid PV Array, battery, and DC load.

DC Micro-Grid	
Nominal voltage	600 V
PV Array Parameters	
Number of series modules per string Ns	10
Number of parallel strings Np	47
Module short circuit current (STC) $I_{sc,r}$	7.84 A
Module open-circuit voltage (STC) $V_{oc,r}$	36.3 V
Module current at maximum power (STC) $I_{mp,r}$	7.35 A
Module voltage at maximum power (STC) $V_{mp,r}$	29 V
Module maximum power P_m	213.15 W
Boost converter inductance L_{Boost}	1.5 mH
Boost converter Capacitance C_{Boost}	3300 μF
PV boost converter switching frequency	5000 Hz
Battery Parameters	
Type	Li-ion
Nominal voltage	240 V
Rated capacity Q	800 Ah
Battery converter inductance	5 mH
Battery converter series resistance	0.1 Ω
Battery converter capacitance	1 mF
Battery converter parallel resistance	1×10^{-4} Ω
GS-VSC Parameters (PWM IGBT)	
DC Voltage V_{Dc}	600 V
Line to line AC voltage Voltage $V_{L-L,rms}$	400 V
Filter inductance, resistance and capacitance L_f, R_f, C_f	0.5 mH, 1 mΩ, 15 μF
DC Load	
Constant resistance	36 Ω
Constant power	10 kW

3.1. Grid-Tied PV Microgrid

In this simulation, the PV microgrid is connected to the utility grid and VSC control is responsible for regulating DC load and DC bus voltage. When the PV generation is more than the load demand in cases of high irradiance, surplus power goes to the grid. However, when it is below load demand, the utility grid supplies the deficiency in power generated by the PV system to the load. The load consumes constant power in all irradiance changes. At instants of sudden changes in irradiance, DC bus voltage is maintained within the permissible limits, ±5%, consequently, load voltage remains in the allowed range which is (600 V ± 30 V). However, there are tiny fluctuations and sudden drops and rises in irradiance for both the DC bus voltage and power provided to the DC load. Therefore, voltage stability is controlled by grid VSC as shown in Figure 8.

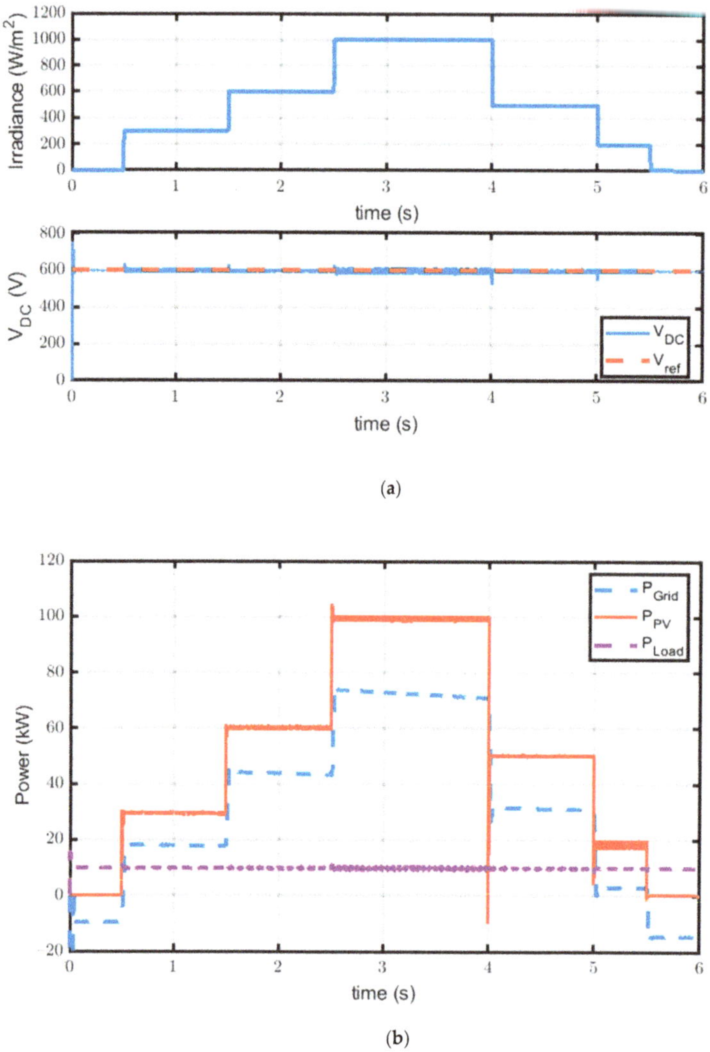

Figure 8. Grid-tied PV microgrid response; (**a**) Irradiation & DC voltage at load point, and (**b**) Power flow through DC microgrid.

3.2. Islanded PV Microgrid

In this simulation, the PV microgrid is disconnected from the utility grid, and the battery with the bidirectional converter control becomes responsible for regulating DC load voltage. The battery discharges to maintain DC load voltage stability and to supply power in case of low power generation by the PV system. When PV power generation increases above the load demand, the battery starts charging from the excess power generated by the PV system as illustrated in Figure 9. Voltage spikes and sags are observed at sudden changes of irradiance, as a result of the fast change of battery current, which causes a voltage increase or decrease due to the flow of momentary current through the parallel diode during switching operations of converter switches.

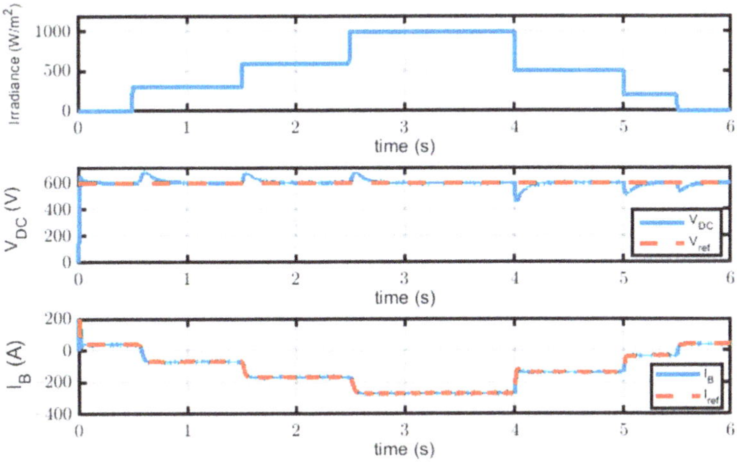

(a)

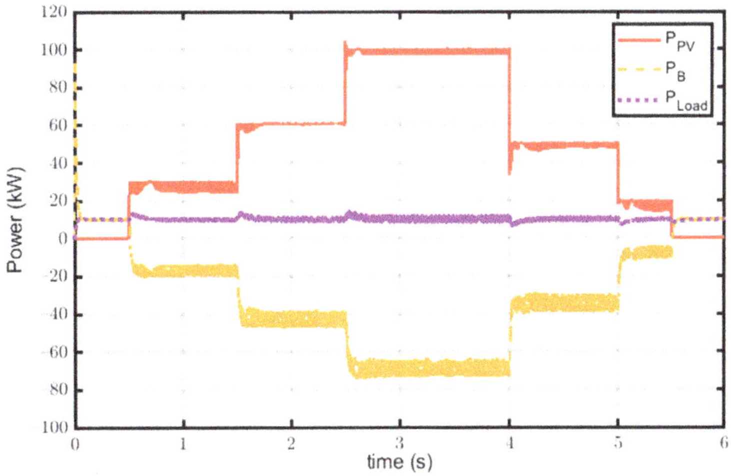

(b)

Figure 9. Islanded PV microgrid response; (**a**) Irradiation, DC voltage at load point and battery current, and (**b**) Power flow through DC microgrid.

3.3. Grid-Tied PV Microgrid with Constant Grid Power

The constant power mode of the utility grid is presented in this case, during which the influence of the microgrid on the utility power system is reduced. Figure 10 shows that the grid supplies constant power to the microgrid by controlling the direct current i_d to track reference positive current i_d^*. Hence, DC voltage is not controlled using VSC control. Therefore, the battery converter regulates DC load voltage and deals with the power generated from the PV module to make the battery charge during excess power generation from the PV system and discharge during PV low power generation. The presence of voltage fluctuations at every sudden change in irradiance level is shown in this case, as with the islanded mode of operation response, because here the battery converter controller is also responsible for DC voltage regulation but voltage is quickly established to track the reference DC voltage. Furthermore, the battery bank responds to changes in the power imbalance between power generation and load demand, thus supplying almost stable power to the load.

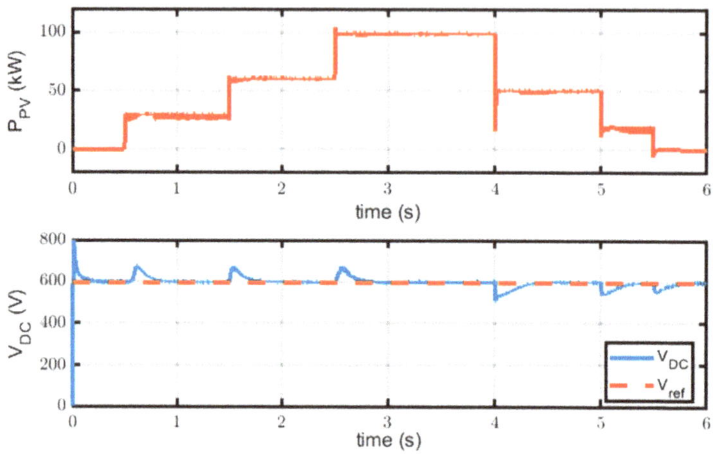

(a)

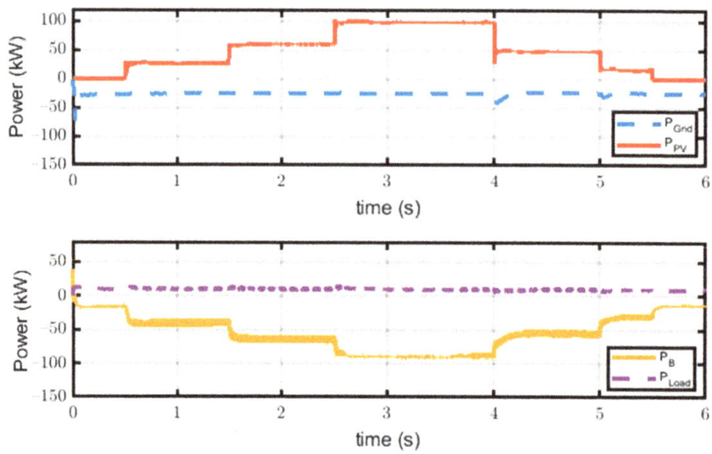

(b)

Figure 10. Response of grid-tied PV microgrid with constant grid power; (**a**) PV power and DC voltage at load point, and (**b**) Power Transfer through microgrid.

3.4. Grid-Tied PV Microgrid with Constant Battery Discharge

Figure 11 shows the battery discharge by constant rate through controlling battery current i_B to positive reference current i_B^*. Battery power is the constant positive power and grid powDer transfer to load is regulated by VSC control. It is also observed that DC-bus power is not affected by the variations.

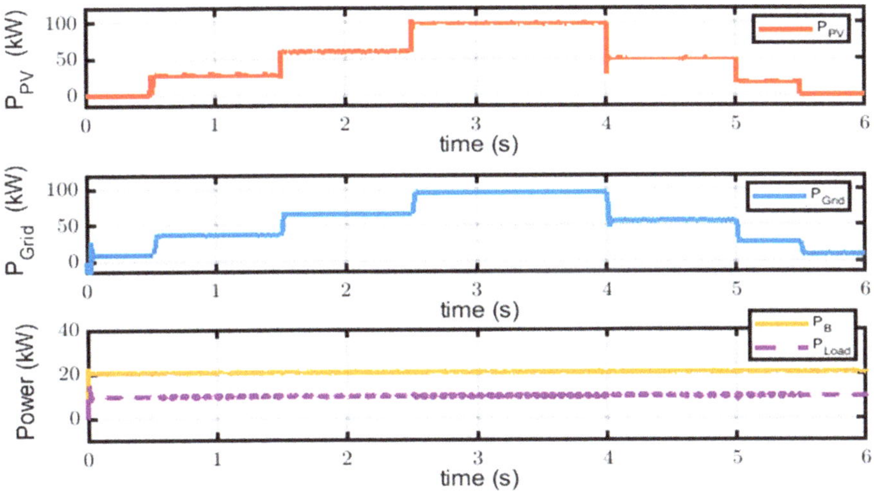

Figure 11. Power flow in grid-tied PV microgrid with constant battery discharge.

3.5. Islanded PV Microgrid with Different Load Demands

For this case, the bidirectional converter is responsible for controlling the charge and discharge of the battery. The power transfer illustrated in Figure 12 shows the response of the DC microgrid in islanded mode with different load demands. It is observed that at instants t = 2 s and t = 4 s the load power is suddenly increased by 10 kW to evaluate the performance of the system at different operating conditions. Therefore, at t = 2 s the load is suddenly increased but PV power generation still exceeds the load demand, so the battery continues to be charged; battery power is negative, therefore, the converter is in buck mode but its power decreases as the load consumes the difference in power. At t = 4 s, the load demand increases by 10 kW, and PV power generation is still higher than demand, so the battery continues to be charged while at t = 5 s, PV generation is decreased past load demand, consequently, the battery responds to meet load demand, where the bidirectional converter is put into boost mode. The system maintains its stability and supply load at different load changes using the control strategy of a battery bidirectional converter. The settling time at transient moments is slightly high but the system quickly restores its stability. When the battery is full, the PV system only supplies the load with no extra energy. In other words, the PV system does not operate at maximum power point but will operate according to load demand.

3.6. Grid-Tied PV Microgrid with Different Load Demands

For the different load demands and variable PV power generation due to different irradiance levels, the utility grid is responsible for supplying the load when demand is increased over PV generation in the grid-tied mode of operation as shown in Figure 13. It is observed that when irradiance level is low during the night or when it is cloudy, grid power is negative to supply the load instead of the PV system. Hence, the grid VSC control is the main controller in this case. Furthermore, power stability is enhanced for the system when tied to the grid rather than in the islanded mode.

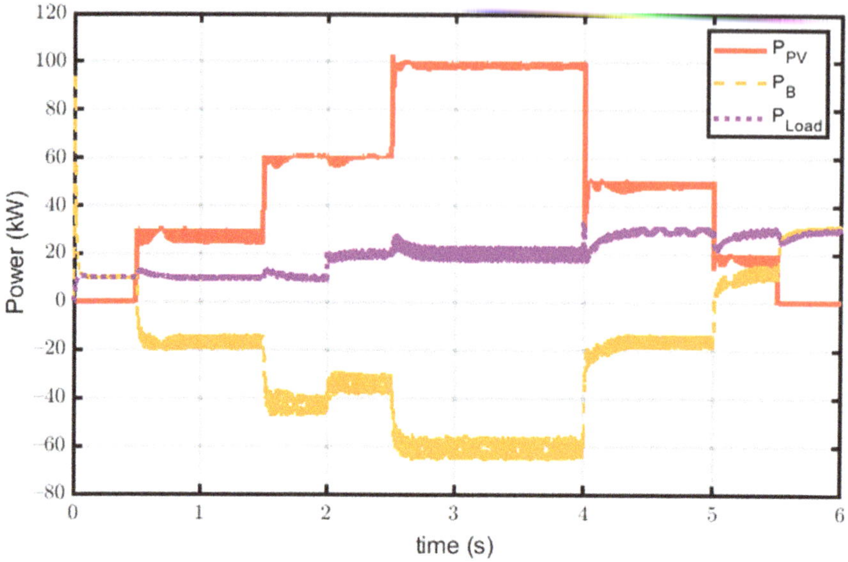

Figure 12. Power flow in islanded PV microgrid with different load demands.

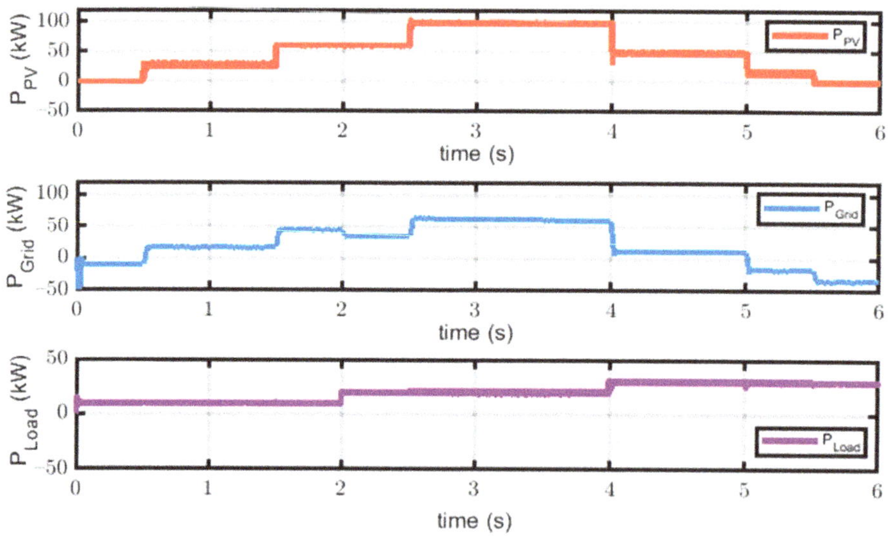

Figure 13. Power flow in Grid-Tied DC PV microgrid with different load demands.

4. Conclusions

This paper presents the enhanced operation of DC microgrid with PV generation as RES and battery as the energy storage system. The grid is connected and disconnected according to the mode of operation. Local control units of VSC and battery bidirectional converters are used to attain the required references for the different cases of simulation of the DC microgrid. The system is simulated for 6 s and the results are analyzed for each case. Results show that an integrated DC microgrid with batteries achieves more flexibility and reliability in the system by balancing power demand and generation. The stability of the DC microgrid is studied to test the reliability of the system during different modes of operations and different load changes. Through the simulation, discussion and results, it can be concluded that whether the system operates in normal cases or abnormal cases, different control strategies can regulate stable DC bus voltage. Additionally, it is observed that the grid-tied mode of operation regulated by VSC control offers more stability than islanded mode. However, battery converter control introduced a stable operation and regulated DC voltage but with a few voltage spikes.

Author Contributions: All authors have contributed to the preparation of this manuscript. D.E. and M.E. designed the idea strategy, wrote the draft manuscript, and studied the data. M.M.F.D. and K.M. wrote the manuscript and designed some figures related to microgrids and introduction. Finally, A.Y.A. and M.L. reviewed, edited, and supported different improvements in the manuscript. All authors have read and agreed to the published version of the manuscript.

Funding: This research was supported by the Department of Electrical Engineering and Automation, School of Electrical Engineering, Aalto University, Espoo, Finland.

Data Availability Statement: The data presented in this study are available on request from the corresponding author.

Conflicts of Interest: The authors declare no conflict of interest.

References

1. Lee, D.; Lee, D.; Jang, H.; Joo, S.-K. Backup Capacity Planning Considering Short-Term Variability of Renewable Energy Resources in a Power System. *Electronics* **2021**, *10*, 709. [CrossRef]
2. Ali, E.; El-Sehiemy, R.; El-Ela, A.A.; Mahmoud, K.; Lehtonen, M.; Darwish, M. An Effective Bi-Stage Method for Renewable Energy Sources Integration into Unbalanced Distribution Systems Considering Uncertainty. *Processes* **2021**, *9*, 471. [CrossRef]
3. Elsisi, M.; Tran, M.-Q.; Mahmoud, K.; Lehtonen, M.; Darwish, M.M.F. Robust Design of ANFIS-Based Blade Pitch Controller for Wind Energy Conversion Systems Against Wind Speed Fluctuations. *IEEE Access* **2021**, *9*, 37894–37904. [CrossRef]
4. Grumm, F.; Schumann, M.; Cosse, C.; Plenz, M.; Lücken, A.; Schulz, D. Short Circuit Characteristics of PEM Fuel Cells for Grid Integration Applications. *Electronics* **2020**, *9*, 602. [CrossRef]
5. Zhou, J.; Sun, H.; Xu, Y.; Han, R.; Yi, Z.; Wang, L.; Guerrero, J.M. Distributed Power Sharing Control for Islanded Single-/Three-Phase Microgrids with Admissible Voltage and Energy Storage Constraints. *IEEE Trans. Smart Grid* **2021**, *1*, 1. [CrossRef]
6. Hirsch, A.; Parag, Y.; Guerrero, J. Microgrids: A review of technologies, key drivers, and outstanding issues. *Renew. Sustain. Energy Rev.* **2018**, *90*, 402–411. [CrossRef]
7. Lv, J.; Wang, X.; Wang, G.; Song, Y. Research on Control Strategy of Isolated DC Microgrid Based on SOC of Energy Storage System. *Electronics* **2021**, *10*, 834. [CrossRef]
8. Guerrero, J.M.; Chandorkar, M.; Lee, T.-L.; Loh, P.C. Advanced Control Architectures for Intelligent Microgrids—Part I: Decentralized and Hierarchical Control. *IEEE Trans. Ind. Electron.* **2013**, *60*, 1254–1262. [CrossRef]
9. Lotfi, H.; Khodaei, A. AC Versus DC Microgrid Planning. *IEEE Trans. Smart Grid* **2017**, *8*, 296–304. [CrossRef]
10. Blaabjerg, F.; Chen, Z.; Kjaer, S. Power Electronics as Efficient Interface in Dispersed Power Generation Systems. *IEEE Trans. Power Electron.* **2004**, *19*, 1184–1194. [CrossRef]
11. Chakraborty, S.; Kramer, B.; Kroposki, B. A review of power electronics interfaces for distributed energy systems towards achieving low-cost modular design. *Renew. Sustain. Energy Rev.* **2009**, *13*, 2323–2335. [CrossRef]
12. Elsisi, M.; Tran, M.-Q.; Mahmoud, K.; Lehtonen, M.; Darwish, M.M.F. Deep Learning-Based Industry 4.0 and Internet of Things Towards Effective Energy Management for Smart Buildings. *Sensors* **2021**, *21*, 1038. [CrossRef] [PubMed]
13. Elsisi, M.; Mahmoud, K.; Lehtonen, M.; Darwish, M.M.F. Reliable Industry 4.0 Based on Machine Learning and IoT for Analyzing, Monitoring, and Securing Smart Meters. *Sensors* **2021**, *21*, 487. [CrossRef] [PubMed]
14. Elsisi, M.; Mahmoud, K.; Lehtonen, M.; Darwish, M.M.F. An Improved Neural Network Algorithm to Efficiently Track Various Trajectories of Robot Manipulator Arms. *IEEE Access* **2021**, *9*, 11911–11920. [CrossRef]
15. Elsisi, M.; Tran, M.-Q.; Mahmoud, K.; Mansour, D.A.; Lehtonen, M.; Darwish, M.M.F. Towards Secured Online Monitoring for Digitalized GIS Against Cyber-Attacks Based on IoT and Machine Learning. *IEEE Access* **2021**. accepted. [CrossRef]
16. Elsisi, M.; Mahmoud, K.; Lehtonen, M.; Darwish, M.M.F. Effective Nonlinear Model Predictive Control Scheme Tuned by Improved NN for Robotic Manipulators. *IEEE Access* **2021**, *9*, 64278–64290. [CrossRef]
17. Ghoneim, S.S.M.; Mahmoud, K.; Lehtonen, M.; Darwish, M.M.F. Enhancing Diagnostic Accuracy of Transformer Faults Using Teaching-Learning-Based Optimization. *IEEE Access* **2021**, *9*, 30817–30832. [CrossRef]
18. Ward, S.; El-Faraskoury, A.; Badawi, M.; Ibrahim, S.; Mahmoud, K.; Lehtonen, M.; Darwish, M. Towards Precise Interpretation of Oil Transformers via Novel Combined Techniques Based on DGA and Partial Discharge Sensors. *Sensors* **2021**, *21*, 2223. [CrossRef]
19. Alshehawy, A.; Mansour, D.-E.; Ghali, M.; Lehtonen, M.; Darwish, M. Photoluminescence Spectroscopy Measurements for Effective Condition Assessment of Transformer Insulating Oil. *Processes* **2021**, *9*, 732. [CrossRef]
20. Ghoneim, S.; Dessouky, S.; Boubakeur, A.; Elfaraskoury, A.; Sharaf, A.A.; Mahmoud, K.; Lehtonen, M.; Darwish, M. Accurate Insulating Oil Breakdown Voltage Model Associated with Different Barrier Effects. *Processes* **2021**, *9*, 657. [CrossRef]

21. Abouelatta, M.A.; Ward, S.A.; Sayed, A.M.; Mahmoud, K.; Lehtonen, M.; Darwish, M.M.F. Fast Corona Discharge Assessment Using FDM integrated With Full Multigrid Method in HVDC Transmission Lines Considering Wind Impact. *IEEE Access* **2020**, *8*, 225872–225883. [CrossRef]
22. Abouelatta, M.A.; Ward, S.A.; Sayed, A.M.; Mahmoud, K.; Lehtonen, M.; Darwish, M.M.F. Measurement and Assessment of Corona Current Density for HVDC Bundle Conductors by FDM Integrated with Full Multigrid Technique. *Electr. Power Syst. Res.* **2021**, *199*, 107370. [CrossRef]
23. Mansour, D.-E.A.; Abdel-Gawad, N.M.K.; El Dein, A.Z.; Ahmed, H.M.; Darwish, M.M.F.; Lehtonen, M. Recent Advances in Polymer Nanocomposites Based on Polyethylene and Polyvinylchloride for Power Cables. *Materials* **2021**, *14*, 66. [CrossRef] [PubMed]
24. Bendary, A.; Abdelaziz, A.; Ismail, M.; Mahmoud, K.; Lehtonen, M.; Darwish, M. Proposed ANFIS Based Approach for Fault Tracking, Detection, Clearing and Rearrangement for Photovoltaic System. *Sensors* **2021**, *21*, 2269. [CrossRef]
25. Ali, M.; Mahmoud, K.; Lehtonen, M.; Darwish, M. Promising MPPT Methods Combining Metaheuristic, Fuzzy-Logic and ANN Techniques for Grid-Connected Photovoltaic. *Sensors* **2021**, *21*, 1244. [CrossRef]
26. Traube, J.; Lu, F.; Maksimovic, D.; Mossoba, J.; Kromer, M.; Faill, P.; Katz, S.; Borowy, B.S.; Nichols, S.; Casey, L. Mitigation of Solar Irradiance Intermittency in Photovoltaic Power Systems With Integrated Electric-Vehicle Charging Functionality. *IEEE Trans. Power Electron.* **2013**, *28*, 3058–3067. [CrossRef]
27. Al-Gabalawy, M.; Mahmoud, K.; Darwish, M.; Dawson, J.; Lehtonen, M.; Hosny, N. Reliable and Robust Observer for Simultaneously Estimating State-of-Charge and State-of-Health of $LiFePO_4$ Batteries. *Appl. Sci.* **2021**, *11*, 3609. [CrossRef]
28. Mostafa, M.H.; Abdel Aleem, S.H.E.; Ali, S.G.; Ali, Z.M.; Abdelaziz, A.Y. Techno-Economic Assessment of Energy Storage Systems using Annualized Life Cycle Cost of Storage (LCCOS) and Levelized Cost of Energy (LCOE) Metrics. *J. Energy Storage* **2020**, *29*, 101345. [CrossRef]
29. Abbas, A.S.; El-Sehiemy, R.A.; El-Ela, A.A.; Ali, E.S.; Mahmoud, K.; Lehtonen, M.; Darwish, M.M.F. Optimal Harmonic Mitigation in Distribution Systems with Inverter Based Distributed Generation. *Appl. Sci.* **2021**, *11*, 774. [CrossRef]
30. Bayoumi, A.; El-Sehiemy, R.; Mahmoud, K.; Lehtonen, M.; Darwish, M. Assessment of an Improved Three-Diode against Modified Two-Diode Patterns of MCS Solar Cells Associated with Soft Parameter Estimation Paradigms. *Appl. Sci.* **2021**, *11*, 1055. [CrossRef]
31. Abaza, A.; El-Sehiemy, R.; Mahmoud, K.; Lehtonen, M.; Darwish, M. Optimal Estimation of Proton Exchange Membrane Fuel Cells Parameter Based on Coyote Optimization Algorithm. *Appl. Sci.* **2021**, *11*, 2052. [CrossRef]
32. Ali, M.N.; Mahmoud, K.; Lehtonen, M.; Darwish, M.M.F. An Efficient Fuzzy-Logic Based Variable-Step Incremental Conductance MPPT Method for Grid-Connected PV Systems. *IEEE Access* **2021**, *9*, 26420–26430. [CrossRef]
33. Said, M.; Shaheen, A.; Ginidi, A.; El-Sehiemy, R.; Mahmoud, K.; Lehtonen, M.; Darwish, M. Estimating Parameters of Photovoltaic Models Using Accurate Turbulent Flow of Water Optimizer. *Processes* **2021**, *9*, 627. [CrossRef]
34. Jyothi, V.M.; Muni, T.V.; Lalitha, S.V.N.L. An Optimal Energy Management System for PV/Battery Standalone System. *Int. J. Electr. Comput. Eng. (IJECE)* **2016**, *6*, 2538–2544. [CrossRef]
35. Kumar, D.; Zare, F.; Ghosh, A. DC Microgrid Technology: System Architectures, AC Grid Interfaces, Grounding Schemes, Power Quality, Communication Networks, Applications, and Standardizations Aspects. *IEEE Access* **2017**, *5*, 12230–12256. [CrossRef]
36. Chao, K.; Tseng, M.-C.; Huang, C.; Liu, G.; Huang, L.-C. Design and Implementation of a Bidirectional DC-DC Converter for Stand-Alone Photovoltaic Systems. *Energy* **2013**, *4*, 8.
37. Eghtedarpour, N.; Farjah, E. Control strategy for distributed integration of photovoltaic and energy storage systems in DC micro-grids. *Renew. Energy* **2012**, *45*, 96–110. [CrossRef]
38. Yi, Z.; Dong, W.; Etemadi, A.H. A Unified Control and Power Management Scheme for PV-Battery-Based Hybrid Microgrids for Both Grid-Connected and Islanded Modes. *IEEE Trans. Smart Grid* **2018**, *9*, 5975–5985. [CrossRef]
39. Merabet, A.; Qin, Z.; Ghias, A.M. Control of Simulated Solar PV Microgrid Operating in Grid-Tied and Islanded Modes. In Proceedings of the IECON 2018-44th Annual Conference of the IEEE Industrial Electronics Society, Washington, DC, USA, 21–23 October 2018; pp. 1729–1734.
40. Kumar, J.; Agarwal, A.; Agarwal, V. A review on overall control of DC microgrids. *J. Energy Storage* **2019**, *21*, 113–138. [CrossRef]
41. Choi, J.-C.; Jeong, H.-Y.; Choi, J.-Y.; Won, D.-J.; Ahn, S.-J.; Moon, S.-I. Voltage Control Scheme with Distributed Generation and Grid Connected Converter in a DC Microgrid. *Energies* **2014**, *7*, 6477–6491. [CrossRef]
42. Xiao, L.; Xu, Z.; An, T.; Bian, Z. Improved Analytical Model for the Study of Steady State Performance of Droop-Controlled VSC-MTDC Systems. *IEEE Trans. Power Syst.* **2016**, *32*, 2083–2093. [CrossRef]
43. Khazaei, J.; Beza, M.B.; Bongiorno, M. Impedance Analysis of Modular Multi-Level Converters Connected to Weak AC Grids. *IEEE Trans. Power Syst.* **2017**, *33*, 4015–4025. [CrossRef]
44. Harnefors, L.; Finger, R.; Wang, X.; Bai, H.; Blaabjerg, F. VSC Input-Admittance Modeling and Analysis Above the Nyquist Frequency for Passivity-Based Stability Assessment. *IEEE Trans. Ind. Electron.* **2017**, *64*, 6362–6370. [CrossRef]
45. Peyghami, S.; Mokhtari, H.; Davari, P.; Loh, P.C.; Blaabjerg, F. On Secondary Control Approaches for Voltage Regulation in DC Microgrids. *IEEE Trans. Ind. Appl.* **2017**, *53*, 4855–4862. [CrossRef]
46. Yazdani, A.; Di Fazio, A.R.; Ghoddami, H.; Russo, M.; Kazerani, M.; Jatskevich, J.; Strunz, K.; Leva, S.; Martinez, J.A. Modeling Guidelines and a Benchmark for Power System Simulation Studies of Three-Phase Single-Stage Photovoltaic Systems. *IEEE Trans. Power Deliv.* **2011**, *26*, 1247–1264. [CrossRef]

47. Luceño Sánchez, J.A.; Díez-Pascual, A.M.; Capilla, R.P. Materials for Photovoltaics: State of Art and Recent Developments. *Int. J. Mol. Sci.* **2019**, *20*, 976. [CrossRef]
48. Tian, H.; Mancilla-David, F.; Ellis, K.; Muljadi, E.; Jenkins, P. A cell-to-module-to-array detailed model for photovoltaic panels. *Sol. Energy* **2012**, *86*, 2695–2706. [CrossRef]
49. Eltawil, M.A.; Zhao, Z. MPPT techniques for photovoltaic applications. *Renew. Sustain. Energy Rev.* **2013**, *25*, 793–813. [CrossRef]
50. Reddy, D.C.; Narayana, S.S.; Ganesh, V. Design of Hybrid Solar Wind Energy System in a Microgrid with MPPT Techiques. *Int. J. Electr. Comput. Eng. (IJECE)* **2018**, *8*, 730–740. [CrossRef]
51. Putri, R.I.; Wibowo, S.; Rifa'I, M. Maximum Power Point Tracking for Photovoltaic Using Incremental Conductance Method. *Energy Procedia* **2015**, *68*, 22–30. [CrossRef]
52. Safari, A.; Mekhilef, S. Incremental conductance MPPT method for PV systems. In Proceedings of the 2011 24th Canadian Conference on Electrical and Computer Engineering (CCECE), Niagara Falls, ON, Canada, 8–11 May 2011; pp. 345–347.
53. Lokanadham, M.; Bhaskar, K.V. Incremental Conductance Based Maximum Power Point Tracking (MPPT) for Photovoltaic System. *Int. J. Eng. Res. Appl.* **2012**, *2*, 1420–1424.
54. Jin, C.; Wang, P.; Xiao, J.; Tang, Y.; Choo, F.H. Implementation of Hierarchical Control in DC Microgrids. *IEEE Trans. Ind. Electron.* **2014**, *61*, 4032–4042. [CrossRef]
55. Tremblay, O.; Dessaint, L.-A.; Dekkiche, A.-I. A Generic Battery Model for the Dynamic Simulation of Hybrid Electric Vehicles. In Proceedings of the 2007 IEEE Vehicle Power and Propulsion Conference, Arlington, TX, USA, 9–12 September 2007; pp. 284–289.
56. Yazdani, A.; Dash, P.P. A Control Methodology and Characterization of Dynamics for a Photovoltaic (PV) System Interfaced With a Distribution Network. *IEEE Trans. Power Deliv.* **2009**, *24*, 1538–1551. [CrossRef]
57. Gao, F.; Kang, R.; Cao, J.; Yang, T. Primary and secondary control in DC microgrids: A review. *J. Mod. Power Syst. Clean Energy* **2019**, *7*, 227–242. [CrossRef]

electronics

MDPI

Article

Proposal of a Decoupled Structure of Fuzzy-PID Controllers Applied to the Position Control in a Planar CDPR

Marco Carpio [1,2,*], Roque Saltaren [1], Julio Viola [2], Cristian Calderon [2] and Juan Guerra [2]

1 Centro de Automática y Robótica, Universidad Politécnica de Madrid, 28006 Madrid, Spain; roquejacinto.saltaren@upm.es
2 Grupo de Investigación en Interacción Robótica y Automática (GIIRA), Universidad Politécnica Salesiana, 010105 Cuenca, Ecuador; jviola@ups.edu.ec (J.V.); ccalderonl1@est.ups.edu.ec (C.C.); jguerraj@est.ups.edu.ec (J.G.)
* Correspondence: mcarpio@ups.edu.ec

Abstract: The design of robot systems controlled by cables can be relatively difficult when it is approached from the mathematical model of the mechanism, considering that its approach involves non-linearities associated with different components, such as cables and pulleys. In this work, a simple and practical decoupled control structure proposal that requires practically no mathematical analysis was developed for the position control of a planar cable-driven parallel robot (CDPR). This structure was implemented using non-linear fuzzy PID and classic PID controllers, allowing performance comparisons to be established. For the development of this research, first the structure of the control system was proposed, based on an analysis of the cables involved in the movement of the end-effector (EE) of the robot when they act independently for each axis. Then a tuning of rules was carried out for fuzzy PID controllers, and Ziegler–Nichols tuning was applied to classic PID controllers. Finally, simulations were performed in MATLAB with the Simulink and Simscape tools. The results obtained allowed us to observe the effectiveness of the proposed structure, with noticeably better performance obtained from the fuzzy PID controllers.

Keywords: CDPR; fuzzy control; PID; topology control

1. Introduction

In recent years, research in the field of robotics has focused on the study of cable-driven parallel robots (CDPR), with the control stage being very important, and involving a significant choice in the structure of the robot. In this way, in [1], the control of a CDPR to simulate movements of a satellite, allowing experimentation with a vibration control caused by external disturbances and by autorotation is developed. Additionally, in [2], a coordinated dynamic control in the task space (CDCT) was proposed for a CDPR to guarantee high-precision control. By analyzing the contour error, a new timing error was introduced to represent the coordination relationship between axes, and an additional robust compensation using the defined timing error was designed. In [3], a robust torque control scheme for a CDPR based on a PD controller was designed with real-time mass estimation and path compensation for pick-and-place tasks with different masses. In [4], the use of a CDPR for 3D printing with concrete was reported. The proposed concept was used to test the possibility of constructing a house with high precision and a stable trajectory. In [5], a review of the state of the art of fully constrained cable-actuated parallel mechanisms and cable-suspended parallel mechanisms was presented, recalling the basic kinematic architecture and briefly exposing the associated static and kinematic models. For its part, in [6], a prototype CDPR was used to 3D print a wall made of glass powder for an artistic exhibition. The position of the robot was measured by 3 on-board lidars and its operation over 174 working hours was evaluated. Additionally, in [7], the application of a CDPR as a 3D printer was proposed, using a retractable end-effector to avoid the collision of the cables with the printed objects and to increase the working space, with a stiffness analysis of the disturbance present in the end-effector.

While the mathematical modeling of the mechanism is relatively complex due to the non-linearities of the components that make it up, such as cables and pulleys, empirical tuning controllers can be chosen, among them the fuzzy and classic PID. That is the case reported in [8], where a fuzzy control was used with an adaptive feedback method for non-linear systems, the controller helps the following error tend towards zero. In [9], a Sugeno-type controller was used for the independent design of the controller and the fuzzy observer. This was achieved through the development of a separation property which obtained satisfactory results from the non-linear systems. For its part, in [8], a fuzzy controller was coupled to highlight the characteristics of a PID controller, improving both the transient and steady-state responses [10]. Fuzzy controllers were also applied for speed and direction control in [11], where an investigation of fuzzy speed control was carried out for a frequency inverter connected to a permanent magnet (PM)-synchronous motor, where fuzzy logic was used based on the speed error. Other applications are in the area of mobile robots, as in [12], where fuzzy control rules were used to heuristically adjust the angles of the wheels and the data from an encoder used in the balance and drive of the mechanical wheel of a ball robot. Something similar was proposed in [13], where a fuzzy controller was used to control the speed and direction of an intelligent mobile robot that tracked and obtained the trajectory of a specific target. While in [14], a fuzzy adaptive PI controller for the non-linear control of the motion of a four-wheeled omnidirectional mobile robot was employed, the fuzzy adaptive algorithm adjusted the PI controller's parameters, and the fuzzy inference rules were set using the tracking error and its derivative.

Several articles analyze ways to tune and apply a classic PID. In [15] the three main control effects were examined for the experimental or calculated values of the delay and the unit reaction rate of the process to be controlled. In [16], a controller based on a classical PID was designed and simulated to regulate the position and orientation of a six degrees-of-freedom (DOF) quadrotor. The control parameters were obtained according to the simulation results. In [17], some rules for the adjustment of the PID of a two-DOF robot manipulator were proposed. This adjustment procedure was extracted from the stability analysis using a Lyapunov function and the LaSalle invariance principle. Finally, in [18], the semi-global stability of robotic manipulators under classical PID control was demonstrated. Based on model compensation techniques, the non-linearities were grouped into a single function and are estimated using a reduced-order observer.

Prior to the control stage, a trajectory planner is required. In [19], the dynamic path planning (DPP) of a planar robot arm was described, non-heuristic algorithms to plan collision-free trajectories with information obtained from the environment by feedback. In the case shown in [20], a Catmull-Rom spline-based path planning scheme was proposed, which allowed a robot to move through several points with a method of speed limitation used at the beginning and end of each node, optimized through time scaling to keep speed and acceleration separated. Finally, in [21], a CDPR was used to simulate underwater conditions on a humanoid robot planning a dynamic polygonal 6-1-6 trajectory, to set the necessary speed and acceleration of the system tracking the humanoid robot.

For the most part, the research and design of control strategies in CDPRs involve the mathematical model, which demands effort in its modeling due to the non-linearities incorporated in the components of the mechanism. From the foregoing, it is important to have alternatives for controller structures that are easy and fast to tune and implement. With the aim of contributing to the field of CDPR control, a decoupled control structure proposal based on fuzzy PID and classic PID controllers was developed and studied, the results were analyzed and their performance was evaluated. The effectiveness of the fuzzy PID controller is demonstrated as having better tracking and less error compared to the classic PID. The main contribution of this research is to provide a decoupled structure for the position control of a CDPR requiring almost no mathematical analysis. The novelty consists in using a well-known design technique for controllers acting independently to control the position of the CDPR in each axis, which has not been previously reported in the literature.

The paper is structured as follows: in Section 2, the structure and equations of forces of the CDPR are presented, as well as the topology of the position control and trajectory planning. The tuning of the PID controller and the design of the fuzzy controller are also developed. In Section 3, the operation of PID and fuzzy PID controllers are simulated and the results are compared. In Section 4, a discussion on the obtained results is presented and, conclusions are established finally, in Section 5.

2. Materials and Methods

2.1. Structure of the Parallel Cable Mechanism

The planar CDPR mechanism shown in Figure 1 is made up of a fixed structure with two posts, and a mobile effector to which the cables are anchored allows for the application of force to generate movement in the vertical plane.

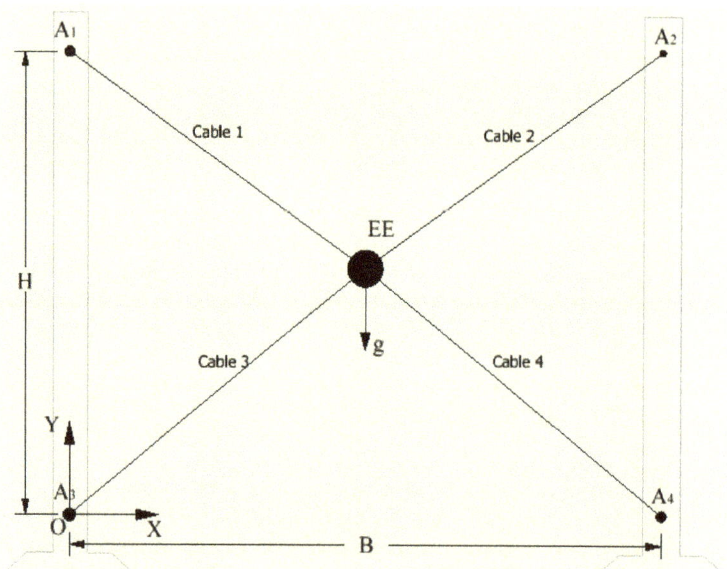

Figure 1. Planar CDPR structure.

In Figure 1, A1, A2, A3, and A4 are the anchor points on the fixed structure, EE is the anchor point on the end-effector, B is the robot base, defined as the distance between the posts supporting the robot cables, and H is the robot height, defined as the height of the posts supporting the robot cables.

The robot workspace is delimited by the anchor points of the pulleys that guide the cable in the fixed structure. A hypothetical case of a mechanism with B = 3 m and H = 2.5 m, with an end-effector of 5 kg in weight and light nylon cables whose characteristics allow the robot to ignore catenary effects was considered [22].

The robot dynamic model is presented in Equation (1) through Equation (4) [23], which consider: the external forces at the EE, the weight of the EE, the friction damping forces of the environment where the robot works, and the forces developed in the robot cables.

$$fd_x - Bd \cdot \dot{x}_G - \sum_{i=1}^{4} \{ (\tau_i - P_i) S_{ix} + Q_i S_{iy} \} = M\ddot{x}_G \quad (1)$$

$$fd_y + M(g{\cdot}y) - Bd{\cdot}\dot{y}_G - \sum_{i=1}^{4}\{(\tau_i - P_i)S_{iy} + Q_iS_{ix}\} = M\ddot{y}_G \tag{2}$$

where:

$$P_i = \rho_m\left(L_ig^S - L_i\ddot{L}_i + \frac{1}{2}(L_i\dot{\alpha}_i)^2\right) \tag{3}$$

$$Q_i = \rho_m\left(\frac{1}{2}L_ig^N - \frac{3}{4}L_i\dot{L}_i\dot{\alpha}_i - \frac{1}{3}L_i^2\ddot{\alpha}_i\right) \tag{4}$$

The different external forces and moments (wrenches) that affect the end-effector correspond to external forces (fd), gravitational forces $(M{\cdot}g)$, forces impressed on the effector due to its acceleration $(M{\cdot}\ddot{x}_G,\ M{\cdot}\ddot{y}_G)$, and damping forces due to friction in the environment where the robot moves $(Bd{\cdot}\dot{x}_G,\ Bd{\cdot}\dot{y}_G)$. The wires have constant density ρ_m, and are actuated by means of force τ_i, $\dot{L}_i$ is recollection or extension speed, and $\dot{\alpha}_i$ is the angular speed of each wire. The speed of the cable's center of mass in direction S_i was considered. The robot model was developed in the MATLAB Simscape toolbox.

2.2. Motion Control Topology

Parallel robots are designed for various applications, among which are those where the end-effector does not exert contact or force with the environment, in which case a position control is required [24]. The position control of the robot can be approached in two ways, one referring to the joint space and the other to the task space. The choice of the control topology depends on the accessibility of the measurement of the signals and the demands of the robot application.

For position control in task space, the position of the end-effector is fed back directly. The control topology is shown in Figure 2, where the effect of a disturbance (representing a displacement in the position of the end-effector) is added for the purpose of evaluating the responses of the control system.

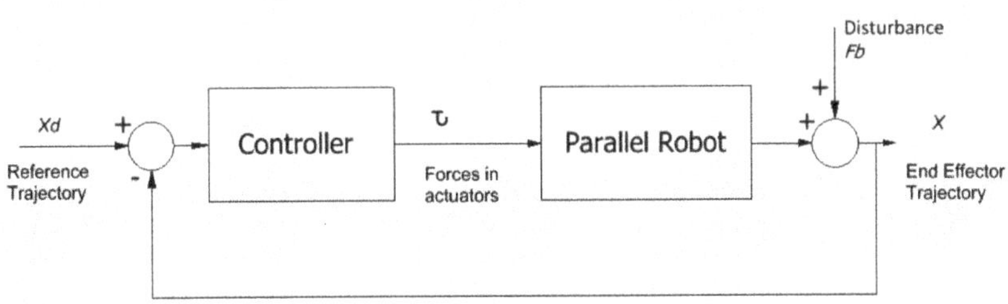

Figure 2. Topology of position control in task space.

General control topologies used in robotics can be structured based on coupled or decoupled control schemes, as feasible [24].

For the case of the planar CDPR in Figure 1, a mixed controller structure was proposed for use in the task space under the following considerations:

- One controller performs the X-axis positioning control. For positive displacement, force is applied to cables 2 and 4, while for negative displacement, force is applied to cables 1 and 3.
- Another controller performs the Y-axis positioning control. For positive displacement, force is applied to cables 1 and 2, while for negative displacement, force is applied to cables 3 and 4.

The control structure for decoupled axis movement is shown in Figure 3, where the X-axis controller and the Y-axis controller are implemented as decoupled controllers with independent tuning.

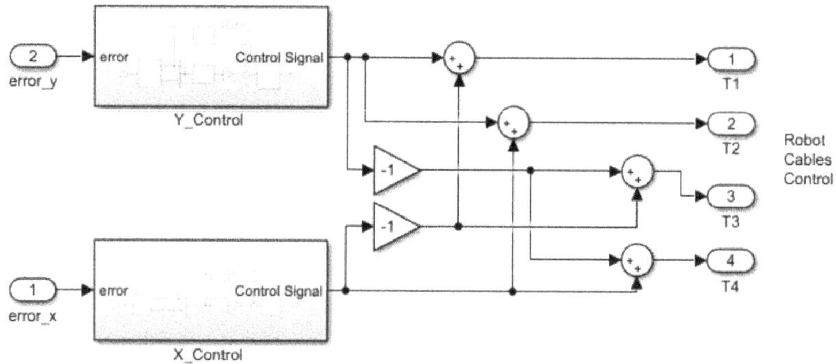

Figure 3. Control structure for the positioning of a planar CDPR.

2.3. Trajectory Planning

The trajectory planning of a robot allows us to determine the continuous position paths that will guide the end-effector of the robot, either in the presence or absence of defined obstacles in its workspace. In this sense, trajectory planning seeks to determine continuous and smooth trajectories in position, speed, acceleration, and jerk for each active joint of the robot, guaranteeing their physical integrity [25].

To meet the expressed requirements of path continuity and smoothness, a 6-1-6 polynomial path can be adjusted [21]. This position path has a sixth-order polynomial in the acceleration and deceleration section, while the middle section guarantees constant speed with a first-order polynomial. The generic polynomial structure 6-1-6 is:

$$h_A(t) = \frac{v_{max}}{t_{ac}{}^5}t^6 - \frac{3v_{max}}{t_{ac}{}^4}t^5 + \frac{5v_{max}}{2t_{ac}{}^3}t^4 + X_0 \tag{5}$$

$$h_B(t) = v_{max}t + \frac{v_{max}t_{ac}}{2} + X_0 \tag{6}$$

$$h_c(t) = -h_A(t) + v_{max}t + \left(tt - \frac{3v_{max}}{2}t_{ac}\right)v_{max} + 2X_0 \tag{7}$$

The values considered along each axis of the robot are:

- h_A, h_B, and h_C: positions reached during the sections of acceleration, constant speed, and deceleration, respectively.
- v_{max}: maximum speed that can be developed.
- t_{ac}: acceleration and deceleration time.
- tt: total time required to develop the whole trajectory.

In Figure 4, the graph of the trajectories 6-1-6 in the task space can be seen, which was used for the robot as positional references. In Figures 5–7, the curves for speed, acceleration, and jerk are shown, which were derived from the position curve, showing that in all cases they were smooth paths that did not present discontinuities [21].

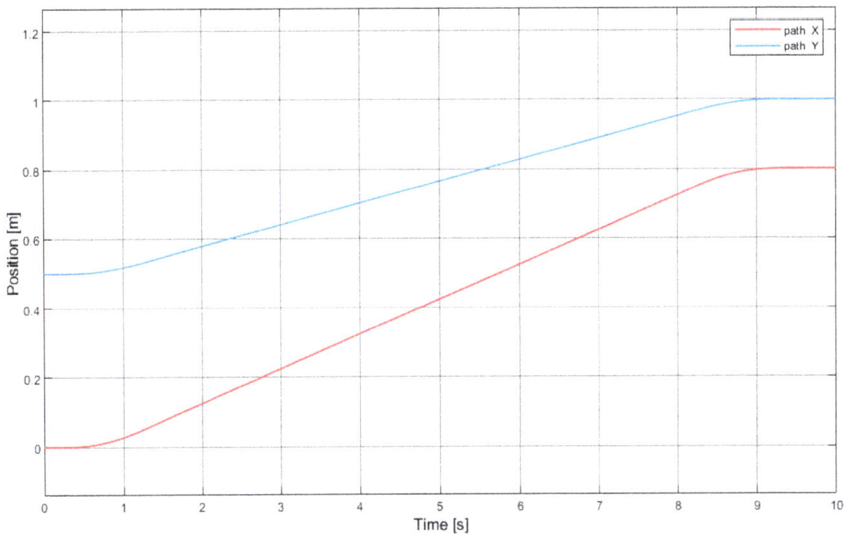

Figure 4. Trajectory for position using 6-1-6 polynomials for the planar CDPR.

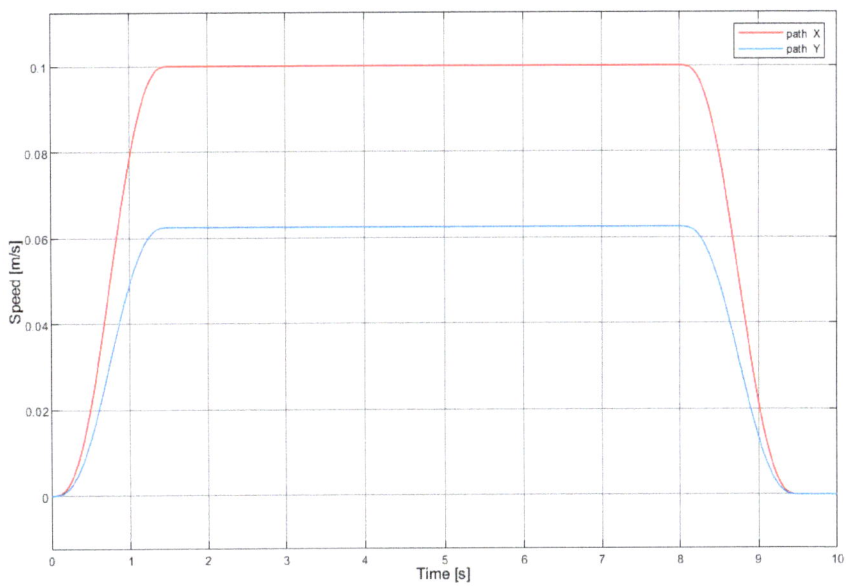

Figure 5. Trajectory for speed using 6-1-6 polynomials for the planar CDPR.

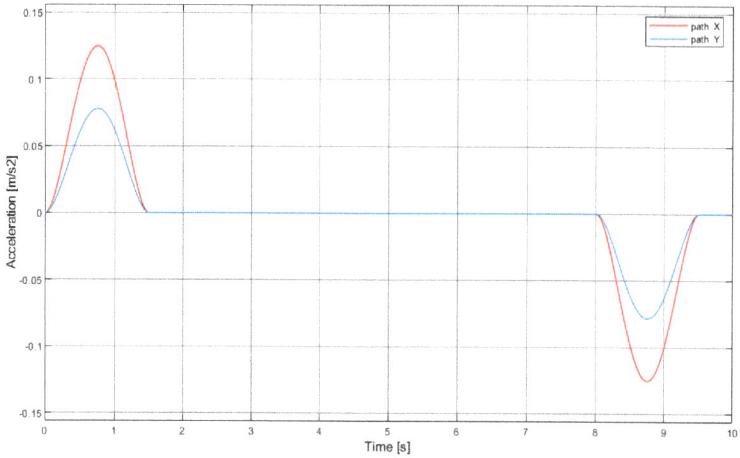

Figure 6. Trajectory for acceleration using 6-1-6 polynomials for the planar CDPR.

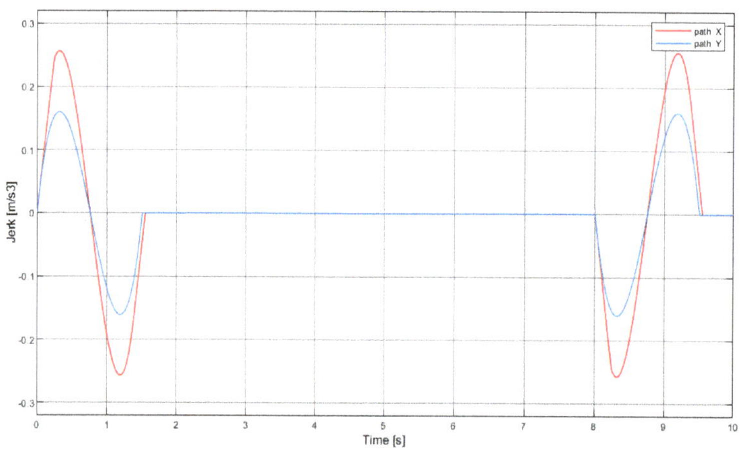

Figure 7. Trajectory for jerk using 6-1-6 polynomials for the planar CDPR.

2.4. Controller Tuning

Based on the dynamic behavior of the system, various controller structures can be adopted for the implementation of the control block, among them PID controllers and fuzzy PID control, which were chosen for this work due to their advantages in tuning and robustness.

2.4.1. PID Control

One of the most used controllers in the industry is the proportional, integral, and derivative (PID) controller.

In Figure 8 the structure of a PID is shown, whose general equation is:

$$U(s) = \mathrm{KP}\left(1 + \frac{1}{\mathrm{Tr} * \mathrm{s}} + \mathrm{Td} * \mathrm{s}\right)E(s) \tag{8}$$

where:

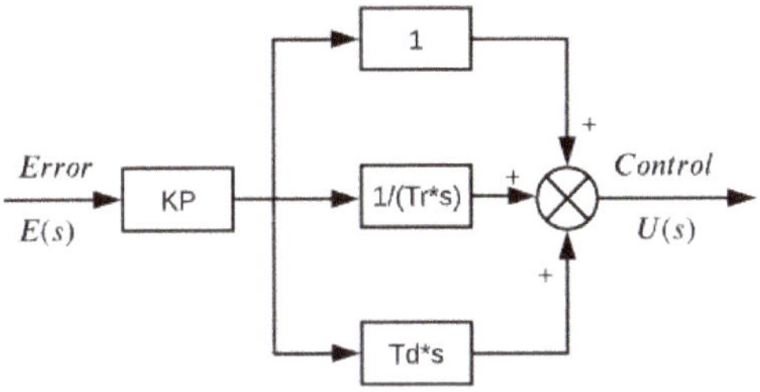

Figure 8. General structure of a PID controller.

U(s): Control signal
KP: Proportional constant.
E(s): Error signal (difference between reference and controller response).
Tr: Adjustment constant for integral action.
Td: Adjustment constant for derivative action.

Based on the Ziegler–Nichols [13] tuning technique, the constants KP, Tr and Td are proposed as a function of the critical period (Pc) and the critical gain (Kc). For the controller structure shown in Equation (8), the PID constants are obtained from Equations (9)–(11):

$$\mathrm{KP} = 0.6 \times \mathrm{Kc} \tag{9}$$

$$\mathrm{Tr} = \mathrm{Pc}/2 \tag{10}$$

$$\mathrm{Td} = \mathrm{Pc}/8 \tag{11}$$

Through the simulation, the critical force value was found in the upper cables, which allow for the balance of the robot in the center of the work plane, for which an approximate force of 2.7 N resulted. This value of the force will be considered as the operating point around which the control signal will act. The proposed control structure has a block that compensates for the forces of the effector's weight, which in this case corresponds to forces of 2.7 N for each upper cable.

In order to generate an oscillation of the system, a force slightly greater than the force that stabilizes it is applied. In this case, a force of 3 N was applied to the upper cables, so that with the robot originally positioned in the center of the plane, oscillations were produced in the vertical axis, allowing the critical period (Pc) to be obtained for the calculation of the controller's parameters. According to Figure 9, the period of oscillation was Pc = 4 s. In the first instance, a critical gain Kc = 1 was assumed, since it used forces very close to the forces that balance the robot in the center of the plane. This gain can be adjusted based on the response of the system.

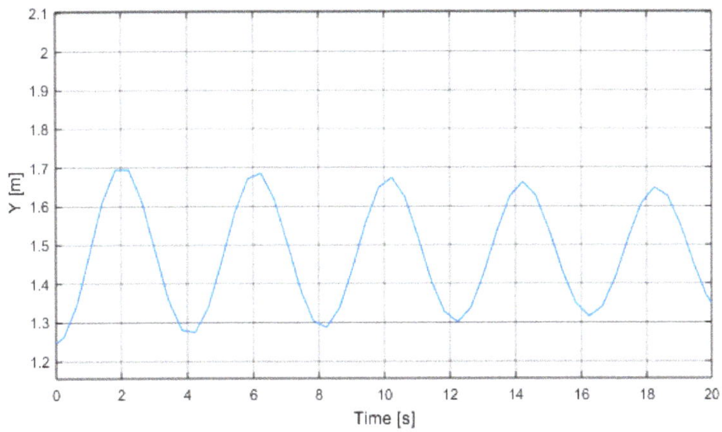

Figure 9. Oscillation response of the robot in the presence of 3 N forces in the upper cables.

The PID parameters shown in Equation (8), resulted in Kp = 0.6, Tr = 2, and Td = 0.5. These constants were configured in the two control blocks shown in the structure of Figure 3, which, including the gravitational forces compensation stage, remains as shown in Figure 10.

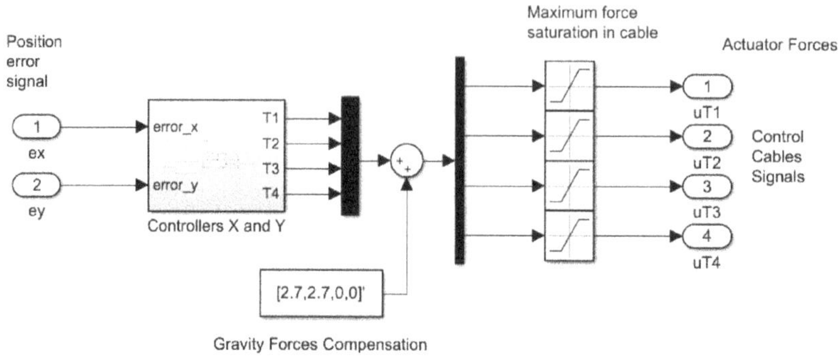

Figure 10. Structure of a decoupled control system for a planar CDPR.

2.4.2. Fuzzy Control

The fuzzy controller is by nature a non-linear controller whose most relevant characteristics are:

- It does not require knowledge of the mathematical model of the plant to be controlled.
- The control output is generated by inference of the input signals based on the membership functions defined for each variable, establishing its form and respective universe of discourse.
- The inference is developed through a rules table of query and decision.

For fuzzy controller tuning, it is very important to define the universe of discourse of each membership function according to the knowledge of the system's operation (operator experience).

A fuzzy logic controller can adopt the structure of a PID controller with the generation of output functions derived from PD action and an adaptation for the integrating signal, as can be seen in Figure 11.

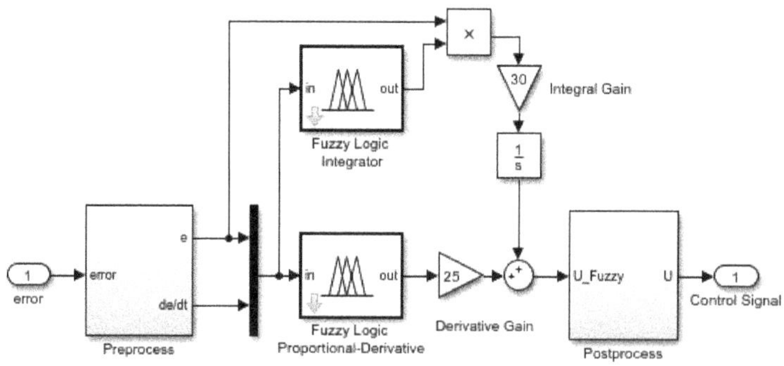

Figure 11. Structure of a fuzzy PID controller.

An independent control structure was chosen for the proportional–derivative and the integral terms, which provided us the possibility of separately adjusting the incidence of each stage according to the response requirements that were presented in the fine-tuning process of the controller by modifying the gain value during each stage. This action replaces the effect of having to make multiple modifications in the universe of discourse of the variables.

For the control of a planar CDPR by means of a fuzzy PID controller, the error signals and their derivatives were considered as inputs to the controller. The selection of the rules and the number and form of the membership functions were based on expert knowledge acquired in the operation of a didactic planar CDPR belonging to Salesian Polytechnic University, as shown in Figure 12. The structure of the model shown in Figure 1, as well as its physical dimensions, were also based on this didactic CDPR. The inference process in the set of rules was of the Mamdani type [26].

The physical dimensions of the robot's workspace described above were directly involved in the choice of the universe of discourse of the error variables. Additionally, with the intention of achieving a more effective action when the robot approached the desired position, it was decided to concentrate the membership functions in the universe of discourse between −0.5 m and 0.5 m, taking into account that if the error were greater it, would be captured by the lateral membership functions which have open trapezoidal characteristics. On the other hand, in the case of the universe of discourse for the signal of the derivative of the error, the maximum speed of movement of the robot was considered, which is 2 m/s in the end-effector. Therefore, using a similar criterion for the action of the membership functions that focused their action on when the robot approached the desired position, a universe of discourse ranging from −1 m/s to 1 m/s was defined.

Figure 12. Planar CDPR assembled in the labs of Salesian Polytechnic University in Ecuador.

Seven membership functions were considered for each input signal to the controller (error signal and derivative of the error), of which the intermediate five were triangular type and those at the ends were open-wing trapezoidal type, as shown in Figures 13 and 14. These membership functions were distributed evenly throughout the universe of discourse and named: large negative (NG), negative (N), small negative (NP), zero (Z), small positive (PP), positive (P), and large positive (PG).

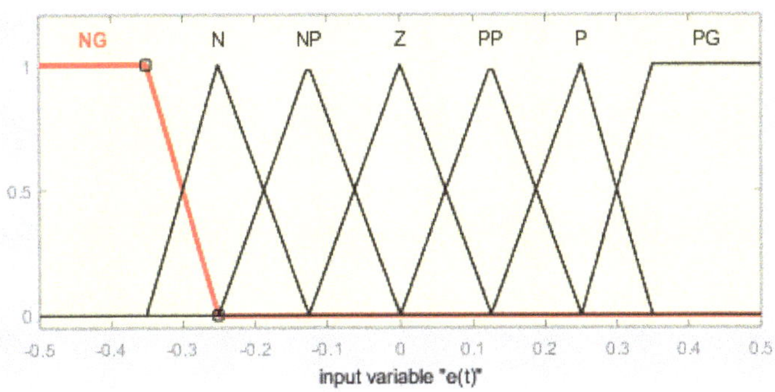

Figure 13. Membership functions and universe of discourse of the error input signal.

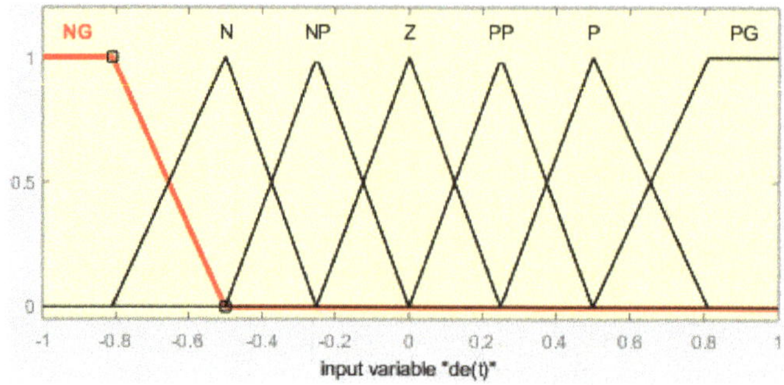

Figure 14. Membership functions and universe of discourse of the error derivative input signal.

These seven membership functions were equidistant in distribution, with each corresponding to 14.2% of the universe of discourse. In the case of the error signal, each membership function was equivalent to approximately 14 cm, and in the case of the derivative of the error, it corresponded to 0.28 m/s. These ranges and the number of membership functions were considered acceptable as they generated control surfaces requiring a moderate amount of computation.

The control output was generated by the inference of seven triangular membership functions, as seen in Figure 15 [26,27]. These membership functions represent the characteristics of the control signal and were named: large negative control (uNG), negative control (uN), small negative control (uNP), zero control (uZ), small positive control (uPP), positive control (uP), and large positive control (uPG).

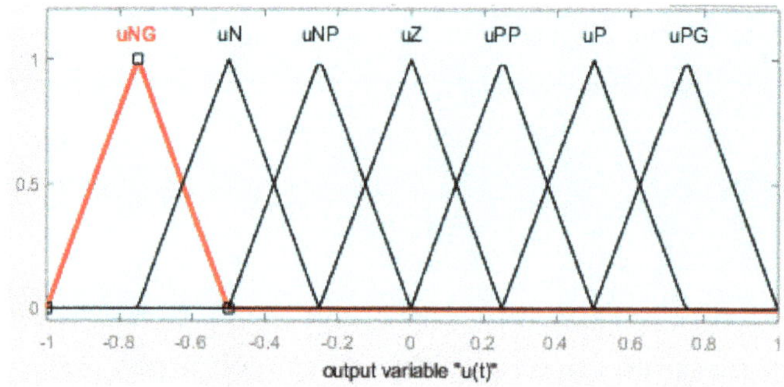

Figure 15. Membership functions and universe of discourse of the control output signal.

The choice of the triangular shape of the membership functions used for the inputs and output was intended to decrease the processing time, understanding that the generated control surfaces would not be physically smooth. It should be noted that the general context of the smooth motion of the robot was considered in the design of the trajectory planner.

The output signal of both the proportional–derivative stage and the integrating stage was derived from an inference process based on AND operations that had a total of 49 rules, whose details are shown in Figures 16 and 17. Each rule was constructed based on expert knowledge of CDPR behavior, and some examples are explained:

- For the output of the proportional–derivative action when the error signal and the error derivative are close to zero, the rule can be stated as: **IF** *e(t)* is **"Z" AND** $\dot{e}(t)$ is **"Z" THEN** *u(t)* is **"uZ."** The same situation for the output of the integrative action can be stated as: **IF** *e(t)* is **"Z" AND** $\dot{e}(t)$ is **"Z" THEN** *u(t)* is **"uPG."** In this case, the idea is that the integrative action is in charge of outputting the required control signal that maintains the tracking error near zero.
- If a small positive error is now considered with a small negative error derivative, a small positive action would be required at the output of the proportional–derivative action and this rule can be stated as: **IF** *e(t)* is **"PP" AND** $\dot{e}(t)$ is **"NP" THEN** *u(t)* is **"uPP."**

- If again, a small positive error is considered, but now a small positive error derivative is present, then the output of the proportional-derivative action must be reinforced, and this can be stated as: **IF** $e(t)$ is "**PP**" **AND** $\dot{e}(t)$ is "**PP**" **THEN** $u(t)$ is "**uP.**"

The defuzzification process of the Mamdani fuzzy inference system is based on the centroid calculation, where the defuzzified value x^* for a fuzzy input is obtained by:

$$x^* = \frac{\int_a^b x\mu(x)dx}{\int_a^b \mu(x)dx} \tag{12}$$

where $\mu(x)$ is the fuzzified input, and $[a,b]$ is the interval where the fuzzy set is defined [28].

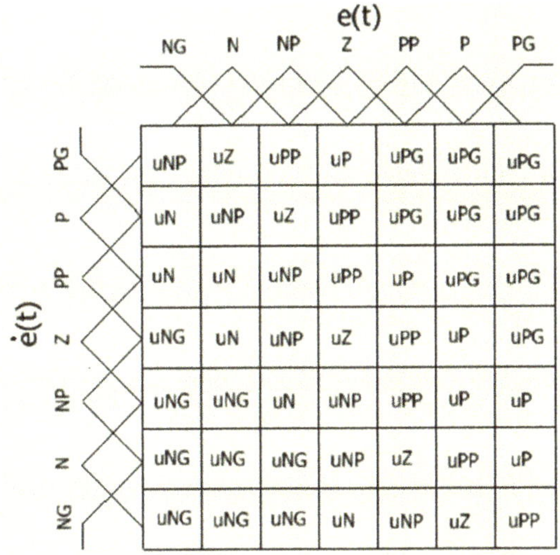

Figure 16. Matrix of rules for the proportional–derivative action.

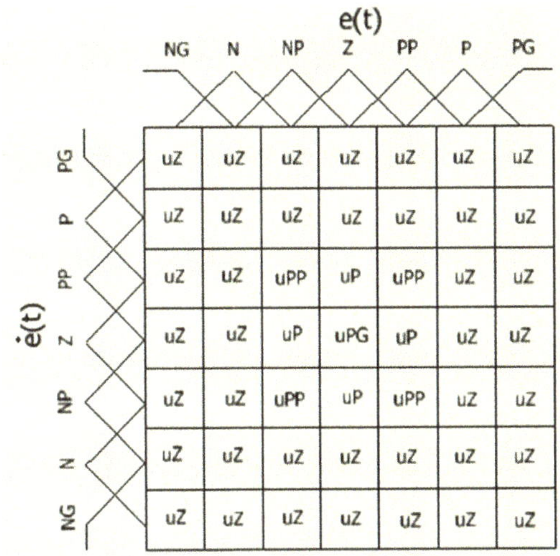

Figure 17. Matrix of rules for the integrative action.

Once the set of rules was implemented, the control surfaces obtained for each stage were observed, as shown in Figures 18 and 19.

The structure and tuning of the fuzzy controller can be implemented in an equivalent way for the control of the X-axis and the Y-axis, according to the planar CDPR decoupled control system structure shown in Figure 3.

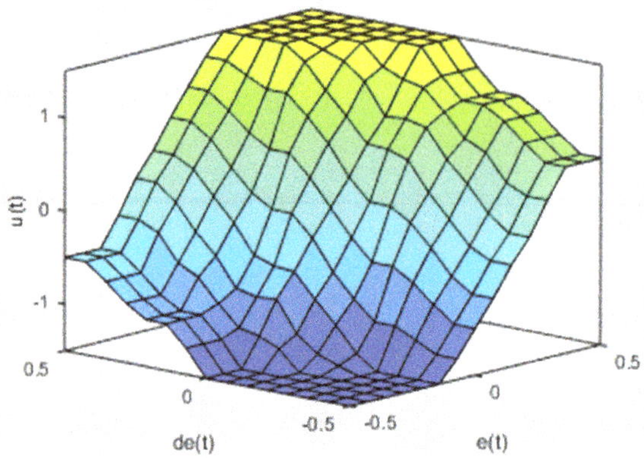

Figure 18. Control surface of the proportional-derivative action.

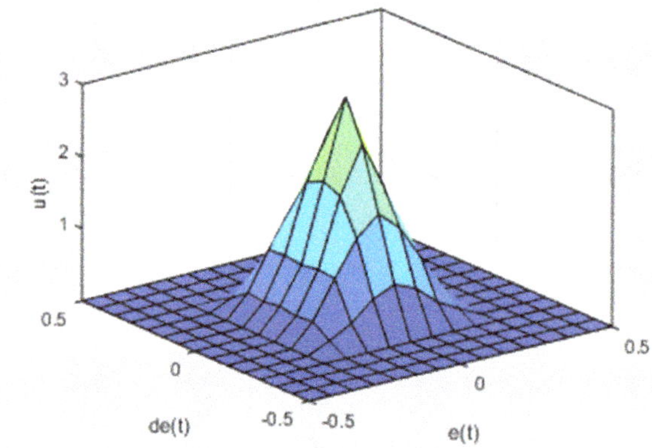

Figure 19. Control surface of the integrative action.

3. Results

The CDPR planar control system is shown in Figure 20, which includes a disturbance signal input that allows for the validation of the results of the controllers in the presence of any external signal that may deviate it from the objective position of the robot. The simulations were developed in MATLAB/Simulink using continuous-time mode, with fixed step size and an ode4 (Runge–Kutta) solver.

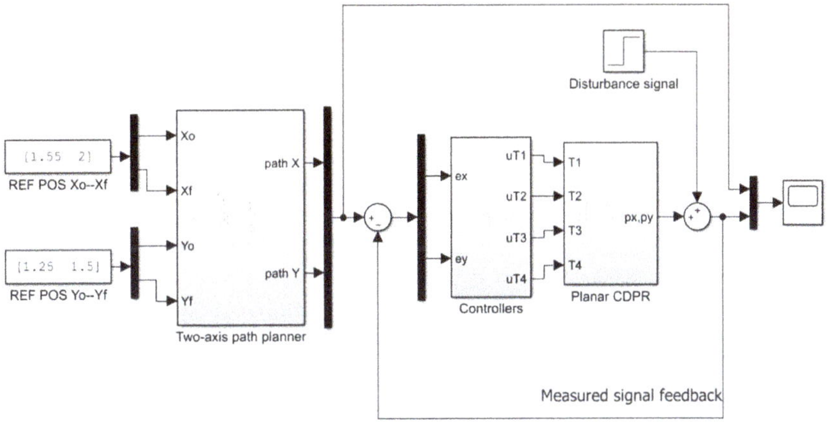

Figure 20. Control system of a planar CDPR.

3.1. Simulation Results for a Control Structure Based on PID Controllers

The results of the simulations for the control structure of Figure 10 based on PID controllers are presented below.

The position in the X and Y axes of the end-effector of the robot is represented by XG and YG. The references generated by the trajectory planner are called Ref. XG and Ref. YG.

Figure 21 shows the robot's positioning response in the absence of disturbance actions, while Figure 22 shows the results in the presence of 10 cm step disturbance actions in the position of each axis.

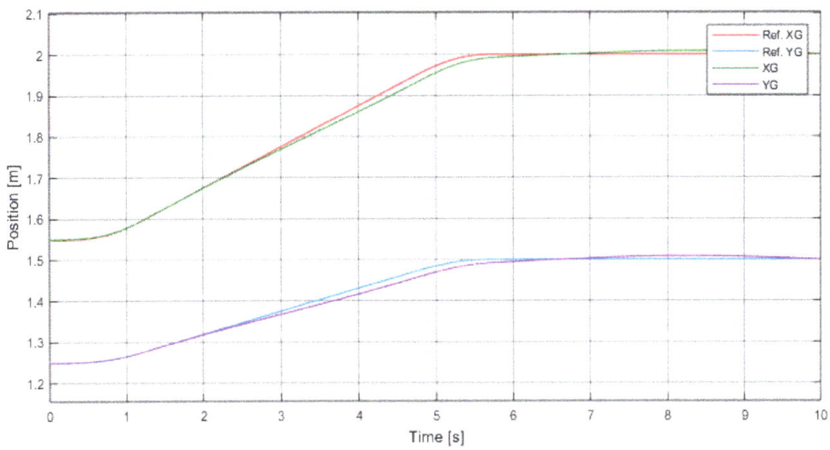

Figure 21. Planar CDPR positioning response of a PID controller.

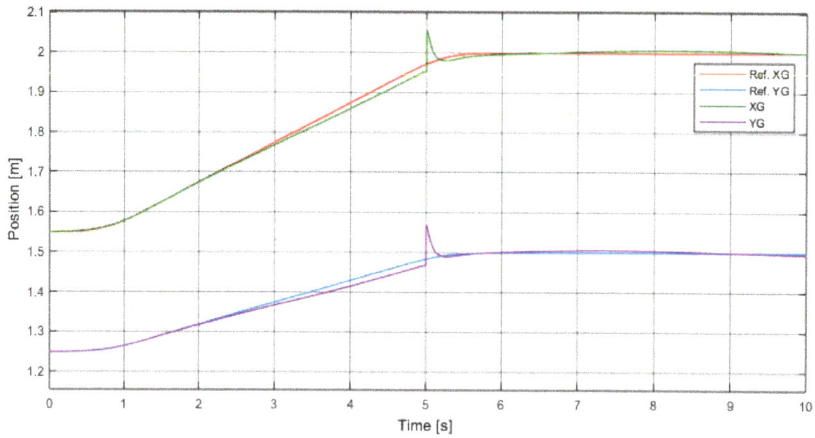

Figure 22. Positioning response of the planar CDPR in the presence of disturbance of a PID controller.

In Figures 21 and 22, it can be seen that the robot followed the positional reference, establishing itself with relative precision, and was also capable of overcoming the disturbance present after 5 s of simulation.

3.2. Simulation Results for Control Structure Based on Fuzzy-PID Controllers

The results of the simulations for the control structure of Figure 10 based on fuzzy PID controllers are presented below.

In Figure 23, the response of positioning and orientation of the robot can be observed in the absence of disturbance actions, while in Figure 24 the results are observed in the presence of 10 cm step disturbance actions in the position of each axis.

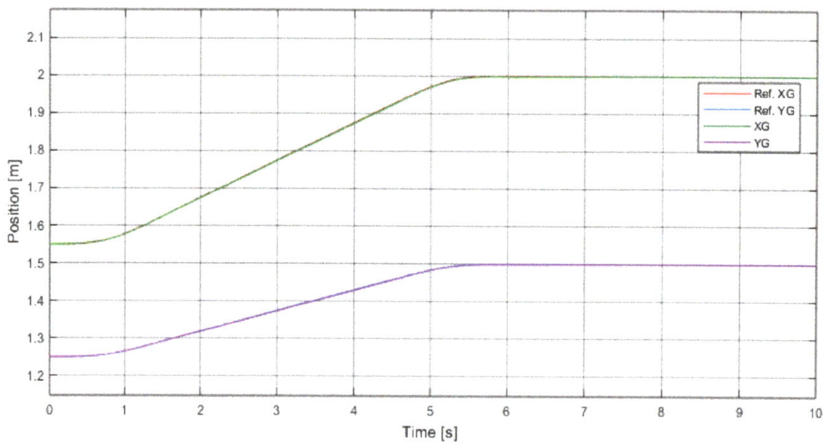

Figure 23. Planar CDPR positioning response of a fuzzy PID controller.

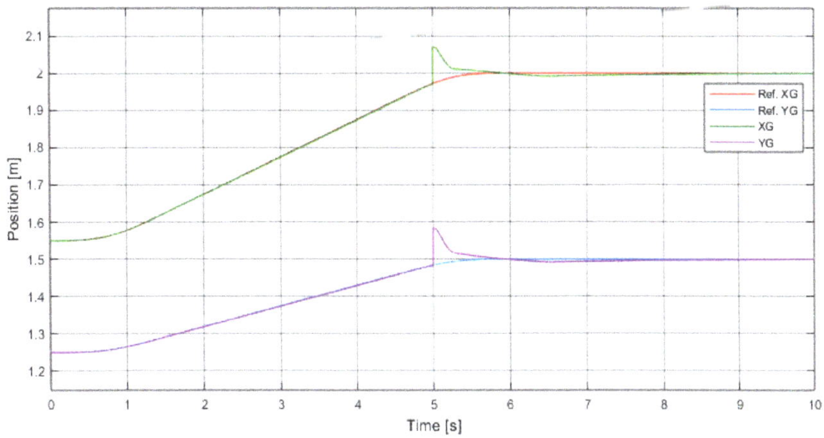

Figure 24. Positioning response of the planar CDPR in the presence of disturbance of a fuzzy PID controller.

In a similar way to the case of control with a PID, it is observed in Figures 23 and 24 that the robot followed the position reference, was established with better precision and was able to overcome the disturbance presented through 5 s of simulation. Although the disturbance rejection was no better than that of a classic PID, a lower tracking error was observed throughout the path. In order to compare the performances of both controllers, the cumulative quadratic error (CQE) between responses and their corresponding references was computed in MATLAB. For the test of the PID shown in Figure 21, the CQE was 0.41 for the response on the X-axis and 0.37 for the response on the Y-axis. The same index calculated for the response of the fuzzy PID shown in Figure 23 gave 0.0056 in the X-axis and 0.0058 in the Y-axis.

4. Discussion

According to the results, it was determined that the decoupled control structure proposed in this document, which considers the movements in the axes of the robot plane as independent, was effective when implemented with both classic and fuzzy PID controllers. During a combined movement on both axes, each controller was influenced by the signals generated because of the movement on the other axis. This influence is assumed as a disturbance that will be controlled by the controller. The effectiveness of the control depends on the distance between the end-effector and the center of the plane of movement, being lower as the end-effector moves away from the center.

The fuzzy PID controller had notably better performance compared to the classic PID, as shown previously with the calculated values of the CQE. These can be also observed in the error signals of the evolutions shown in Figures 21 and 23, which are plotted in Figures 25 and 26.

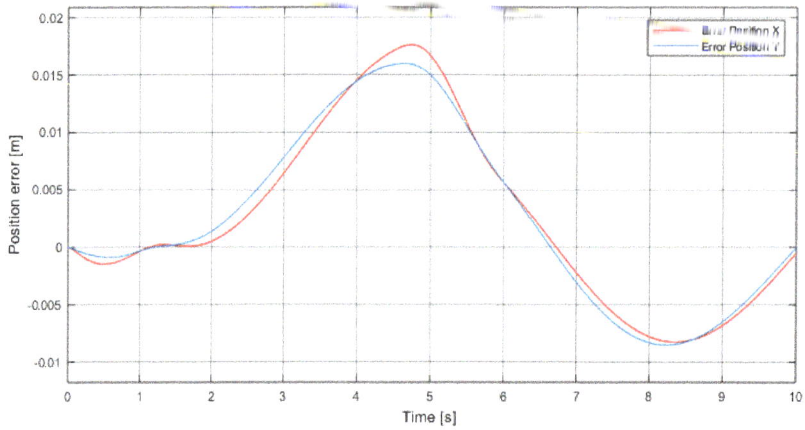

Figure 25. Error signal developed during robot movement under the action of a PID controller.

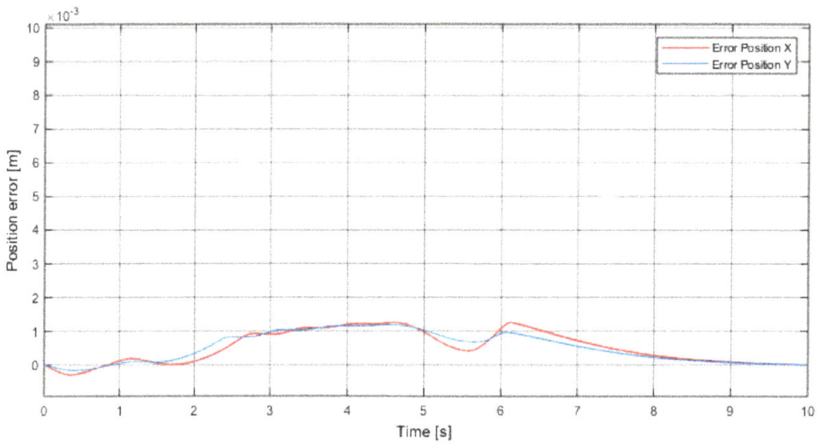

Figure 26. Error signal developed during robot movement under the action of a fuzzy PID controller.

It is important to highlight that compensation for gravitational forces calculated in the center of the workspace was proposed. The non-linearity of the system restricted the performance of the controllers to an area close to this point of operation. Therefore, the workspace under the proposed control structure was affected. In this sense, a point more distant from the center of the robot [X, Y] = [2.6, 2.3] was explored, with the disturbing position signal acting after 15 s. Figures 27 and 28 show the responses of the PID control system and the fuzzy PID, respectively, in which it can be seen that the PIDs did not present an adequate control action.

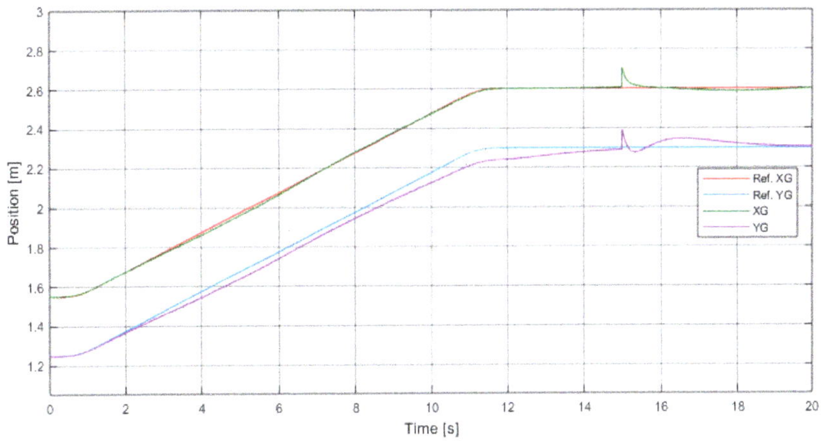

Figure 27. Positioning response of the planar CDPR (away from the center) with disturbance at 15 s of simulation, with a PID controller.

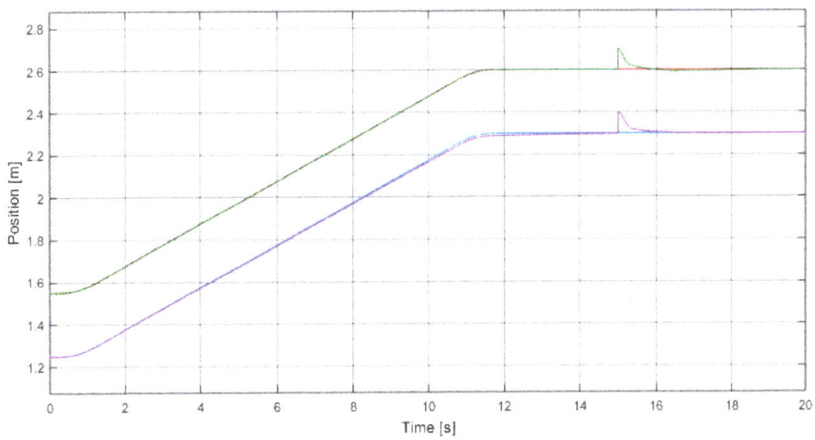

Figure 28. Positioning response of the planar CDPR (away from the center) with disturbance at 15 s of simulation, with a fuzzy PID controller.

5. Conclusions

The results show that PID controllers with linear characteristics correctly control the non-linear mechanism under a decoupled structure for each axis of the end-effector. However, by having a defined operation point at the center of the robot, these controllers lose effectiveness at positioning the robot at extreme points of the work plane, reducing the effective working space of the robot.

It was observed that the fuzzy PID controllers, having non-linear characteristics, controlled the non-linear mechanism with greater accuracy, and presented smaller error signals than those of the control case based on classic PID controllers. Additionally, it was shown that fuzzy PID controllers presented an adequate level of performance in extreme positions of the robot, allowing us to effectively take advantage of a wider workspace with respect to the case of the PID controllers.

As was shown, when analyzing the behavior of the error signal developed by the control system for each case, the control system based on fuzzy PID presented better results in terms of the amplitude of the error and the stabilization time.

The decoupled control structure proposed for each axis of the planar CDPR has proven to be effective even when it was experimented upon using trajectories of simultaneous movement between the two axes.

Future work should include an experimental test of the proposed CDPR method shown in Figure 12. Also, future work should extend the application of this structure to the case of a spatial CDPR in which decoupled movements are assumed for the three axes.

Author Contributions: Conceptualization, M.C. and R.S.; methodology, M.C. and R.S.; Investigation, M.C., C.C. and J.V.; Software, R.S and M.C.; Writing—Review & Editing, M.C., C.C., J.G. and J.V. All authors have read and agreed to the published version of the manuscript.

Funding: This research was supported by the Spanish Government Projects under Grant DPI2014-57220-C2-1-P, Grant PGC2018-095939-B-I00, in part by the RoboCity2030 DIH-CM Madrid Robotics Digital Innovation Hub, S2018/NMT-4331, and funded by the Programas Actividades I+D en la Comunidad de Madrid, in part by the Structural Funds of the EU, and the GIIRA research group at Universidad Politécnica Salesiana, Ecuador.

Conflicts of Interest: The authors declare no conflict of interest. The funders had no role in the design of the study; in the collection, analyses, or interpretation of data; in the writing of the manuscript, or in the decision to publish the results.

References

1. Sun, H.; Tang, X.; Cui, Z.; Hou, S. Dynamic Response of Spatial Flexible Structures Subjected to Controllable Force Based on Cable-Driven Parallel Robots. *IEEE/ASME Trans. Mechatron.* **2020**, *25*, 2801–2811. [CrossRef]
2. Zhang, B.; Shang, W.; Cong, S.; Li, Z. Coordinated Dynamic Control in the Task Space for Redundantly Actuated Cable-Driven Parallel Robots. *IEEE/ASME Trans. Mechatron.* **2020**. [CrossRef]
3. Picard, E.; Caro, S.; Franck, P.; Claveau, F. Control Solution for a Cable-Driven Parallel Robot with Highly Variable Payload. *Mech. Robot. Conf.* **2018**, *5B*, 26–29.
4. Tho, T.P.; Thinh, N.T. Using a Cable-Driven Parallel Robot with Applications in 3D Concrete Printing. *Appl. Sci.* **2021**, *11*, 563. [CrossRef]
5. Gosselin, C. Cable-driven parallel mechanisms: State of the art and perspectives. *Mech. Eng. Rev.* **2014**, *1*, DSM0004. [CrossRef]
6. Merlet, J.; Papegay, Y.; Gasc, N. The Prince's tears, a large cable-driven parallel robot for an artistic exhibition. In Proceedings of the IEEE International Conference on Robotics and Automation, Paris, France, 31 May–31 August 2020; pp. 10378–10383.
7. Jung, J. Workspace and Stiffness Analysis of 3D Printing Cable-Driven Parallel Robot with a Retractable Beam-Type End-Effector. *Robotics* **2020**, *9*, 65. [CrossRef]
8. Chen, Y.; Shao, L.; Liu, S.; Zhang, Y.; Wang, H. Adaptative Fuzzy Control for a Class of Nonlinear Time-Delay Systems. In Proceedings of the IEEE Data Driven Control Learn. Syst. Conf. (DDCLS), Cairo, Egypt, 14–16 December 2020; pp. 1125–1130.
9. Ma, X.-J.; Sun, Z.-Q.; He, Y.-T. Analysis and design of fuzzy controller and fuzzy observer. *IEEE Trans. Fuzzy Syst.* **1998**, *6*, 41–51.
10. Erenoglu, I.; Eksin, I.; Yesil, E.; Guzelkaya, M. An Intelligent Hybrid Fuzzy PID Controller. In Proceedings of the 20th European Conference on Modelling and Simulation, Bonn, Germany, 28–31 May 2006; pp. 1–5. [CrossRef]
11. Dewantoro, G.; Kuo, Y. Robust speed-controlled permeant magnet synchronous motor drive using fuzzy logic controller. In Proceedings of the IEEE International Conference on Fuzzy Systems (FUZZ-IEEE), Taipei, Taiwan, 27–30 June 2011; pp. 884–888.
12. Yunong, Y.; Ha, H.M.; Kim, Y.K.; Lee, J. Balancing and driving Control of a ball robot using fuzzy control. In Proceedings of the International Conference on Ubiquitous Robots and Ambient Intelligence (URAI), Goyangi, Korea, 28–30 October 2015; pp. 492–494.
13. Zabbah, I.; Foolad, S.; Chaharaqran, B.; Mazlooman, R. Design and making the intelligence assistant robot and controlling it by the fuzzy procedure. In Proceedings of the International Conference on Electronics, Computer and Computation (ICECCO), Ankara, Turkey, 7–9 November 2013; pp. 168–171.
14. Sheikhalr, A.; Fakharian, A.; Adhami, A. Fuzzy adaptative control of omni-directional mobile robot. In Proceedings of the 13th Iranian Conference on Fuzzy Systems (IFSC), Qazvin, Iran, 27–29 August 2013; pp. 1–4.
15. Ziegler, J.G.; Nichols, N.B. Optimum settings for automatic controllers. *Trans. ASME* **1942**, *64*, 759–765. [CrossRef]
16. Li, J.; Li, Y. Dynamic analysis and PID control for a quadrotor. In Proceedings of the IEEE International Conference on Mechatronics and Automation, Beijing, China, 7–11 August 2011; pp. 573–578.
17. Kelly, R. A tuning procedure for stable PID control of robot manipulators. *Robotica* **1995**, *13*, 141–148. [CrossRef]
18. Cervantes, I.; Alvarez, J. On the PID tracking control of robot manipulators. *Syst. Control Lett.* **2001**, *42*, 37–46. [CrossRef]
19. Lumelsky, V. Effect of kinematics on motion planning for planar robot arms moving amidst unknown obstacles. *IEEE J. Robot. Autom.* **1987**, *3*, 207–223. [CrossRef]
20. Kim, J.; Jin, M.; Park, S.; Chung, S.; Hwang, M. Task Space Trajectory Planning for Robot Manipulators to Follow 3-D Curved Contours. *Electronics* **2020**, *9*, 1424. [CrossRef]

21. Barroso, A.; Saltaren, R.; Portilla, G.; Cely, J.; Carpio, M. Smooth Path Planner for Dynamic Simulators Based on Cable-Driven Parallel Robots. In Proceedings of the International Conference on Smart Systems and Technologies (SST), Osijek, Croatia, 10–12 December 2018; pp. 145–150.
22. Max, H. *Cable Structures*, 1st ed.; The MIT Press: Cambridge, MA, USA, 1981; pp. 2–255.
23. Taghirad, H. *Parallel Robots: Mechanics and Control*, 1st ed.; CRC Press: Boca Raton, FL, USA, 2013; pp. 1–533.
24. Merlet, J. *Parallel Robots*, 2nd ed.; Springer: Paris, France, 2006; pp. 4–320.
25. Macfarlane, S.; Elizabeth, A. Jerk-Bounded Manipulator Trajectory Planning: Design for Real-Time Applications. *Trans. Robot. Autom.* **2003**, *19*, 42–51. [CrossRef]
26. Kaur, A.; Kaur, A. Comparison of Mamdani-Type and Sugeno-Type Fuzzy Inference Systems for Air Conditioning System. *Int. J. Soft Comput. Eng. (IJSCE)* **2012**, *2*, 323–325.
27. Carpio, M.; Orozco, W.; Betancur, M. Design and Simulation of a Fuzzy Controller for Vertical Take off and Landing (VTOL) Systems. In Proceedings of the International Autumn Meeting on Power, Electronics and Computing (ROPEC), Ixtapa, Mexico, 9–16 November 2016.
28. Ponce, P. *Artificial Intelligence with Applications to Engineering*, 1st ed.; Alfaomega: Mexico City, Mexico, 2010; pp. 72–75.

electronics

MDPI

Article

Artificial Neural Network Controller for a Modular Robot Using a Software Defined Radio Communication System

Luis Fernando Pedraza [1,*], Henry Alberto Hernández [2] and Cesar Augusto Hernández [3]

1 Telecommunications Engineering Department, Universidad Distrital Francisco José de Caldas, Bogotá 11021-110231588, Colombia
2 Control and Automation Engineering Department, Universidad Distrital Francisco José de Caldas, Bogotá 11021-110231588, Colombia; hahernandezm@udistrital.edu.co
3 Electrical Engineering Department, Universidad Distrital Francisco José de Caldas, Bogotá 11021-110231588, Colombia; cahernandezs@udistrital.edu.co
* Correspondence: lfpedrazam@udistrital.edu.co

Received: 11 July 2020; Accepted: 12 August 2020; Published: 2 October 2020

Abstract: Modular robots are flexible structures that offer versatility and configuration options for carrying out different types of movements; however, disconnection problems between the modules can lead to the loss of information, and, therefore, the proposed displacement objectives are not met. This work proposes the control of a chain-type modular robot using an artificial neural network (ANN) that enables the robot to go through different environments. The main contribution of this research is that it uses a software defined radio (SDR) system, where the Wi-Fi channel with the best signal-to-noise Ratio (SNR) is selected to send the information regarding the simulated movement parameters and obtained by the controller to the modular robot. This allows for faster communication with fewer errors. In case of a disconnection, these parameters are stored in the simulator, so they can be sent again, which increases the tolerance to communication failures. Additionally, the robot sends information about the average angular velocity, which is stored in the cloud. The errors in the ANN controller results, in terms of the traveled distance and time estimated by the simulator, are less than 6% of the real robot values.

Keywords: artificial neural network (ANN); modular robot; software defined radio (SDR); signal-to-noise ratio (SNR)

1. Introduction

Today, modularity is present in numerous areas of industry and robotics; therefore, modular systems offer benefits such as versatility, robustness and low-cost manufacturing compared to fixed-parameter conventional designs [1]. This has driven the use of modular robots whose structure is made up of multiple modules that are combined in different configurations to carry out various kinds of tasks. Some of these tasks include simple movements such as spinning or moving forward and complex movements such as walking or crawling [2,3]. The scope and movements of the robotic structure depend on the shape and number of degrees of freedom of each module, since these variables can increase the processing capacity required to synchronize the articulations of each module [4,5].

The techniques to control a modular robot can be centralized, decentralized or hybrid. In the first case, structure control is embedded in a single device [6]. In the second case, the controller can be any module in the structure [7,8]. In the third case, the controller incorporates features of the previous controllers; that is, there is a central controller that sends parameters to the modules that translate said information to perform a task [9–11].

The artificial neural network (ANN) has been used in robotics applications due to the high computation rate and capacity to support nonlinear functions. The uses of ANN controllers in robotics include the support of wireless connections for underwater swarm robots [12], the control of a five-degrees-of-freedom robot [13] and a neural-learning-based sensorless control scheme in the presence of an input dead zone for a robotic arm [14].

Furthermore, the evolution of communication systems throughout the years has led to their application in robots to enhance their performance [15]. One of the more novel approaches in communication systems corresponds to the development of software defined radio (SDR) technology, which is a radio system where the components are implemented using software to interact with hardware [16,17]. In this project, the Raspberry Pi 3 device was used to implement the SDR since it allows for the development of wireless applications with a robust low-cost embedded system, which has been used as a communication system for robot control in the monitoring and storage of data in real time [18]. It has also been used for the control and communication of a robot that produces basic motions and sends a video to an Android device [19]. Typically, communication in modular robots is based on infrared or wired communication; however, some initiatives have been developed to communicate the modules wirelessly using ZigBee [20] and Wi-Fi [21] technologies, although to date, there are no reports on the use of SDR communication.

This work contributes to the literature with the use of a wireless ANN controller that builds the path of an EMERGE modular robot in a simulator and sends the information to the modular robot through an SDR communication network implemented in a Raspberry Pi 3. The result of this is the approximation of the behavior of the robot before its start-up and in the use of a communication channel that causes fewer errors and has a higher speed than those around it, at a low cost. This paper is organized as follows: Section 2 describes the structure and operation of the system, while Section 3 presents and discusses the results obtained with the controller executed in the simulator and the robot. Lastly, Section 4 presents the conclusions derived from the overall work.

2. System Development

The elements that compose the system are described below: the EMERGE modular robot, the simulator, the ANN controller and the SDR communication platform, as shown in Figure 1. Furthermore, this section details the concepts required to understand the operation of the EMERGE modular robot, the control method and an explanation of the experiments carried out to evaluate the controller.

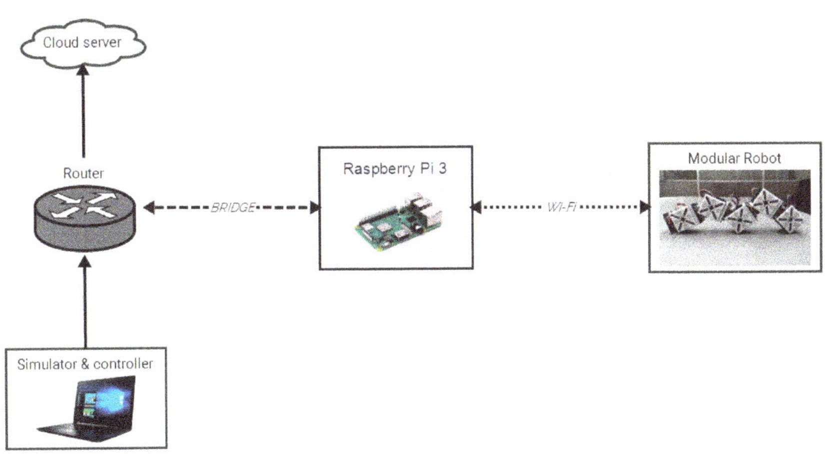

Figure 1. General diagram of the developed system.

2.1. EMERGE Modular Robot

The EMERGE robot seen in Figure 2a is an open-use prototype; that is, the materials, electrical circuits and procedure necessary for its assembly can be found in a repository [22]. Additionally, this prototype is flexible, which allows the user to adapt the circuits to particular needs [23–25]. For instance, in this case, a printed circuit was added to the robot with the ESP32 microcontroller, which allows it to communicate with the Raspberry Pi using Wi-Fi wireless technology.

(a) (b)

Figure 2. EMERGE modular robot: (**a**) Assembly; (**b**) Individual module.

This robot is basically composed of various modules, such as the one shown in Figure 2b, where the user defines the grouping. Each module has four sides with magnets that can be connected to other modules. The information is shared using the controller area network (CAN) protocol, which can package, send and receive the information from or towards a specific module or device [23–25].

Although, in this application, chain-type morphologies were considered to carry out the experiments, the CAN communication protocol and the structure of each module are flexible, which allows the robot modules to be grouped with different types of morphologies and, therefore, perform various tasks [22].

The traditional method to control the EMERGE robot is based on a centralized controller such as the one in Figure 3a, that is implemented in the platform, so the controller has an embedded control algorithm that is executed in real time during the operation of the platform [23]. However, when the platform is turned off or a module is disconnected, the controller is desynchronized and the robot stops moving. This is avoided with the control and communication strategy proposed in this paper.

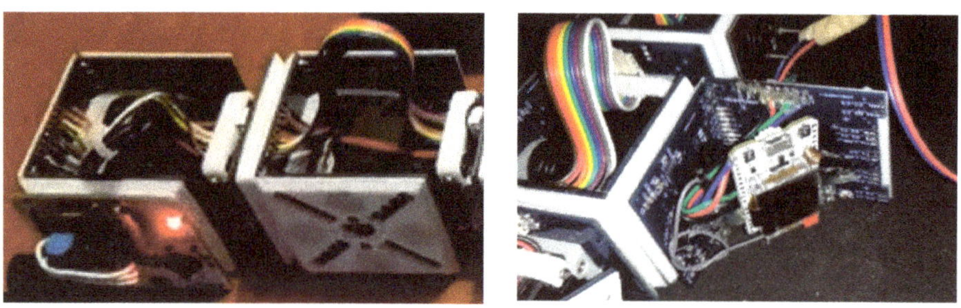

(a) (b)

Figure 3. Local controllers: (**a**) Traditional; (**b**) Wi-Fi module.

The proposed controller modifies the centralized control technique using an evolutionary algorithm that is executed locally in the controller. This is achieved by generating the control parameters on the computer, in which the parameters are simulated and sent to the robot through the SDR network, which connects to the robot's Wi-Fi module (ESP32 microcontroller), presented in Figure 3b. This device sends the received information to each module through the CAN bus [23].

2.2. Modular Robot Simulator

The simulation environment was developed in the 3D World Editor application in Matlab [26]. The dynamic interactions between the module chains, the environment and simulated obstacles are displayed in the editor. This allows the user to know in advance the real movements of the robot. Figure 4a shows the virtual module of the robot implemented in the 3D simulation. This module was created in the SolidWorks software. The virtual modules are coupled to create the robot morphology as shown in Figure 4b, and the movement is produced according to the rotation and translation data received from the controller.

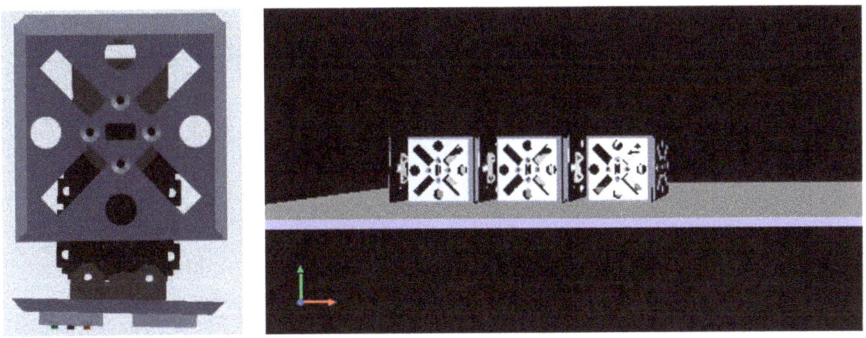

(a) (b)

Figure 4. Virtual simulator: (**a**) Module developed in SolidWorks; (**b**) Design and assembly of the robot in the 3D World Editor environment.

The sequence of movements in the simulator is generated using the motion control tables, which were designed based on a sine function with an amplitude, frequency and phase shift for each module. As a result of this function, values between 0 and π are obtained, and then a conversion is performed for the start-up of the actuator of the module, which receives values between 0 and 1024 as shown in Figure 5. The conversion is limited in the range of $[\frac{\pi}{4}, \frac{3\pi}{4}]$, since any value outside this range would compromise the mechanical structure of the robot.

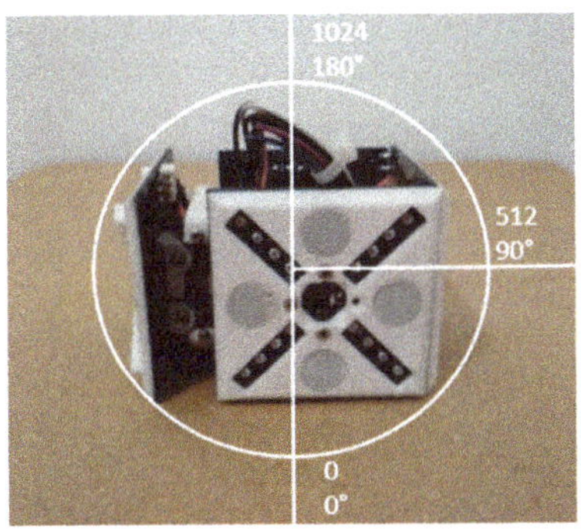

Figure 5. Motion range for the module actuator.

The simulator user interface shown in Figure 6 allows the selection of the morphology and environment to simulate the path. Three designed morphologies are available with 3 to 5 modules, as well as three environments: a flat surface, a ladder as an obstacle and an L-shaped path. Then, the ANN controller is executed to determine the position of each module of the robot. The data are represented graphically in the virtual environment, and, if needed, these are sent to the real robot through the SDR communication network.

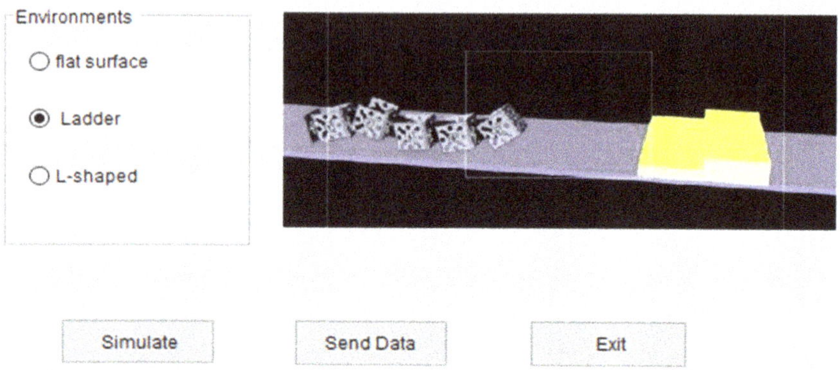

Figure 6. The simulator user interface.

2.3. *Artificial Neural Network Controller*

The ANN controller calculates the position of each robot module [27–30]. In this case, a backpropagation ANN was implemented as shown in Figure 7a, which uses a training algorithm based on the correction of the mean squared error. Basically, it is a margin of error ($\in$) that is estimated as the average of the squares of the errors, as shown in the following equations—that is, the difference between the expected value ($\hat{y}_i$), contained in a dataset, and the estimated value (y_i), calculated by the ANN. This difference is adjusted in each training iteration based on the weights (w_i) of each ANN neuron, with an activation function f_i, until the error is close to zero (in this case, a threshold of $\tau = 4 \times 10^{-8}$ is established).

$$y_i = f_i(w_i \times y_i + \epsilon) \quad (1)$$

$$\in_i = \frac{1}{n}\sum_{i=1}^{n}(\hat{y}_i - y_i)^2 \quad (2)$$

In this case, the training dataset, presented in Table 1, is a database containing the following information: the number of modules, type of environment and position of the modules. Furthermore, this dataset contains 1000 records of samples taken during the operation of the robot modules in different environments, 750 records to be used for ANN training and 250 for validation of the estimated results. The ANN controller inputs are the type of environment and the number of modules, while the positions of the modules are the outputs. Afterward, the ANN is trained to reproduce the set of movements in the simulator and, if required, in the robot, as shown in Figure 7b. The number of hidden layers of the ANN was established as 25 since that is the minimum number to estimate a set of continuous and stable movements with a low error, as is analyzed in chapter 3, and using moderate computational resources during training. The training time is approximately 430 s.

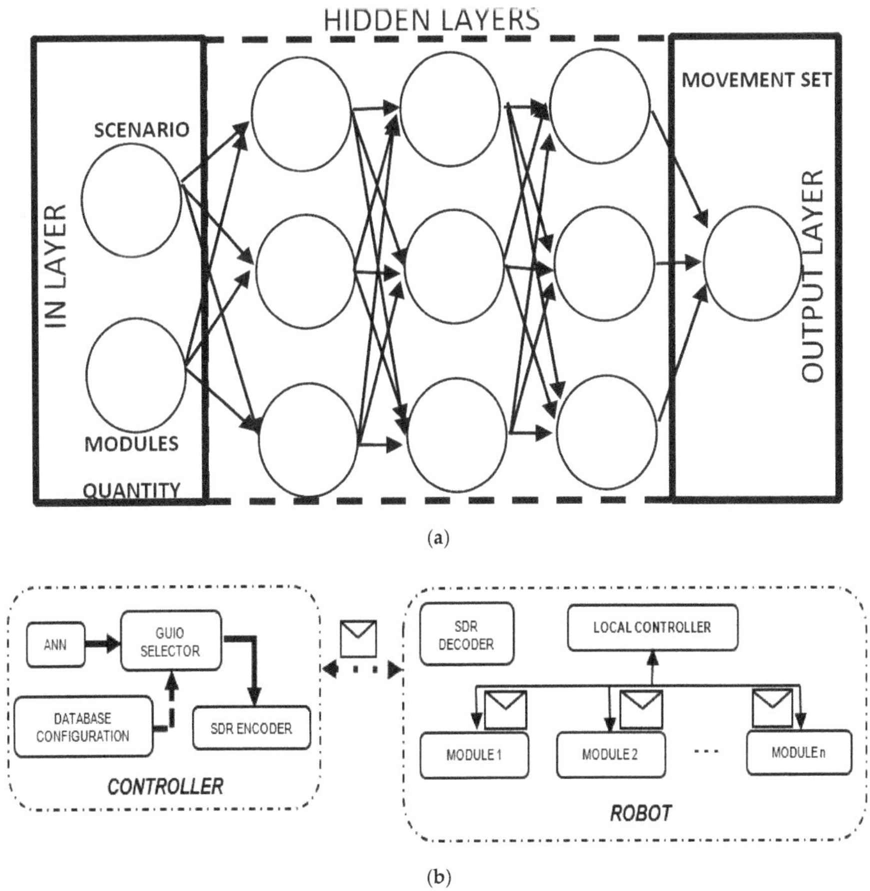

Figure 7. Artificial neural network (ANN) configuration: (**a**) Implementation of the layers; (**b**) Robot controller.

Table 1. Database segment used to train the ANN.

Inputs		Outputs				
Scenario	Number of Modules	Module 1	Module 2	Module 3	Module 4	Module 5
Flat surface	3	300	320	340	-	-
Flat surface	4	325	345	365	385	-
Ladder	4	350	370	390	410	-
L-shaped	4	375	395	415	435	-
Flat surface	5	400	420	440	460	480
Ladder	5	425	445	465	485	505

In Algorithm 1, the instructions of the proposed ANN controller are presented, which delivers the movements to the simulator and, if required, to the robot. The three environments over which the robot can move, to evaluate the algorithm, are shown in Figure 8.

Algorithm 1. Control strategy

```
Function ANN (in i, out o, margin of error ϵ)
    τ = 4 × 10^-8                                   //Threshold as stop condition
    ANN ← Inputs [i][1]                             //In vector layer
    ANN ← Outputs [1][o]                            //Out vector layer
    ANN ← Activation function (f_i)                 //f_i is a gaussian function (Equation (1))
    ANN ← Hidden layers [10][25]                    //Matrix 10 neurons × 25 layers
    ANN ← Initial weights                           //Initial weight assignment function
    While τ < ϵ do
        ANN ← optimize weights (i, o)
        ϵ ← test ANN                                //Validation of results
    End While
    return ANN
End ANN

Function Virtual enviroment ()
    Load libraries 3D enviroment                    //Load virtual objects and robot
    Start SDR port                                  //Open port to establish communication
    Create communication port read thread           //Start communication routine
    Create communication port send thread
    Start GUIO (Graphical User Interface Objects)   //Start program
    i ← number of modules                           //Select robot morphologie
    j ← select escenario                            //Select enviroment
    m ← mode                                        //Select routine test or ANN mode
    epochs ← 0                                      //Start iterations
    If mode == 1 then
        θ_i ← movements database                    //Read predefined movements (Table 1)
    else
        θ_i ← ANN(i, j, inf)                        //Read ANN movements
                                                    //Note: inf is a initial value (can be > 10)
                                                    //for ϵ and start ANN weights
    While epochs < 200 do
        ∝_i← Generate movements in the virtual reality environment (θ_i)
                                                    //Nomalize the θ_i value and fixes it
                                                    //on the actuator scale
          Send via serial port (∝_i)                //Send θ_i to each real module
          Run the move routine for 100 milliseconds //Delay for the next movement
        epochs ++
        ϵ ← MSE(θ_i)                                //Mean Squares Error routine (Equation (2))
        θ_i ← ANN(i, j, ϵ)                          //Simulates the ANN and update weights
    End While
End Virtual enviroment
```

(a) (b) (c)

Figure 8. Environments used to evaluate the controller algorithm: (**a**) Flat surface; (**b**) Ladder as an obstacle; (**c**) L-shaped path.

2.4. Software-Defined Radio Communication System

The communications system developed, presented in Figure 1, is composed of the following. First, there is a Raspberry Pi 3, which is configured as a wireless access point (WAP) in which the SDR is performed and the wireless network is used to measure the power level of the channels of the Wi-Fi network. Second, there is a router that provides an internet connection and sends the information generated from the robot to the cloud. This router is also connected to a computer in which the ANN controller is simulated and developed to send movements to the robot. Third, there is an ESP32 microcontroller that communicates bidirectionally with the Raspberry, transmitting the motion sequence to the robot and the angular velocity to the Raspberry, to be sent and stored in the cloud.

In the WAP configuration of the Raspberry, the name of the wireless network (SSID), the channel, and the level of security, among other settings, are edited. To provide internet access through the WAP, a bridge between the Raspberry's wireless interface and the ethernet network adapter is created. Hence, the traffic is redirected through the network cable that is connected to the router to access to the Internet.

The Raspberry Pi has limitations in the network interface, so a USB dongle is used to measure the power of the surrounding wireless networks. After measuring the power of the channels in the 2.4 GHz band, this information is sent to the Raspberry Pi to start the SDR.

The SDR system establishes the Wi-Fi transmission between the Raspberry and the ESP32, from the beginning, using the channel with the highest SNR. To achieve this, the powers or received signal strength indicators (RSSI) are captured from the channels of the access points found in the Raspberry environment, which are measured by the USB dongle. Then, the power per channel is averaged based on the RSSI measurements of the access points, as shown below:

$$\overline{P}_{channel} = \frac{\sum_{i=1}^{N} P_{channel}}{N} \tag{3}$$

where $\overline{P}_{channel}$ is the average power of the Wi-Fi channel in dBm, $P_{channel}$ is the channel power for a wireless access point in dBm and N is the number of wireless access points that are present in the same channel. The Gaussian white noise power is now calculated [31]:

$$P_{white\_noise} = 10 \log (kTB) \tag{4}$$

where k is the Boltzmann constant $1.3806852 \times 10^{-23}$ J/K; T is the ambient temperature in degrees Kelvin—in this case, it is 298.15 °K; and B is the bandwidth of each Wi-Fi channel in Hz (20 MHz). Therefore, P_{white_noise} is −131 dBm. Finally, the SNR of each channel can be determined as [32]:

$$\text{SNR} = \overline{P}_{channel} - P_{white\_noise} \quad (5)$$

Then, the channel with the highest SNR is chosen and set to the access point.

The communication between the Raspberry and the ESP32 is bidirectional. The Raspberry sends the sequence of movements to the ESP32 located in the modular robot. The ESP32 sends the robot's average angular velocity to the Raspberry. The user datagram protocol (UDP) is used in this task.

The routine program in the Raspberry Pi was developed in Python, which directs the packets of the robot's motion sequence to the IP address of the ESP32, enables the input buffer to receive packets from the ESP32, and executes a sub-process to connect to the *ThingSpeak* servers and thus send the robot's performance parameters to the cloud, which, in this case, are the average angular velocity of each movement.

The programming algorithm contained in the ESP32 was developed in the Arduino IDE. This contains the necessary instructions to interpret the commands sent from the Raspberry Pi to move the robot, while it also collects and sends the data obtained by the robot connecting to the Raspberry's WAP.

The connection to the *ThingSpeak* server is established through a script that is executed as a sub-process within the main UDP communication routine in the Raspberry, to store the data on the server. The identification and password provided by the platform are used to access the previously created channel. Subsequently, when the data transmission between the WAP and the ESP32 microcontroller is successful, the routine sends the performance parameter to the server to be visualized after a delay of around one minute.

3. Results and Discussion

The ANN controller simulation delivered results close to those obtained with the modular robot, with the robot moving through the proposed environments in virtual and real scenarios as shown in Figure 9. In each proposed environment, the modular robot with five modules traveled a distance of 1.8 m. In the ladder environment, the robot surpassed the obstacle. In the L-shaped path, the modular robot turned 45° to the right after advancing 1.05 m. The times and distances obtained in the simulator and the real modular robot are compared in Tables 2 and 3.

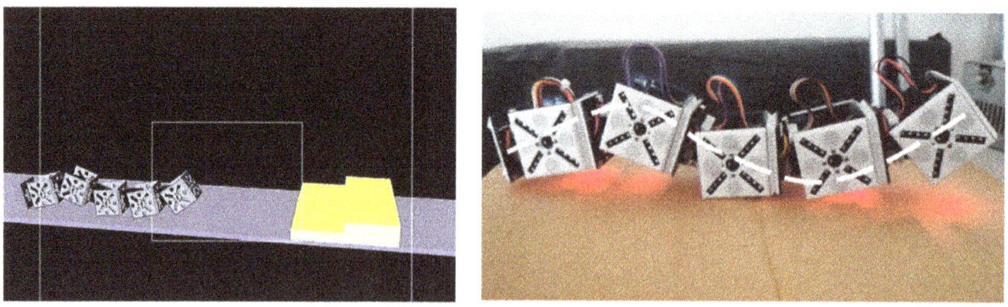

(a) (b)

Figure 9. Modular robot movement with five modules: (**a**) Virtual environment; (**b**) Real environment.

Table 2. Comparison of the travel times for each environment in the simulator and the real scenario.

Environment	Time Estimated by the Simulator	Time in Real Scenario	Error
Flat surface	11 min	11.6 min	5.45%
Ladder	13 min	13.75 min	5.76%
L-shaped	13 min	13.7 min	5.38%

Table 3. Comparison of the traveled distances for each environment in the simulator and the real scenario.

Environment	Distance Estimated by the Simulator	Distance in Real Scenario	Error
Flat surface	1.8 m	1.77 m	1.66%
Ladder	1.8 m	1.71 m	5%
L-shaped	1.8 m	1.73 m	3.88%

Figure 10 shows the margin of error between the training data and the real data during the ANN training, as well as the results of the movement of a module compared to the information stored in the database.

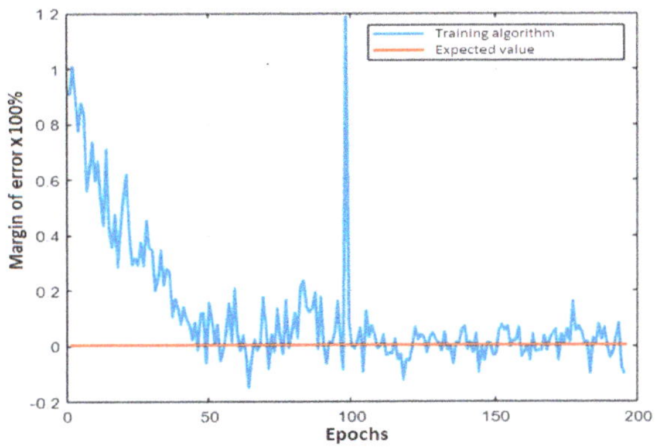

(**a**)

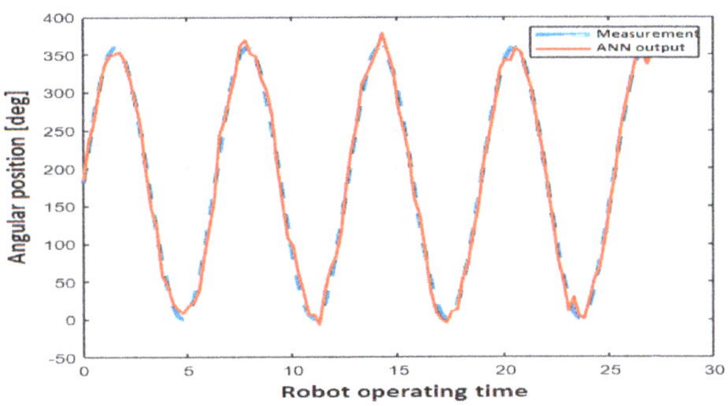

(**b**)

Figure 10. ANN training: (**a**) Margin of error; (**b**) Movement result vs. measured value, for a single module.

Initially, the most appropriate ANN configuration for robot control was established. Then, the same ANN was tested by changing the number of hidden layers. The results in Figure 11 show that the lowest error was obtained for 25 layers.

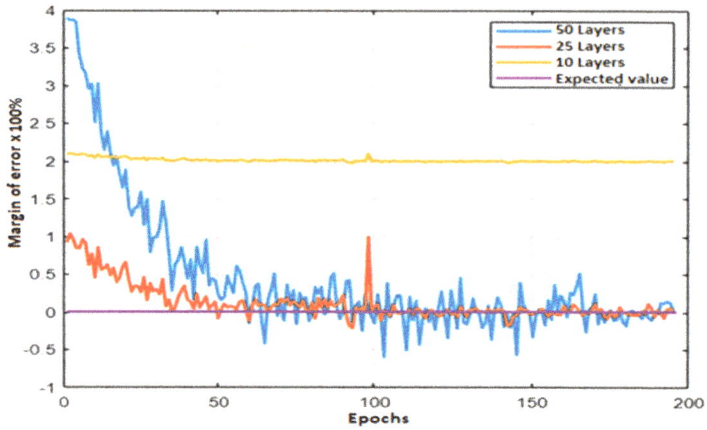

Figure 11. ANN margin of error for different numbers of hidden layers.

Finally, the communications network based on SDR was tested. For this, the SNR at different sites was obtained for the Wi-Fi channels connected to the Raspberry Pi, as seen in Table 4, and with a Wi-Fi sensitivity, in the best scenario, of −98 dBm [33]. An adequate SNR value must be above 40 dB, which occurs for most selected channels.

Table 4. Average signal-to-noise ratio (SNR) for selected Wi-Fi channels at different sites.

Place Number	Average SNR (dB)
1	69
2	46
3	66
4	36
5	58
6	49
7	59
8	53
9	46

The Wireshark software was used to find the lost packets and the latency between the Raspberry Pi and the ESP32 module located in the modular robot, for approximately one hour of communication tests. Out of 1647 transmitted and received packets, 0.162% were lost, and the average latency was 12.23 ms.

The average angular velocity information of the modular robot is stored in the cloud through a server hosted by ThingSpeak, as presented in Figure 12.

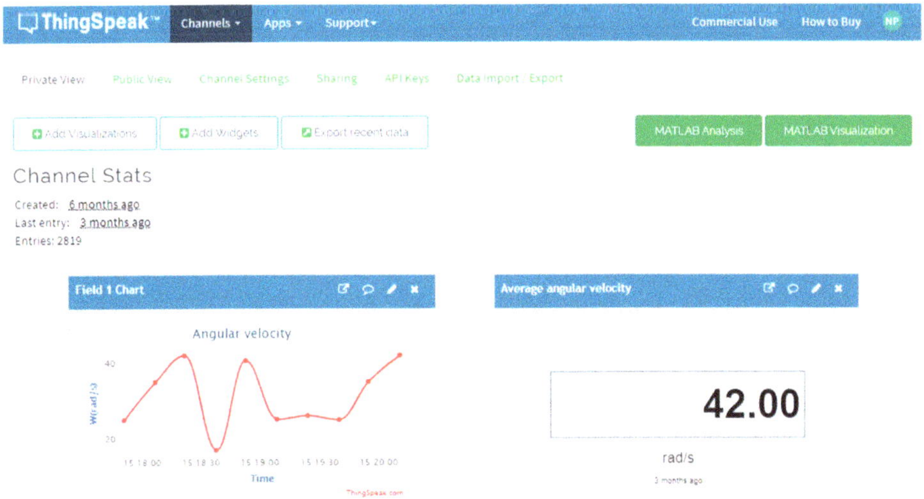

Figure 12. Average angular velocity of the modular robot stored in the cloud.

4. Conclusions

In this paper, an ANN controller for a modular robot that uses an SDR communication network was presented, where the Wi-Fi channel with the best SNR was selected, and then the information regarding the simulated movements and obtained by the controller was sent to the modular robot, as a contribution to the literature. The distance and time estimated by the simulator did not exceed an error of 6% when compared to those of the real robot, as evidenced in Tables 2 and 3.

The developed ANN controller has 25 layers, two inputs and one output. It predicted the movements of the robot with a training margin of error less than 5%, as seen in Figure 10. Furthermore, this type of strategy is adaptive, which means that a single ANN configuration was required for the robot to move around the environment. Another advantage of this control strategy is that the robot can go through the path even when a module fails, given that the parameters are sent from an external device, such as the Raspberry Pi.

The behavior of the ANN with different configurations of hidden layers showed an optimal operation region for generating the robot controller. This region was found between 20 and 30 hidden layers, since more than 50 layers or fewer than 10 layers caused the training algorithm to not converge satisfactorily. This is depicted in Figure 11. Selecting a number of hidden layers outside the optimal region implies that the controller cannot find an appropriate set of movements for the robot to use to move from one place to another.

The innovative SDR communications network developed transmitted the information corresponding to the robot movements from the simulator to the modular robot, using a WAP developed with the Raspberry Pi and the ESP32 microcontroller located in the robot. This reduced the controller disconnection, and the fault tolerance of the robot was increased. The Raspberry chose, from the establishment of communication, the Wi-Fi channel with the highest SNR, which caused little information loss and low transmission latency compared to in other channels with a lower SNR. Furthermore, the transmitted information was stored and displayed in the cloud, corresponding to the average angular velocity with which the robot moved.

Author Contributions: The modular robot and artificial neural network controller were made by H.A.H.; the software-defined radio system was implemented by L.F.P.; the simulator was designed by H.A.H. and executed by C.A.H.; and H.A.H., L.F.P., and C.A.H. performed the experiments, analyzed the results, drew conclusions, and reviewed and edited the paper. All authors have read and agreed to the published version of the manuscript.

Funding: This research was funded by Centro de Investigaciones y Desarrollo Científico (CIDC)—Universidad Distrital Francisco José de Caldas with the project code: 1-273-597-19.

Acknowledgments: We express our gratitude to CIDC—Universidad Distrital Francisco José de Caldas for the support. We also appreciate the recommendations of the reviewers.

Conflicts of Interest: The authors declare no conflict of interest.

References

1. Baca, J.; Ferre, M.; Campos, A.; Fernandez, J.; Aracil, R. On the Analysis of a Multi-task Modular Robot System for Field Robotics. In Proceedings of the 2010 IEEE Electronics, Robotics and Automotive Mechanics Conference, Morelos, Mexico, 28 September–1 October 2010; pp. 475–480.
2. Zhao, J.; Wei, Y.; Fan, J.; Shen, J.; Cai, H. New Type Reconfigurable Modular Robot Design and Intelligent Control Method Research. In Proceedings of the 6th World Congress on Intelligent Control and Automation, Dalian, China, 21–23 June 2006; pp. 8907–8911. [CrossRef]
3. Jingtao, L.; Tianmiao, W.; Yongling, H. The Modular Approach Based on Functional Components Division for Modular Reconfigurable Walking Robot. In Proceedings of the International Conference on Reconfigurable Mechanisms and Robots, London, UK, 22–24 June 2009; pp. 540–544.
4. Hayakawa, T.; Kamimura, T.; Kaji, S.; Matsuno, F. Autonomous Distributed System for Gait Generation for Single-Legged Modular Robots Connected in Various Configurations. *IEEE Trans. Robot.* **2020**, 1–20. [CrossRef]
5. Ye, C.; Chen, N.; Chen, L.; Jiang, C. A Variable-Scale Modular 3D Printing Robot of Building Interior Wall. In Proceedings of the 2018 IEEE International Conference on Mechatronics and Automation, Changchun, China, 5–8 August 2018; pp. 1818–1822. [CrossRef]
6. Giusti, A.; Althoff, M. On-the-Fly Control Design of Modular Robot Manipulators. *IEEE Trans. Control Syst. Technol.* **2017**, *26*, 1484–1491. [CrossRef]
7. Zhao, B.; Liu, D. Event-Triggered Decentralized Tracking Control of Modular Reconfigurable Robots through Adaptive Dynamic Programming. *IEEE Trans. Ind. Electron.* **2019**, *67*, 3054–3064. [CrossRef]
8. An, T.; Men, X.; Zhang, X.; Li, Y.; Dong, B. Adaptive Dynamic Programming-based Decentralized Sliding Mode Optimal Control for Modular and Reconfigurable Robots. In Proceedings of the 2019 IEEE Symposium Series on Computational Intelligence (SSCI), Xiamen, China, 6–9 December 2019; pp. 31–36.
9. Alattas, R. Hybrid evolutionary designer of modular robots. In Proceedings of the 2016 Annual Connecticut Conference on Industrial Electronics, Technology & Automation (CT-IETA), Bridgeport, CT, USA, 14–15 October 2016; pp. 1–4.
10. Karimoddini, A.; Karimadini, M.; Lin, H. Decentralized hybrid formation control of Unmanned Aerial Vehicles. In Proceedings of the 2014 American Control Conference, Portland, OR, USA, 4–6 June 2014; pp. 3887–3892.
11. Ahmad, S.; Aminnuddin, M.; Shukor, M.A.S.M. Modular hybrid control for double-link two-wheeled mobile robot. In Proceedings of the 2012 International Conference on Computer and Communication Engineering (ICCCE), Kuala Lumpur, Malaysia, 3–5 July 2012; pp. 807–813.
12. Vicmudo, M.P.; Dadios, E.P. Artificial neural network controller for maintaining underwater swarm robots' wireless connections. In Proceedings of the 2015 International Conference on Humanoid, Nanotechnology, Information Technology, Communication and Control, Environment and Management (HNICEM), Cebu City, Philippines, 9–12 December 2015; pp. 1–6.
13. Kern, J.; Jamett, M.; Urrea, C.; Torres, H. Development of a neural controller applied in a 5 DOF robot redundant. *IEEE Lat. Am. Trans.* **2014**, *12*, 98–106. [CrossRef]
14. Peng, G.; Chen, C.L.P.; He, W.; Yang, C. Neural-Learning-Based Force Sensorless Admittance Control for Robots with Input Deadzone. *IEEE Trans. Ind. Electron.* **2020**, 1. [CrossRef]
15. Wan, J.; Tang, S.; Shu, Z.; Li, D.; Wang, S.; Imran, M.; Vasilakos, A.V. Software-Defined Industrial Internet of Things in the Context of Industry 4.0. *IEEE Sens. J.* **2016**, *16*, 1. [CrossRef]
16. Ulversoy, T. Software Defined Radio: Challenges and Opportunities. *IEEE Commun. Surv. Tutor.* **2010**, *12*, 531–550. [CrossRef]

17. Muñoz, E.C.; Martínez, L.F.P.; Hernandez, C. Rényi Entropy-Based Spectrum Sensing in Mobile Cognitive Radio Networks Using Software Defined Radio. *Entropy* **2020**, *22*, 626. [CrossRef]
18. Li, X.-Q.; Ding, X.; Zhang, Y.; Sun, Z.-P.; Zhao, H.-W. IoT Family Robot Based on Raspberry Pi. In Proceedings of the 2016 International Conference on Information System and Artificial Intelligence (ISAI), Hong Kong, China, 24–26 June 2016; pp. 622–625.
19. Guleci, M.; Orhun, M. Android based WI-FI controlled robot using Raspberry Pi. In Proceedings of the 2017 International Conference on Computer Science and Engineering (UBMK), Antalya, Turkey, 5–8 October 2017; pp. 978–982.
20. Cabrera, M.; Trifonov, R.S.; Castells, G.A.; Stoy, K. Wireless communication and power transfer in modular robots. In Proceedings of the IEEE/RSJ IROS: Workshop on Reconfigurable Modular Robotics: Challenges of Mechatronic and Bio-Chemo-Hybrid Systems, San Francisco, CA, USA, 21 September 2011.
21. Haxhibeqiri, J.; Jarchlo, E.A.; Moerman, I.; Hoebeke, J. Flexible Wi-Fi Communication among Mobile Robots in Indoor Industrial Environments. *Mob. Inf. Syst.* **2018**, *2018*, 1–19. [CrossRef]
22. Easy Modular Embodied Robot Generator. Available online: https://sites.google.com/view/emergemodular/home?authuser=0 (accessed on 20 June 2020).
23. Hernández, H.; Moreno, R.; Faina, A.; Gomez, J. Design of a Bio-Inspired Controller to Operate a Modular Robot Autonomously. In *Lecture Notes in Computer Science;* Springer Science and Business Media LLC: Berlin, Germany, 2018; pp. 314–325.
24. Liu, C.; Liu, J.; Moreno, R.; Veenstra, F.; Faíña, A. The impact of module morphologies on modular robots. In Proceedings of the 2017 18th International Conference on Advanced Robotics (ICAR), Hong Kong, China, 10–12 July 2017; pp. 237–243.
25. Moreno, R.; Liu, C.; Faina, A.; Hernandez, H.; Gomez, J. The EMeRGE modular robot, an open platform for quick testing of evolved robot morphologies. In Proceedings of the Genetic and Evolutionary Computation Conference, Berlin, Germany, 15–19 July 2017; pp. 71–72. [CrossRef]
26. 3D World Editor. Available online: https://la.mathworks.com/help/sl3d/the-3d-world-editor.html (accessed on 5 May 2020).
27. Hellebrekers, T.; Chang, N.; Chin, K.; Ford, M.J.; Kroemer, O.; Majidi, C. Soft Magnetic Tactile Skin for Continuous Force and Location Estimation Using Neural Networks. *IEEE Robot. Autom. Lett.* **2020**, *5*, 3892–3898. [CrossRef]
28. Li, C.; Fahmy, A.; Sienz, J. Development of a Neural Network-Based Control System for the DLR-HIT II Robot Hand Using Leap Motion. *IEEE Access* **2019**, *7*, 136914–136923. [CrossRef]
29. Mano, M.; Capi, G.; Tanaka, N.; Kawahara, S. An Artificial Neural Network Based Robot Controller that Uses Rat's Brain Signals. *Robotics* **2013**, *2*, 54–65. [CrossRef]
30. Korovesis, N.; Kandris, D.; Koulouras, G.; Alexandridis, A. Robot Motion Control via an EEG-Based Brain-Computer Interface by Using Neural Networks and Alpha Brainwaves. *Electronics* **2019**, *8*, 1387. [CrossRef]
31. Penttinen, J.T.J. *The Telecommunications Handbook: Engineering Guidelines for Fixed, Mobile and Satellite Systems*, 1st ed.; Wiley: Chichester, UK, 2015; p. 785.
32. Dolińska, I.; Masiukiewicz, A.; Rządkowski, G. The mathematical model for interference simulation and optimization in 802.11n networks. In Proceedings of the International Workshop CS&P' 2013, Warsaw, Poland, 25–27 September 2013; pp. 99–110.
33. Behzad, A. *Wireless LAN Radios: SYSTEM Definition to Transistor Design*, 1st ed.; Wiley: Hoboken, NJ, USA, 2007; pp. 73–75.

electronics

MDPI

Article

Prediction of Critical Flashover Voltage of High Voltage Insulators Leveraging Bootstrap Neural Network

M. Tahir Khan Niazi [1], Arshad [2,*], Jawad Ahmad [3], Fehaid Alqahtani [4], Fatmah AB Baotham [5] and Fadi Abu-Amara [6]

1 Department of Electrical Engineering, HITEC University Taxila, Punjab 47080, Pakistan; tahirniazai@yahoo.com
2 Institute for Energy and Environment, University of Strathclyde, Glasgow G1 1XQ, UK
3 School of Computing, Edinburgh Napier University, Edinburgh EH10 5DT, UK; Jawadkhattak@ieee.org
4 Department of Computer Science, King Fahad Naval Academy, Al Jubail 35512, Saudi Arabia; fehaidb00282066@gmail.com
5 Faculty of Computing and Information Technology, King Abdul Aziz University, Jeddah 21431, Saudi Arabia; fbaothman@kau.edu.sa
6 Computer & Information Science Department, Higher Colleges of Technology, Abu Dhabi 25026, UAE; fabuamara@hct.ac.ae
* Correspondence: arshadali.giki@gmail.com

Received: 19 August 2020; Accepted: 24 September 2020; Published: 2 October 2020

Abstract: Understanding the flashover performance of the outdoor high voltage insulator has been in the interest of many researchers recently. Various studies have been performed to investigate the critical flashover voltage of outdoor high voltage insulators analytically and in the laboratory. However, laboratory experiments are expensive and time-consuming. On the other hand, mathematical models are based on certain assumptions which compromise on the accuracy of results. This paper presents an intelligent system based on Artificial Neural Networks (ANN) to predict the critical flashover voltage of High-Temperature Vulcanized (HTV) silicone rubber in polluted and humid conditions. Various types of learning algorithms are used, such as Gradient Descent (GD), Levenberg-Marquardt (LM), Conjugate Gradient (CG), Quasi-Newton (QN), Resilient Backpropagation (RBP), and Bayesian Regularization Backpropagation (BRBP) to train the ANN. The number of neurons in the hidden layers along with the learning rate was varied to understand the effect of these parameters on the performance of ANN. The proposed ANN was trained using experimental data obtained from extensive experimentation in the laboratory under controlled environmental conditions. The proposed model demonstrates promising results and can be used to monitor outdoor high voltage insulators. It was observed from obtained results that changing of the number of neurons, learning rates, and learning algorithms of ANN significantly change the performance of the proposed algorithm.

Keywords: critical flashover voltage; Artificial Neural Networks (ANN); Gradient Descent (GD); Levenberg-Marquardt (LM); Conjugate Gradient (CG); Quasi-Newton (QN); Resilient Backpropagation (RBP); Bayesian Regularization Backpropagation (BRBP)

1. Introduction

Outdoor high voltage insulators are exposed to various types of stresses. Stresses include mechanical, electrical, thermal, and environmental stresses. To simulate the effect of these stresses in the laboratory, different types of techniques are used. High-voltage stresses and artificial rain and fog are a few examples. The critical flashover voltage of insulators depends on the insulator design, surface roughness, orientation, rain, humidity, temperature, fogs, Ultraviolet (UV) radiations, wind speed, direction, and distance from the pollution source [1,2]. Although the performance of outdoor insulators is affected by many parameters, pollution deposition on the insulator surface is considered a major factor in the deteriorating performance of insulators. Pollution deposition on outdoor insulators surface may be due to industrial emissions, salt spray from the sea, and chemicals' emissions from vehicles and or agriculture. The change in the performance of outdoor insulators due to pollution deposition depends on the type of pollution constituents. Generally, pollution deposited on the insulator surface is classified into two major types: inert pollution and active pollution. The effect of active and inert pollution on the insulator performance is different resulting in errors of flashover voltage calculations [3].

Intelligent techniques such as fuzzy logic [4], Support Vector Machine (SVM) [5], Artificial Neural Networks (ANN) [6–8], Hidden Markov Model (HMM) [9], K-means clustering [10], Discrete Wavelet Transform (DWT) [11], S-Transform [12], have been extensively used in electrical power system and high voltage engineering problems. These intelligent systems can be successfully utilized for the condition monitoring of high-voltage outdoor insulators to increase the reliability of power system transmission and distribution as well as minimize human efforts and cost [13].

With the increase in transmission line voltages and increased distance of renewable power sources from the loads, the importance of research on the pollution performance of insulators has significantly increased. The mechanism of flashover in high voltage porcelain, glass, and ceramic insulators under contamination has been studied extensively in the past [14–16]. Many researchers have proposed mathematical models to predict the critical flashover voltage under uniform and non-uniform pollution [17,18]. An improved mathematical model has been proposed in Reference [19] to estimate pollution flashover voltage of ceramic insulators based on dimensional analysis of the flashover influencing parameters. Shahabi et al. [20] studied the flashover process of outdoor insulators by adding a random value to the discharge length to account for wind speed, direction, and thermal convection on the discharge. Palangar et al. [21] proposed an improved dynamic model for predicting the critical flashover parameters of ceramic insulators by incorporating capacitance in the equivalent circuit of the dry band.

Apart from mathematical and numerical modeling, many researchers have proposed intelligent systems such as ANN for flashover voltage prediction [6,8,22]. Salem et al. [22] combined Adaptive Neuro Fuzzy Inference System (ANFIS) with ANN and used insulator height, diameter, form factor, creepage distance along with Equivalent Salt Deposit Density (ESDD) as input parameters to train the model. In Reference [23], the authors applied dimensional analysis to the proposed ANFIS-based ANN network by establishing a relationship between critical flashover voltage and leakage current. The arc constant of the mathematical model for obtaining the test data was optimized using a Genetic Algorithm (GA) for improved results.

Another important intelligent technique used for flashover prediction is SVM, which offers the advantage of global optimality. Least Square SVM (LS-SVM) was proposed in Reference [24] for prediction of pollution severity and critical flashover voltage based on insulator diameter, height, ESDD, and form factor. Ming-Yuan et al. [25] estimated insulator leakage current using SVM by finding correlation between weather conditions and leakage current. Different meteorological parameters were combined with leakage current parameters generated from different types of insulators. Gencoglu et al. [26] proposed LS-SVM for prediction of flashover voltage by generating the training data set from numerical models based on Finite Element Method (FEM). The LS-SVM parameters were tuned using a grid search algorithm for improved accuracy.

Saranya et al. [27,28] proposed a new method for condition monitoring of outdoor insulators by identifying insulator arc faults using phasor angle measurements. The insulator arcs have been classified using SVM to support the design of improved protection schemes for smart grids. A modified LS-SVM scheme has been proposed by applying a fixed set of support vectors to predict the critical flashover voltage under polluted conditions [5]. The Quadratic Renyi Criterion (QRC) is used to select support vectors from the training data set.

The existing literature demonstrates considerable work on the application of intelligent systems in predicting the flashover voltage of outdoor high voltage insulators. However, there are specific gaps in the current knowledge which need to be further investigated. The existing ANN algorithms used the Gradient Descent (GD) algorithm due to its faster convergence and lower computation time by compromising the prediction accuracy. The current literature also considered insulator height, diameter, form factor, and ESDD as input parameters for flashover prediction, while the flashover voltage also depends on environmental conditions such as temperature, humidity, and non-soluble pollution. Apart from that, fixing the number of neurons, learning rates, and the number of hidden layers significantly changes the prediction accuracy of ANN, which needs to be investigated. One of the major limitations of existing ANN-based prediction models is that most of them rely on data from mathematical models which are based on a particular assumption. Additionally, current mathematical models are applicable to porcelain and glass insulators and cannot be applied to polymeric insulators without modification due to the different flashover mechanism of polymeric insulators as compared to porcelain and glass insulators.

2. Materials and Methods

ANN and other machine learning algorithms have been used to predict critical flashover voltage, leakage current, and ESDD. However, there are some limitations of the existing literature such as; (1) use of insulator dimensions and pollution severity as input parameters for learning and ignoring the environmental conditions (humidity and temperature); (2) using a single learning algorithm for training, for example, GD in most cases; (3) the training data set is either small or generated from mathematical models. This paper presents an intelligent system for flashover voltage prediction of polymeric insulators using experimental results as a training data set for training the ANN. The experimental results of critical flashover voltage are obtained under controlled environmental conditions. To increase the sample space and accuracy of the proposed model, bootstrapping is applied to the actual data set. The proposed NN model is tested for different learning algorithms such as GD, Levenberg-Marquardt (LM), Conjugate Gradient (CG), Quasi-Newton (QN), Resilient Backpropagation (RBP) and Bayesian Regularization Backpropagation (BRBP). The number of neurons in the hidden layer, the number of hidden layers, as well as learning rate, are varied to obtain the optimum parameters. The prediction accuracy of each model is tested using Root Mean Square Error (RMSE), Mean Absolute Percentage Error (MAPE), Regression Value (R) and Normalized Mean Square Error (NRMSE).

2.1. Experimental Setup and Test Methods

High voltage tests were performed on rectangular samples of HTV silicone rubber under controlled environmental conditions. The clean fog method (solid layer) based on modified IEC 60507 was used to apply soluble and non-soluble pollution on the insulator samples. The test setup and sample configuration are shown in Figures 1 and 2, respectively. The insulator samples were energised using a power frequency 0–100 kV test transformer. Before energising, samples were placed in the climate chamber for a considerable amount of time to make sure no dry bands were present, and the samples were properly wetted. Initial tests were performed on a uniformly polluted sample to determine the probable flashover voltage. Once the probable flashover voltage was determined, the remaining tests were performed by applying voltage in steps of 5% of the probable flashover voltage. Each step was maintained for 2 min, and if no partial arcs appeared, the voltage was increased further. In the case of appearance of a partial arc, the voltage was kept constant at that step until the partial arc vanished or lead to flashover. This process was repeated for each sample. As silicone rubber loses its hydrophobicity under energization, the sample was replaced after every two tests. This helped in maintaining the uniform pollution layer and the hydrophobic nature of silicone rubber.

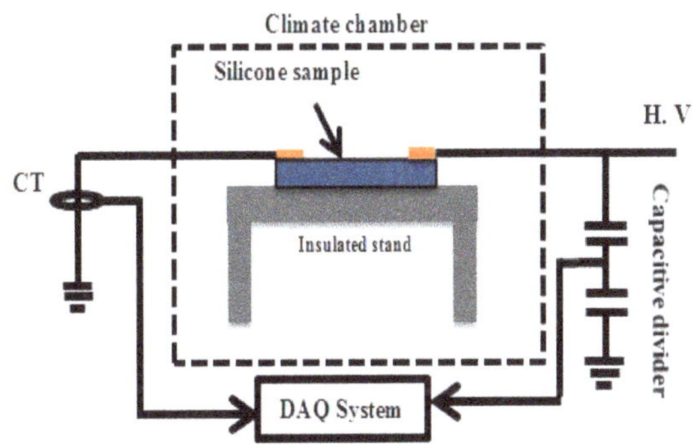

Figure 1. The high-voltage test setup.

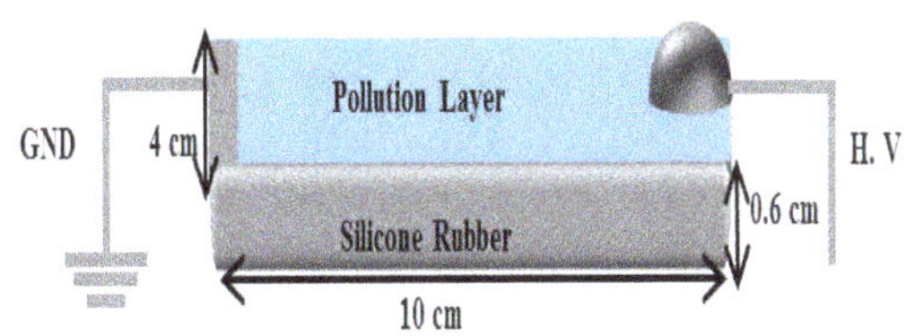

Figure 2. The electrode setup and sample configuration.

Experimental Results

Air pollution deposited on the insulator surfaces can be broadly classified into two major types: active and inert. Active pollution is represented with ESDD, while inert pollution is represented with NSDD. NSDD is the non-soluble part of pollution such as dust, cement, or sand, which does not dissolve in water but forms a thick layer on the surface of the insulator, which may affect the flashover behavior. The effect of ESDD and NSDD is different on flashover voltage of polymeric insulators as presented in Reference [1]. Figure 3 shows the relationship between critical flashover voltage and ESDD at different values of NSDD. A total of 16 tests were performed at different combinations of ESDD and NSDD. The results show that as the value of ESDD and NSDD increases, the critical flashover voltage decreases. This is mainly due to the increase in leakage current due to the increased conductivity of the pollution layer, as well as the increased thickness of the pollution layer when NSDD is increased. The increase in the thickness of the pollution layer resists the recovery of hydrophobicity and facilitates uniform wetting of the pollution layer, resulting in increased leakage current. The temperature and humidity were kept constant during these tests to minimize the effect of environmental conditions.

The effect of relative humidity on critical flashover voltage is shown in Figure 4. The relative humidity was varied within the climate chamber, while temperature and NSDD were kept constant. Samples with different ESDD values were tested. The critical flashover voltage decreased as humidity and ESDD increased. This may be due to the increase in pollution constituent dissolving in the humid air surrounding the insulator.

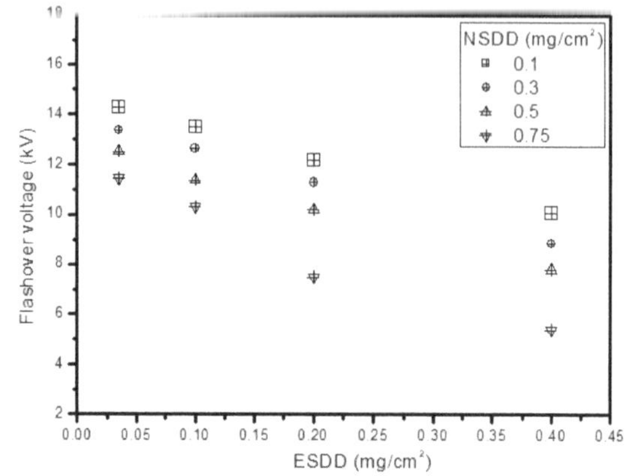

Figure 3. The relationship between NSDD and critical flashover voltage at moderate humidity and 10 °C temperature.

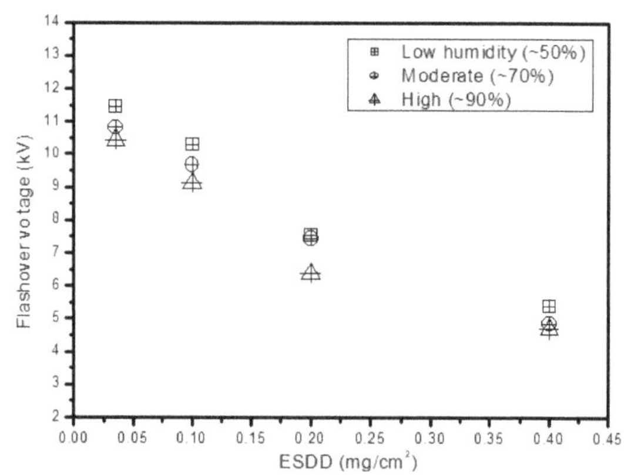

Figure 4. The relationship between relative humidity and critical flashover voltage at 10 °C temperature and NSDD of 0.75 mg/cm^2.

Apart from humidity, inert, and active pollution, ambient temperature also affects the flashover process. The influence of high temperature on insulator performance in desert conditions has been investigated in the literature. However, here, the focus is on the effect of temperature under polluted and humid conditions, which influence the hydrophobicity loss and recovery process of polymeric insulators. The results of the critical flashover voltage at four different temperature values are shown in Figure 5. It can be observed that critical flashover voltage decreases with an increase in temperature and ESDD. There can be multiple explanations, such as a change in the hydrophobicity recovery process and conductivity of the pollution layer. However, the obtained results show that as the temperature increases, the conductivity of the pollution layer increases, which leads to an increase in leakage current, decrease in surface resistance, and critical flashover voltage.

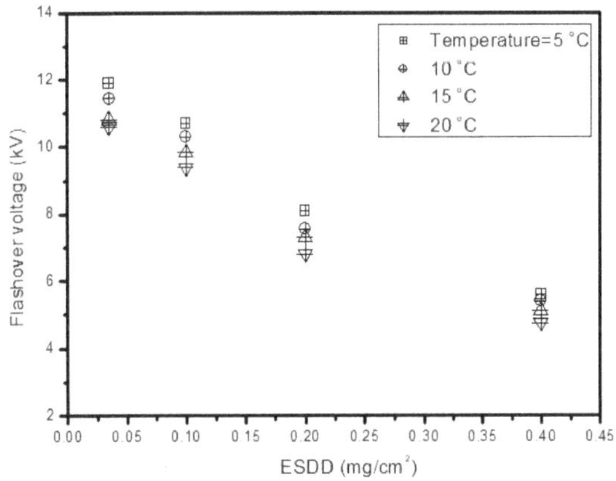

Figure 5. The relationship between ambient temperature and critical flashover voltage at moderate humidity and NSDD of 0.75 mg/cm^2.

2.2. Proposed Artificial Neural Network Algorithm

Machine learning algorithms such as ANN can be effectively used in high voltage engineering to minimize cost and time of experimentation. In this work, we proposed a machine learning algorithm based on NN to predict the critical flashover voltage of outdoor high voltage insulators. Details about the proposed machine learning algorithm are given in the following section.

2.2.1. Bootstrapping Method

Bootstrapping, or sometimes called bagging, is a statistical technique to increase the sample space when a limited number of data samples are available for training machine learning algorithms. Apart from increasing the number of observations, bootstrapping also offers the advantage of improved accuracy as well as increased effectiveness of percentage estimation. A bootstrap sample is a random sample conducted with replacement; it means the number of times a random observation is selected from the real data. Rather than relying on the theory, which gives the sets of all possible estimates, the bootstrap generates estimates through re-sampling distribution named bootstrap distribution, and the standard deviation of all estimates is called the bootstrap standard error. There are two main reasons to use the bootstrap approach instead of large sample theory approach: one is the lack of large sample data, and the other is to workout with the standard error of the estimates.

In this technique, sampling is performed by extracting only one sample at a time from a given data, and the selected sample is returned to the data set. In this way, the sample appears more than once in the given test data in the next iteration. This method of sampling is known as sampling with replacement. The bootstrap method can be summarized as [29]:

- Select the number of samples which need to be extracted from given data
- Select the appropriate size of selected samples
- For each selected sample, perform sampling with replacement
- Compute the various statistical parameters of the given data
- Lastly, compute the mean of all statistical parameters.

In this paper, a two-dimensional chaos map known as Tangent Delay Ellipse Reflecting Cavity Map System (TD-ERCS) was applied for the random selection of samples. This technique is used widely for the generation of random numbers and permutations. This type of chaos system is preferred for the bootstrapping method because of its equiprobability and nonlinear nature [30]. TD-ERCS can be generalized as:

$$x_n = -\frac{2k_{n-1}y_{n-1} + x_{n-1}\left(\mu^2 - k_{n-1}^2\right)}{\mu^2 + k_{n-1}^2} \quad (1)$$

$$y_n = k_{n-1}(x_n - x_{n-1}) + y_{n-1} \quad (2)$$

where $n = 1, 2, 3, \ldots$

$$k_n = \frac{2k'_{n-m} - k_{n-1} + k_{n-1}(k'_{n-m})^2}{1 + 2k_{n-1}k'_{n-m} - k(k'_{n-m})^2} \quad (3)$$

$$k'_{n-m} = \begin{cases} -\frac{x_{n-1}}{y_{n-1}}\mu^2 & n < m \\ -\frac{x_{n-m}}{y_{n-m}}\mu^2 & n \geq m \end{cases} \quad (4)$$

$$y_0 = \mu\sqrt{1 - x_0^2} \quad (5)$$

$$k'_0 = -\frac{x_0}{y_0}\mu^2 \quad (6)$$

$$k_0 = -\frac{tan\alpha + k'_0}{1 - k'_0 tan\alpha} \quad (7)$$

$$\begin{cases} \mu \in (0,1) \\ x_0 \in [-1,1] \\ \alpha \in (0,\pi) \\ m = 2,\ 3,\ 4,\ 5,\ldots \end{cases} \quad (8)$$

Here μ, x_o, α and m are the seed parameters. These seed parameters are used as the key in random number generation from the TD-ERCS map. Random sequences are denoted by x_n and y_n in Equations (1) and (2). Machine learning algorithms were trained by taking 100 bootstrap samples, and 44 observations were made for each bootstrap sample. Given data was tested by using unselected observations. For each chosen sample, performance matrices as well as average value ($\overline{y}$) were computed. Moreover, the deviation of each value from the average value was described in terms of standard deviation (STD). A schematic diagram of the bootstrapping method is shown in Figure 6.

$$\overline{y} = \frac{1}{B}\sum_{b=1}^{B} y \quad (9)$$

$$\text{STD} = \sqrt{\frac{\sum_{b=1}^{B}(y - \overline{y})^2}{B - 1}} \quad (10)$$

2.2.2. Artificial Neural Network

ANN is a specialized computer program that is trained through various learning algorithms for the identification of any linear or non-linear relationship between variables of interest in any raw data set. ANN is gaining importance in almost every field of life, ranging from business, social sciences, to engineering and sciences, mainly because of its exceptional large data handling and analyzing capability. A significant amount of research work has already been conducted, both for offline and online state monitoring, in power engineering through ANN [31,32]. In the implementation of ANN analysis, it is very crucial to devise a suitable ANN model with valid input and output variables. Proper scrutiny of data is very important as it ensures the preciseness of acquired results. Once the ANN model is developed, it can then be utilized for accurate estimation of an output variable by using a given set of input values.

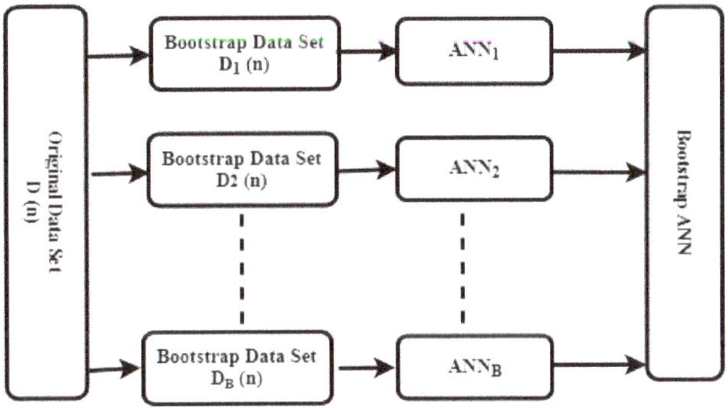

Figure 6. Bootstrap ANN architecture.

The main processing entity in the ANN model is the neuron. ANN contains many neurons which are linked to each other through specialized information-carrying pathways known as interconnections. There can be multiple inputs to a single neuron, and it can have one or more outputs. Generally, external stimuli or outputs of any other neuron act as the input to the given neuron. One possibility is that output of a neuron is fed back as the input to the same neuron. Each interconnection of neurons is associated with a weight. The output is produced only if the weighted sum of all neurons acting as input to a certain neuron crosses a predefined weighted sum limit. The ANN model contains three basic layers: the input layer, output layer, and one or more hidden layers. The number of neurons in each layer should be decided while implementing the ANN [33]. A schematic diagram of a typical ANN network is shown in Figure 7.

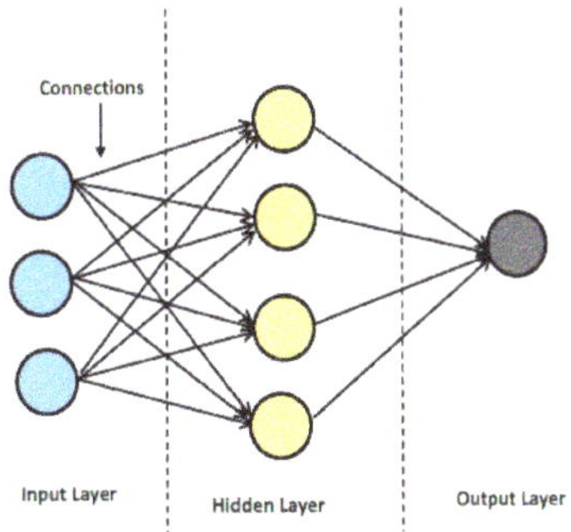

Figure 7. Generic diagram of an ANN network.

The ANN model used in this work has four inputs (ESDD, NSDD, humidity, temperature) and one output (Flashover voltage), as shown in Figure 8. The number of neurons in the hidden layer and the number of hidden layers were varied to study the effect of varying the number of neurons and hidden layers on the performance of each algorithm. Apart from that, six different types of training algorithms were used.

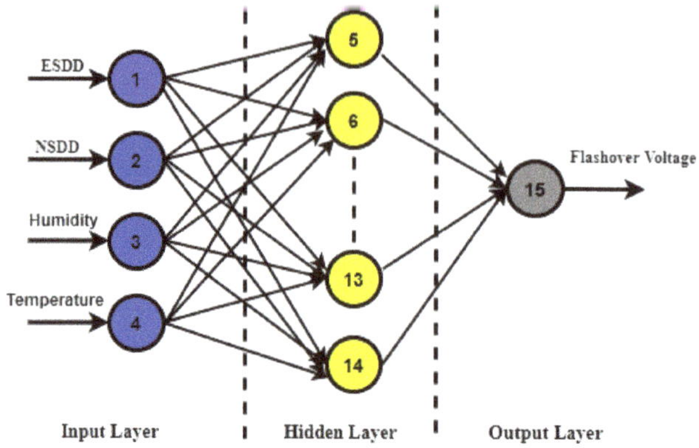

Figure 8. Schematic diagram of the proposed ANN network.

To avoid saturation while training the ANN model, it is important to perform normalization of the given data set. There are two different ways in which normalization can be performed. In the first method, normalization is achieved by considering only maximum values of input and output variables, while in the second method, both maximum and minimum values are considered. In this case, we used the first method of normalization as described below. If there are $p = 1, 2, 3 \ldots, n_p$ number of patterns, $i = 1, 2, 3, \ldots, n_i$ number of input values, and $k = 1, 2, 3, \ldots, n_k$ the number of output values. Then,

$$n_{i,max} = \max(n_i(p)) \tag{11}$$

$$O_{k,max} = \max(O_k(p)) \tag{12}$$

Therefore, normalized values are

$$n_{i,nor(p)} = \frac{n_i(p)}{n_{i,max}} \tag{13}$$

$$O_{k,nor(p)} = \frac{O_k(p)}{O_{k,max}} \tag{14}$$

After normalization, the input and output values will be between 0 and 1. The different types of learning algorithms used in this study such as GD, LM, CG, QN, RBP and BRBP are given in Appendix A.

3. Results

In this paper, various machine learning tools were applied to predict the critical flashover voltage of HTV silicone rubber outdoor insulators. A comparison between the predicted and actual value of flashover voltage obtained through the LM algorithm is shown in Figure 9. It can be observed from Figure 9 that forecasted values for flashover voltage are closer to the actual values. A similar comparison for the prediction of critical flashover voltages using machine learning techniques was done in Reference [34], which validates the results presented in Figure 9. For better visualization and comparison of these machine learning algorithms, it would be more appropriate to use some matrices for describing the accuracy and validity. In this paper, the accuracy and preciseness of the implemented algorithms were described in four matrices. These are Root Mean Square Error (RMSE), Normalized RMSE (N-RMSE), Mean Absolute Percentage Error (MAPE) and R value. RMSE is the square root of the average of squared errors, while NRMSE is the normalized value of RMSE. In MAPE, the percentage of the average of the error value is calculated. Mathematically, these matrices can be described as:

$$\text{RMSE} = \sqrt{\frac{1}{n}\sum_{i=1}^{n}(FV_{Ai} - FV_{Pi})^2} \tag{15}$$

$$\text{NRMSE} = \sqrt{\frac{1}{n}\sum_{i=1}^{n}(\frac{FV_{Ai} - FV_{Pi}}{FV_{Ai}})^2} \tag{16}$$

$$\text{MAPE} = \frac{1}{n}\sum_{i=1}^{n}\left|\frac{FV_{Ai} - FV_{Pi}}{FV_{Ai}}\right| \times 100\% \tag{17}$$

$$\text{R} = 1 - (\frac{\sum_{i=1}^{n}(FV_{Ai} - FV_{Pi})}{\sum_{i=1}^{n}FV_{Ai}})^2 \tag{18}$$

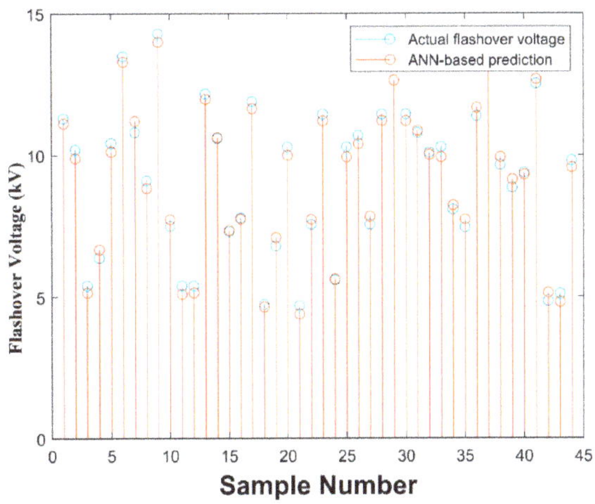

Figure 9. Comparison of the predicted and actual flashover voltage using the LM learning algorithm and 10 neurons in the hidden layer.

Here, 'n' is the number of samples, 'FV_{Ai}' and 'FV_{Pi}' are actual and forecasted critical flashover voltage values. The values of these performance metrics must be close to some definite value. Usually, values of RMSE, NRMSE, and MAPE, which are approaching zero imply the efficient operation of a machine learning algorithm. In other words, the machine learning algorithm will be considered reliable only if its error values obtained through RMSE, NRMSE, and MAPE are approaching zero, while in terms of the R parameter, the machine learning would be rated as good enough if its error value in terms of R is closer to 1.

A performance comparison, based on variation in the number of neurons in the hidden layers of different machine learning algorithms, is depicted in Figure 10. For the GD algorithm, the error value for RMS, NRMSE, and MAPE decreases with the increasing number of neurons from 5 to 15. However, a further increase in the number of neurons to 20 results in an increase of error values. The R-value for GD first increases from 5 to 15 neurons, and further increment to 20 neurons results in a decrement of the R value. Thus, increasing the number of neurons from 15 to 20 adversely affects the performance of GD. In the case of the RP algorithm, error values for RMS, NRMSE, and MAPE first decrease on increasing neurons from 5 to10. Further increase in the number of neurons leads to an increase of error values (RMS, NRMSE and MAPE). A similar trend is followed by the R-value where the increase of the number of neurons beyond 10 decreases the R value.

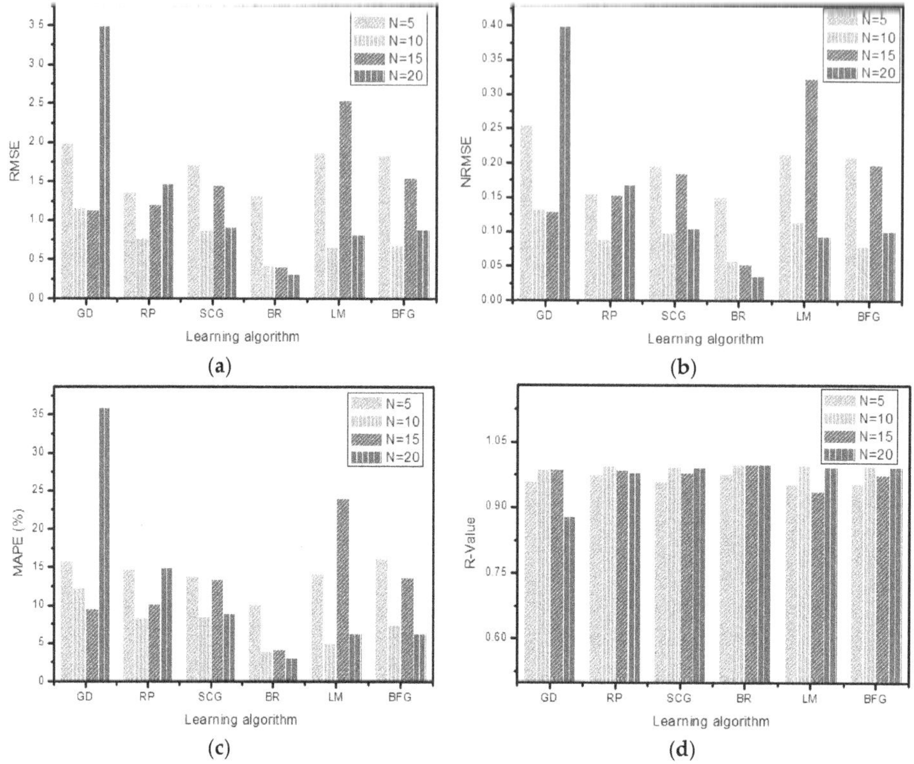

Figure 10. Performance parameters comparison of the different learning algorithms on the basis of changes in the number of neurons in the hidden layer. (**a**) RMSE; (**b**) NRMSE; (**c**) MAPE (%); (**d**) R value.

Thus, increasing the number of neurons from 10 to 20 adversely affects the performance of RP. The SCG, LM and BFG Quasi newton algorithms exhibit rather random behavior. In these algorithms, an increase in the number of neurons from 5 to 10 strengthens the efficiency of the given machine learning algorithm. A further increase in neurons from 10 to 15 overshoots the error values for RMSE, NRMSE, and MAPE and decreases the regression value, R. The behavior of the BR backpropagation algorithm is quite distinct from the above-stated algorithms where an increase in the number of neurons boosts the performance of ANN. Overall, it can be concluded that increasing the number of neurons to a certain limit has a healing effect on the GD algorithm and BR backpropagation algorithm. For the rest of the algorithms, the number of neurons must be chosen as the optimum, and a general trend should not be followed.

The above-mentioned results are based on a single hidden layer, and only the number of neurons in the hidden layer was varied. Increasing the number of hidden layers also effects the performance of the neural network. In this paper, three hidden layers with different numbers of neurons were considered. The results obtained are shown in Figure 11, where [x, y, z] in the legend represents the number of neurons in each hidden layer. It was noted that by increasing the number of hidden layers, the computational complexity of the proposed neural network increased; however, the computational performance of proposed algorithms was not tested in this work. Comparing the results shown in Figure 11 to that of Figure 10, it can be noted that the performance of some algorithms improved with the increased number of hidden layers, while others deteriorated at the same time. The BR backpropagation algorithm which performed better for a single hidden layer worsened when increasing the number of hidden layers and neurons. In other words, increasing the number of hidden layers caused overfitting of the given data. Similarly, the performance of the RP algorithm is also adversely affected. On the other hand, the performance of the remaining algorithms has improved as indicated by their error values. It is very important to note here that the performance of any algorithm is also dependent on the number of neurons in that layer. All these algorithms exhibit random behavior. For example, in the case of the SCG algorithm, increasing the number of neurons in the hidden layer from [20, 10, 5] to [30, 20, 10] reduces the RMSE from 1.22 to 0.59, NRMSE from 0.19 to 0.069, and MAPE from 10.93 to 5.09%.

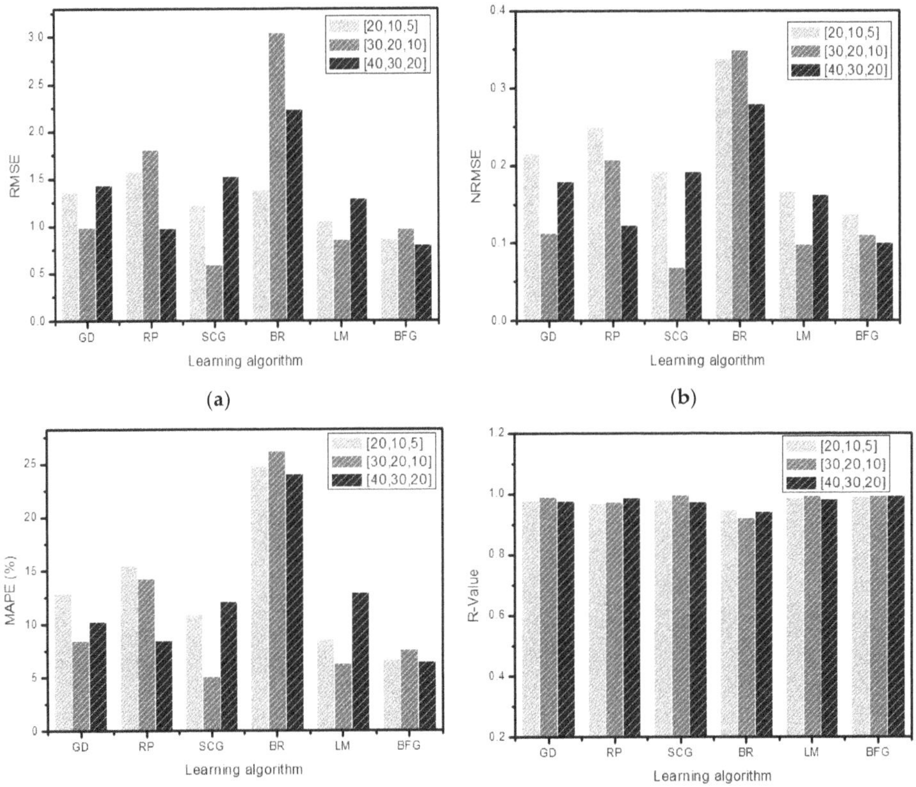

Figure 11. Performance parameters comparison of the different learning algorithms based on changes in the number of neurons and using three hidden layers. (**a**) RMSE; (**b**) NRMSE; (**c**) MAPE (%); (**d**) R value.

Choosing a certain learning rate for a neural network algorithm is also very important for improved performance. The learning rate is considered a hyperparameter in neural networks, and it accounts for alterations that should be made in the current model in response to calculated errors. A small value of the learning rate requires a large number of training epochs, whereas a large learning rate value may cause convergence of the algorithm rapidly to the local minima or maxima. Figure 12 shows the performance comparison of the GD algorithm for different learning rates. It can be observed from these plots that increasing the learning rate from 0.0025 to 0.0075 apparently does not have any significant effect on error values obtained through RMS, N-RMS, and MAPE. However, a further increase in the learning rate value depicts the dominant increment in the value of these matrices, therefore indicating a drastic deterioration of the GD algorithm. On the other hand, the R-value did not account for any variation in the learning rate value, and it remains constant.

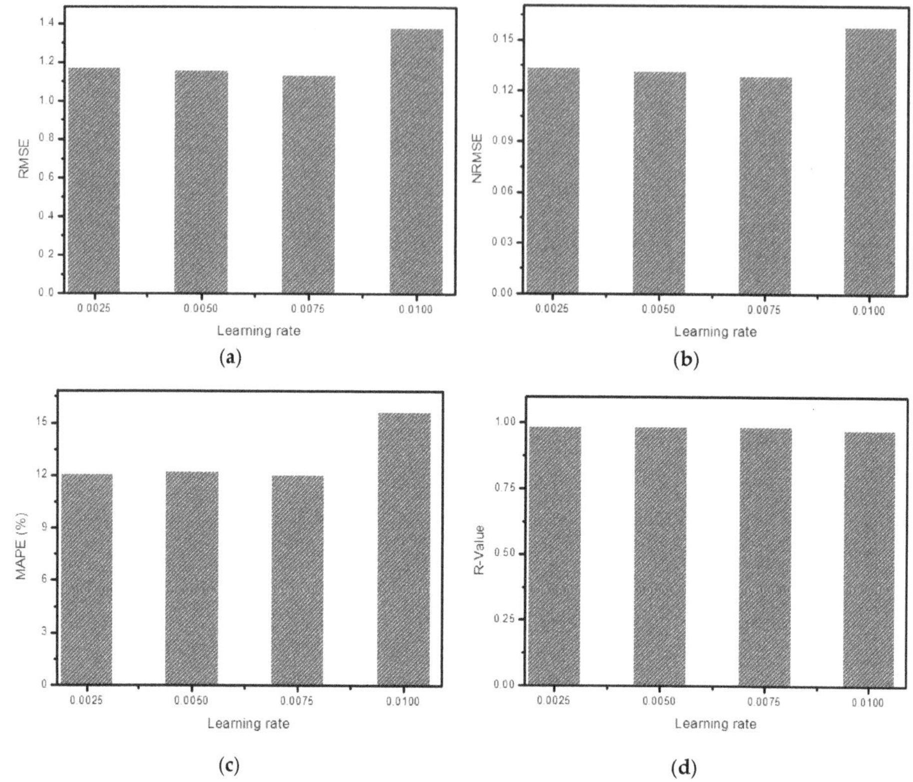

Figure 12. Performance parameters comparison of the GD algorithm for different learning rates. (**a**) RMSE; (**b**) NRMSE; (**c**) MAPE (%); (**d**) R value.

4. Conclusions

In this paper, different training algorithms of ANN were applied for the prediction of critical flashover voltage of insulators. These learning algorithms were applied by varying various parameters like the number of neurons, hidden layers, and learning rate. It was found that increasing the number of neurons to a certain limit can boost the performance of the machine learning algorithm for accurate prediction of flashover voltage, but after crossing a certain threshold, any further increase deteriorates the performance. Similarly, increasing the number of hidden layers had a positive influence on machine learning algorithms, except BR backpropagation, whose performance was affected badly with increasing hidden layers. The performance of the GD algorithm changed with the changing learning rate. Any inappropriate value may lead to large prediction errors of deployed algorithms. Therefore, it is important to choose the optimum values of the learning rate, number of neurons, and hidden layers for better performance of the machine learning algorithm. Additionally, the performance of the ANN algorithm is related to the type of learning algorithm utilized. These results can help scientists and engineers choose the best learning algorithm and associated parameters while predicting the critical flashover voltage of outdoor polymeric insulators.

Author Contributions: Data curation, J.A., F.A., F.A.B. and F.A.-A.; Investigation, A.; Methodology, M.T.K.N., A. and J.A.; Project administration, F.A., F.A.B., and F.A.-A.; Software, J.A.; Validation, J.A., A., F.A.-A.; Visualization,

F.A. and F.A.B.; Writing—original draft, M.T.K.N., and A.; Writing—review & editing, A., F.A.B. and F.A.-A. All authors have read and agreed to the published version of the manuscript.

Funding: This research received no external funding.

Acknowledgments: In this section, you can acknowledge any support given, which is not covered by the author contribution or funding sections. This may include administrative and technical support, or donations in kind (e.g., materials used for experiments).

Conflicts of Interest: The authors declare no conflict of interest.

Appendix A

This section describes the details of the learning algorithms used to train the neural network.

Appendix A.1. Gradient Descent

The GD method is usually applied for maximization or minimization of any n-dimensional function. It is described in the form of a gradient vector 'g' that points towards the steepest point of the given n-dimensional function $f(x\_n)$, given that 'g' is differentiable on that point. Mathematically, it can be written as:

$$g(x_1,\ x_2,\ x_3, \ldots .x_n) \ = \ \nabla\ f(x_1, x_2, x_3, \ldots .x_n) \tag{A1}$$

where '∇' is the gradient operator. The gradient is equivalent to the derivative of that point, therefore, a negative gradient will always point to the steepest point (minima) of the given function '$f(x_n)$'. In physical terms, gradient descent means moving downwards in steps proportional to the magnitude of gradient vector '$|g|$'. There are many shortcomings associated with this algorithm, like convergence to local minima instead of global and a low convergence rate. But due to low memory requirements, it is still considered a good algorithm for processing large data sets.

Appendix A.2. Conjugate Gradient Descent (CGD)

For quadratic functions, the GD algorithm exhibits slow convergence and involves many iterations. Therefore, to overcome this shortcoming, the CDG method was introduced in Reference [35]. This algorithm detects the minimum of any quadratic function 'f' by searching in orthogonal directions.

Let $f(x)$ be the function to be minimized, with 'x' being a vector of 'N' variables. The CGD algorithm consists of the following steps:

The CGD Algorithm

1. Start with initial set point of 'x_0' (iteration = k = 0).
2. In the second step, direction is computed as given below:

$$g(k) = \frac{\partial f(w(k))}{\partial w(k)}$$

   i- If $g(k) = 0$, then $x(k)$ is already present at optimal minimum point.
   ii- If $g(k) \neq 0$ and $k = 0$, then $r(k) = -g(k)$, move to step 3.
   iii- If $g(k) \neq 0$ and $k > 0$, then $r(k)$ can be calculated as:

$$r(k) = -g(k) + \frac{g^H(k).g(k)}{g^H(k-1).g(k-1)} \times r(k-1)$$

3. In this step, $w(k+1)$ is calculated, which steers to the minima of function 'f' in the direction $w(k) + \alpha \times r(k)$.
4. $k = k + 1$, move back to step 2.

Optimal point is obtained in K iterations where $K \leq N$

Appendix A.3. Quasi Newton Method

The Quasi-Newton method is an improved form of Newton's method. Newton's method requires a lot of computational space as it involves calculation of the Hessian matrix. In the Quasi-Newton method, an approximation of the inverse Hessian matrix is made at each iteration step. Newton's method initiates by finding out first derivative '$\nabla_x f(x)$', with an initial estimate of 'x^k'. This nonlinear function '$\nabla_x f(x^k + u)$' can be expanded by applying the Taylor series, up to two terms only:

$$\nabla_x f\left(x^k + u\right) = g\left(x^k + u\right) = g\left(x^k\right) + \nabla_x g\left(x^k\right)u \tag{A2}$$

Further, setting it equal to zero and assuming $u = u^k$

$$g\left(x^k\right) + \nabla_x g\left(x^k\right)u = 0 \tag{A3}$$

$$\nabla_x g\left(x^k\right)u = -g\left(x^k\right) \tag{A4}$$

where '$\nabla_x g\ (x^k)$' is Hessian matrix. As stated above, the Quasi-Newton calculates only the approximate value for the Hessian matrix. This approximation is made possible by making use of Broyden–Fletcher–Goldfarb–Shanno (BFGS) algorithm. By applying the Quasi-Newton BFGS algorithm, the following secant condition is obtained:

$$\nabla_x^2 f\left(x^{k+1}\right).\left(x^{k+1} - x^k\right) \approx \nabla_x f\left(x^{k+1}\right) - \nabla_x f\left(x^k\right) \tag{A5}$$

Hessian matrix '$\nabla_x^2 f\ (x^{k+1})$' is replaced by approximation 'H^{k+1}'.

$$H^{k+1}d^k = y \tag{A6}$$

where, $d^k = \left(x^{k+1} - x^k\right)$, and $y = \nabla_x f\left(x^{k+1}\right) - \nabla_x f\left(x^k\right) = g^{k+1} - g^k$.

Hessian matrix 'H^{k+1}' can be calculated by an earlier computed Hessian matrix 'H^k' as follows:

$$H^{k+1} = H^k + \frac{g^k g^{kT}}{d^k g^{kT}} + \frac{y^k y^{kT}}{d^k y^{kT}} \tag{A7}$$

Moreover, further simplification to the given problem is made by assuming $A^k = H^{-k}$
And A^{k+1} can be computed as:

$$A^{k+1} = \left(I - \frac{d^k y^{kT}}{d^{kT} y^k}\right)A^k\left(I - \frac{y^k d^{kT}}{d^{kT} y^k}\right) + \frac{d^k d^{kT}}{d^{kT} y^k} \tag{A8}$$

Appendix A.4. Levenberg-Marquardt (LM)

The LM algorithm is widely used for solving nonlinear least-squares problems. It is also termed as the damped least-square method. This algorithm does not involve the computation of the Hessian matrix. However, it incorporates the Jacobean matrix and gradient vector for obtaining the optimal point of any function 'f'. The optimal point is calculated using the following steps:

Calculate Steps

1. Let j_k denotes Jacobian matrix, d_k indicates search direction, the initial iteration parameter value is set to greater than zero ($a_1 > 0$):
$$0 \le p_0 \le p_1 \le p_2 \le 1$$
2. If $||j_k^T F_k|| \le \varepsilon$, terminate the criteria here. Otherwise
$$\mu_k = \alpha_k(\theta||F_k|| + (1+\theta)||j_k^T F_k||$$
compute d_k as:
$$\left(j_k^T j_k + \mu_k I\right)d = -j_k^T F_k$$
3. Then solve the following equation
$$r_k = \frac{||F_k||^2 - ||F(x_k + d_k)||^2}{||F_k||^2 - ||F_k + j_k d_k||^2}$$
$$x_{k+1} = \begin{cases} x_k + d_k & if\ r_k > p_0 \\ x_k & else \end{cases}$$
$$\alpha_{k+1} = \begin{cases} 4\alpha_k & if\ r_k < p_1 \\ \alpha_k & if\ r_k \epsilon [p_1, p_2] \\ \max\left\{\frac{\alpha_k}{4}, m\right\} & else \end{cases}$$
$k = k + 1$, move back to step 2.

Appendix A.5. Resilient Backpropagation

The RBP algorithm is one of the most widely deployed learning algorithms in neural networks. In this algorithm, the magnitude of the partial derivative is ignored, and only its sign is used as an indication for introducing any alterations in weights. An update in the weight is made only if the sign of partial derivative changes. The work of this algorithm can be summarized as [36]:

The RBP Algorithm

1. If the sign of derivative of the given function does not change in the next succeeding iterations, then an update in the weight is made as indicated below.

If $\left(\frac{\partial E}{\partial wk_j}(t-1) \times \frac{\partial E}{\partial wk_j}(t)\right) > 0$

Then

$$\Delta k_j(t) = minimum\left(\Delta k_j(t-1) \times \eta +, \Delta \max\right)$$

$$\Delta wk_j(t) = -sgn\left(\frac{\partial E}{\partial wk_j}(t)\right) \times \Delta k_j(t)$$

$$\Delta wk_j(t+1) = wk_j(t) + \Delta wk_j(t)$$

2. But, if the sign of derivative changes in the next iteration then weight decreases as shown below.

If $\left(\frac{\partial E}{\partial wk_j}(t-1) \times \frac{\partial E}{\partial wk_j}(t)\right) < 0$, **Then**

$$\Delta k_j(t) = maximum\left(\Delta k_j(t-1) \times \eta -, \Delta \min\right)$$

$$\Delta wk_j(t+1) = wk_j(t) - \Delta wk_j(t-1)$$

$$\frac{\partial E}{\partial wk_j}(t) = 0$$

3. In case, derivative is equal to zero then no changes are made to the weight value:

If $\left(\frac{\partial E}{\partial wk_j}(t-1) \times \frac{\partial E}{\partial wk_j}(t)\right) = 0$, **Then**

$$\Delta wk_j(t) = -sgn\left(\frac{\partial E}{\partial wk_j}(t)\right) \times \Delta k_j(t)$$

$$\Delta wk_j(t+1) = wk_j(t) + \Delta wk_j(t)$$

Where Δk_j= size of update

Appendix A.6. Bayesian Regularization Backpropagation

Traditional backpropagation method performs the task of minimization of given function

$$F = E_d, \tag{A9}$$

where

$$E_d = \sum_{i=1}^{n} (t_i - a_i)^2 \tag{A10}$$

In this equation, 'n' denotes the number of training inputs, 't_i' indicates anticipated output and 'a_i' is the ith output obtained as a result of neural network operation.

In regularization problems, the objective function is described as.

$$F = \alpha E_w + \beta E_d \tag{A11}$$

$$E_w = \sum_{i=1}^{n} w_i^2 \tag{A12}$$

Here, 'E_w' is the penalty factor and is equivalent to the addition of the squares of all network weights and 'α and β' are regularization parameters. It is very important to obtain optimal values for these regularization parameters. Generally, smaller weights for these parameters are preferred as it enhances the generalization capability of the given network. Too large a value of α ($\alpha \gg \beta$) results in tolerance to higher errors. The converse condition ($\alpha \ll \beta$) may lead to overfitting. In Reference [37], David Mackay presented a methodology for obtaining optimum weights of regularization parameters, commonly known as Bayesian regularization.

In the Bayesian regularization algorithm, a network's weights are considered as random variables. Let '*D*' indicate a training data set for a particular neural network model '*M*', then the posterior distribution for network's weights can be written as;

$$P(w|D,\ \alpha,\beta,M\ ) = \frac{P(D|w,\beta,M)P(w|\alpha,M)}{P(D|\alpha,\beta,M)} \tag{A13}$$

Here, 'w' is the vector containing network's weights, $P(w|\alpha, M)$ is prior distribution, $P(D|w,\beta,M)$ is likelihood function and $P(D|\alpha,\beta,M)$ is a normalization term. Normalization factor $P(D|\alpha, \beta, M)$ can be expressed as;

$$P(\ D|\alpha,\beta,M\ ) = \int\ P(D|w,\beta,M)P(w|\alpha,M)dw \tag{A14}$$

By considering the nature of noise in training data and prior distribution to be Gaussian in nature, we can write then,

$$P(D|w,\beta,M) = \frac{1}{Z_D(\beta)}\exp(-\beta E_d) \tag{A15}$$

$$P(w|\alpha,M) = \frac{1}{Z_w(\alpha)}\exp(-\alpha E_w) \tag{A16}$$

where

$$Z_D(\beta) = \left(\frac{\pi}{\beta}\right)^{\frac{n}{2}} \tag{A17}$$

$$Z_w(\alpha) = \left(\frac{\pi}{\alpha}\right)^{\frac{N}{2}} \tag{A18}$$

$$P(w|D,\ \alpha,\beta,M)\ \ = \frac{exp(-F(w))}{Z_F(\alpha,\beta)} \tag{A19}$$

$$Z_F(\alpha,\beta) = Z_D(\beta) + Z_w(\alpha).\ P(D|\alpha,\beta,M) \tag{A20}$$

The main purpose is to find out the values or weights that will cause minimization of '$F(w$'). In other words, this is analogous to maximization of $P(w|D, \alpha, \beta, M)$. So, by Baye's rule:

$$P(\alpha,\beta|D,M) = \frac{P(D|\alpha,\beta,M)P(\alpha,\beta|M)}{P(D|M)} \tag{A21}$$

By considering the prior density $P(D|\alpha, \beta, M)$ to be uniform, then maximization of posterior $P(\alpha, \beta|D, M)$ will be equal to the maximization of $P(D|\alpha, \beta, M)$.

$$P(D|\alpha,\beta,M) = \frac{\left(\frac{1}{Z_D}(\beta)\right)\exp(-\beta E_D)\left(\frac{1}{Z_w}(\alpha)\right)\exp(-\alpha E_w)}{\left(\frac{1}{Z_F}(\alpha,\beta)\right)\exp(-F(w))} \tag{A22}$$

$$P(D|\alpha,\beta,M)= \frac{Z_{F(\alpha,\beta)}}{Z_D(\beta)Z_w(\alpha)} \tag{A23}$$

$Z_w(\alpha)$ and $Z_D(\beta)$ are already known values. '$Z_{F(\alpha,\beta)}$' can be estimated by Taylor expansion. For normalization constant, we can solve it as:

$$Z_F = 2\pi^{\frac{N}{2}}\left(det\left(H^{MP}\right)^{-1}\right)^{\frac{1}{2}} \exp\left(-\mathrm{F}(w)^{MP}\right) \tag{A24}$$

Here, 'H' is Hessian matrix and can be calculated as

$$H = \beta\nabla^2 E_D + \alpha\nabla^2 E_w \tag{A25}$$

Putting the value of 'Z_F' and further solving it gives us the optimum weight of 'α' and'β'at 'w_{MP}'. So,

$$\alpha^{MP} = \frac{\gamma}{2E_w(w^{MP})} \tag{A26}$$

And

$$\beta^{MP} = \frac{n-\gamma}{2E_D(w^{MP})} \tag{A27}$$

References

1. Arshad; Nekahi, A.; McMeekin, S.G.; Farzaneh, M. Flashover characteristics of silicone rubber sheets under various environmental conditions. *Energies* **2016**, *9*, 683. [CrossRef]
2. Hamza, A.-S.H.; Abdelgawad, N.M.; Arafa, B.A. Effect of desert environmental conditions on the flashover voltage of insulators. *Energy Convers. Manag.* **2002**, *43*, 2437–2442. [CrossRef]
3. Farzaneh, M.; Chisholm, W.A. *Insulators for Icing and Polluted Environments*; John Wiley & Sons: Hoboken, NJ, USA, 2009; Volume 47.
4. Asimakopoulou, G.E.; Kontargyri, V.T.; Tsekouras, G.J.; Elias, C.N.; Asimakopoulou, F.E.; Stathopulos, I.A. A fuzzy logic optimization methodology for the estimation of the critical flashover voltage on insulators. *Electr. Power Syst. Res.* **2011**, *81*, 580–588. [CrossRef]
5. Mahdjoubi, A.; Zegnini, B.; Belkheiri, M.; Seghier, T. Fixed least squares support vector machines for flashover modelling of outdoor insulators. *Electr. Power Syst. Res.* **2019**, *173*, 29–37. [CrossRef]
6. Samakosh, J.D.; Mirzaie, M. Flash-over voltage prediction of silicone rubber insulators under longitudinal and fan-shaped non-uniform pollution conditions. *Comput. Electr. Eng.* **2019**, *78*, 50–62. [CrossRef]
7. Belhouchet, K.; Bayadi, A.; Bendib, M.E. Artificial neural networks and genetic algorithm modelling and identification of arc parameter in insulators flashover voltage and leakage current. *Int. J. Comput. Aided Eng. Technol.* **2019**, *11*, 1–13. [CrossRef]
8. Kamarudin, M.S.; Othman, N.A.; Jamail, N.A.M. Artificial Intelligence Techniques for Predicting the Flashover Voltage on Polluted Cup-Pin Insulators. *Emerg. Trends Intell. Comput. Inform. Data Sci. Intell. Inf. Syst. Smart Comput.* **2019**, *1073*, 362.
9. Lu, S.; Lin, G.; Liu, H.; Ye, C.; Que, H.; Ding, Y. A weekly load data mining approach based on hidden Markov model. *IEEE Access* **2019**, *7*, 34609–34619. [CrossRef]
10. Farshad, M. Detection and classification of internal faults in bipolar HVDC transmission lines based on K-means data description method. *Int. J. Electr. Power Energy Syst.* **2019**, *104*, 615–625. [CrossRef]
11. Narayanan, V.J.; Sivakumar, M.; Karpagavani, K.; Chandrasekar, S. Prediction of Flashover and Pollution Severity of High Voltage Transmission Line Insulators Using Wavelet Transform and Fuzzy C-Means Approach. *J. Electr. Eng. Technol.* **2014**, *9*, 1677–1685. [CrossRef]
12. Natarajan, A.; Narayanan, S. S-transform based time-frequency analysis of leakage current signals of transmission line insulators under polluted conditions. *J. Electr. Eng. Technol.* **2015**, *10*, 616–624. [CrossRef]
13. Prasad, P.S.; Rao, B.P. Review on Machine Vision based Insulator Inspection Systems for Power Distribution System. *J. Eng. Sci. Technol. Rev.* **2016**, *9*, 135–141. [CrossRef]
14. Lan, L.; Gorur, R.S. Computation of AC wet flashover voltage of ceramic and composite insulators. *IEEE Trans. Dielectr. Electr. Insul.* **2008**, *15*, 1346–1352. [CrossRef]
15. Venkataraman, S.; Gorur, R.S. Prediction of flashover voltage of non-ceramic insulators under contaminated conditions. *IEEE Trans. Dielectr. Electr. Insul.* **2006**, *13*, 862–869. [CrossRef]

16. Zhang, D.; Zhang, Z.; Jiang, X.; Yang, Z.; Zhao, J.; Li, Y. Study on Insulator Flashover Voltage Gradient Correction Considering Soluble Pollution Constituents. *Energies* **2016**, *9*, 954. [CrossRef]
17. Li, Y.; Yang, H.; Zhang, Q.; Yang, X.; Yu, X.; Zhou, J. Pollution flashover calculation model based on characteristics of AC partial arc on top and bottom wet-polluted dielectric surfaces. *IEEE Trans. Dielectr. Electr. Insul.* **2014**, *21*, 1735–1746. [CrossRef]
18. Hadjrioua, F.; Mahi, D.; Slama, M.E.A. Application of the analytical arc parameters on the dynamic modeling of HVDC flashover of polluted insulators. In Proceedings of the 2014 International Conference on Electrical Sciences and Technologies in Maghreb (CISTEM), Tunis, Tunisia, 3–6 November 2014; pp. 1–5.
19. Badachi, C.; Dixit, P. Prediction of pollution flashover voltages of ceramic string insulators under uniform and non-uniform pollution conditions. *J. Electr. Syst. Inf. Technol.* **2016**, *3*, 270–281. [CrossRef]
20. Shahabi, S.; Gholami, A. Dynamic model to predict AC critical flashover voltage of nonuniformly polluted insulators under thermal ionization conditions. *Turk. J. Electr. Eng. Comput. Sci.* **2017**, *25*, 2322–2335. [CrossRef]
21. Palangar, M.F.; Mirzaie, M.; Mahmoudi, A. Improved flashover mathematical model of polluted insulators: A dynamic analysis of the electric arc parameters. *Electr. Power Syst. Res.* **2020**, *179*, 106083. [CrossRef]
22. Salem, A.A.; Abd Rahman, R.; Kamarudin, M.S.; Othman, N.A.; Jamail NA, M.; Hamid, H.A.; Ishak, M.T. An alternative approaches to predict flashover voltage on polluted outdoor insulators using artificial intelligence techniques. *Bull. Electr. Eng. Inform.* **2020**, *9*, 533–541. [CrossRef]
23. Salem, A.A.; Abd-Rahman, R.; Al-Gailani, S.A.; Kamarudin, M.S.; Othman, N.A.; Jamail, N.A.M. Artificial Intelligence Techniques for Predicting the Flashover Voltage on Polluted Cup-Pin Insulators. In *International Conference of Reliable Information and Communication Technology*; Springer: Cham, Switzerland, 2019; pp. 362–372.
24. Zegnini, B.; Mahdjoubi, A.H.; Belkheiri, M. A least squares support vector machines (LS-SVM) approach for predicting critical flashover voltage of polluted insulators. In Proceedings of the 2011 Annual Report Conference on Electrical Insulation and Dielectric Phenomena, Cancun, Mexico, 16–19 October 2011; pp. 403–406.
25. Cho, M.Y.; Lin, P.S. Using Support Vector Machine for Classifying Insulator Leakage Current. *Intl. J. Electr. Comput. Sci. IJECS-IJENS* **2015**, *15*, 30–38.
26. Gencoglu, M.T.; Uyar, M. Prediction of flashover voltage of insulators using least squares support vector machines. *Expert Syst. Appl.* **2009**, *36*, 10789–10798. [CrossRef]
27. Saranya, K.; Muniraj, C. A SVM Based Condition Monitoring of Transmission Line Insulators Using PMU for Smart Grid Environment. *J. Power Energy Eng.* **2016**, *4*, 47–60. [CrossRef]
28. Govindaraju, P.; Saranya, K.; Muniraj, C. Condition monitoring of transmission line insulators using PMU for smart grid environment. In Proceedings of the 2016 6th International Conference on Intelligent and Advanced Systems (ICIAS), Kuala Lumpur, Malaysia, 15–17 August 2016; pp. 1–6.
29. James, G.; Witten, D.; Hastie, T.; Tibshirani, R. *An Introduction to Statistical Learning*; Springer: New York, NY, USA, 2013; Volume 112.
30. Khan, J.S.; Ahmad, J.; Khan, M.A. TD-ERCS map-based confusion and diffusion of autocorrelated data. *Nonlinear Dyn.* **2015**, *87*, 93–107. [CrossRef]
31. Jeyasurya, B. Application of artificial neural networks to power system transient energy margin evaluation. *Electr. Power Syst. Res.* **1993**, *26*, 71–78. [CrossRef]
32. Daut, M.A.M.; Hassan, M.Y.; Abdullah, H.; Rahman, H.A.; Abdullah, M.P.; Hussin, F. Building electrical energy consumption forecasting analysis using conventional and artificial intelligence methods: A review. *Renew. Sustain. Energy Rev.* **2017**, *70*, 1108–1118. [CrossRef]
33. Nielsen, M.A. *Neural Networks and Deep Learning*; Determination Press: San Francisco, CA, USA, 2015; Volume 2018.
34. Arshad; Ahmad, J.; Tahir, A.; Stewart, B.G.; Nekahi, A. Forecasting Flashover Parameters of Polymeric Insulators under Contaminated Conditions Using the Machine Learning Technique. *Energies* **2020**, *13*, 3889. [CrossRef]
35. Cheney, E.W.; Kincaid, D.R. *Numerical Mathematics and Computing*; Cengage Learning: Boston, MA, USA, 2012.

36. Patil, S., Naik, G.M., Pai, K.R. An application of wavelet transform and artificial neural network for microarray gene expression based brain tumor sub-classification. *Int. J. Emerg. Technol. Adv. Eng.* **2015**, *5*, 410–414.
37. MacKay, D.J. Bayesian interpolation. *Neural Comput.* **1992**, *4*, 415–447. [CrossRef]

MDPI AG
Grosspeteranlage 5
4052 Basel
Switzerland
Tel.: +41 61 683 77 34

Electronics Editorial Office
E-mail: electronics@mdpi.com
www.mdpi.com/journal/electronics

www.ingramcontent.com/pod-product-compliance
Lightning Source LLC
Chambersburg PA
CBHW040834250926
51850CB00007BA/1312
* 9 7 8 3 7 2 5 8 4 8 0 7 2 *